Answers to Questions About

Old Jewelry

1840 - 1950

5th Edition

C. Jeanenne Bell, G.G.

Published by

 **krause
publications**

700 E. State Street • Iola, WI 54990-0001
Telephone: 715/445-2214

Please, call or write us for our free catalog of antiques and collectibles publications.
To place an order or receive our free catalog, call 800-258-0929.
For editorial comment and further information,
use our regular business telephone at (715) 445-2214.

Library of Congress Catalog Number: 99-62391
ISBN: 0-87341-731-3

Printed in the United States of America

Dedication

The One from Whom all good things cometh
and
my parents
Anne Hooper Noblitt
Aaron Belton Noblitt
and
my children
Lisa Anne Underwood
Sally Jeanenne Stites
Donald Louis Bell, II
Amanda Aaron Bell
and
my husband
Michael Marshall
With Love

Contents

A Note From The Author

Welcome to the 5th edition of *Answers to Questions about Old Jewelry*. I am delighted to have the opportunity to update, revise and add to a book that has brought me so many new friends. In this edition, I have included a new section to answer your questions regarding, "How Was It Made?" Additionally, I have answered your questions on the making of the beautiful work referred to as filigree in the 1920s and 1930s. Hopefully, this edition will answer many of your other questions about jewelry manufacturing and construction techniques.

Once again, I have updated all the prices except those from auction house sales. Please be aware of the date a piece was sold and take this into account when considering the price realized.

As I was preparing this book for the new millennium, it was only natural for me to compare the end of the 20th century with that of the 19th century. There are so many parallels to ponder. In the last decade of the 19th century advertisements advocating magnets for better health and spirituality and symbolism were common topics of conversation. In the last decade of the 20th century, magnets were touted again as the answer to many health problems and "new age" religious thought was again in the minds and hearts of individuals throughout the country.

In jewelry, the parallels were just as obvious. Platinum became the most favored metal at the end of the 19th century. Today, it has again gained national acceptance as the premier metal. The Arts and Crafts Movements of the 19th century stressed some of the same qualities that hand crafters do today. People are once again concerned with artistry and craftsmanship. Cameos, mosaics, and anything with enamel work are the most collectible items.

This is a wonderfully exciting time to start or add to a collection of antique jewelry. May this book add to your enjoyment of an interesting hobby or profession.

Happy hunting!

C. Jeanenne Bell

Please address your correspondence to:

C. Jeanenne Bell
c/o Jewelry Box Antiques, Inc.
7325 Quivira Road, Ste. 238
Shawnee, KS 66216

Introduction

Almost everyone is curious about old jewelry. Maybe it's because most people have a piece or two tucked away somewhere. It could be a locket that belonged to a grandmother or a pin that has been handed down in the family. Along with most jewelry comes unanswered questions, "How old is it? Is it valuable? What is the material?" Whether you are a serious collector or a curious owner, this book will help answer these questions.

Section I deals with jewelry styles from 1840-1950. To make looking at each style easier, they are divided into the following historical periods:

1840-1860	Victoria and Albert
1861-1889	Victoria
1890-1915	Edwardian; Art Nouveau
1920-1930s	Art Deco
1940-1950s	Modern; Retro Modern

Jewelry has always had definite period styles. These were reflected in jewelry motifs in much the same manner as they were reflected in furniture. Consequently, if you can identify a piece of Art Nouveau furniture, you can probably recognize a piece of jewelry from that same period.

Period styles have a way of overlapping and changes happened gradually. A style that was waning in 1860s England could still be in its peak of popularity in the United States. As communications improved and travel made the world seem smaller, these changes took place more rapidly. This will be more evident as the later periods are examined.

A study of jewelry is incomplete unless it includes information about the lives and times of the people who wore it. How they lived and what they experienced was reflected in their clothes and accessories. For this reason, each period begins with a short historical synopsis.

Since jewelry was used to complement clothing, it is impossible to fully understand jewelry styles without relating them to the fashions they accessorized. Fashion plates are included in each time period to make the period's clothing real. Many period quotes from publications are included, not only to supply information on the styles, but also to provide a flavor of the times. In each period, certain pieces and materials were in vogue. These were determined by many things: the neckline, the hem line, the hairstyles, and even the economy.

The historical information, the magazine quotes, and the many photographs included in Section I should help provide answers to the questions: "When was it made & what is it worth?"

Section II is an overview of one hundred years of cameos. They have become so fashionable and collectible that many readers requested more information on the subject. This section is included to fill this need.

Section III answers questions about jewelry manufacturing and construction techniques.

The appendices deal with the different types of metal used in jewelry making. Gold, silver, pinchbeck, gold filled, gold plated, and platinum are some of the topics discussed. Many questions concerning a piece of jewelry can be answered by learning to identify its metal content.

Maker's marks, trademarks and designer marks can make a vast difference in the value of the piece. The appendices also contain a listing of collectible marks and background information about many of the designers and companies that produced today's collectible pieces.

Finding answers to questions about old jewelry is an interesting hobby. It can be an adventure into the past that can be a big investment in the future. Happy hunting and remember: stay curious!

Acknowledgments

Dan Alexander, President of Books Americana for his friendship and positive motivation.

Gemological Institute of America and its President Richard I. Liddicoat, Jr. for allowing us to reprint illustrations from their course on colored gems.

Gem Media, a division of The Gemological Institute of America for providing photographs for the "Is It Real?" section.

William Doyle Galleries, 175 East 87th St., New York, New York for supplying photographs, descriptions and prices, and for granting permission for their use in this book.

Phillips, Blenstock House, 7 Blenhein St., New Bond St., London W1YOAS and Mr. John Condrop and Mr. A. Spice for their assistance and permission to use photographs, descriptions and prices from their auction catalogues.

Sotheby's, 1334 York Ave., New York, for granting us permission to use photographs, descriptions and prices from their auction catalogue.

Sotheby's & Co., Bloomfield Place, Off Bond Street, London WIA2AA, Mr. David Bemmett, F.G.A. Head of Jewelry Dept. and his secretary, Joan Marchant, for permission to use auction photographs, descriptions and realized prices and for their assistance in supplying this information.

Mr. T. Roe of Jowsey & Roe, #7 Sandgate, Whitby, North Yorkshire, England, for allowing me to photograph the Jet jewelry in his shop and for sharing his memories of the history of the Whitby Jet Industry.

Norm Williams and King Features Syndicate, NY, for permission to use illustrations from their 1949-50 pattern book.

Camille Grace, "Stuff" dealer, K. C., MO, for allowing me to take her jewelry across the country to be photographed.

Wayne Baldwin, Peggy Carlson, Mary Holloway, Anne Noblitt, A. B. Noblitt, Lela Reed, Margaret Sorrell and Mignon Stufflebam for sharing pieces from their collections.

Lucille and Sam Mundorff of "The Old 'n You Antiques Mart Inc.", Kansas City, MO, for allowing us to photograph some of their pieces.

Edward J. Tripp, Blue Ridge, Texas for sharing his knowledge of Ivory.

Marilyn Roos, "Natural Amber", St. Louis, MO, for an informative interview on Amber.

Bob P. Holloway, Kansas City, MO, artist, for the excellent Hallmark example in the "What Is This Metal?" section.

Amanda Bell for her able assistance on the microfilm machine.

Skinner Co., Boston, Massachusetts, for allowing us to reproduce the picture's from their catalogue.

My daughter, Lisa Bell Underwood, for her unlimited help on the Fifth Edition. It may not have been possible without her.

Christie's East, 219 East 67th Street, NY, NY, for allowing us to include pictures from their auction catalogs.

Butterfield and Butterfield, 220 San Bruno Avenue, San Francisco, CA, for allowing us to include items from their auction catalogs.

Peter DiCristafaro, President, and Al Weisberg, Exec. Dir. of the Providence Jewelry Museum, 88 Spectacle Street, Cranston, RI, for their willingness to share their knowledge of die-striking and jewelry manufacturing. Special thanks preserve our jewelry history and heritage for future generations.

Michael Salvadore, Jr., President of American Jewelry Products, Inc., 100 Bellows Street, Bldg. 13, Warwick, RI, for sharing his knowledge of white metal spin-casting and allowing us to photograph some of his operations and use some of his slides.

Ralph Flemming, III, of Carla Corp., East Providence, RI, for providing information about electroforming and allowing us to include photographs of some of their pieces.

Salvadore Tools and Findings, Providence, RI, for allowing us to photograph their machines in action for this book.

Section 1:

When was it made & what is it worth?

Chapter One: 1840-1860

The American & English Historical Period

The years from 1840-1860 were exciting times in which to be alive. Changes were taking place at a rapid pace. The fruits of the Industrial Revolution were bringing about new social and economic conditions.

The American spirit of creativity was boundless. These were the years in which Horace Greeley founded the New York Tribune (1841), Goodyear patented his rubber making process (1844), Howe invented the sewing machine (1846), Tiffany opened his first store (1849), and Gail Borden patented his process for condensing milk (1856).

On January 24, 1848, gold was discovered in California. As the eyes of the world turned toward Sutter's Mill, people headed in that direction. They went by wagon, by horse, and by foot, seeking their fortune. This migration led to new towns all across the country. California's population increased 2,500% in one year.

As a result of this migration, railroads were expanding. In 1840, there were 3,000 miles of track. By 1860, the total had grown to 30,000. Railroads were definitely on the move, bringing economic success along with them.

During this period fortunes were being made. In 1845, New York had twenty-one millionaires and many more would be added to the list before 1861. The showman P. T. Barnum made his fortune promoting amusements. He sponsored period celebrity Jenny Lind's American debut in 1850. The editor of *Godey's Lady's Magazine* had this to say about the trend it set:

> Of course now that Jenny Lind is more widely known to the American Public, shopkeepers lose no time in making the most out of the popular tastes for novelties. Jenny Lind bandeaux, were the only things extensively copied among us, until she had absolutely arrived and then the furor commenced. At Stewarts', Beck's and Levy's there was no difference, but in the Bowery, Canal Street, or Eight and Second Streets, in Philadelphia, Jenny Lind plaids, combs, slides, earrings, work baskets, bonnets, and even hair-pins were advertised and recommended. Now, these had no legitimate claim to the title inasmuch as we do not believe Mademoiselle Lind had ever seen, much less worn, the articles in question. It was a barefaced shopkeeping ruse, but nevertheless it succeeded. Half the American public is now wiping their heated brows with Jenny Lind pocket-handkerchiefs, or dressing their hair with Jenny Lind's combs.

For the first time the average person was allowed the luxury of leisure time activities. Baseball clubs sprang up in towns across the country. In 1858, the National Association of Baseball Players was formed. Trotting races, boxing, and even football games were popular. (Of course, these activities were for men only.)

In England, these years were also filled with changes. These were the years in which Britain became known as a nation immersed in both industry and the arts. Already the undisputed leader in steam navigation and railway construction, by staging the first International Exposition of Arts and Industry in 1851, England also became known as a patron of the arts.

With the exception of the years 1842 and 1848, when there was a depression, the nation flourished with unprecedented economic success. Cottage industries were becoming a thing of the past. More and more people went to work in factories. Factory-made goods were cheaper and more plentiful than their handmade predecessors, and most people had the money to buy them.

Social conditions were improving. The Shaftesbury Act of 1842 made it illegal for the mines to hire children under ten years of age. In 1847, the Fielden Act made it against the law for a child to work more than ten hours a day.

No longer was a person destined to stay in the social class to which he had been born. Victorians were beginning to believe that with education, hard work, and the proper fear of God, a person's opportunities were unlimited. Even the young aristocrats were going into trade and industry.

Religion was an important element in Victorian life. On "Census Sunday" in 1851, it was estimated that five out of every twelve people attended a worship service. Most Sundays were spent attending church, reading the Bible, and refraining from worldly activities.

Quite often when things are changing too fast, society looks to the past for inspiration. This was the case with the Victorians. They looked back to the middle ages and were enchanted by armor wearing knights, fair maidens, and chivalry. They wanted to emulate these romantic ideals for their generation. Medieval balls became the highlight of the social circle, giving everyone an opportunity to don the costume of the period. There was even talk of having a medieval ball as part of the queen's coronation, but the idea was dropped because of the enormous expense involved.

Queen Victoria's exemplary lifestyle gave the country an opportunity to once again experience pride in its royal family. With her stable influence and the guidance of superb prime ministers, Britain expanded its imperialistic power and became a great nation. With the exception of the Crimean War (1854-56), this was a time of peace and prosperity.

Victoria

Queen Victoria was born on May 24, 1819, at Kensington Palace. Her father was the Duke of Kent, the fourth son of George III. At birth, there seemed to be little prospect of her ever becoming Queen of England. However, fate would have it otherwise.

Victoria led a very sheltered life. Her father died when she was a baby. Her German mother, Victoria Maria Louise, raised her in England, anticipating the day when she would inherit the crown. Victoria was never allowed time to herself. Someone was with her at all times. She even slept in the room with her mother. Always protected, she was never left alone.

It is little wonder that Victoria's first request, after being crowned queen in 1838, was to spend time alone. Her request was granted. Later her bed was moved to a room of her own. She was the queen, and it was exhilarating!

The people of England were anxious for the young queen to marry and have children to insure the throne. Victoria, happy with her first taste of freedom, was totally against the idea until her cousin came to visit. She had met Albert a few years earlier when he and his brother came for a two-week stay. At that time, she had been impressed with his blue eyes and engaging smile.

When she saw him again, all her reservations vanished and she was in love.

The marriage was a happy one. The children, a total of nine, came one after another. Holidays were spent on the seashore at Osborne or in their Balmoral House in Scotland. Victoria was a loving, giving person, who placed a high regard on sentiment. Her life centered around her God, her God-given duties as queen, her beloved Albert, and her children.

Albert

Prince Albert should share equal billing with Queen Victoria in this time period. He was very instrumental in the impact England had on the world during these years. Francis Charles Augustus Albert Emmanuel was born on August 26, 1819, in Colburg, Germany. His father was the Duke of Saxe-Coburg-Gotha. His aunt was Victoria Maria Louise of Saxe-Coburg, the mother of Queen Victoria. From early childhood he had been groomed as a possible husband for his cousin.

After the marriage, Albert worked as an aid and advisor to Victoria. Although some people worried about the queen taking advice from someone who was not English, the nation grew to love and respect him.

He was as sentimental as his wife in many respects. The engagement ring he gave her was in the form of a serpent (an ancient symbol of eternal love). For their sixth anniversary he presented her with a wreath for her hair made of porcelain and enameled gold which he had designed himself. The orange blossom wreath had four enameled oranges, each representing one of their children. He also designed a brooch the queen presented to Florence Nightingale commemorating her services in the Crimean War.

Albert loved art, and one of his favorite ways to spend an afternoon was to browse through art studios and museums. This interest led to his appointment as head of a commission to encourage art in England. In 1844, he became president of "A Society For Improving The Conditions Of The Working Classes." He was very concerned and often personally inspected sites that needed improving or were in the process of being improved.

Albert was a firm believer in the importance of education. In 1847, he was elected Chancellor of Cambridge University. Many of his ideas were incorporated into the university's programs. Some of these ideas were even imitated by Oxford University.

One of the most exciting contributions Albert made to the Victorian era was his part in the Great International Exposition of 1851. There had been other expositions, but this was the first of international scope. The *Crystal Palace Exhibitions Illustrated Catalogue* speaks glowingly of his help.

> If, therefore, the merit of having originated exhibitions of her own manufacture belongs to France, it is to his Royal Highness Prince Albert that the more noble and disinterested plan of throwing open an institution of this description to all the competition of the whole world, is exclusively due; and his suggestion has been carried out in a spirit every way worthy its grandeur and generosity.

Further into the history we find these words:

> But indeed, for his (Prince Albert) indefatigable perseverance, his courageous defiance of all risks of failure, his remarkable sagacity in matters of business, and the influence which attached to his support the whole project, notwithstanding the great exertions which had been made to secure its realization, must have fallen to the ground.

Lest we think these kind words were given because Albert was the queen's husband, the article makes it very plain that this was not the case:

> It is difficult to assign to Prince Albert the degree of praise which is really due on this occasion without incurring the suspicions of being in some degree influenced by the exalted position he holds in the country...Rather than incur the imputation of sycophancy, his admirers have sometimes been led to do less than justice to the very prominent part he has

taken in this project, and to the consummate skill with which he has smoothed down all opposition to it. In a word, for the World's Exposition, the world is entirely indebted to the Prince Consort.

The Great Exhibition

The Great Exhibition of the Industry of all Nations' purpose was to provide an arena for the celebration of the arts and industry of man. Each country displayed its newest and best in the four divisions: raw materials, machinery and mechanical inventions, manufactures, sculpture and plastic art. Prizes were awarded in each category.

The exhibition was housed in a building designed by Joseph Paxton and built by the firm of Fox and Henderson. Its glass and iron construction made it look like a gigantic greenhouse. Dubbed "The Crystal Palace," it was truly a wonder to behold. Built in the shape of a parallelogram, it had an enclosed area of 772,284 square feet (about nineteen acres). The construction utilized 9,000,000 feet of glass, 550 tons of wrought iron, and 3,500 tons of cast iron. But the building had such a light and airy look, that people were concerned about its safety. After several tests proved the strength and safety of the design, the public could hardly contain their excitement until opening day.

Interior of the Transept, as seen from the South Entrance.

The Queen and her husband presided at the official opening on May 1, 1851. The Archbishop of Canterbury gave the invocation and a huge, combined choir sang the Hallelujah Chorus. The procession was regal. Clearly, this was the event of the decade, and only season ticket holders were allowed to attend this ceremony. An estimated 25,000 people were present.

After opening day, the general public came. Using England's excellent railroads, they flocked from all over to see the Crystal Palace and its contents. It was the place to see and be seen. Many days were required to view the exhibition properly. There were literally miles of things to see. For a small fee, the average working man or woman could see sights normally reserved for royalty.

The largest section in the building housed machinery. Machines for making rope, lace, silk, flax, and furniture could be seen in operation. Steam hammers, hydraulic presses, and fire engines were on display. Power for the machinery was furnished by an engine house built one hundred and fifty-five feet from the main building. Its five boilers produced enough steam power to serve the entire exhibition.

Each country had a section in which to show the best of its machinery, inventions, art, and products. There were musical instruments, furniture, carpets, vases, china, laces, clocks, watches, toys, stained glass, and much, much more. The jewelry and precious stones attracted much attention. The 280 carat "Kah-i-Norr" diamond and Adrian Hope's 177 carat diamond were on display along with everyday items such as chatelaines and brooches.

A.W.N. Pugin, an Englishman, designed the medieval court section of the exhibition. Here he displayed the jewelry collection he had designed using Gothic motifs. There were bracelets, brooches, earrings, and necklaces featuring lovely blue and green enameling. They were encrusted with pearls, turquoise and cabochon garnets (cabochon cut stones in a medieval style setting were popular). These ecclesiastical, medieval designs appealed to the romantic nature of the Victorians. The novels of Sir Walter Scott had enticed their imaginations to medieval times. This jewelry made tangible the beauty already associated with that period. The collection caused a revival in enameling techniques. Crosses, quatre-foils, and many other architectural details became popular jewelry motifs.

Jewelry designs based on nature were much in evidence at the exhibition. The *Art-Journal Illus-*

Western entrance to the Great Exhibit. (Courtesy *Art-Journal Illustrated Catalogue*)

trated Catalogue made this comment about the new styles:

> The taste for floral ornament in jewelry has been very prevalent of late, and it's a good and happy taste, inasmuch as an enameled leaf or floret brilliant color is an excellent foil to a sparkling stone. We have scarcely seen the design for jewelry at any period more tasteful, elegant, and appropriate than they are at the present day.

The Crystal Palace Exhibition was a success from every point of view. The queen and royal children enjoyed it so much that they visited many times. This was an added incentive for the public. It was estimated that over six million people visited the exhibition.

This success instigated a series of exhibitions. The United States had a Crystal Palace Exposition in 1853. It was promoted by P.T. Barnum, and yes, it was called the Crystal Palace Exposition. In 1855, an International Exhibition was staged in Paris, and England scheduled another one for 1861.

Fashions in Clothing & Jewelry

England and America looked to Paris for fashion. These were always seasoned by the English form for "correctness," and "Americanized" for the United States. In January 1850, *Godey's Lady's Book* found it necessary to print the following:

> We have always taken care in preparing our descriptions of fashion and fashion from foreign authorities, to translate, as far as possible, the French terms and idioms, for as a correspondent justly says 'it is presumed the Lady's Book is read and intended more for American than French ladies.' Moreover, it may be noticed that our magazine is the only one that does this among all the numerous pretenders in the same path. It is true, there are, now and then, names of articles that have naturalized into our language, for

Illustration from *Godey's Lady's Book*, August, 1850.

which there is no translation. For instance, the Spanish, mantilla; the French mantelet, berthé; a raché or glacé silk; tulle, etc., etc. With these exceptions, if our friends, and of them, will take the trouble to look back through the last volume, they will find no other foreign word introduced. The importance of this, in magazines destined for circulation in remote districts, where no language but our own is spoken or written, will at once be recognized. For those whom a city life had not made familiar with the proper names of articles, we annex a collection of terms most generally in use.

The *Godey's Lady's Book* also included the following explanation of terms:

Berthé is cape of lace, of almost the shape of those so fashionable a few years since, and called "low capes," in common parlance.

Tulle: or illusion-common fine silk net lace.

Ruché: a ruffle or quilling of lace or ribbon.

Corsage: waist of a dress.

Boquet de Coeffure and boquet de carrsage: bouquets for the waist and head.

Glacé silk: a summer or thin silk.

In the 1840s and 1850s, as in all Victorian times, it was highly improper for "Meladies" ankles to show. Therefore, dresses were long and full with two or three flounces. Daytime (or morning) dresses usually had high necklines, pointed waists, and long sleeves even in the summer. Over this one wore a decorative apron and a berthé. During the day, bonnets snugly covered the head and ears. For evening, dresses were cut low and the arms were exposed. The head was uncovered and flowers and fruit were woven into the hair.

Throughout this period, women kept their ears covered. During the day, they were hidden under a bonnet; for evening they were covered with clusters of curls. As *Godey's Lady's Book* stated in 1855:

We give up the ear. Pretty or not, it cannot afford to be shown. Any face in the world looks bold with the hair put away so as to show the ears. They must be covered. The curving of the jaw needs the intersecting shade of the falling curl, or of the plait of braid drawn across it. So evident is it to us that nature intended the female ear to be covered-(by giving long hair to women, and making the ears concealment almost inevitable as well as necessary to her beauty)-that we only wonder the wearing of it covered, by hair or cap, has never been put down among the rudiments of modesty.

Very little jewelry was worn during the day. Since bonnets or curls covered the ears, earrings were primarily worn only for state events. Jewelry was limited to hair ornaments, brooches, and bracelets. Of these, bracelets were by far the most popular. An article in the *World of Fashion* states:

Bracelets are now considered indispensable; they are worn in the following manner: on one arm is placed the sentimental bracelet, composed of hair and fastened with some precious relic; the second is a silver enameled one, having a cross, a cassolette, or anchor and heart, as sort of a talisman; the other arm is decorated with a bracelet of gold network fastened with a simple nœud, similar to one of narrow ribbon; the other composed of medallions of blue enamel, upon which are placed small bouquets of brilliants, the fastening being composed of a single stone; lastly a broad gold chain, each link separated with a ruby and opal alternate.

Yes, you read it correctly! The women actually wore five bracelets (two on one arm and three on the other), and mixed a variety of materials such as hair, silver, gold net, gold chain, enameled medallions, brilliants, rubies, and opals. The arms were available to decorate so they used them to the fullest.

By the end of 1855, the neckline was worn lower. Necklaces once again came into fashion. According to the December issue of *Godey's*, the most popular ones were made of hair.

Now that dresses are cut away from the throat more than for many years past, necklaces are once more in vogue. Hair necklaces are made in transparent globules or beads, and united in a continuous chain, or separated by a gold bead, either plain or chased, with a handsome gold clasp. Pendants of hair are almost necessary to this style of necklaces. One of the most effective, and apparently most simple, is a cross woven of hair and enframed by small diamonds; this is suspended on a narrow black velvet ribbon, a band always enhances the purity of a white throat and neck. A simple gold chain the light Venetian link, with no pendant but a small medallion passing once around the neck, is very suitable for a young girl. Nothing can be more in taste than a necklace on a thin, bony or discolored neck. Very few women in our country should venture upon one after thirty.

In 1855, *Godey's Magazine* stated:

Skirts are made very full. Fashion exacts an immense use of crinoline. Many are gathered at the waist into large round and hollow plaits. The front of the skirt is not as full or as long as the back; the first should leave the foot visible, while the second just clears the ground, or, for every dress, forms a demi-rounded train. Underskirts are arranged so as to meet the exactions of the modern hoop. Corsets are cut much shorter, no longer compressing the hip. Crinoline is worn with one or two flounces, the object being as much breath as possible to the figure.

By January 1859, skirts had become so wide *Godey's* complained that, "Young ladies are now presenting a very formidable appearance of amplitude. The wand of fashion has transformed the most slender girls into the appearance of haystacks." However, this obvious disapproval did not deter their announcement, in the next issue, of a new "self supporting tournure." They enthusiastically stated:

That this invention should not have been made long ago, is surprising, for it is very simple and yet the best article to give beauty to the human figure. All other devices to give rotundity to the shape betray themselves, while this yields to the figure and makes no sign of its existence in the gait of a lady. The light pliant springs which proceed from the steel waistband, below or above the edge of it. As may be needed by short or long waists, perform their office admirably. These are represented by the vertical bands. The horizontal ones represent broad tapes, which sustain the general drapery. Nothing could be invented so well calculated to meet the demands of those who, in full dress, wish to present the realization of a well shaped and graceful figure. This tour-

nure is now generally adopted by fashionable ladies in all parts of the country, and is prized because it never loses its ability to sustain and round the skirts. Without suggesting that it is employed for such a purpose. The demand for it is very great, but the large manufactures in this city will be able to supply every dress and millinery establishment in the country, during the present season. Ladies will be delighted to throw away the cumbersome articles hitherto used to improve the figure, and adopt this admirable invention, which has been patented.

Though *Godey's Lady's Magazine* was known for its beautifully-colored fashion plates, not every department was pleased with women's styles. Dr. Jno. Stainback Wilson, editor of the magazine's Health Department wrote:

While we are no Bloomerite, we must enter our protest against the very long dresses of the present day.

Illustration from *Godey's Lady's Book*, August, 1850.

They are cumbersome, uncleanly, and wastefully extravagant. They prevent freedom of motion in walking; they gather the dirt from the roads and streets as they drag their beautiful lengths along; and they cannot possible last. In view of all these things, then, and others that might be mentioned, our verdict is; let the skirts of dresses be sufficiently bloomerized to swing clear of the ground, at any rate. Pointed waists are nearly as bad as corsets. They compress and paralyze the muscles beneath them; while the internal organs, the stomach, liver, spleen, etc. are crowded downward, thus causing a train of most common and serious disorders to which women are subject.

Death was a very real and present part of life in Victorian times. It demanded respect not only for the departed, but also for the feelings of the living. A death was always followed by a period of mourning. This usually consisted of a year spent in full mourning and another in half mourning. Some widows were known to mourn the rest of their lives.

During this mourning time women were subject to very rigid dress codes. These applied not only to widows, but also to daughters, aunts, sister-in-laws, and cousins. *Godey's Lady's Book* helped keep the ladies up-to-date on what was appropriate. Their March 1855, fashion section carried these recommendations:

Mourning attire for a daughter-mourning dress of parametta cloth trimmed with robins of crepe; small crepe collar with cuffs. **Walking-Dress**-dress of black silk and an overskirt of crepe; crepe collar and sleeves, crepe and silk bonnet with fall, entirely black inside; black parasol; jet brooch and chain; black kid gloves. **Attire for an Aunt**-black poplin dress for the street; black velvet bonnet and black cloth mantle; white collar and sleeves. **Evening Dress**-barege or glacé silk flounces; collar and sleeves, with little but rich embroidery; white kid gloves.

Godey's Lady's Book made the following comments on the wearing of fur:

Furs are at the height of favor and were never more universally worn. Ermine bands are used for trimming opera-cloaks, or sorties du bal; dark fur, and sable, and mink for velvet cloaks, etc., intended for the street. A Victorian, or cape with lappets, or round cloak, with cuffs and a small muff, are considered a full set. The Victorians are usually quite deep, coming half way to the waist behind-the cape to the waist and below it. The cloaks are as deep as ordinary talmas, and with the capes, have a collar. The muffs are still quite small. Furs are lined usually with quilted silk, and ornamented by rich cords and tassels. Sable, Hudson's Bay, and mink are the favorites among the expensive furs-Siberian squirrel, and a mixture of the gray and white fur in stripes, are among the less expensive ones.

Cameos

When Victoria ascended to the throne, cameos were already immensely popular. Excavations had awakened interest in this old art, and Napoleon I had initiated "a Prix de Rome" in 1805, to encourage stone engraving. About that same time a public school was opened in Rome for the study of cameo engraving. It was founded by Pope Leo XII and met with much success.

The early cameos were made from stone. In the sixteenth century workmen turned to shell to meet the demand for more cameos at less expensive prices. Cameos were set in rings, brooches, earrings, and bracelets. The men wore them in watch fobs, rings, and pins. Stone cameos were cut from onyx, agate, sardonyx, cornelian, coral, lava, and jet. The carvers of shell cameos used the shells of the Black Helmet and the pink and white Queen's Conches which were so plentiful in the seacoast towns in Italy.

Cameos made lovely, portable souvenirs for tourists visiting the ruins of Pompeii and Hercelium. When the travelers returned home, their friends were enchanted with these small works of art. Within a short time, Italian cameo artists had shops in England, France, and America. These craftsmen carved cameos in the ancient styles or any other designs the purchaser might select. The January 1850 issue of *Godey's Magazine* included the following note, "Peabody the celebrated Cameo Portrait Cutter, 140 Chestnut Street, is kept busily engaged with the portraits of some of our most eminent citizens."

Cameos are made by cutting away background material to make a design in relief. In stone cameos, a banded agate is often used. The lighter band is used for the figure of the cameo. The remainder is carved away to expose the darker ground. In shell and stone cameos, the true artist takes advantage of different layers and faults in the material to enhance the design.

Stone cameos are generally more valuable than those made of shell. But the medium is not nearly as important as the artistry. The best way to judge a cameo is to examine it with a good magnifying glass. Graceful, smooth-flowing lines with much detail are signs of a good one. The inferior ones seem to have sharper lines, fewer details, and a harsh look. Be sure to hold the cameo to the light and examine it for possible cracks.

Many antique cameos were reset in the late seventeen and early eighteen hundreds. Some craftsmen were expert at copying antique pieces. This makes accurate dating almost impossible. However, there are usually some clues to help determine age.

If a cameo is made of lava, it is almost certainly Victorian. Other clues are the style of design (Greek, Roman, etc.), types of clothing and hair styles on the figures, and the type of mounting. If the cameo is mounted as a brooch, carefully examine the pin and hook. Safety catches are a twentieth century adaptation. If the cameo has one, then it is either not older than the early nineteen hundreds or a new catch has been added.

If it is an addition, this can usually be ascertained by more careful examination. Look for signs of soldering. Often the new catch is attached to a small plate jointed to the back of the brooch. Next look closely at the pin and notice what kind of hinge it has. If the sharp point of the pin extends past the body of the brooch, it is an "oldie."

Gold, silver, pinchbeck, gold filled, cut-steel, and jet were some of the materials used for mounting cameos. The type of metal used can often give an indication of when it was made. If the mounting is pinchbeck it was probably made between the early seventeen and the mid-eighteen hundreds.

Gold electroplating was patented in 1849 so, if the piece was plated, it was made after that date. Nine karat gold was legalized in 1854. A piece in 9K would have to be made after that date. A popular metal used for mountings in the 1880s was silver, but this does not mean that all cameos mounted in silver were made at that time. All the clues have to be examined before a judgment on age can be made.

Scenic cameos are generally more expensive than bust cameos. A very popular motif around 1860 was what is known as "Rebecca at the Well." There are many variations on this theme, but they usually include a cottage, a bridge, and a girl.

Technically, a cameo is made by cutting away the background of a material to make a design in relief, but there are some items called cameos that do not fit this description. Josiah Wedgewood's factory produced jasperware plaques in blue and white and black and white. These had the look of a cameo, but they were molded. These mass produced cameos were originally very inexpensive, but today they are quite collectible. Fine examples of cameos are pictured throughout this book.

Chatelaines

Chatelaines were a very necessary accessory for the Victorian matron. Considered a vital part of home management, they were also ornamental and prestigious. The chatelaine consisted of a large central piece which was either hooked or pinned at the waist. From this extended chains with swivel attachments for hanging a variety of household necessities such as a pair of scissors, a sewing case with needles and thread, a knife, a vinaigrette, a coin purse, a pencil, a note case, a scent bottle, and a watch and key.

Inspiration for this type of accessory may be traced to medieval times when the keeper of the keys, which were usually worn on a chain around the waist, was the person with authority. Chatelaines were in and out of fashion for several hundred years. The *Art-Journal Illustrated Catalogue* of 1851 made this comment about them:

> The modern chatelaine is but a reproduction of an article of decorative ornament, worn by ladies in our own country more than a century and a half ago. The watch, the scissors, etui, and pincushion were then ostentatiously appended to the dresses of the ladies, quite as much for ornament as for use.

Chatelaines were made from gold, pinchbeck, silver, silver plate, stamped metal, and cut-steel. They are quite collectible.

Cut-Steel

England was well known for its cut-steel industry. The most noted producer was Mathew Boulton of Birmingham. He made beautiful rings and brooches, using Wedgewood cameos in cut-steel frames.

A piece of cut-steel is made by riveting rosettes fashioned from thin metal to another metal plate that has been cut in a design. Although it is called cut-steel, the metal could be silver alloy or even tin. The glitter of cut-steel comes from light reflecting off the rosettes. Imitation cut-steel is made by stamping the rosettes from a sheet of metal. The best way to determine the authenticity of a piece is by looking at the back. If there are two pieces of metal and one is a solid plate with rivets showing, chances are that the piece is genuine.

Even though cut-steel glittered, it was not flashy, so the Victorians considered it proper for day wear. Many lovely cloak clasps, shoe buckles, brooches, and chatelaines were made.

Daguerreotypes & Gutta-percha

In the 1840s, everybody who was anybody had a photographic sitting. A sitting was an accurate description since the subject had to sit in the sun for up to thirty minutes in order to get the proper exposure. Louis J. M. Daguerre perfected this photographic process. In 1839, he sold it to the French government. That same year Samuel F. B. Morse, inventor of the telegraph, saw these new daguerreotypes and was fascinated. On his return to the United States, he shared his new interest and soon photography was flourishing.

Thanks to daguerreotypes, we have pictures of notable people such as John Quincy Adams,

Andrew Jackson, Daniel Webster, Henry Wadsworth Longfellow, and Harriet Beecher Stowe. It is estimated that by 1849, Americans were being photographed at the rate of three million a year.

The daguerreotype is identified by the mirror-like reflection of its background. Since the pictures were under glass, a proper container was an important consideration. Thus the daguerreotype case and locket came into existence.

Materials most often used for these cases were molded paper, composition, and gutta-percha. The latter two materials are of the greatest interest to the jewelry and accessory minded, because many decorative articles were made from them.

In 1854, Samuel Peck of Connecticut patented a composition case made of shellac, sawdust, and coloring matter. When this mixture was heated, it could be pressed in a mold to create many pleasing designs.

Although many of today's generation have never heard of gutta-percha, it was very prevalent during the Victorian era. Made from the sap of a Malayan tree, its usefulness was discovered during the rubber making process and introduced to Paris in 1842. The *Crystal Palace Catalogue of 1851* included this definition: "The Isonandra Gutta, the source of the gum-elastic, known as gutta-percha, one of the most useful substances introduced into the arts during the present century-."

Because it was very durable and highly impressionable, it lent itself well to the Victorian taste for embellishment. In its finished state the color is black or brownish. This dark color made it a natural material for mourning jewelry, but it was by no means used exclusively for that purpose. Lockets, brooches, bracelets, and walking cane heads were just a few of its many uses. The October 1855 *Godey's* listed this unique use, "Gutta-percha for a Decayed Tooth-Procure: a small piece of gutta-percha, about as much as will fill the cavity in your tooth, nearly level; drop it into boiling water, and while in the soft state press it into the tooth; then hold in the mouth cold water to harden the gutta-percha."

The Gutta Percha Company displayed many items at the Crystal Palace Exposition in 1851. Included were a sculptural-like group entitled the "Deer and Hounds," a huge, highly embellished sideboard, a chaise lounge with a back of gutta-percha elastic, and even printing type. This wonderful new material was one of the first natural plastics.

Many pieces of gutta-percha are still available at reasonable prices. As more people become aware of this unique material, prices are sure to rise.

Garter Jewelry

Victorian jewelers took designs from a variety of sources. One popular motif stemmed from the Royal Order of the Garter. This Order, founded by King Edward III in 1348 to strengthen military leadership, is the highest honor a British monarch can bestow. Members of the order wear a blue garter buckled on their knee. Victoria was much too modest for this tradition. Instead she chose to wear it on her arm. Thus the garter became a very fashionable jewelry motif.

Bracelets displaying this design were most plentiful. Rings were made in the form of a garter, and lockets were engraved with this motif.

Hairwork Jewelry

Victorian women wore jewelry not only as a decorative accessory but also as an outward expression of their inner most feelings. To them it was perfectly natural for Queen Victoria to have a bracelet made from her children's baby teeth. This may seem far-fetched to today's generation, but in those days it was a high privilege to have a part of a loved one near. To have carelessly disposed of the teeth would have been throwing away a part of her children.

This sentimental nature fostered an increasing interest in hairwork jewelry. For years it had been popular to own a lock of a loved one's hair. This was usually kept in a special compartment in the back of a brooch, a locket, a ring, or even in a watch fob. In the early years of the nineteenth century, hair began to be used for the actual making of jewelry.

Hairwork became a drawing room pastime, just as popular as crocheting or tatting. What could be more rewarding than working with the hair of a loved one. This pastime spread throughout Europe. In December 1850, *Godey's Lady's Book* introduced it to American women:

Of the various employments for the fingers lately introduced among our country women, none is, perhaps more interesting than that we are about to describe, via. hairwork; a recent importation from Germany, where it is very fashionable. Hitherto almost exclusively confined to professed manufactures of hair trinkets, this work has now become a drawing-room occupation, as elegant and as free from all annoyances and objections of litter, dirt, or unpleasant smells, as the much practiced knitting, netting or crochet can be; while a small handkerchief will at any time cover the apparatus and materials in use. By acquiring a knowledge of this art, ladies will be themselves enabled to manufacture the hair of beloved friends, and relatives into the bracelets, chains, rings, earrings, and devoices, and thus insure that they do actually wear the memento they prize, and not a fabric substituted for it, as we fear has sometimes been the case.

The hairwork was done on a round table while sitting or standing, depending on the table's height. Many ladies preferred to stand because their full dresses sometimes interfered with the dangling weights on the hair.

Hair preparation was most important. Not only must it be boiled in soda water for fifteen (15) minutes, but it also had to be sorted into lengths and divided into strands containing from twenty to thirty hairs. All this had to be done before the actual work began! This was a true labor of love.

Godey's article gave complete directions for preparing the hair and included patterns for two types of chains and bracelets. Working with these directions and subsequent patterns in *Godey's Lady's Book* and *Peterson's Magazine*, many finely executed pieces were made.

The watch chain was by far the most popular piece of hairwork jewelry. By providing her love with a chain from her hair, a young lady was assured that she would be in his thoughts many times a day. Hair bracelets combining the hair of each child were a popular keepsake for a mother. A guard chain was always useful, and openwork crosses and earrings were quite lovely.

When the hair work was completed, it was sent to the jeweler for fittings. Beautiful clasps with compartments for photographs, closures mounted with stones, and even miniatures were used to complete bracelets. A variety of fittings were available for finishing brooches and earrings. To make long necklaces or guard chains, the jeweler used small gold tubes to join the sections of hair.

If the lady did not trust her own talents for doing hairwork, there were other methods for obtaining this jewelry. The monthly issues of *Godey's Lady's Book* included illustrations of hair jewelry that could be ordered through the editor. One had only to choose from the many designs and send in the hair along with the proper amount of money. Below are two price lists from *Godey's Lady's Book*:

	August 1855	**March 1859**
Breast Pins	from $4.00 to $12.00	$4.00 to $12.00
Ear Rings	from $4.50 to $10.00	$4.50 to $10.00
Bracelets	from $3.00 to $15.00	$3.00 to $15.00
Rings	from $1.00 to $ 2.00	$1.50 to $ 3.00
Necklaces	from $4.50 to $ 7.00	$6.00 to $15.00
Fob Chains	from $4.00 to $ 8.00	$6.00 to $12.00
The Charms of Faith, Hope and Charity		$4.50
Hair Studs		$5.50 to $11.00 (set)
Sleeve Buttons		$6.50 to $11.00 (set)

There were jewelers in London and New York whose primary business was to make the hairwork jewelry that was so much in demand. Linherr and Company of New York was one of the most famous. At the Crystal Palace Exposition of 1853, in addition to their full line of hair bracelets, brooches, necklaces, and chains, they displayed a full-size tea set made entirely of hair. The October 8, 1853 issue of *Gleason Pictorial Drawing-Room Companion* spoke highly of this display. The following excerpt from this article gives an indication of how popular hairwork jewelry had become.

> It is a very modern fashion to so braid and form the hair as to make not only an outside ornament of itself, but also to produce the most beautiful and delicate effect. The perfection to which this new art has been brought, has led to the general adoption of these ornaments by the ladies, and they are now almost as much worn by the "upper ten" as are golden ornaments; and that the effect-to say nothing of the pleasant ideal of thus wearing the hair of those we love and cherish-is incomparably superior to metallic jewelry, no person of good taste will venture to deny.

Some hairwork pieces were made of horsehair. Because it was coarser than human hair, it was easier to work. Consequently, it became the perfect material for a beginner. After mastering the art in horsehair, one was then ready to proceed to work the precious hair of a friend or a relative. Indeed it was precious and not only because of the sentiment involved. In the 1850s, hair was an expensive commodity with a vast array of commercial uses. Every spring hair merchants visited festivals, fairs, and markets throughout France and Germany. They offered young girls ribbons, combs, and trinkets in exchange for their hair, "The quantity of hair produced by the annual harvest was calculated at 200,000 pounds weight."[2] This hair was made into artificial ringlets, false plaits, beards, moustaches, perukes, and jewelry. Its value was often triple that of silver.

The comment by Leigh Hunt that appeared in the May 1855 *Godey's* sums up beautifully the Victorian's love of hair, "Hair is at once the most delicate and lasting of our materials, and survives us, like love. It is so light, so gentle, so escaping from the idea of death, that with a lock of hair belonging to a child or friend, we may almost look up to heaven and compare notes with the angelic nature-may almost say, 'I have a piece of thee here, not unworthy of thy being now.'"

Scottish Jewelry

Queen Victoria loved Scotland and all things Scottish. Her pride in her Stuart ancestry and the popularity of Sir Walter Scott's novels made Scottish jewelry a fashionable accessory.

In 1848, the Royal couple purchased "Balmoral" to use as a summer home. Since this home closely resembled the home of Sir Walter Scott, it held a romantic fascination for the young Queen and her subjects. This led to a new country house design known as Scottish Baronial. The desire for things Scottish became even more apparent.

As early as 1851, people were wearing tartans. On their arms were flexible bracelets enameled with matching plaid designs. At a state ball in Buckingham Palace, celebrating the opening of the Crystal Palace Exposition, the royal children wore tartans and the guests wore Stuart tartans. When the Queen visited the Emperor and Empress of France in 1855, her entire family wore kilts. The tartans fascinated the Empress, and she introduced them to Paris.

Brooches and pins were the most popular form of Scottish jewelry. Mountings were usually silver, but some gold and even enameled ones were used. Moss agate, bloodstone, cornelian, and other stones native to Scotland were popular. The most popular stone, by far, was the Cairngorm, named for the Cairngorm Mountains of Scotland in which it is found. This smokey yellow quartz is often incorrectly called smokey topaz or Scotch topaz.

Scottish jewelry was popular throughout England until the death of Albert in 1861. After his mourning period, though the jewelry continued to be made, it was never again quite as popular.

Serpent Jewelry

When Albert gave Victoria an engagement ring in the form of a serpent, he generated a revival of this ancient decorative motif. The Queen was particularly fond of this design. She owned several serpent pieces, including a bracelet, which she wore at her first council meeting.

The Snake motif, believed to be a symbol of eternal love, was used throughout the Victorian period. On a stroll through London, ladies could be seen wearing serpent rings, serpents entwined around their arms, and serpents coiled on their brooches.

In the book *David Copperfield*, by Charles Dickens, which was published in 1850, a character tells of window shopping with his wife, "We look into the glittering windows of the jeweler's shops and I show Sophy which of the diamond-eyed serpents, coiled up on white satin rising-grounds, I would give her if I could afford it."

The style was so accepted that the 1855 *Godey's Magazine* gave complete instructions for making a serpent bracelet using skeins of gold twist, dark green cord, and violet and green silk. It was to be

worked "in imitation of hair." Four number six steel beads were used for eyes. This enabled ladies who could not afford good serpent bracelets to wear the latest design.

Popular Stones & Materials

Amethyst

The amethyst was a very fashionable stone throughout the Victorian era. Because of its ecclesiastical association, it was acceptable to wear in the latter stages of mourning. Since amethysts were plentiful, they were affordable and could be worn by all classes. In a yellow gold or pinchbeck mounting, surrounded by seed pearls, they were quite lovely.

The amethyst is a member of the quartz family of stones. It is known for its violet to red-purple hue. In fact, the name amethyst is now synonymous with the color. The finest colored and most valuable are known as Siberian amethyst. This refers to the quality of the stone and not the location from which it comes.

In olden days the amethyst was believed to possess the power to protect the wearer and bring good luck. The person born in February is fortunate to be able to claim this as their birth stone.

Bloodstone

Victorians wore and admired the bloodstone. This ancient stone, also known as heliotrope (Heel-ee-trope), is actually a dark green chalcedony with flecks of red. The ancients believed the red to be drops of blood; hence the name bloodstone. Many magical powers were ascribed to it including the power to stop bleeding and preserve health. Even though it is one of the birth stones for March, it is seldom used today. When a piece of jewelry contains bloodstone, it is usually old.

Coral

The Victorians had a special love for coral jewelry. Since Roman times it was believed to possess the power to ward off evil and danger. Consequently, it was a favorite christening present. A look at any family portrait of the period will show this popularity. Every baby and young child pictured will be wearing a coral necklace. These were added to as the child grew, as we do the "add a bead" and "add a pearl" necklaces today. Baby rattles with coral stems, and coral teething rings were also popular.

Coral was not limited to the young. In 1845, the Prince of the Two Sicilies gave his bride, the Duchess d' Aumale, a beautiful parure of coral jewelry.

This started a fashion among women of all ages that continued to the late 1860s. The November 1855 *Godey's* contained this comment on coral:

> Coral ornaments are the favorite style of jewelry. The bracelets are formed of strands of coral passing round the arm several times, and finished with a long tassel of the same beads. The bracelet sultan forms a pretty summer ornament; it is composed of strands of gold cord intermixed with green silk and coral beads, wide and worked in a Gothic pattern, from which hang five small coral balls, attached to the bracelet by gold ribbons.

Robert Phillips, an English jeweler, did much to popularize coral. He encouraged Italian craftsmen to come to England, and he entered coral jewelry in all the important exhibitions. This did so much for the economy of Naples, where most coral is found, that the King of Naples honored him for his contribution to the industry.

Coral is the calcareous skeletons of marine animals. It is found in abundance in the Naples' area. The most prized colors are deep red and angel skin pink. Because coral is easy to work, it is used for designs which call for a profusion of flowers and leaves.

Many Victorian brooches and earrings were made using the natural or branch coral. This was a less expensive way to use the stone. Consequently, there are more of these pieces available than the highly carved ones.

Goldstone

Goldstone is quite often encountered in old jewelry. It was used for the ground of some mosaics and as a stone for cuff links or stick pins. Since it is neither gold nor a stone, it can be added to the list of misnomers in the jewelry field. Goldstone is an imitation aventurine made of glass to which copper crystals have been added. It has a gold spangled look that is quite attractive. Once seen it is very easy to recognize.

Code in Front of Name

(A) Auction House - Auction Price
(C) Collector - Collector Asking Price
(D) Dealer - Dealer's Asking Price

Bracelets

(C) (W. Baldwin)

1850-1860 bracelet, 14K with taille d' epergne enameling and pearls. Widest point 1-3/4" dia., 6-1/4" long.
Price: $1,395

(D) (Jewelry Box Antiques)

1860s bracelet, hinged, gilt on brass, note granulation, 1/2" w.
Price: $225

(C) (W. Baldwin)

Scottish bracelet, silver with agates and cornelian, head 1-1/8" x 1-3/8", length 6-3/4".
Price: $625

(A) (Photo courtesy of Skinner, Inc., Boston, Mass - 12-04-90)

Circa 1860, Etruscan Revival gold bracelet, Castellani, each link with wire twist detail is mounted on fetter-shaped loops (some floral cluster missing).
Price: $10,500

(C) (Jeanenne Bell)

1840-1850s bracelet, 18K yellow hollow gold set with baroque pearl, approx. 7" long and the largest plaque, 1-3/4" x 1-3/4".
Price: $1,800

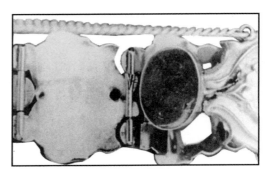

Back view of bracelet showing construction method.

1850-1860 bracelet, gold fittings, hairwork, engraved "Sister Hair." **Price: $485**

(C) (Jeanenne Bell)

1850s bracelet, gilt brass mtg., lava cameos, colors are black, putty, reddish brown, and gold brown (no two alike), 3/8" x 7/8". **Price: $1,850**

(D) (Jewelry Box Antiques)

1850s bracelet, silver mtg., nine lava cameos, 5/8" x 7/8". **Price: $500**

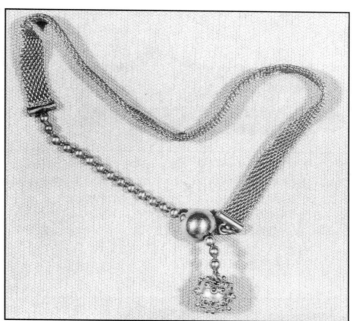

(D) (Jewelry Box Antiques)

1860-1880 bracelet, gold-filled. Note Etruscan work on drop, 3/4" wide. **Price: $150**

(C) (Dr. Betty Walls)

Bracelet, 18K yellow gold set with diamonds, embellished with royal blue enameling. **Price: $3,000**

(A) (Photo courtesy of Sotheby's, New York 10-6-83)

Circa 1840 bracelet, gold with cabochon garnets. Reverse of center garnet is a compartment for hair. Scale type band is flexible. **Price: $1,430**

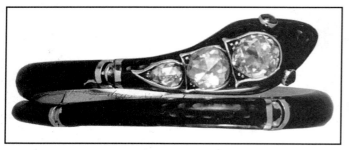

Circa 1844 bracelet, gold snake motif. The articulated body is decorated with ultra-marine guilloche enameling. Head set with three rose diamonds and cabochon ruby eyes (slightly imperfect). £2,530.   **Price: $4,500**

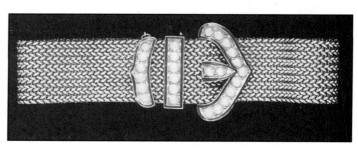

Mid 1800s bracelet, gold with half pearl and royal blue enamel, £880.   **Price: $1,570**

Mid 19th century bracelet, gold hinged bangle with royal blue enameling with approx. 6 cts. of old mine cut diamonds.   **Price: $3,080**

Circa 2nd half of the 19th century bracelet, gold set with pink topaz, rose diamonds and cushion-shaped diamonds. The topaz and diamond cluster can be detached and worn as a brooch, £3,740.   **Price: $6,660**

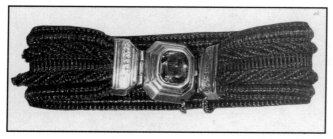

1850-1860 bracelet, 15K fittings, hairwork with amethyst in clasp, 3/4" x 6".   **Price: $475**

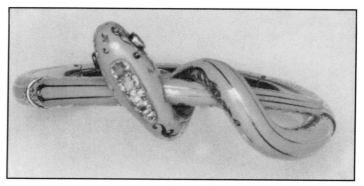

Early Victorian bracelet, yellow gold hinged bangle, serpent motif with Cambridge-blue enamel. The head is set with 5 diamonds and ruby eyes, £650.   **Price: $1,160**

Brooches & Pins

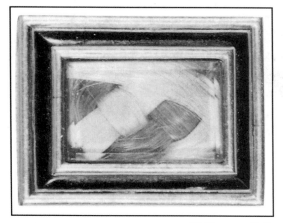

(C) (Jeanenne Bell)

1840-1850 brooch, 18K memorial pin with black enameling, white and brown hair under beveled glass, 1" x 7/8". **Price: $300**

(C) (Jeanenne Bell)

1850-1870 brooch, jet-matte and shiny finish, 1-1/4" x 1-3/4".
Price: $180

(D) (Jewelry Box Antiques)

1850s-1860s cameo brooch, yellow gold-filled, 2-5/8" x 1-3/4". **Price: $395**

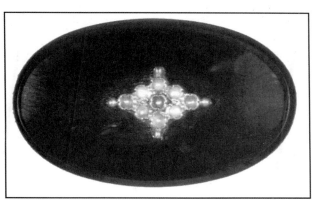

(D) (Jewelry Box Antiques)

1840-1860 brooch, 18K jet with seed pearl, 1-1/2" x 5/8". **Price: $295**

(D) (Jewelry Box Antiques)

1850-1860 brooch, gold over brass with some gold ornamentation, stone cameo, 3" x 1-1/4". **Price: $325**

(D) (Jewelry Box Antiques)

1840-1860s brooch, 14K yellow gold set with coral. approx. 1-1/8" dia.
Price: $395

(D) (Jewelry Box Antiques)

1840-1850 brooch, 15K grapes of seed pearls. 1" dia. **Price: $395**

(D) (Jewelry Box Antiques)

1840-1860 brooch, yellow rolled gold mounting set with "Three Graces" shell cameo, 2-1/4" x 2-1/8".
Price: $695

(C) (W. Baldwin)

1850-1860 brooch, gold-filled, angel-skin carved coral, 2-1/2" x 1-1/2". **Price: $1,800**

(C) (Jeanenne Bell)

1850-1860 brooch, 15K yellow gold fittings with open weave hairwork, engraved "Mary," 1-3/4" x 1". **Price: $495**

(C) (Jeanenne Bell)

Circa 1840-1860 brooch, 18K yellow gold with table worked hair, 3-1/2" long. **Price: $350**

(D) (Jewelry Box Antiques)

1840-1850 brooch, gilt mtg. with enameled leaves and molded cameo. **Price: $95**

(D) (Jewelry Box Antiques)

1850-1860 brooch, Pinchbeck mtg., shell cameo, 1-1/4" x 1-1/2". **Price: $295**

(D) (Jowsey & Roe, Whitby, England)

Circa 1840-1860 brooch, jet, "IN MEMORY OF MY DEAR BROTHER," glass center for hair, 1-1/2" x 1-1/8". **Price: $250**

1850-1860 brooch, angel-skin carved coral, 2-3/4" x 3/4". **Price: $525**

1840s brooch, 10K yellow hollow gold, 1-5/8 x 1-1/8". **Price: $300**

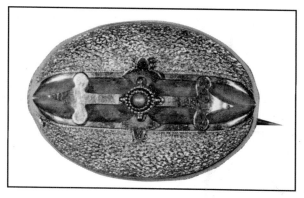

1850-1860 brooch, gold-filled with gold ornamentation and seed pearl. Made to hold watch. **Price: $165**

1850-1860 brooch, 15K fittings, open weave light brown hairwork with leaf ornamentation, 2" x 1". **Price: $450**

Circa 1850-1870 hair brooch, 18K yellow gold. **Price: $400**

1850-1860 brooch, gutta-percha, angel holding baby, 1-3/4" x 2". A popular biblical reference. **Price: $300**

(C) (Jeanenne Bell)

1850-1860 brooch, gutta-percha pair of birds, 1-1/4" x 2".
Price: $95

(C) (Jeanenne Bell)

Early 1800s brooch, 18K surrounded by pearls, rock crystal covers flowers made of hair, 1-1/4" x 1-1/8".
Price: $650

(D) (Jewelry Box Antiques)

1840-1860s brooch, jet and yellow gold-filled bow-shaped with hairwork.
Price: $300

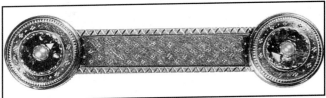

(C) (W. Baldwin)

Mid 1800s brooch, yellow gold with amethyst and pearls, 2-1/2" x 5/8".
Price: $495

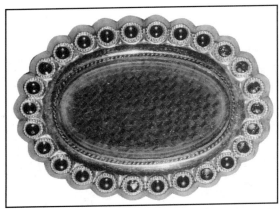

(C) (Jeanenne Bell)

1850-1870 brooch, gold-filled with black enameling, hair in flat weave under beveled glass, 1-3/8" x 1-1/8".
Price: $175

(A) (Photo courtesy of Sotheby's, Park Bernet and Co., London 12-15-83)

Circa 1860 brooch, gold with banded agate, £440.
Price: $780

(C) (Jeanenne Bell)

Early 1800s brooch, Pinchbeck memorial piece with black enameling, braided hair under crystal, 1-1/4" x 1".
Price: $200

(D) (Jowsy & Roe, Whitby, England)

Circa 1840 brooch, jet memorial piece, some damage to reverse, 2" x 2-1/2". **Price: $295**

(A) (Photo courtesy of Sotheby's, London 12-15-83)

Circa 1840 brooch, gold with attractive colored step-cut emerald and cushion-shaped diamonds, £27,500. **Price: $48,950**

(A) (Photo courtesy of Sotheby's, London 4-14-83)

Circa 1840 brooch, cabochon sapphire with rose cut and cushion-shaped diamonds, £7,480. **Price: $13,315**

1850-1860 brooch, gilt mtg., gold stone front, glass covered compartment in rear, 1-1/2" x 1-1/4".

Price: $135

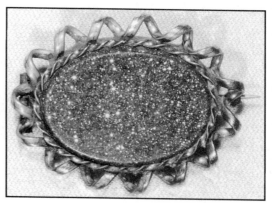

(C) (Jeanenne Bell)

(D) (Camille Grace)

1850-1860 brooch, gold-filled with amethyst, 1-1/4" x 1". **Price: $195**

(D) (Jewelry Box Antiques)

1850-1870 brooch, gold-filled, jet cross, 1" dia. **Price: $175**

(A) (Photo courtesy of Phillips, London 12-24-83)

Mid 19th century brooch, gold-shaped enameled plaques with pearls and diamonds, detachable fittings, £850.
Price: $1,525

(C) (W. Baldwin)

Scottish brooch, silver with cairngorm stone, 3-1/2" dia.   **Price: $675**

(D) (Camille Grace)

Scottish brooch, English sterling hallmark, Scottish with agate and amethyst, 7/8" x 7/8".   **Price: $295**

Scottish Brooch, silver with cairngorm, 3-1/2" dia.   **Price: $675**

(C) (W. Baldwin)

(D) (Camille Grace)

Scottish brooch, silver-Scottish agate and cairngorm, 1-1/8" dia.   **Price: $375**

(A) (Photo courtesy of Sotheby's, New York 10-6-83)

Mid 19th century brooch, silver and gold with carved black and white onyx "Moonface" cameo, embellished with rose cut diamonds.   **Price: $1,760**

(C) (Jeanenne Bell)

1850-1860 brooch, yellow gold mtg. with hairwork, 1-1/2" x 7/8". **Price: $495**

(D) (Jewelry Box Antiques)

Mid 1800s brooch, yellow rolled gold mounting set with beautifully done shell cameo. Center section is reversible so that the glazed compartment (reverse) can be worn in front, 2-3/4" x 2-1/4". **Price: $750**

1850-1860 brooch, yellow gold with a compartment in back for hair, 1-5/8" x 1-3/8". **Price: $475**

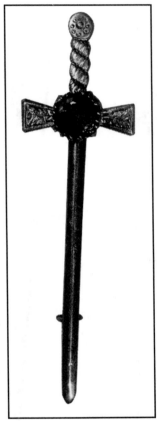

(C) (W.Baldwin)

Scottish Brooch, hallmarked sterling, cairngorm stone, 3" x 3/4". **Price: $250**

(C) (W.Baldwin)

(D) (Jewelry Box Antiques)

Mid 1800s brooch, hairwork on black, 2" x 1-9/16". **Price: $225**

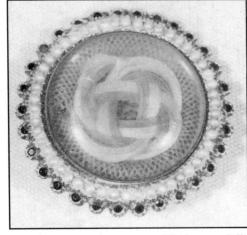

(C) (Jeanenne Bell)

Early 1800s brooch, 18K with pearls and jet, hair under rock crystal, also woven hair background, 1-3/8" diameter. **Price: $595**

Mid-19th century brooch, gold oval with shell cameo of Bacchante, signed with mark of Castellani on the cone-shaped pin cap, £900. **Price: $1,600**

Circa 1865 micro-mosaic pin, Italy, yellow gold depicting Raphael's, "Madonna of the Chair." **Price: $3,600**

Circa 1840-1860 brooch, 10K yellow gold with hand-carved shell cameo depicting a scene of boys with a bird, approx. 2-1/4" x 2". **Price: $995**

Circa 1840-1860 brooch/pendant, hand-carved biblical scene in new 14K yellow gold mounting, overall approx, 2-1/4" x 1-3/8". **Price: $995**

(C) (Jeanenne Bell)

Circa 1840-1860 snake pin, 18K yellow gold.
Price: $400

(A) (Photo courtesy of William Doyle Galleries 9-21-83)

Circa 1840s eye pin, yellow gold with blue enamel snake.
Price: $900

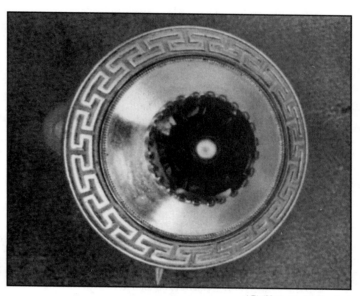

(C) (Vernetta McCarthy)

1860s pin, yellow gold-filled, glass purple stone set with pearl in Grecian key design, 1-3/8" dia.
Price: $165

(D) (Jewelry Box Antiques)

1840s pin, hollow gold-filled, 1-11/16" x 1-1/4".
Price: $95

Code in Front of Name

(A) Auction House - Auction Price
(C) Collector - Collector Asking Price
(D) Dealer - Dealer's Asking Price

Chatelaines

(A) (Photo courtesy William Doyle Galleries, New York 9-19-90)

Circa 1860 French chatelaine, yellow gold and silver, suspending a pair of ornamented lidded perfumes and centered by an Etui. The richly scrolled and foliated frame surrounds agate fields decorated with rose diamond and ruby nature scenes with birds and flowers.

Price: $20,000

(A) (Photo courtesy of Phillips, London 7-28-83)

Early 19th century chatelaine, gold with enameling, appendages include a locket base seal, locket globe fob, a seal, a watch (a later addition), and a watch key, £2,200.

Price: $3,925

Crosses

(C) (Jeanenne Bell)

1850-1860 gutta-percha cross, 1-1/2" x 2-1/2". **Price: $195**

(D) (Jewelry Box Antiques)

1840-1860 gutta-percha cross, gold-filled, 7/8" x 1-3/4". **Price: $90**

(D) (Jewelry Box Antiques)

1850-1870 cross, gilt on brass with gold ornamentation, 1-1/3" x 2-3/8", note trefoils. **Price: $150**

Victorian cross, set with round and oval-shaped turquoise cabochon, highlighted by mine-cut diamonds, 15 ct.
Price: $800

(A) (Photo courtesy of Skinner, Inc., Boston, Mass-9-25-90)

Code in Front of Name

(A) Auction House - Auction Price
(C) Collector - Collector Asking Price
(D) Dealer - Dealer's Asking Price

(C) (Jeanenne Bell)

1850-1870 necklace with cross, yellow gold fittings all hairwork cross, 1-1/4" x 2", chain 18" l.

Price: $550

(D) (Jewelry Box Antiques)

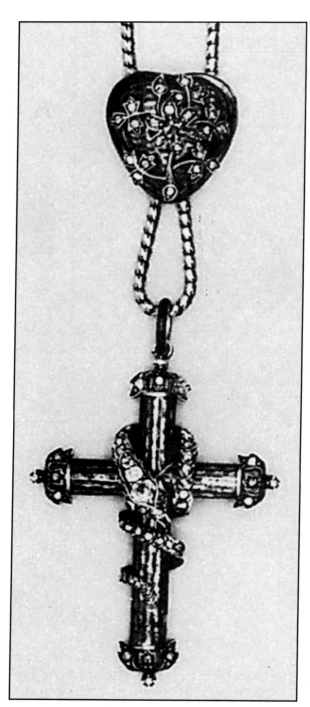

(A) (Photo courtesy of Sotheby's, London 4-14-83)

Circa 1835, Croiz-a-La-Jeanette, gold with royal blue enamel and rose-cut diamonds, serpent has ruby eyes, some enamel damage, £1,100.

Price: $2,000

1840-1860 necklace, 18K yellow gold cross, approx. 1-3/8" x 1-1/2" on 14K yellow gold chain 16". **Price: $1,175**

Lockets

(A) (Photo courtesy of William Doyle Galleries New York 12-7-83)

Mid-1800s gold, coral and emerald locket, 18K yellow gold containing pink coral, white enamel, and four square emeralds.
Price: $950

(C) (W. Baldwin)

1840-1850 locket, pinchbeck contains daguerreotype, 1" x 1-1/2". **Price: $300**

(C) (Jeanenne Bell)

1850-1860 locket, gutta-percha with a tin type and ornate interior, 1-3/4" x 2". **Price: $195**

Interior view of locket.

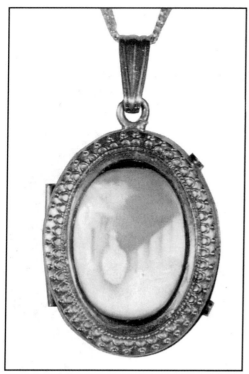

(D) (Jewelry Box Antiques)

1850-1860 locket, yellow gold-filled, variation of "Rebecca at the Well," new G.F. chain and bale, 1" x 1-1/2".

Price: $325

(C) (Jeanenne Bell)

1840-1850 locket, pinchbeck-Prince of Wales, made of feathers, 3/4" x 1". **Price: $250**

(D) (Jewelry Box Antiques)

1840-1860 locket, gilt over brass with glass insets and tintype of baby, 5/8" x 7/8". **Price: $165**

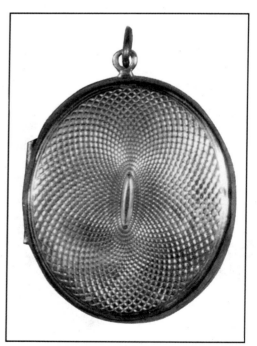

(D) (Jewelry Box Antiques)

1840-1860 locket, gold-filled glass insets, depth indicates it originally contained a daguerreotype, 1-1/4" x 1-1/2".

Price: $130

(D) (Jewelry Box Antiques)

1850-1860 locket, gold-filled with 5 turquoise stones, 1" x 2". **Price: $195**

(D) (Camille Grace)

1840-1860 locket, yellow gold with 5 pearls, 5/8" x 3/8". **Price: $495**

(C) (Jeanenne Bell)

1850-1860 locket, gold-filled glass insets, 1" x 1-1/2". **Price: $155**

(C) (Jeanenne Bell)

1850-1860 locket, gold-filled hand-engraved, button on top activates latch similar to a mechanism in hunting case watch, 1-1/4" dia., has obvious repair. **Price: $150**

1850-1860 locket, gold over brass rim with gold top, cross enameled cobalt blue, back has glass covered opening with lock of hair, 5/8" x 7/8". **Price: $195**

1850-1870 locket, gold over brass, cross in blue enamel, leaf design in black enamel, cross has "in memory of." Back has garter motif, inside are pressed flowers under glass enclosure, 1" x 1-1/8". **Price: $125**

1850-1870 locket, gutta-percha on original black ribbon, 1-1/4" x 1-1/2". **Price: $165**

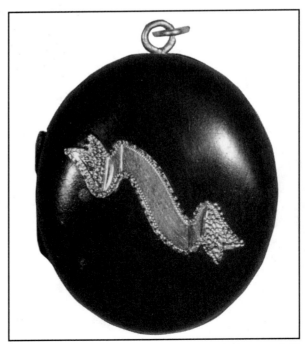

1845-1855 locket, gutta-percha with gold ornamentation, 1" x 1-1/4". **Price: $165**

1860 locket, composition same design on inside as the one pictured below, 1-1/2" x 2". **Price: $125**

1859-1860 locket, 10K gold locket on new 14K chain, 1" x 1-1/4". **Price: $340**

Early 1800s locket, pinchbeck, hand-engraved, 1-5/8" dia. **Price: $325**

Necklaces

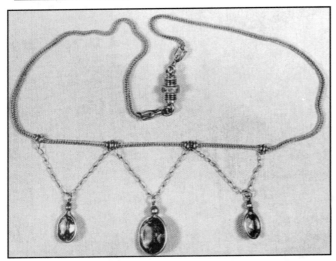

(C) (W. Baldwin)

1840-1850 necklace, yellow gold, amethyst, 16" l.
Price: $925

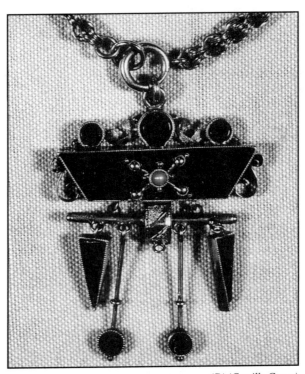

(D) (Camille Grace)

1850-1860 necklace, 14K onyx and seed pearl chain, 14-1/2" l, drop 1-3/8" x 2". **Price: $895**

(A) (Photo courtesy William Doyle Galleries, New York 9-19-90)

Micro-mosaic pendant necklace, 18K granular yellow gold. **Price: $13,000**

(A) (Photo courtesy of Sotheby's, London 7-28-83)

Circa 1840 necklace, gold and turquoise serpent, head is pavé set with turquoise and rose diamonds, in fitted case, £2,090. **Price: $3,720**

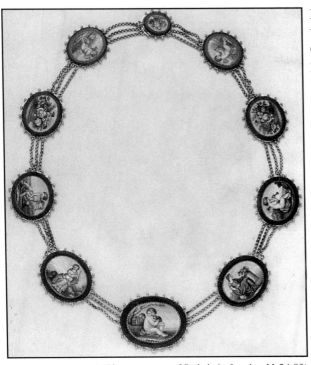

Mid-19th century necklace with matching brooch and earrings (necklace only pictured). Features gold with Roman mosaics of putti, muses and flowers, £3,740. **Price: $6,670**

(A) (Photo courtesy of Sotheby's, London 11-24-83)

Circa 1840 necklace, gold with moonstones and garnets.
Price: $1,650

(A) (Photo courtesy of Sotheby's, New York 10-3-83)

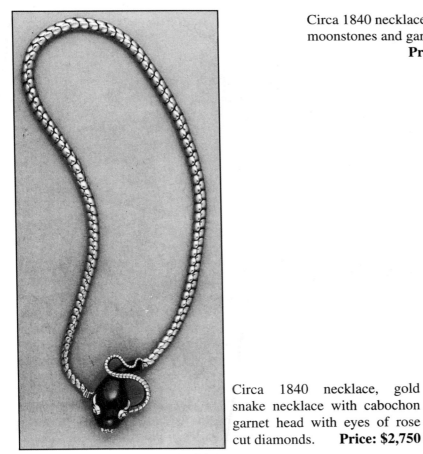

Circa 1840 necklace, gold snake necklace with cabochon garnet head with eyes of rose cut diamonds. **Price: $2,750**

(A) (Photo courtesy of Sotheby's, New York 12-7-83)

(A) (Photo courtesy of William Doyle Galleries, New York)

Victorian coral necklace. **Price: $625**

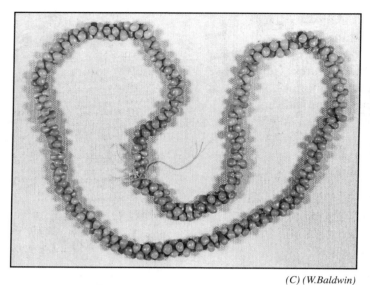

Necklace, coral beads, 19" l. **Price: $350**

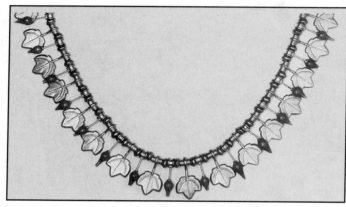

Mid-19th century necklace, gold Etruscan style, £1,500.
Price: $2,670

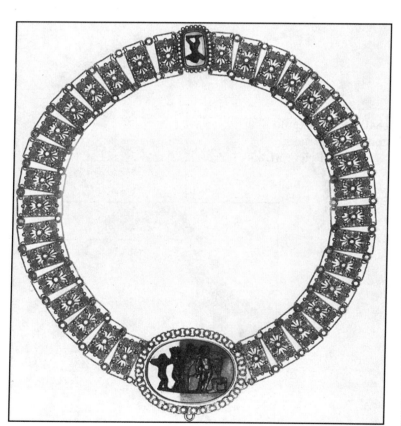

Early 19th century necklace, gold panel links with a central mount set with oval brown and black agate cameo "Captor and Captive," clasp has a cushion-shaped agate cameo, £1,050.
Price: $1,875

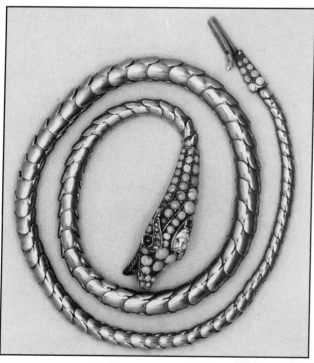

Circa 1840 necklace, gold snake, head and tail set with turquoise, head set with pear-shaped diamond, missing two stones, £1,760. **Price: $3,140**

Pendants

Early 1800s cut-steel pendant, painting on ivory. 1-5/8" x 2". **Price: $350**

Circa 1840 pendant, gold and silver with lapis and agate stones, reverse has a miniature compartment, French, £935. **Price: $1,665**

Early Victorian pendant, yellow gold with floral spray of diamonds on dark blue enamel, embellished with pearl set bud drops, locket on reverse side, £1,600.
Price: $2,850

1840-1860 pendant, gilt brass mtg., Cornelian cameo, 3/4" x 1-1/3". **Price: $295**

Early 1800s pendant, pinchbeck with beveled glass front and back, front glass is hinged and opens, 1-5/8" x 2-1/2".
Price: $350

45

(D) (Jewelry Box Antiques)   Pendant-reverse.

1860s pendant 18K yellow gold set with cabochon cut banded agate and pearls, back has glazed compartment for hair, approx. 1-1/2" x 2-1/4".
Price: $800

(C) (Jeanenne Bell)

1860s brooch/pendant, 15K beautiful sardonyx cameo with graduation, 1-1/8" x 1-7/8".
Price: $1,400

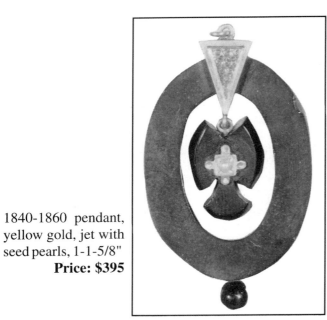

1840-1860 pendant, yellow gold, jet with seed pearls, 1-1-5/8"
Price: $395

(D) (Jewelry Box Antiques)

1790-1840 pendant, 18K yellow gold set with diamond and pearl.   **Price: $895**

(C) (Mary Farlish)

46

Rings

(C) (Patricia Horton)

Late 1700s ring, 14K yellow gold set with citrine 18.64 ct. and 10 rose-cut rubies and 10 rose-cut diamonds. **Price: $3,000**

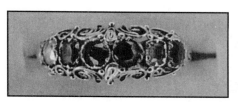

(D) (Jewelry Box Antiques)

1840-1860s ring, 18K yellow gold, acroptic ring, ruby, emerald, garnet, amethyst and diamond, spells "Regard" **Price: $995**

(C) (Cindy Milliron)

1840s-1860s ring, 18K yellow gold set with hand-carved coral cameo. **Price: $795**

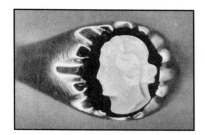

(D) (Jewelry Box Antiques)

1840-1860s ring, cameo, mounting 1940s, 10K yellow gold, Belcher black and white cameo. **Price: $450**

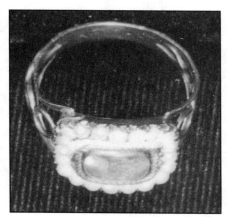

(C) (Jeanenne Bell)

Early 1800s ring, 18K with pearls and compartment for hair under crystal, 1/2" x 1/2". **Price: $475**

(D) (Jewelry Box Antiques)

1850-1860 ring, 10K flexible band made like a bracelet, clasp in head of ring, probably held a handkerchief. **Price: $295**

(C) (Jeanenne Bell)

1850-1860 ring, 14K fitting, hairwork, 1/8" wide. **Price: $300**

Code in Front of Name

(A) Auction House - Auction Price
(C) Collector - Collector Asking Price
(D) Dealer - Dealer's Asking Price

Watches & Watch Accessories

Victorian silver watch chain with small silver acorn and ball drop, has 1842 four pence coin and souvenir coin, 5" l. **Price: $95**

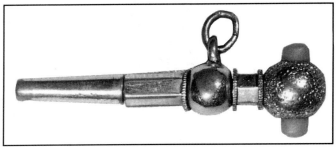

1840-1860 watch key, gold over brass with coral, 1-1/2" l, looks great worn on neck chain or watch chain. **Price: $225**

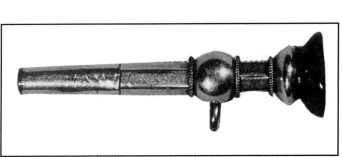

1850-1860 watch key, gold-filled with bloodstone, 1-1/2" l. **Price: $295**

1840-1860 watch chain, gilt fittings, two pieces of hairwork intertwined, snake and early swivel, 3/4" x 8-1/2". **Price: $175**

1850-1860s watch pin, gold-filled with taille d' epergne enameling. 1" x 7/8". **Price: $125**

1840-1860 watch chain, gold fittings with two hair patterns. Note snake and early swivel, 3/8" dia. x 8-1/2" l. **Price: $175**

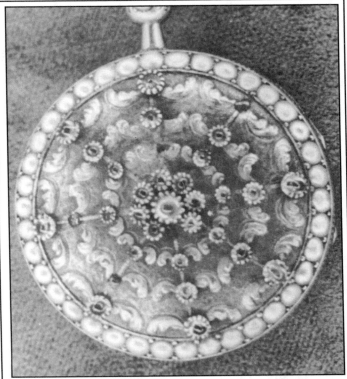

(D) (Jewelry Box Antiques)

Mid-1800s watch, 14K yellow gold key wind & key set embellished with half pearls and cabochon cut rubies.

Price: $2,600

Front of watch.

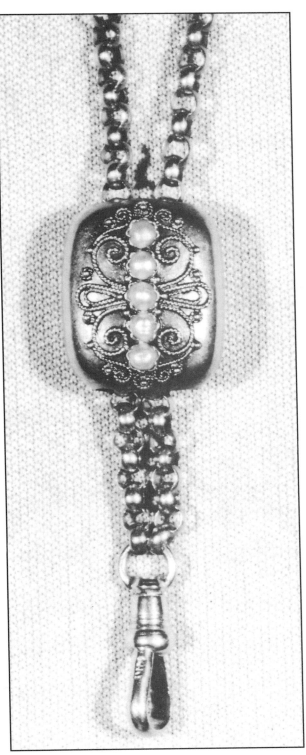

(D) (Jewelry Box Antiques)

1850-1860 slide chain, 18K gold, slide with four pearls and granulation, chain 39" l, 1/2" x 3/4".

Price: $2,350

Sets

(D) (Jewelry Box Antiques)

1860 brooch and earrings, gold over brass, note Etruscan influences, granulation, brooch 2-1/2", earrings 3/4" dia., screw backs not original. **Price: $350**

(D) (Jewelry Box Antiques)

1860 brooch and earrings, gold-filled with enameling. Earrings were originally collar buttons, pin 1-1/4" x 1", earrings 1/2" x 5/8". **Price: $395**

(C) (Jeanenne Bell)

Circa 1870s brooch and earrings, gold top with gold over brass backs and taille d' epergne enameling, centered with black/white stone cameos. **Price: $1,100**

(A) (Photo courtesy of Sotheby's, London 11-24-83)

Circa 1875-1880, DemParure, pendant and earrings, gold with Roman mosaic of bouquet of flowers, £935. **Price: $1,665**

50

(A) (Photo courtesy of Sotheby's, London 7-28-83)

Circa 1840, brooch/pendant and earrings, gold with cabochon garnets, £495.   **Price: $881**

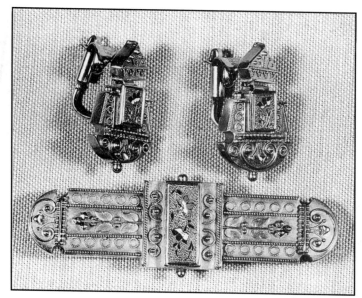

(C) (W. Baldwin)

1860-1870 brooch and earrings, yellow gold with granulations and enameled flowers, brooch 2-3/8" x 7/8".

Price: $995

(A) (Photo courtesy William. Doyle Galleries, New York 12-7-89)

Cameo and half pearl brooch and earrings, 14K yellow gold (earrings not pictured). **Price: $2,100**

(A) (Photo courtesy of Sotheby's, London 4-14-83)

Circa 1835, DemParure, necklace, earrings, and brooch, gold cannetille set with pink topaz, £1,540.   **Price: $2,740**

(C) (B. Morrison)

1860-1870 necklace and earrings, 14K sardonyx cameo, new wires on earrings, necklace drop 1" x 2", earrings 3/8" x 1". **Price: $1,600**

(D) (Jewelry Box Antiques)

1860s pin and earring set, 18K yellow gold petra-dura in original box (2" x 1-5/8"). **Price: $1,800**

(A) (Photo courtesy of Phillips, London)

1820s DemParure consisting of necklace, brooch, and earrings, early 19th century-gold cannetille set with rubies and diamonds, original case, £2,800. **Price: $4,985**

Code in Front of Name

(A) Auction House - Auction Price
(C) Collector - Collector Asking Price
(D) Dealer - Dealer's Asking Price

Miscellaneous

(C) (Jeanenne Bell)

Early 1800s eyeglass, glass 1-1/2" dia., overall length 3-1/4".   **Price: $225**

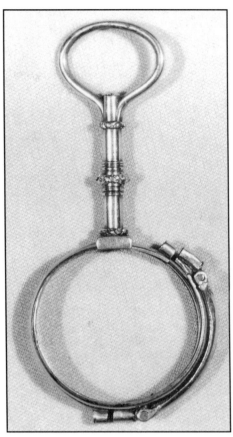

(C) (Jeanenne Bell)

1850-1860 eyeglasses, can be used either opened or closed. Glass portion 1-1/4" dia., length 3-1/8", width opened 3-1/2".   **Price: $225**

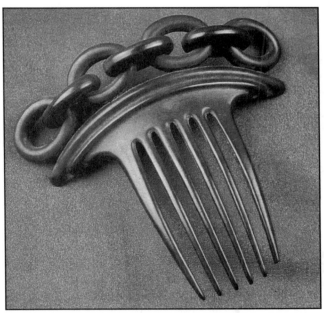

(A) (Skinner Auction, Boston 9-26-94)

1840-1860 Victorian vulcanite hair comb, signed Goodyear 1851.   **Price: $430**

(A) (Skinner Auction, Boston, 12-13-94)

1840-1860 Victorian micro-mosaic earpendants depicting a dove.   **Price: $920**

Chapter Two: 1861-1889

The American & English Historical Period

These years were filled with growth and change. In America, the first shots of the Civil War were fired in April 1861. Neither side expected it to last long. The mood was almost jovial as the men rushed off to battle, but this changed as the days and weeks turned into years. There was much bloodshed and the country experienced pain and suffering. People came to realize that a country at war with itself could never have a true victory. Both sides were relieved when the fighting finally came to an end.

The war created a significant change in the role of women. More than that, it had actually changed their opinion of themselves. They realized that they were not delicate flowers, but could withstand any trials that war could bring.

In the North, women worked in offices and Washington was a favorite location because it was close to the troops. The Treasury Department and other government agencies hired hundreds of women to replace the men who were off fighting for the Union.

The government needed uniforms quickly, so it bought a lot of new sewing machines and offered their use to any person or group who would agree to sew uniforms. Volunteers came forward quickly, and the uniforms were made. In the process, the American woman grew to like the sewing machine. It became an accepted tool in the construction of clothing.

Because women were concerned about the sanitary conditions of their fighting men, they decided to raise money for improvements. Sanitary Fairs, as they came to be called, became the most popular way to provide these funds. Almost every town and village sponsored at least one a year. They ranged from the church bazaar in small towns to huge fairs. Philadelphia's Fair in 1864 netted a million dollars. It included a Horticultural Department and a Picture Gallery.

Southern Belles were also becoming independent. They worked wherever needed: in the fields, overseeing large farms, or raising money for their men in uniform. The "clinging vines" learned to shoot a rifle when it became necessary to protect their home. Many women found themselves doing things that would have been considered unladylike in times of peace. Of course, they also had their sewing circles, and provided much needed items for their soldiers.

When the war ended, many men returned home with a different perspective on life. The women they came home to were also changed. Never again would they see themselves as they were before the war. The South would rebuild, and the nation would heal its wounds; but the women had found themselves, and nothing would ever be quite the same.

Interest in women's education grew. In 1865, Vassar Female College was founded. Many other female colleges were also opened, and in addition to their regular academic studies, young ladies were taught independent sports such as archery, skating, tennis, and swimming.

Croquet became a popular pastime. *Peterson's Magazine* published an article in 1864 giving complete instructions for playing the game, so women knew how to play before the men returned home. It provided a charming excuse for ladies and gentlemen to engage in an outdoor sport.

When time permitted, baseball was played between the soldiers. After the war, it grew into a consuming passion. Everything that pertained to baseball or its players was a subject for comment. The January 5, 1878 issues of *Leslie's Illustrated Newspaper* contained this interesting bit of gossip, "Mr. Sutton, a well-known professional baseball player was converted at a revival meeting in Philadelphia not long ago. He arose to address the meeting, and said 'I have made the first base, and, by the help of the Lord, will make a home run.'"

Horseback riding became a very fashionable exercise. Fashion magazines were filled with the latest attire for riding. *Leslie's Illustrated Newspaper* even sketched a prominent socialite taking her daily horseback ride down Fifth Avenue.

In the 1870s, the Women's Property Act was passed. This allowed married women to own property. No longer did a woman's holdings automatically pass into her husband's ownership after the wedding. Not everyone viewed this as progress. *Leslie's Illustrated Newspaper*, June 1878, complained, "Her legal rights have become so preponderant that those of her hitherto recognized lords and masters are insignificant in comparison."

The 1880s brought more marvelous new things. The light bulb Edison invented in 1879 came into use, the Brooklyn Bridge was completed, the fountain pen was perfected, the first skyscraper was built, the Statue of Liberty was unveiled, the adding machine was patented, the New York Museum was opened, and George Eastman made photography available to the masses by introducing the Kodak Camera. A period that began with war and violence ended with optimism and hope.

In England, the year 1861 began sadly for the Queen. Her mother, the Duchess of Kent, died. For the first time, Victoria experienced a personal loss. She had been so happy, so complete, that she had forgotten death could not be ruled away at her will as other things could.

Just as she was beginning to come out of her grief, another even more terrible event happened. Toward the end of November, Albert became ill. His condition became increasingly worse. On December 14th, he died, and Victoria was grief-stricken. The nation was stunned and everyone went into a state of mourning.

Victoria's mourning lasted for years. It turned into an obsession to do things as Albert would have wanted them done. The remaining years of her life were dedicated to his memory. She wanted her country to know and appreciate him as she did. Writers were commissioned to record the story of his life. Monuments were built and dedicated to her dear Albert's memory.

In 1863, Edward married Princess Alexandra, the daughter of the King of Denmark. The women of Great Britain were glad to have someone to whom they could look who was not in mourning. Because Alexandra was young and attractive, she influenced fashion. She frequently wore a "dog-collar" (a necklace containing several strands that fit snugly around the neck). It was so fetching that soon all the ladies were wearing them.

From 1874 through 1880, Benjamin Disraeli was Prime Minister of England. He enjoyed a fine relationship with Queen Victoria, and was responsible for getting her active again. Under his influence, England expanded its imperialistic powers. Disraeli was instrumental in acquiring controlling interest in the Suez Canal for Britain. In 1877, he played a major role in having Victoria proclaimed "Empress of India."

In 1887, the English celebrated their "Jubilee Year." The good Queen had reigned for fifty years, and that was reason to rejoice! Many items added the word "Jubilee" to their product as an extra enticement to buy. There was even a "Jubilee Rug Machine" for use in the home. In May of that year, J. Theobald and Company advertised a "Grand Jubilee Prize Picture Puzzle Contest." To enter this competition one had only to purchase one of the Grand Jubilee Packets, "...which have been specially prepared in celebration of Her Majesty's Jubilee. This Packet contains the most marvelous value for the money, as we have determined to make it the most successful that we have ever offered. Everyone who has seen it wonders how we can possibly sell it at the price. As these articles are specially Jubilee goods, every loyal patriotic person ought to possess a parcel, and treasure up the articles as mementos of this most auspicious occasion."

How could any loyal subject resist that offer? The packet contained "The Queen's Jubilee Album" and, "...an elegant Jubilee Brooch being a beautiful heavily gold-plated brooch in the shape of an extended fan, with the word 'Jubilee' across it; this is no common loud cheap jewelry, but finished in the highest style of art, and could not be detected from a brooch costing a guenia."

Also included in the package was a, "Jubilee fancy scarf pin, most richly finished, the center of the pin represents the Royal Arms of England in brilliant colors, surrounded by a gold-plated band bearing the motto 'Honi qui mal y Pense,' surmounted with the Royal Crown in gold and crimson colours and crossed by two scepters; besides this also a handsome Jubilee Medal bearing the queen's head as a medallion, and the words 'Queen Victoria's Jubilee, 1887' set in a handsome star." Surely some of these pieces are still in existence today. Many collectors would love to acquire them.

Ten years later, the queen celebrated her sixty-year reign with a Diamond Jubilee. Lytton Strachey in his book, *Queen Victoria*, sums it up beautifully:

> As the splendid procession passed along, escorting Victoria through the thronged re-echoing streets of London on her progress of thanks giving to St. Pauls' Cathedral, the greatness of her realm and the adoration of her subjects blazed out together. The tears welled to her eyes, and while the multitude roared round her, 'how kind they are to me! How kind they are!' she repeated over and over again. That night her message flew over the Empire: 'From my heart I

thank my beloved people. May God bless them!' The long journey was nearly done. But the traveler, who has come so far, and through such strange experiences, moved on with the unflattering step. The girl, the wife, the aged woman, were the same: vitality, conscientiousness, pride, and simplicity were hers to the latest hour.

The Centennial International Exposition

In 1876, America celebrated its one hundredth birthday. This long awaited event was several years in the planning, "In 1872, Congress passed an act creating the Centennial Board of Finance with the authority to receive subscriptions to the capital stock not exceeding ten million dollars, to be divided into shares of not more than ten dollars each, and to use the proceeds for the erection of the buildings and all suitable fixtures and appurtenances for carrying on the exhibition to its close."[3]

Because of its historical significance, Philadelphia was chosen as the site for this great Centennial International Exposition. On July 5, 1873, Secretary Fish invited foreign nations to participate. Great Britain, France, Denmark, Germany, Switzerland, Mexico, Turkey, Brazil, Venezuela, Peru, Chile, The Sandwich Islands, Argentine Confederation, Japan, China, Australia, Bolivia, Canada, Columbia, Nicaragua, Equador, Liberia, Orange Free State, Guatemala, Honduras, and Salvador accepted the invitation.

The site of the exposition was two hundred and thirty-six beautiful acres that bordered on the Scheylkill river. Ground was broken on July 4, 1874, and the exposition opened on May 10, 1876. *Harper's New Monthly Magazine* made small note of the momentous occasion, "The Centennial Exposition was opened at Philadelphia May 10, by an address from President Grant. The Emperor Dom Pedro assisted the President in setting the machinery in motion by starting the Corliss Engine."

It was an exciting place to think about, to write about, and to visit. For months before the opening, articles were written about the country's past and future. How the early Americans lived, what they wore, and how they furnished their homes were topics for study. The country had indeed survived and prospered.

People from far and near poured into Philadelphia. Many came by railway. The Centennial had two depots to receive them. Some utilized the steamboats that made regular runs from downtown to the exposition. Others took the numerous horse cars and hack lines. In 1878, *Leslie's Illustrated Newspaper* made this comment concerning transportation to the Centennial, "As many as 250,000 persons were conveyed in one day from Philadelphia to the Centennial Exposition grounds and the facilities were even then not sufficient to meet the demand made of the transportation."

As early as 6:00 A.M., the lines would start forming at the ticket booths. Admission was a half dollar (50¢) and the people were more than eager to pay it. There were so many things to see that one hardly knew where to begin. There was the Main Exposition Building with exhibits from all over the world, the Machinery Hall where machinery could be seen in operation, Memorial Hall with all its wondrous works of art, the Shoe and Leather Building where one could view the actual making of shoes, the Brewers Building, the Photographic Building, and many, many more. There was a Japanese Bazaar for buying gifts and a Photographic Studio. If all the walking worked up an appetite, there were restaurants where foods from all over the world could be sampled.

The exposition had its own railroad that circled the exhibitions. It provided a way to get a general feeling of the layout of the buildings and gave one's feet a much needed rest. The cost of the four-mile trip was five cents, and people were allowed to ride as long as they liked.

One of the most visited buildings was the Department of Public comfort. Reception rooms, washrooms, toilets, barber shops, and dressing rooms were located here. It provided a good meeting place. Additionally, lunch baskets could be checked until needed, and there were umbrellas and wheelchairs available for rental.

> The Women's Building was of special interest. Women had played a large part in raising money for the Centennial. Without their support, it might never have taken place. The Women's Centennial committee decided to go a step further and have their own building. They wanted, "a place to exhibit work of women in such a manner as would display to advantage the individual taste and manufacture, and artistic skill of the sex."[4]

One of the more costly buildings, the Women's Pavilion, had 30,000 square feet of display area, "The walls were painted a light color, neatly paneled with blue upon the ceilings. The panels on the side walls were decorated with groups allegorical of Faith, Hope, and Charity, Art, Labor, Instruction, and the Family." It was a perfect setting for displaying their many talents. The building was lovely and displays were well done.

Not everyone shared this opinion. William Dean Howell made his views quite clear in his book, *A Sennight of the Centennial*, "It seems not yet the moment for the better half of our species to take their stand apart from the worst upon any distinct performance in art and industry; even when they have a building of their own, some organizing force to get their best work into it is lacking; many of those pictures and pincushions were no better than if men had made them."

Several other articles shared thoughts on the event such as, "The governments of England, France, Germany, Brazil, Spain, Sweden, and Japan built buildings to represent their countries. Japan also built a Japanese dwelling. During its erection it 'created more curiosity and attracted infinitely more visitors than any other building on the grounds. It was erected by native Japanese workmen, with materials brought from home, and built in their own manner with curious tools and yet more curious manual processes."[5]

There were many jewelry displays at the Centennial, but none as striking as the Tiffany Exhibit. Their display was filled with watches, silver, jewelry, and stationery. They not only received special recognition but were presented with a gold medal.

The Centennial celebration had many positive results. The nation took pride in its achievements and was favorably recognized by the rest of the world for its famous "Yankee ingenuity." Even more important was the opportunity that the exposition allowed the average person contact with other countries' cultures.

Fashions in Clothing & Jewelry

Thanks to the movie "Gone With the Wind," most people are familiar with the clothing and hair styles of the 1860s and 70s. It made real the beautiful dresses and manicured coiffures worn by the ladies of the period. Who could ever forget the elegant dress that Scarlett made from her green velvet draperies? The scene in which Scarlett, dressed in mourning clothes, danced with Rhett Butler is still imprinted in many minds.

The jewelry of the 60s and 70s is best described as heavy, massive, and solid. Massiveness was equated with well-made and sturdy. The bigger a piece of furniture or jewelry, surely better it must be. Colors were also visually heavy. Rich red velvets covered not only furniture and windows, but also "meladies" as well. The feeling of opulence was everywhere.

The most outstanding feature of fashion was the hoop skirt which was introduced by the Princess Eugunie in Paris. It was not unusual to use as many as thirty yards of material for one skirt. Still, they did tend to make the waist appear smaller, and small waists were definitely in fashion. Laced corsets were also used to minimize the waist. Some ladies wore their lacing so tight they were subject to fainting spells. To further emphasize the waist,

buckles came into favor. "Buckles for waist bands have now attained colossal proportions, but these are generally imitation, and not genuine gold and silver...," *Peterson's Magazine* from November 1864 went on to say, "The chased buckles are more distinguished than the plain dead ones, as the workmanship adds to their beauty. The mother-of pearl buckles are worn with white dresses; and it is fashionable to wear a buckle both at the front and back of the waist."

Necklaces adorned every neck. "Necklaces or very thick chains have become indispensable with a low dress, and are also worn with high chemisettes and Swiss bodices," said the January 1864 *Petersen's Magazine*. "The large round jet or coral beads are preferred for demi-toilet and married ladies' often wear the thick gold chains."

These gold chains, combined with other pieces, were the heights of fashion. In November of 1864, Peterson's noted:

> Jewels are of a very massive description, and set flat in the Cameo style; pearls and precious stones are often laid upon enamel, which has a very good effect. Necklaces are almost indispensable now with low dresses. Bold chains are six and eight times doubled and fastened here and there with thick round balls of gold, inlaid with jewels; the same style with pendant ornaments, is pretty for bracelets. Brooches are mostly round in the shape of small shields and very massive; they are made of different shades, some inclining to green, some to red and some of a deep burnish color. Pearls or smaller stones are arranged in a pattern over them.

A new way to wear chains became popular during the 1865-70 period. Instead of being worn around the neck in the traditional way, they were suspended from over the top of the bonnet and draped over the bust. They were known as Benoiton Chains because a character in the play "La Famille Benoiton" wore her necklace in this manner. These long chains were made of gold, pearls, beads, or most any kind of material.

Jewelry was being worn at all times and in all places. The pieces were enormous, and many were in the costume jewelry category. The *Godey's Lady's Book* of January 1864 comments:

> Jewelry is now being worn in out-of-door dress. The style in Vogue is the Oriental-crescents, large round sequins, and long drooping ornaments being preferred. Very large earrings, brooches, clasps and studs are worn to match, in dimensions hitherto unheard of, and either in plain gold, or in gold and coral, or enameled. These jewels, being but a passing whim of fashion, need not be of the purest gold or precious gems. Even French ladies who have always been very particular on this point, now wear imitation jewels without the least scruple.

With loved ones off to war, everyone wanted a keepsake close at hand. The locket came to be considered an important part of the total fashion picture. The May 1864 *Peterson's Magazine* confirms this:

Lockets, medallions, etc. are still being worn around the neck attached to narrow velvet ribbons. Black ribbon velvet is generally used for this purpose, as well as to tie the lace tucker which may be worn with a low-necked dress. But frequently the velvet is selected to match the trimming of the dress-a white dress trimmed with a scarlet velvet ribbon, both for

the locket and tucker, would be used, and with a blue dress-blue velvet etc. Two yards of ribbon velvet will be sufficient to suspend the locket, as long ends are worn. Many ladies especially in Paris, have latterly adopted the plan of mounting precious stones upon black velvet for the throat, a style that will be found advantageous around throats which are neither round nor fair. Necklaces of all descriptions are greatly in vogue but many ladies still retain the simple locket and velvet, in preference to more costly necklets. Rosettes for the shoes made to correspond with the trimmings of the dress, likewise velvet ribbon for the locket are now usually sent home with the dress by the generality of our best dress makers.

Because the women were involved in working for the war efforts, hair styles became less complicated. The hair was often worn pulled back, and nets came into fashion. In February 1864, *Peterson's Magazine* gave complete instructions for making a hairnet. The article was introduced by these words:

The hairnet is a very pretty article of dress, and useful also where the hair is redundant. It is one of those classical fashions, revived, with advantage, in the present day, when the stiff modes are entirely out of favor. The materials are as simple as possible, being nothing more than a good netting silk. Brown is the prettiest color for the general wear; but if a more dressy style is desired, the color should be selected to suit the costume with which it is to be worn.

Nets were so widely accepted, that soon they were being used with evening attire. This was noted in the April edition of the same magazine, "For small evening parties, dinners, or the opera, nets, when made of fine gold braid, are very becoming and give additional smartness to the toilet. Many young ladies are satisfied with gold braid, fastened to the center of the net and the hair-dress is finished; others add flowers."

The ears were no longer considered unattractive. With the hair worn back, earrings became fashionable again. The November issue of *Peterson's Magazine* stated, "Earrings are worn extremely large and weighty in the Grecian style; bonnets now being so small, the earrings are allowed to show outside them, and have in consequence acquired more importance than ever."

Combs became a very popular adornment for the hair. Not only were they utilitarian, but they could also be an asset to the overall fashion picture. *Peterson's Magazine* stated, "Combs for the hair now come within the sphere of jewels. They are made with a wide,

Peterson's January, 1864.
Fig. I - Ball dress of white silk, trimmed with black and white lace.
Fig. II - Evening dress of blue silk, trimmed, around the bottom, with a deep flounce, headed by a thick chenille cord. Above the flounce is a deep white chenille fringe, headed by a cord of the same. Backs of white chenille.

flat piece turned back from the teeth, and composing a very rich ornament, set with gold and precious stones; these combs are worn in the back hair; smaller ones are also sometimes used to keep back the hair in the front."

The war helped prove to women just how impractical their clothes were. When one had to get up each morning and ride the omnibus to work it was painfully apparent that huge hoops had no place on public transportation. The skirts were also much too long. They were a nuisance when walking on muddy streets, which every working woman had to do on occasion.

As early as 1874, women were holding dress reform meetings. Something had to be done. By the 1880s the hoops were gone, but they were replaced by the bustle. The skirts were much narrower, but the bustle did protrude, "How well the bustle performed may be judged by the story of the Washington lady who walked to church and home again with a toy rooster perched on her bustle."[6] Many women wanted to do away with this contraption. In April of 1887, the fashion editor of the *Young Ladies' Journal* wrote, "We are told by competent authorities that steel tournures, and all the metallic appliances which are so uncomfortable, are going out of fashion."

Things improved very quickly. Two months later the same writer made this comment:

Fashion is really becoming quite rational, after all the extravagances and eccentricities with which has too justly been charged. It has now become quite quiet and reasonable.

The ridiculous tournures, enormously protruding, which vexed seriously inclined spirits for the last few years are now almost forgotten; they have been transformed into a modest cushion, scarcely apparent, which offers a timid support to the skirt, making the bend of the waist. Our shoes and boots, with stilt-like heels, have long been exchanged for rational chaussures with low square heels; an absurd peak by which they terminated hurt so many feet that it has been found quite necessary to change it for a rational shape, neither square nor pointed, but something between the two, which looks graceful without being uncomfortable.

What else were we blamed for? Extravagant chapeaux, which towered high above the head-inconvenient hats,

which at the theater played the troublesome part of screens for these spectators who were unfortunate enough to sit behind them. Well here reason is triumphant, and our capotes are perfectly charming; small and well posed upon the head, they form a most becoming frame to the face.

What, therefore, can modern Fashion be accused of now? It is quite rational and practical and logical as most things are in the "Age of Realism."

Hair styles evolved from being pulled back in the 1860s and 1870s, to being put up in the 1880s. Everyone was hair conscious. Switches of extra hair were worn by most women to supplement what Mother Nature had given them. The new hair styles were identified by name. The *Young Ladies' Journal* described three of the most popular styles of 1887:

Illustration from *The Young Ladies' Journal*, July, 1887.

"The Diana Coiffure" is much in vogue. For this coiffure the hair is turned straight up from the roots, and arranged on the top of the head into a sort of rouleau, which is fashioned with a small tortoiseshell comb. Two tortoiseshell pins to match are used to fasten the ends of the front hair into loops at the sides quite high on the head.

"The Marie-Antionette Coiffure" is also much in vogue. For this coiffure the hair is arranged in a rouleau; it is not brushed straight off from the face and fastened straight down, but merely rolled off and attached with pins, but so as to remain loose. This style does not suit all faces but is becoming to ladies who have a low broad forehead, and straight eyebrow.

"The Psyche Coiffure" is also very fashionable. The hair is also combed up from the roots, but it is then twisted and arranged into two loops, fastened with a small comb and pins of light-colored tortoiseshell.

In 1885, Charles Dana Gibson drew his first Gibson Girl. She became the epitome of what was most desirable. Women all over the country emulated her dress, hair style, manners and even her drooped eyelid, head-tilted-back poses. Alice Roosevelt, the President's daughter, gave the American public an opportunity to vicariously experience the thrill of a real live Gibson type. They were shocked by her flaunting of the rules, such as smoking in public. But since she did things they did not have the courage or the money to do, it made her even more endearing. T.R. loved her and was proud of her independent spirit, even though he once stated, "I can be President or I can handle Alice. I can't possibly do both."

The mood of the world was reflected in these new up-sweep hair fashions. In England, people were ready to shed the heavy mood that Victoria's mourning had spread across the country. They were ready for some gaiety in their lives.

Americans were beginning to feel carefree and optimistic. Women were experiencing an unprecedented freedom in fashion. This lightness began to be reflected in jewelry. By December of 1887, a new style of jewelry was emerging. These changes were noted in *The Young Ladies' Journal*:

These are a few changes to note in fashionable jewelry, the solid, massive portebonheur is quite out of fashion; bracelets are all made in the chain style, or else composed of a fine circle with diamonds and precious stones; gold chains and lockets for the neck are things of the past; brooches are of the most fanciful and dainty type, and are fastened here, there, and everywhere, among lace folds, close to the shoulder or near the neck; ear drops are as small as possible; diamonds are fixed in close to the ear. Combs and hairstyles are ornamented with pearls and precious stones. Jewels are now required to have at least as much artistic as intrinsic value.

So be it—out went the old and in came the new.

Archaeological Inspirations

Archaeological findings exerted an important influence on jewelry designs of the 1861-1889 period. The digs began in Egypt after Napoleon's conquest in 1798. The findings spurred interest in archaeological artifacts, and from 1806 to 1814, the French excavated Pompeii.

Pompeii had been completely covered by a volcanic eruption in 79 A.D. The excavations uncovered a city that had been caught unaware. It provided a glimpse of an ancient civilization almost beyond belief to the nineteenth century. Beautiful houses with frescoed walls, atriums complete with fountains and mosaic floors, jewelry made with ancient unknown gold work methods, and everyday items made with beautiful skill and craftsmanship—all these discoveries captured the imagination of the people.

Greek artifacts were discovered on the island of Crete and Rhodes. In 1848, Sir Austin Henery Layard wrote *Minevia and Its Remains*, a book about the fascinating archaeological finds in the ancient capital of Assyria. The archaeological motifs of the Egyptians, Etruscans, Greeks, and Romans were popular first in Europe, and then they spread to England. By the 1850s, the theater was using the discoveries to authenticate scenery for plays. In 1853, Charles Dean based his scenery for the play "Sardanapalus" on pieces in the British Museum. This made the public even more aware of the archaeological finds. The ancient motifs were further stimulated in 1862, by the display of Castillani jewelry at The Great Exposition in London. They attracted much attention, and the public went home convinced that the ancient styles were the most suitable for jewelry designs.

By 1864, jewelry designs inspired by the finds, had spread to the United States. The June issue of *Peterson's Magazine* noted, "The new models are all copied from the antique and give one a very good idea of the beautiful gold and jewel ornaments of Old Grecian Art." The same publication made this comment in the November issue, "Earrings are now made in the antique style. They represent a large circle, in the center of which either a large ball of dead gold, or five crescents of pearls is fastened; the crescents diminish in size as they ascend. Sometimes the earring is composed of a large crescent of dead gold studded with coral and fringed with gold."

Interest in archaeological findings continued to increase. The "Treasure of Priam" was discovered by Heinrich Schlieman in 1869. In 1872, the British Museum bought some fine examples of ancient jewelry from the Castillani Collection. This enabled the British to study and admire the archaeological styles. The French could satisfy their curiosity by viewing the Cavalier Company Collection at the Louvre, and the Italians could study pieces by Augusto Castillani in the Capitoline Museum.

It was not until 1877 that people in the United States could boast of a collection of archeological finds. In the early 1870s, Luigi P. do Cesnola, a United States Consul at Larmoce, discovered the treasure vaults of the Temple of Kurium. An account of the discovery was published July 1872, in the *Harper's New Monthly Magazine*. Within the next five years, more discoveries were made on this island of Cyprus. In July of 1877, *Harper's* published another article in which they rejoiced at these findings being displayed in the United States, "The Metropolitan Museum of Art had the wisdom to commence its collection of illustrations of ancient art at the very beginning of all art, and to offer to its visitors and the American public facilities for studying what no European collection illustrates—the birth of art among civilized men, and its growth in the early years."

Harper's went on to say, "The treasure vaults of the Kuruin were vast, "Gold, silver, alabaster, and bronze, the work of artists and artisans dead more than twenty-five centuries ago, are here gathered; not a few specimens, a ring or two and a gem or two, but literally hundreds of ear and finger rings, bracelets, necklaces, amulets and ornaments in vast variety."

Harper's described many of the pieces, and it had this comment on the earrings:

It cannot fail to strike the observer that the present form was a favorite, and many in this form are evidently Phoenician of an early date. Simple crescents of plain gold are numerous. After these came plain crescents with raised edges and wire ornamentations. Then enamels beautify the crescent. Precious stones are placed on them, or form pendants. Then the crescent swells into a solid gold form. Then the hollow gold is shaped in lobes with charming surface ornaments. Then we see agates cut in new-moon form, and set in gold with delicious granulated patterns. There is no end to the varieties of earrings. There are bunches of fruit, rosettes, plaques with impressed images, earrings with pendants in every form, and earrings with pendants, in the modern form, where a small ornament fits close on the lobe of the ear.

The article also gave an excellent description of granulations:

This style of work, known in Etruscan jewelry, characterizes much of this ancient Greek work, and is a puzzle to modern goldsmiths. We illustrate a gold ornament—a round brooch or amulet—for the sake of

describing this remarkable style of work. The surface of this object presents to the eye the appearance of a gold disk stamped in a die, or crossed by numerous fine wires at right angles with each other. On examining it with the magnifying glass, however it is found that the effect is produced by minute globes of gold, each one perfectly round and smooth, soldered on the surface in exact lines, each globe touching the next. There are on the surface of this small object, a little over an inch in diameter, upward of nine hundred of these globes. How were they made, and how were they soldered on in such absolutely true lines? The ablest gold-workers in America (and that is to say the ablest in the world) tell us that they cannot explain it.

Revival jewelry was already in fashion by the time the Metropolitan Museum acquired Cesnola's finds. The *Harper's* article stated, "There are some things here in silver which, were they perfect, would ravish the eyes of our lady readers, and over which some of them who love old art will bend in delighted rapture. These are silver belts worn by the ladies of Cyprus in the ancient years. Within the past year or two, a fashion has prevailed among ladies in America of wearing broad metallic belts of silver or other metal. Could an American lady possess one of these belts of Cypriot made in its original freshness, or its facsimile, she would be very happy."

Ten years later (1887), the ancient style jewelry was still being worn. But instead of being made of gold, the designs were now executed in silver. This is confirmed by an article in the *Young Ladies' Journal* of January 1887, "Jewels of old silver, finely wrought in the imitation of Ancient jewelry, are also among the favorite trinkets of fashion just now. There are beautiful bracelets composed of detached ovals fastened together by very fine chains. Brooches to match, and exquisite chatelaines of the most beautiful workmanship.

Castellani

One of the most familiar names in nineteenth century design is Castellani. Actually there were several Castellanis who played an important role in jewelry styles.

Fortunato Pio Castellani was born in 1793, the son of a goldsmith. In 1814, he went to work for his father and excelled at the craft. He became fascinated with Etruscan jewelry while working in an advisory capacity to the Papal government in 1836. They needed his expertise on gold work to advise them on purchases of artifacts from a tomb discovered at Cervetri.

He was intrigued with the Etruscan art of granulation and wanted to learn this ancient technique. After many unsuccessful attempts to capture the art of the tiny granules he went in search of someone who might have knowledge of this ancient art. In a remote mountain village he found some men and women to whom this art of working gold had been passed from generation to generation. He persuaded them to come to Rome to live and work with him. It was not long before his workshop was known throughout Italy.

Castellani's sons, Alessandro (1824-1883) and Augusto (1829-1914), were both active in their father's business. When the revolutionary upheavals started in 1848, the shop was closed. In 1851, Fortunato retired and turned the business over to his sons. They became involved in the revolution. Eventually Alessandro fled to Paris and Augusto went to London. They took their enthusiasm for Etruscan work with them and shared its technique with other artists in those cities. Thus, the design spread to new areas.

Alessandro became an expert in archaeological artifacts. He was a collector and a dealer. Some of his customers were the museums of England, Europe, and America. In 1868, he published a catalogue entitled, "Italian Jewelry as Worn by the Peasants of Italy, Collected by Signor Castellani."

Augusto was very involved in the business and strove to carry on his father's traditions. Later, his knowledge and interest led him to become the Director of the Capitoline Museum in Rome. He was the author of *Antique Jewelry and Its Revival*, published in 1862.

When the Castellani jewelry was displayed at the 1862 International Exposition in London, it drew much attention. The name Castellani and their crossed capital "C" trademark became known throughout the world.

Popular Stones & Materials

Jet

At the death of her beloved husband, Queen Victoria went into a period of mourning which was to last the rest of her life. This unexpected death left the English subjects shocked and grieved. All the nation went into mourning.

It was customary to be "in mourning" for a period of two years. The first year only black was allowed to be worn. This was a time of full mourning, and elaborate regulations pertained to the appropriate dress for the departed's relatives. The second year was spent in half-mourning. The bereaved could wear a few things that were not black such as amethyst, because of its ecclesiastical associations. However, for the most part, all jewelry and clothes were dark.

Jet was an obvious solution to the problem of jewelry suitable during this period. Victoria had first worn jet during the mourning period for William IV, her predecessor, and it was natural for her to wear it while in mourning for her husband.

Jet is a hard, coal-like material. This is a type of fossilized wood. The finest jet was mined in the town of Whitby, England. The industry started there in the early nineteenth century, and by 1850, there were fifty jet workshops. Because it lent itself well to carving and kept a sharp edge, it was used extensively. By 1873, there were more than two hundred jet shops in this one small town.

Because jet is extremely lightweight, it was the perfect material for making the enormous lockets, necklaces, brooches and bracelets that were so popular in the 1860s and 1870s. The success enjoyed by the jet factories led to many imitations. French jet, which is neither French nor jet (it is black glass), was cheaper to manufacture. It gave the jet industry some competition; but because it is much heavier, it was used mostly in the making of beads and smaller items.

Today, it is illegal to mine jet in Whitby. The jet is in seams in the walls of the cliffs on which parts of the town were built. Consequently, the very existence of the town was threatened by those who extracted the velvety substance. The two jet cutters in the town today have to rely on the pieces that wash up on the shore of this coastal town. This circumstance makes the jet of the Victorian era more precious than ever. Good, well-made examples of Whitby jet are sure to appreciate in value. For ways to differentiate between jet and other visually similar materials such as Gutta-percha, bog oak, glass and onyx, read Section III.

Diamonds

Diamonds were discovered in South Africa in 1867. A peasant boy, playing near a river, found a pretty stone and took it home. A traveler passing through the village saw the boy's prize and suspected what it might be. He was right; it was a diamond valued at $2,500. Word of the find spread, and the diamond rush began. Within a few years, diamonds were very much in fashion, and this new source was supplying the Paris demand.

Diamonds have always been in coveted. The Greeks appreciated the stone's hardness and called it "Adamas," meaning unconquerable. Consequently, it was often worn into battle. The stones were not cut or faceted as they are today, but worn in their natural pointed shape.

These early diamonds were found in streams of India. These alluvial diamonds required no mining because the natural erosion of the earth uncovered them. Until 1871, alluvial diamonds were the only ones available to man.

By chance it was discovered that diamonds were buried deep inside the earth in what is now known as "pipes." These pipes are thought to be part of extinct volcanoes. The rock surrounding the diamond is called "blue ground." It is estimated that an average of two tons of blue ground must be mined to find a single carat of diamonds.

Diamonds are judged by carat weight, cut, clarity, and color. Consequently, three stones each weighing one carat could vary thousands of dollars in price. A carat weighs two hundred (200) milligrams which is equal to one hundred (100) points. Hence a half carat is fifty points, and twenty five points equal a fourth of a carat.

The cut of a diamond is very important. It takes an expert to decide the proper cut for each stone. The proper proportions will enhance the stone's brilliance and increase its value. Most diamonds today are brilliant cut and have fifty-eight facets.

The clarity of a diamond is determined by the purity of the stone. Flaws such as dark inclusions and feathers can greatly decrease the value. A diamond is considered to be flawless if there are no visible flaws when the stone is examined using a ten power loupe.

Diamonds come in a variety of colors. Some are colorless, many have a yellowish tinge, and a few have a bluish tinge. When fancy colors such as green, violet, brown, blue, red, and yellow are found in quality stones, they are very expensive and highly collectible. Since diamonds tend to pick up color from surrounding objects, a white background is best when determining a stone's true color.

From the 1880s through the 1920s, the Tiffany mounting was the most popular setting used for a diamond. Someone at Tiffany came up with a six-prong setting that became known as a "Tiffany" mounting. It became so fashionable, that the average person would ask for it by name and this infuriated the other jewelers. They did not like the fact that a customer had to use a competitor's name to describe the type of setting they wanted.

Because the diamond has always been highly prized, there have been many imitations. These include rock crystal, zircon, spinel, Strass glass, and diamond doublets. Today's popular imitations are cubic zirconia, YAG, and strontium titanate. Because these synthetic stones look very much like diamonds to the untrained eye, it is wise to buy from a reputable source.

Opals

In 1870, a huge opal field was discovered in Australia. This prompted Queen Victoria to try again to lift the veil of superstition that had befallen the stone. The novel, *Anne of Geurstein*, written by Scott and published in 1829, was responsible for the opal being considered bad luck. Lady Heromine, a character in the book, always wore an opal in her hair. Its iridescent glow seemed to reflect her every mood. When she came to a tragic end, the opal's mysterious powers were blamed.

The opal was one of Queen Victoria's favorite stones. She gave them as wedding gifts to her daughters and wore them herself. Still, the superstition remained. When Napoleon presented the Empress Eugenie with a parure of opals, she refused them. Even today some people think it is unlucky to wear an opal unless it is a birthstone. Others believe, as the ancients, did that the stone brings good fortune to its wearer.

There are three types of opals: precious, fire, and common. The precious is the kind most people associate with the word "opal." It has a beautiful multicolored iridescence that changes when exposed to different angles of light. The most common color of precious opal is white. There are also black opals, but they are very rare. Opals may also be found in colors of gray, blue, or green.

The fire opal is named for its orange color. It is not opalescent, and it does not have the rainbow-like colors. The best of this type are clear and transparent. Another variety of the fire opal is the Mexican water opal. It is usually light brown or colorless.

The so-called common opals are varied. There are agate opals, wood opals, honey opals, milk opals, and moss opals. Most of these the average person would never identify as an opal.

Because opals contain as much as thirty percent (30%) water, they require very special treatment. If a stone gets too dry, it tends to crack or lose its iridescent quality. In the book *Gemstones of the World*, Walter Schumann suggests the best treatment is to "...saturate the stone with oil or water and to avoid the aging process by storing the piece in moist absorbent cotton."

Garnets

Throughout the ages garnets have been worn and admired. Although the word garnet usually conjures up pictures of a wine red stone, they can be found in every color except blue. Actually, garnets are a group of stones that have the same structure, but differ chemically. The garnets most associated with the name are almadine and pyrope. They are also the most common.

The pyrope (PIE-rope) garnets were popular during the 1860-1889 period. Their deep rich color was a favorite accessory for the massive clothing of the 1860s and 70s. These Bohemian garnets, fashioned in lighter scale mountings, continued to be popular in the 1880s and 90s. They are red or reddish brown in color and tend to be more transparent than the almadine garnet. Most pyrope garnets are mined in Czechoslovakia, Australia, and South Africa.

The almadine (AL-man-dine) garnet tends to have a slightly purplish tint. The most common variety of garnet, it is found in Brazil, India, Australia, Czechoslovakia, and Sri Lanka.

A lesser known variety of garnet is the demantoid (deh-MAN-toid). Its rich emerald green color and diamond-like luster make it the most valuable of garnets.

The garnet is the accepted January birthstone. Some believe that it empowers the wearer with truth, constancy, and faith. Ancient man wore it for protection against being struck by lightning. No matter what reason is chosen for wearing garnets, they always seem to be admired and enjoyed.

Mosaics

Mosaics were popular souvenirs for the Victorian traveler. Not only did they picture scenes that had been visited, but they were made using ancient methods made popular by the excavations. Most of these tiny works of art were done in Florence and Rome.

The mosaics from Florence are commonly known as "petra dura." These works of art are made by cutting designs out of stones much as malachite and cornelian, and fitting them together in a black background stone. This was done so expertly that a magnifying glass is needed to verify that the design is indeed made from pieces and not painted. Flowers and birds were favorite motifs.

The mosaics from Rome have an entirely different look. They are made of tiny rectangular bricks of glass. As early as the eighteenth century, the Vatican was making pieces to sell to visitors. The motifs are typical Roman ruins and other familiar scenes of Rome. Many designs were taken from mosaics found in the ruins of Pompeii. Again a magnifying glass is needed to fully appreciate the craftsmanship that went into creating these souvenir pieces.

Mosaics are highly collectible. The price depends on the material used for the mounting and the workmanship of the artist.

Pique and Tortoise Shell

The popular French definition of the word Pique is "dotted" or "cracked." This is an apt description of the beautiful work done in tortoise shell or ivory. The most frequently encountered pique is done in tortoise shell, which comes from the hawksbill turtle. Even though this is the smallest of marine turtles, it usually weighs between one hundred and two hundred pounds. Both the mottled upper shell and the lower "yellow belly" are used for ornamental purposes.

Tortoise shell is one of nature's natural plastics. It can be heated and molded or cut into many forms. For pique the shell is heated and a design is formed (star, cross, etc.). Into this design "dots" or "racks" are drilled. These minute spaces are inlaid with silver or gold rods. The hot tortoise shell emits a glue-like film which, along with the natural contraction caused by the cooling shell, snugly seals the metal.

Many lovely pieces were made using this process. Pique has been in and out of fashion since the sixteenth century. In the nineteenth century, it was popular in the 1820s and the 1870s. Today, it is highly collectible. When a piece comes on the market, it is quickly purchased by a collector. Since pique is not being reproduced, it most assuredly will continue to appreciate in value.

(A) (Photo courtesy of Sotheby's, London, 6/30/99)

Gold and malachite demi-parure, Italian, circa 1820 pendant earrings, brooch, and necklace. The necklace features oval cameos showing mythological scenes alternating which alternate with smaller Medusa and Cupid heads. £3,200 **Price: $5,280**

(A) (Photo courtesy of Sotheby's, London, 6/30/99)

Late 19th century diamond brooch with diamond set flowerheads and palmettes. £2,000 **Price: $3,300**

(A) (Photo courtesy of Sotheby's, London, 6/30/99)

Circa 1870 parure comprising a gold hinged bangle (55mm diam.), earrings, and brooch. All pieces are set with diamonds and emeralds. £5,000 **Price: $8,250**

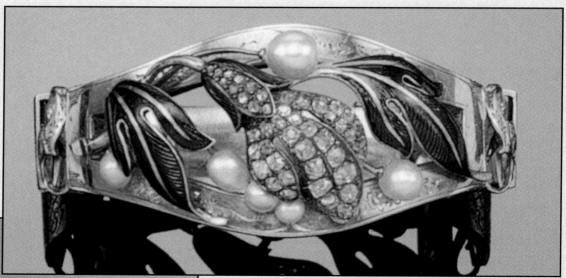

Circa 1870 bangle, diamond set petals, green enamel and pearl leaves, back has engraved rectangular panels joined together by figure-eight links, brooch en suite. £3,500 **Price: $5,775**

Circa 1830 diamond brooch, heart-shaped leaves on diamond studded branch. £1,800 **Price: $2,970**

(A) (Photo courtesy of Sotheby's, London, 6/30/99)

1906 Chaumet fine gold necklace and bangle with turquoise, pearls, and diamonds. Fitted cases and French marks (diamond shoulder missing on bangle). £8,500

Price: $14,025

(A) (Photo courtesy of Sotheby's, London, 6/30/99)

Circa 1880 diamond and turquoise ribbon bow brooch. Set with diamonds and cabochon turquoise. £2,000   **Price: $3,300**

(A) (Photo courtesy of Sotheby's, London, 6/30/99)

Circa 1900 butterfly brooch, enamel, chrysobel and diamonds. Brooch has Child & Child maker's mark on back. £3,500   **Price: $5,775**

Circa 1880 archaeological revival-style gold necklace and earrings, likely by Melillo, 395mm long. £16,500
Price: $27,225

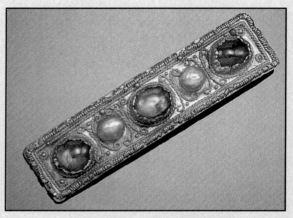

Circa 1880 rare gold, pearl, and sapphire archaeological revival-style Wièse jewel. £1,700
Price: $2,800

Circa 1900 diamond pendant on a slender chain necklet. £3,800   **Price: $6,270**

Circa 1910 seed pearl, sapphire and diamond pendant on a slender chain necklet. £4,000   **Price: $6,600**

Circa 1910 enamel and diamond pendant watch. £1,900   **Price: $3,135**

Circa 1900 yellow sapphire and pendant brooch. £2,600   **Price: $5,940**

(A) (Photo courtesy of Sotheby's, London, 6/30/99)

Left: Circa 1905 seed pearl and diamond necklace. £2,500   **Price: $4,125**

Center: Circa 1909 Wolfers plique-à-jour, baroque pearl, emerald and diamond pendant. £6,000   **Price: $9,900**

Right: Circa 1915 seed pearl, emerald, diamond sautoir (pearl tassel is later replacement). £5,500   **Price: $9,075**

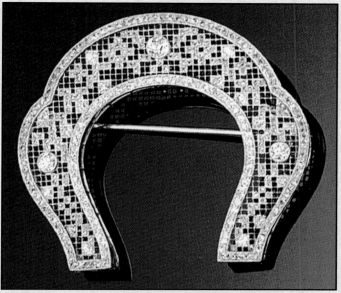

(A) (Photo courtesy of Sotheby's, London, 6/30/99)

Circa 1910 diamond horseshoe-design brooch. £2,400
Price: $3,960

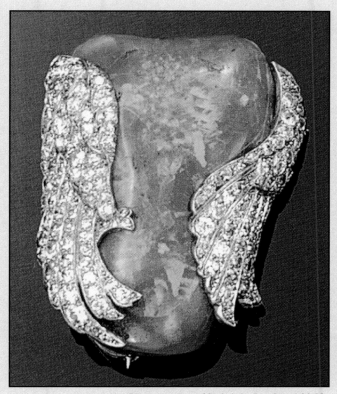

(A) (Photo courtesy of Sotheby's, London, 6/30/99)

Circa 1935 unusual black opal and diamond brooch.
£3,800   **Price: $6,270**

(A) (Photo courtesy of Sotheby's, London, 6/30/99)

Circa 1920 moonstone intaglio, emerald, and diamond pendant.
£3,500   **Price: $5,775**

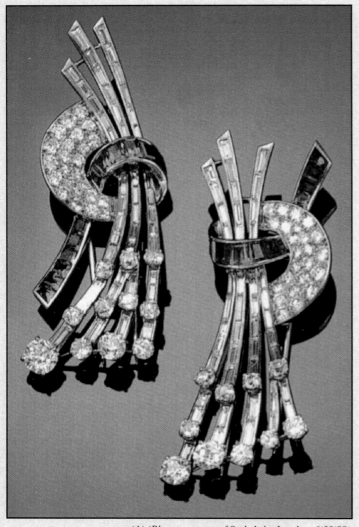

Circa 1930 furled ribbon clips. £27,200   **Price: $11,880**

Circa 1950 emerald and diamond double clip brooch and earclips. £7,000   **Price: $11,500**

Circa 1930 diamond brooch. £2,800   **Price: $4,620**

Bracelets

(D) (Jewelry Box Antiques)

1880s-1890s baby bracelet, gold filled, engraved "baby," black enamel, 1/4" wide, adjustable closure. **Price: $145**

(C) (Jeanenne Bell)

1850s-1870s bracelet, gold over brass with gold ornamentation, quatre foils are pink gold, leaves are green gold, bookchain style, 1/4" x 7" l. **Price: $195**

(D) (Jewelry Box Antiques)

1850s-1870s bracelet, gold filled, bracelet 1/2" wide, slide 7/8". **Price: $375**

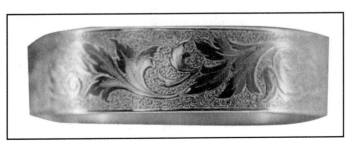

(D) (Jewelry Box Antiques)

1840-1860s bracelet, 14K yellow gold, engraved, 5/8". **Price: $995**

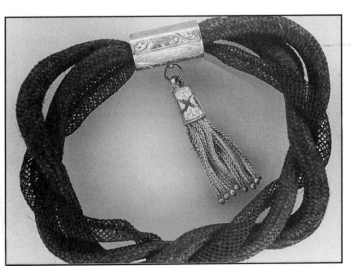

(D) (Jewelry Box Antiques)

Circa 1870s bracelet, yellow gold filled with table-worked hair in original box. **Price: $525**

1860s bracelet, gold embellished with black button pearls, cushion-shaped rubies, and diamonds, £15,400.
Price: $27,410

1860s-1870s bracelet, 10K locket clasp, three strands of hair, 1-1/4" dia. x 6" l.
Price: $525

1860s bracelet, gold snake motif with woven body and eyes set with old mine diamonds.
Price: $2,200

1860s bracelet, gold with Italian mosaics of allegorical figures representing the four seasons, reverse has glazed compartments, fitted case.
Price: $4,950

1860s-1870s bracelet, 10K locket clasp with 4 weaves of hairwork in 3 colors, 1" x 7".
Price: $550

1860s-1870s bracelet, 14K yellow gold hinged bangle, mint condition. **Price: $2,795**

1860s-1870s bracelet, 22K gold lava cameo, 7/8" x 1", band 1" x 1/2". **Price: $1,800**

1860s-1870s bracelet, 18K gold, 8" long, each lava cameo, 1-1/4" l x 1-1/2" w x 7/8" h relief. **Price: $2,800**

1860s-1870s bracelet, 15K gold mtgs., petra dura center plaques, 1-7/8" x 2-1/4"; 2 side pieces, length 6-1/2". **Price: $3,500**

1860s-1870s bracelet, 10K fittings, hairwork, 3/4" x 6-1/2".
Price: $550

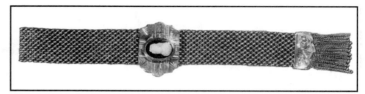

1860s-1870s bracelet, gold filled with stone onyx cameo, bracelet 7/8". **Price: $450**

1860s-1870s bracelet, gutta-percha, 1-1/2" x 2" wide.
Price: $350

1860s-1870s bracelet, 9K locket clasp with 4 weaves of hairwork, 1" w x 7-1/8" l. **Price: $485**

1860s-1870s bracelet, jet strung on elastic with shell cameos, 3/4" x 1-1/2" wide. **Price: $1,500**

1860s-1870s bracelet, jet strung on elastic with petra dura. 1-1/4" wide. **Price: $1,100**

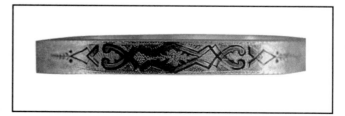

1860s-1870s bracelet, 13K yellow filled 1/4" with taille d' epergne enameling. **Price: $580**

1860s-1880s bracelet, silver chain with gold designed links, 7-1/2" l, note acorn drop. **Price: $225**

1860s-1870s bracelet, yellow gold filled mesh (missing tassel), 10" x 1/2". **Price: $250**

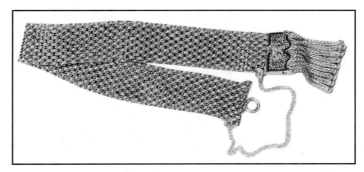

1860s-1880s bracelet, 14K gold clasp has taille d' epergne and seed pearls, 1/2" wide. **Price: $1,800**

1860s-1870s bracelet, yellow gold filled with black taille d' epergne enameling, no hinge, strung on wide elastic. **Price: $325**

1860s-1880s bracelet, jet chain and lock, bracelet 8" long, lock 1/2" x 3/4". **Price: $295**

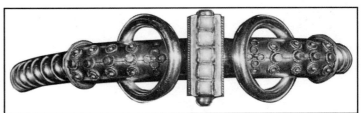

1870s-1880s bracelet, gold over brass with turquoise stones and granulation. **Price: $265**

1870s-1880s bracelet, gold filled mesh, 1/4"
wide with stone cameo, cameo 5/8" x 7/8".
Price: $395

1870s-1880s bracelet, gold filled mesh, 1/2" wide, top
is 1/2" x 1" black enameled. **Price: $395**

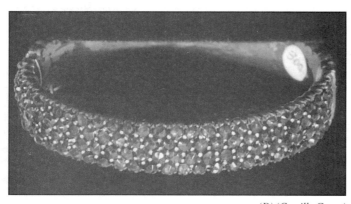

1870s-1890s bracelet, gilted silver with 4 rows of rose-
cut garnets, 1/2" wide. **Price: $995**

1880s-1900s bracelet, silver over brass, mosaic flower
insets, 1/2" x 7" l. **Price: $145**

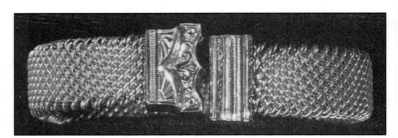

1870s-1880s bracelet, gold over brass, mesh 1/2" wide with
metal core. **Price: $165**

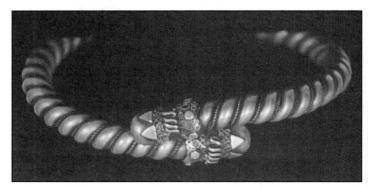

1870s-1880s bracelet, silver, flexible, note Etruscan influence. **Price: $135**

1870s-1890s bracelet, gold hinged bangle set with foiled
backed, rectangular mixed cut 3.8 cts, emerald surrounded by rose-cut diamonds and flanked by pearls,
£2,600. **Price: $4,630**

1870s-1880s bracelet, gold filled, taille d' epergne enameling mkd., "W.E.W. & Co.," 3/8" wide band, glide 5/8" x 1".
Price: $365

1880s-1890s bracelet, gold over brass, 1/8" twisted wire, ends approx. 3/8". **Price: $95**

1880s bracelet, silver, acorn drop. **Price: $115**

1887 bracelet, English hallmark, sterling, hinged bangle, 5/8" wide. **Price: $350**

Bracelet, dated May 13, 1884, gold over brass, 3/8" w, visible repairs. **Price: $325**

1890s bracelet yellow gold filled bangle, oval with red stone, 2-1/2" x 2". **Price: $295**

1880s bracelet, yellow gold filled mesh-style with swan of tri-color gold on the approx. 1" x 1/2" clasp, ptd. July 2, 1884. **Price: $290**

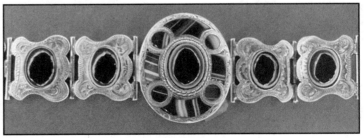

Circa 1870s bracelet, sterling silver with banded agate, cabochon's and inlaid stones. Center plaque, approx. 1-3/8" x 7-1/2" l each length approx. 7/8" x 7/8". **Price: $695**

(A) (Photo courtesy of Phillips, London 1-28-84)

Gold hinged bangle with owl and Latin motto, by Carlo Giulian, £1,800. **Price: $3,200**

(D) (Jewelry Box Antiques)

Bracelet, pat. dates Jan. 1, 1879 and Feb. 26, 1884, gold filled 1/2" wide. **Price: $145**

(D) (Jewelry Box Antiques)

Bracelet, pat. June 19, 1883, flexible gold over brass with embossed design. **Price: $125**

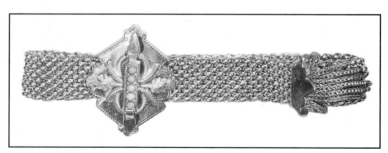

(D) (Jewelry Box Antiques)

Bracelet, patent date Nov. 7, 1871 and June 26, 1872 gold filled, slide clasp has 5 Persian turquoises, 1" x 1/4" mesh bracelet, 1/2" w. **Price: $425**

1870s-1890s pair of bracelets, matte jet balls with shining jet bead spacers, end matte ball 8mm. **Price: $150**

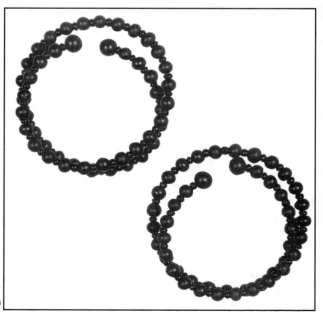

(D) (Jewelry Box Antiques)

(D) (Camille Grace)

1860s-1870s hinged bracelet, gold filled with taille d' epergne enameling.   **Price: $425**

(D) (Jewelry Box Antiques)

1880s-1890s hinged bracelet, yellow gold filled with pink and green gold designs.   **Price: $345**

(D) (Camille Grace)

1860s-1880s pair of bracelets, gold over brass, mkd., "W.E.W. & Co." adjustable band, each bracelet has 3 garnets and 2 pearls, 3/8" wide.   **Price: $395 pair**

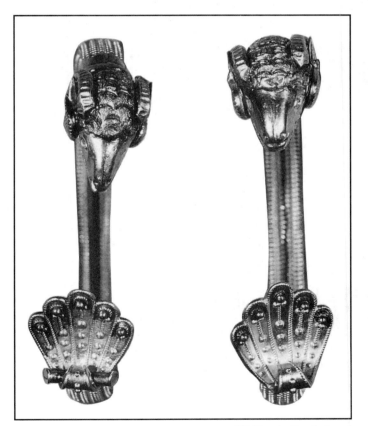

(D) (Jewelry Box Antiques)

1870s-1880s pair of bracelets, gold over silver, ram's head and mesh, 1/4" x 3/4".   **Price: $395 pair**

Code in Front of Name

(A) Auction House - Auction Price
(C) Collector - Collector Asking Price
(D) Dealer - Dealer's Asking Price

(D) (Jewelry Box Antiques)

Hinged bracelet with safety, pat'd. July 21, 1874, H & B Co. gold filled with some gold, beautiful taille d' epergne enameling, 3/4" x 7/8" wide.   **Price: $395**

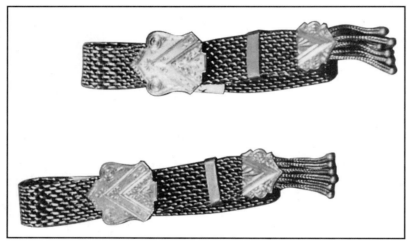

(D) (Jewelry Box Antiques)

1870s-1880s pair of bracelets gold over brass, this type bracelet was usually worn in pairs, one on one arm and one on the other.

Price: $495

(A) (Photo courtesy of Skinner, Inc., Boston, Mass 9-25-90)

Victorian bracelet, centered by round cultured pearl, surrounded by 11 round mine cut sapphires and flanked by rose-cut diamonds, silver and 14K yellow gold, center portion of bracelet converts to a pin, in a fitted box marked "Carrington & Co. Goldsmiths, 150 Regent St. W."

Price: $3,100

Brooches & Pins

(D) (Jewelry Box Antiques)

Circa 1880s brooch, gold over brass, star burst with garnets, approx. 1-3/8" diameter. **Price: $489**

1850s-1870s brooch, 14K gold, stone cameo with enameling, 1-1/4" x 1-1/2". **Price: $975**

(C) (Jeanenne Bell)

Florentine mosaic brooch/pendant, silver mounting. **Price: $1,000**

(A) (Photo courtesy Wm. Doyle Galleries, New York 9-20-89)

(C) (Jeanenne Bell)

1850s-1870s brooch, gold filled fittings and gold ornamentation, hairwork 2-1/4" x 1-1/2".

Price: $325

Circa 1870s brooch, 14K yellow gold with taille d'epergne enamel, approx. 1-1/4" diameter. **Price: $395**

(D) (Jewelry Box Antiques)

(D) (Jewelry Box Antiques)

1860s-1870s brooch, gold top with black taille d' epergne enameling, 2-3/8" x 5/8". **Price: $250**

(D) (Camille Grace)

1860s-1870s brooch, gold filled mounting, shell cameo, 1-3/4" x 2".
Price: $325

(A) (Photo courtesy of Wm. Doyle Galleries, New York 9-21-83)

1860-1870 brooch, yellow gold with cameo and 6 assorted diamonds.
Price: $325

(D) (Jewelry Box Antiques)

1860s-1870s brooch, 14K, 2-1/8" x 1-1/2".
Price: $395

(A) (Photo courtesy of Sotheby's New York 10-6-83)

1850s-1870s brooch, gold with oval sardonyx cameo, embellished with 4 seed pearls and 8 single cut diamonds.
Price: $990

(C) (Camille Grace)

1860s-1880s brooch, silver mtg., shell cameo, 1-3/4" x 2-1/4".
Price: $325

(C) (Jeanenne Bell)

1860s-1870s brooch, 18K mosaic has black onyx background with multicolored flowers beautifully worked cluster of grapes, compartment for hair in rear, piece swivels so that hair can be in front, 2" x 2-1/4".
Price: $1,800

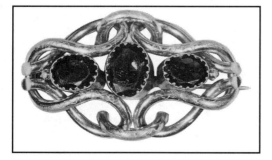

(D) (Jewelry Box Antiques)

1860s-1870s brooch, gold filled with garnet colored stones, typical massive style, 2-3/4" x 1-3/4".
Price: $195

(D) (Jewelry Box Antiques)

1860s-1880s brooch, gold over brass with some gold ornamentation, clear stone and 2 pearls, 2-1/4".
Price: $140

1860s-1870s brooch, gold over brass with garnets, 2" x 1-1/2". **Price: $125**

1860s-1870s brooch, Bog Oak shamrocks, centered with emeralds, 2" x 1-1/2". **Price: $300**

1860s-1870s brooch, jet with painting on porcelain of Vagabond Boy, 2" x 1-1/2". **Price: $345**

1860s-1870s brooch, gold filled with taille d' epergne enameling, 1-1/4" x 1". **Price: $245**

1870s-1880s brooch, gold mtg., garnet with 2 seed pearls, 1-3/8" x 3/8". **Price: $425**

1860s-1880s brooch, gold filled mtg., shell cameo, 2-1/4" x 2-5/8". **Price: $295**

1860s-1880s brooch, gold, agate, 1-1/4" dia.
Price: $240

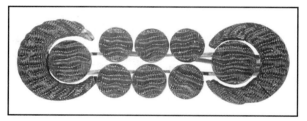

1870s-1880s brooch, gold filled, crepe stone, 2-1/4" x 3/4". **Price: $135**

1860s-1880s brooch, gold with onyx and 1 pearl, 1-3/4" x 1-1/8". **Price: $425**

1870s-1880s brooch, crepe stone, 2-1/2" x 1/2", chipped corner. **Price: $55**

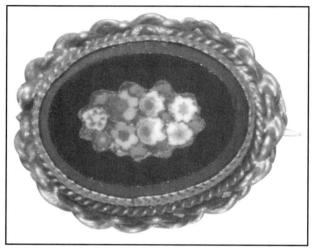

1860s-1880s brooch, gold over brass, mosaic in black onyx with flowers of white, red, and green, 1" x 3/4". **Price: $260**

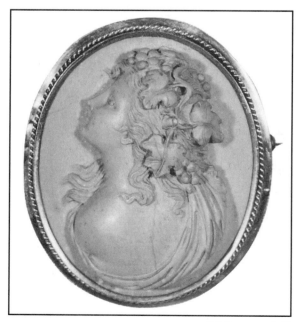

1860s brooch, 18K mtg., lava cameo, 1-3/4" x 2-1/8". **Price: $2,000**

(C) (W Baldwin)

1870s-1880s brooch, gold filled with onyx and pearl, 2-1/4"x 3/8".
Price: $150

(D) (Jewelry Box Antiques)

1870s-1889 brooch, matte jet balls 5mm and crepe stone on Gutta-percha, 2-1/8"x 1/4".　　　　　**Price: $125**

1870s-1880s brooch, gold filled, key motif, 2-3/4" x 3/4".
Price: $145

(D) (Jewelry Box Antiques)

(A) (Photo courtesy of Sotheby's New York 4-14-83)

Brooch 1870s, Girandole style set with rubies and diamonds, £3,520. **Price: $6,265**

(C) (W. Baldwin)

1860s-1880s brooch, yellow gold cabochon garnet and granulation work, glassed compartment in back for hair, 1-1/2" x 1-1/4".
Price: $595

87

1880s-1900s brooch, gold over brass mtg. with Celluloid cameo, 1-1/2" x 2".
Price: $95

1860s-1880s brooch, jet mounting with a painting on porcelain, 1-5/8" x 2".
Price: $345

Pat. June 5, 1887 brooch, gold top, back gold over brass 2" x 5/8".
Price: $125

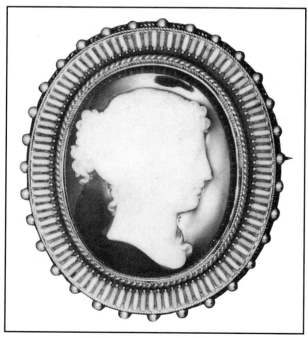

Circa 1860s brooch, by "Castellani," gold centered with a carved ruby cameo Cupid's head with a border of cushion-shaped diamonds, £11,000. **Price: $19,580**

1880s brooch, gold with sardonyx cameo and pale blue and white enameling, £770.   **Price: $1,370**

(C) (W. Baldwin)

1880s-1910s brooch, silver with amethyst and 3 baroque pearls, 1-3/8" x 1-7/8". **Price: $195**

(D) (Jewelry Box Antiques)

1880s-1890s brooch, gold over brass mtg., pyrite, 2-1/8" x 1/4", drop 1/2" dia. **Price: $125**

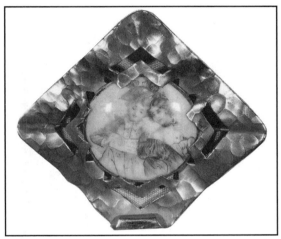

(D) (Jewelry Box Antiques)

1880s-1890s brooch, gold filled mtg., painting on porcelain, 3" x 2-3/4". **Price: $325**

(C) (W. Baldwin)

1870-1890 brooch, gold with onyx and seed pearls, 2-5/8" x 1/2". **Price: $1,575**

Antique diamond and ruby pendant brooch.
Price: $3,450

(A) (Photo courtesy of Christie's East, New York 6-7-99)

(D) (Camille Grace)

1880s-1910s brooch, silver with amethyst and 3 baroque pearls, enameled trim, 1-3/8" x 1". **Price: $245**

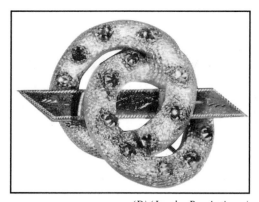

(D) (Jewelry Box Antiques)

1870s-1890s brooch, yellow gold filled with rose-cut imitation garnets and sapphires, 1-3/4" x 1-1/8". **Price: $85**

(D) (Camille Grace)

1880s-1890s brooch, gold over brass, Bohemian garnets, 1-3/8" dia. **Price: $300**

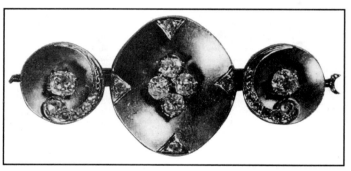

(C) (Camille Grace)

1880s-1890s brooch, 18K gold with 6 diamonds, 1-7/8" x 7/8". **Price: $1,275**

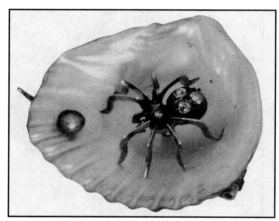

Brooch, 1860 gold, shell and pearl designed as a spider in cockleshell, £385. **Price: $685**

(D) (June O' Donnel)

1880s brooch, sterling, painting on porcelain, 2" x 1-1/2". **Price: $350**

1880s-1890s brooch, gold over brass, Bohemian garnets, 1-1/8"x 1-1/8". **Price: $350**

(D) (Camille Grace)

1880s-1890s brooch, gold over brass, crescent and star, Bohemian garnets, 1-3/8" x 1-1/2". **Price: $325**

1880s-1890s brooch, gold over brass, crown of Bohemian garnets, 1-7/8" x 1". **Price: $395**

1889-1890s hallmarked brooch, sterling, 1-3/4" x 1-1/8". **Price: $165**

1879 brooch, inscribed "Mary," painted carved wood with gold ornamentation, 1-3/8" x 1". **Price: $195**

Brooch, jet marked, "Whitby," 2" x 1-1/2". **Price: $200**

Mid 19th century brooch, gold with oval sardonyx cameo. **Price: $660**

Second half of 19th century brooch, gold with enameled repousse plaque representing St. George and the dragon, cerulean enamel frame, £495. **Price: $880**

1860s-1870s memorial brooch, gold with black enameling, nice tin type. **Price: $325**

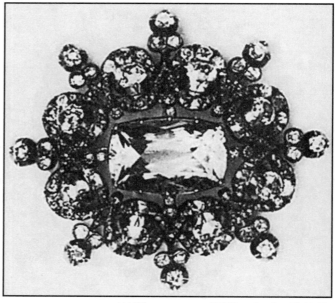

Victorian brooch, gold with cushion-shaped aquamarine set in a pierced silver collet, surrounded with diamonds. £1,500. **Price: $2,670**

1880s-1890s, brooch/pendant, gold filled, shell cameo, 1-1/2" x 2". **Price: $395**

(D) (Camille Grace)

Brooch/pendant, last quarter of 19th century, gold with sardonyx cameo, mounting embellished with rose-cut diamonds. £1,650. **Price: $2,940**

1870s-1880s brooch/pendant, gold with tassels, 1-1/4" x 3-1/8". **Price: $995**

(C) (W. Baldwin)

Victorian Scottish agate pin, 14K yellow gold, in the shape of a dagger, set with smokey quartz, jasper, bloodstone and agate. **Price: $650**

(A) (Photo courtesy of Skinner, Inc., Boston, Mass 9-25-90)

(D) (June O'Donnel)

1860s-1880s pin, yellow gold filled over brass, crescent motif with crystals, 2" x 1".
Price: $125

(D) (Jewelry Box Antiques)

1860s-1880s pin, 14K yellow gold filled with leaf motif and archeological revival design.
Price: $350

(D) (Jewelry Box Antiques)

1860s-1880s pin, mosaic, 1-1/4" dia. **Price: $995**

1860s pin, yellow gold filled, painting on porcelain with twisted mounting design, 1-1/2" x 2". **Price: $345**

1880s pin, yellow gold filled bar style, 2-1/4" x 1/2". **Price: $125**

1890s pin, 9K yellow gold baby with stars, 1-9/16" x 5/16".

Price: $125

1880s pin, yellow gold filled over brass set with petra dura and lava, originally was an earring. **Price: $145**

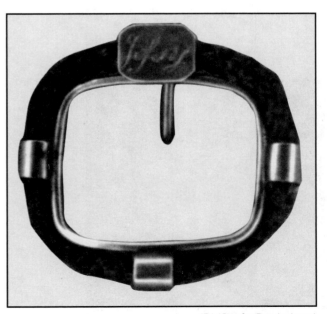

1880s pin, yellow gold approx. 7/8" square, made of hair. **Price: $195**

1860s-1880s scarf pin, gold filled fittings, hairwork is finished all around, harp motif was popular for many years.
Price: $235

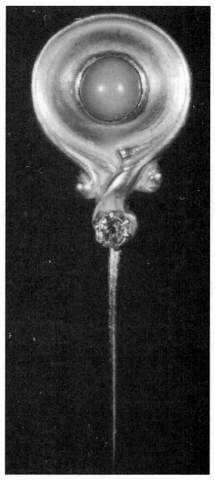

1880-1900 scarf pin, 14K yellow gold with turquoise and diamond. **Price: $135**

1870s-1880s scarf pin, gold filled with blue enameled ground, 5/8". **Price: $55**

1860s-1880s pins, 18K yellow gold set with coral beads.
Top: 2-3/4" x 1-1/4". **Price: $395**
Bottom: 1-1/4" x 1". **Price: $200**

1880s-1890s scarf pin, gold over brass, 3/4" dia. **Price: $58**

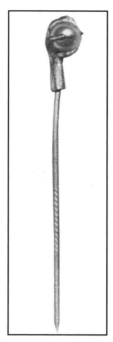

1880s-1890s scarf pin, gold over brass, claw set 6mm pearl. **Price: $58**

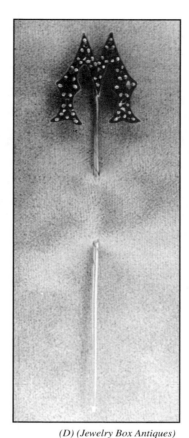

1860s-1880s stick pin, gold over brass, initial "M" set with garnets. **Price: $165**

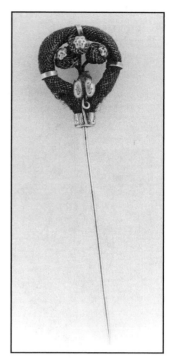

1860s-1880s stick pin, 14K yellow gold, table worked hair (some damage), 3-3/16" l. **Price: $175**

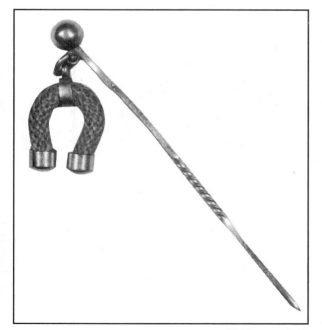

1880s scarf pin, gold over brass fitting, hairwork, popular horseshoe motif, 1/2" x 5/8", pin 2-1/2" l. **Price: $195**

Code in Front of Name

(A) Auction House - Auction Price

(C) Collector - Collector Asking Price

(D) Dealer - Dealer's Asking Price

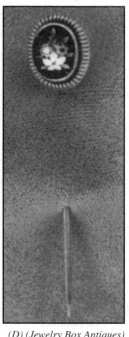

1880s stick pin, mosaic. **Price: $195**

Crosses

1860s-1870s cross, gutta-per-cha with anchor of hope, 2-1/16" x 3-3/4".
Price: $245

(C) (Jeanenne Bell)

1860s-1880s cross, gold top, back is gold over brass, 1-5/8" x 2-3/8". **Price: $160**

(D) (Jewelry Box Antiques)

(D) (June O'Donnel)

1860s cross, gutta-percha, 2-3/4" x 1-3/4". **Price: $225**

(D) (June O'Donnel)

1860s-1880s cross, yellow gold over brass, rose-cut garnets, 3" x 2". **Price: $680**

1880s cross, 14K yellow gold with seed pearls and pink sapphires, 2-1/4" x 1-1/2". **Price: $240**

1860s-1880s cross pendant, jet. 3-1/2" x 2-1/4". **Price: $295**

Cross, jet, 2-1/2" x 4". **Price: $210**

Cross pendant, jet faceted beads, 3-3/4" x 2-1/2". **Price: $125**

1860s-1880s cross pendant, jet, 4-1/4" x 3/4". **Price: $245**

Earrings

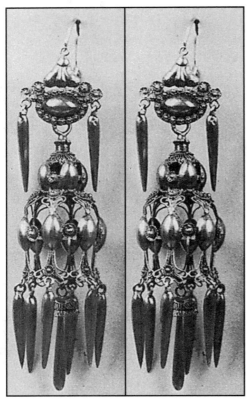

(A) (Photo courtesy of Skinner, Inc., Boston, Mass 9-25-90)

Antique gold earrings, 18K yellow gold filigree openwork with gold tassels. **Price: $375**

(A) (Skinner Auction, Boston 9-26-94)

1870s Victorian 14kt gold earrings, enamel. **Price: $805**

(A) (Photo courtesy of Sotheby Park Bernet & Co. London 12-15-83)

1875-1895 earrings, gold classical Greek style with filigree and granulation, £2,090. **Price: $3,720**

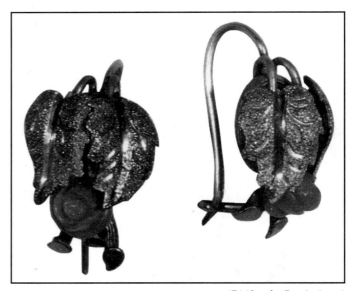

(D) (Jewelry Box Antiques)

1850s-1870s earrings, gold filled, pink and green gold leaves, imitation coral stones, 1/2" x 7/8".

Price: $155

Code in Front of Name

(A) Auction House - Auction Price
(C) Collector - Collector Asking Price
(D) Dealer - Dealer's Asking Price

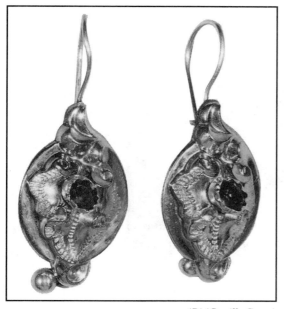

(D) (Camille Grace)

1860s-1870s earrings, gold filled with garnets. 3/4" x 2-1/8". **Price: $295**

1860s-1870s earrings, gold filled with gold ornamentation, taille d' epergne enameling, 1/2" x 1-1/2". **Price: $395**

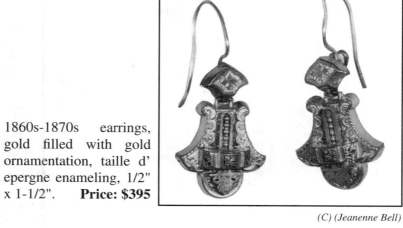

(C) (Jeanenne Bell)

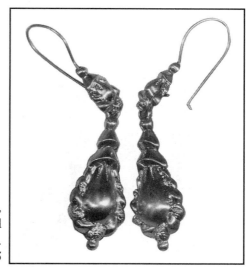

1860s-1870s earrings, gold filled, often called hollow gold. 1-3/4" l. **Price: $225**

(D) (Jewelry Box Antiques)

(D) (Camille Grace)

1860s-1870s earrings, gold with coral, 3/4" x 1-3/4". **Price: $425**

1860s-1870s earrings, 18K yellow gold with pearls and enameling. **Price: $800**

(D) (Jewelry Box Antiques)

(D) (Jowsey & Roe, Whitby, England)

1860s-1870s earrings, jet, 2" x 3/4".
Price: $295

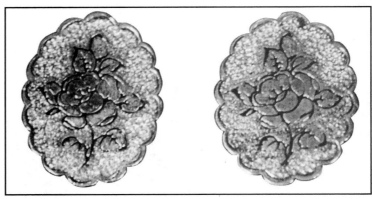

(D) (Jewelry Box Antiques)

1860s-1880s earrings, gold tops, gold over brass backs, black enameling, original collar buttons now have 14K posts.
Price: $395

(C) (Nancy Bechtold)

1860s earrings, pique.   **Price: $800**

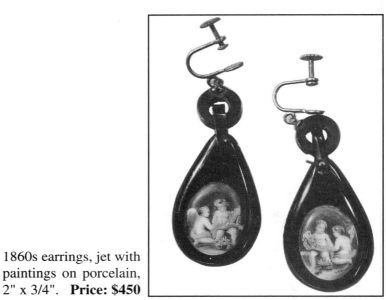

1860s earrings, jet with paintings on porcelain, 2" x 3/4". **Price: $450**

(D) (Jowsey & Roe, Whitby, England)

Late 19th century earrings, gold mountings with grapes of multicolored pearls, leaves are studded with 12 small old European cut old mine diamonds, screw backs added later. **Price: $770**

(A) (Photo courtesy of Sotheby's New York 10-5-83)

1860s earrings, jet with pink shell cameos, 2-1/4" x 1".
Price: $425

(D) (Jowsey & Roe, Whitby, England)

1875-1880s earrings, gold with diamonds and royal blue enameled star within borders of white enamel, £770. **Price: $1,370**

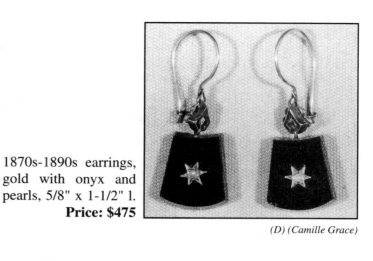

1870s-1890s earrings, gold with onyx and pearls, 5/8" x 1-1/2" l. **Price: $475**

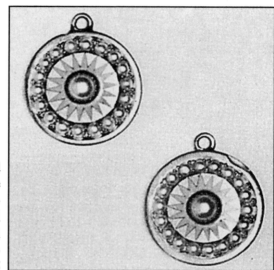

Earrings, gold dish-shaped with half pearl set in blue enamel star centers, surrounded by a half pearl hoop, signed C.G. in oval cartouches, Carlo Guilliano, £400. **Price: $715**

Last quarter of the 19th century earrings, gold with powder blue, crimson and black enamel, £1,320. **Price: $2,350**

Victorian earrings, black onyx set in gold highlighted by half pearls, 9ct. **Price: $375**

Lockets

(C) (Camille Grace)

1870s-1890s locket and chain, 18K gold with 2 rubies, 9 dematoid garnets, 12 pearls, and 4 diamonds with granulation, 1-1/4" x 2-1/4", chain 24". **Price: $1,495**

(C) (Jeanenne Bell)

1850s-1870s locket, gutta-percha with anchor motif, 1" x 1-1/4". **Price: $195**

(D) (Jewelry Box Antiques)

1860s-1870s locket, gilt over brass with some gold ornamentation, two blue stones and two red stones, 1-1/8" x 1-3/8". **Price: $185**

(D) (Camille Grace)

1850s-1870s locket, gold filled with gold top and bottom, taille d' epergne enameling. 1-1/4" x 1-3/4". **Price: $225**

1850s-1870s locket, pinchbeck, 1-1/2" x 2-1/2". **Price: $245**

(C) (Jeanenne Bell)

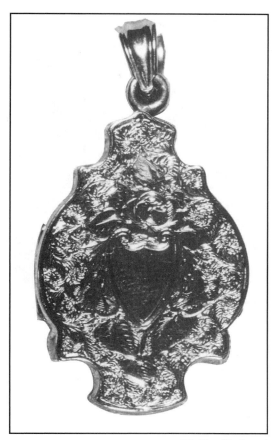

(D) (Camille Grace)

1880s-1890s locket, gold tops, triple picture holder, 7/8" x 1-1/4". **Price: $265**

(C) (Jeanenne Bell)

1860s-1880s locket, gold filled with original mesh chain 1/4" x 19" l, locket 1" x 1-1/2". **Price: $595**

(D) (Jewelry Box Antiques)

1860s-1880s locket, "Mizpah" oval-shaped. **Price: $195**

1860s-1880s locket, gold filled, 7/8" x 1-1/4", mint condition. **Price: $195**

1860s-1880s lockets, yellow gold filled with taille d' epergne enameling. **Price: $225**

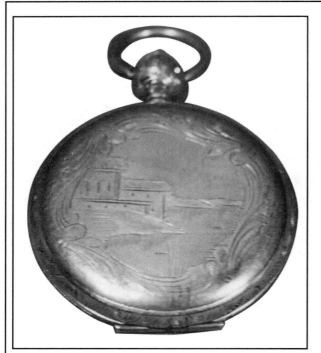

1860s locket, gold filled, contains two tin types. Note the button on top that opens like hunting case watch, 1-1/2" dia. **Price: $250**

Inside view of locket.

1870s-1890s locket, gold navette-shaped with applied floral spray of diamonds on dark blue translucent enamel, £800. **Price: $1,425**

(A) (Photo courtesy of Phillips, London 6-21-83)

(D) (Camille Grace)

1880s-1890s locket, 9K heart, 3/4" x 1". **Price: $245**

(D) (Jewelry Box Antiques)

1860s baby locket, yellow gold filled, 1/2" dia. **Price: $125**

(C) (Jeanenne Bell)

1870s-1880s locket, gold over brass with some gold ornamentation, moonstone in center, contains a lock of hair, 1-1/4" x 2-1/8". **Price: $195**

(D) (Jewelry Box Antiques)

1860s-1870s locket, yellow gold filled, black enameling and 5 seed pearls, 1-1/2" x 1". **Price: $200**

1884 locket, pat'd., yellow gold filled with hunting case motif on one side and engraving on back, holds 4 photos. **Price: $195**

1879 Hallmarked locket, sterling, 1-1/4" x 1-3/4". **Price: $165**

1880s-1890s locket and bookchain, gold filled locket, 1-1/8" x 1-1/2", chain 1/2" x 18" l. **Price: $495**

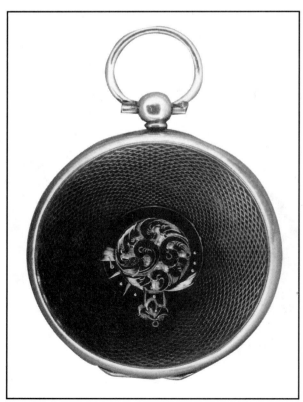

1860s locket, 1-3/4" dia. **Price: $195**

(D) (Jewelry Box Antiques)

1870s-1880s locket and chain, gold over brass with banded agate and seed pearls, 1-3/8" x 2". **Price: $150**

(D) (Camille Grace)

1860s-1880s locket fob, gold filled with 1" x 1-5/8" gold stone attached to book-chain, 1/2" x 16" l. **Price: $425**

(D) (Jowsey & Roe, Whitby, England)

1870s locket/pendant, jet, (does not open), photo in back compartment, 2" x 1-3/4". **Price: $225**

(C) (Ms. Marietta)

Circa 1870s locket, sterling silver with engraved links. Locket is embellished with pink gold and green gold birds, locket overall 1-3/8" x 2-3/8", chain length approx. 18 in. **Price: $895**

Necklaces

(D) (Jowsey & Roe, Whitby, England)

1860s necklaces (2), jet (1) (inside necklace) 18" long, 1/2" dia.; (2) (outside necklace) 23" long.
Price: $250 ea.

(C) (W. Baldwin)

1870s-1880s bookchain, silver, originally had a locket attached, 5/8" x 16-1/2" l.   **Price: $425**

(C) (W. Baldwin)

1870s-1880s bookchain, silver, 1/2" x 17-1/2" l.
Price: $400

(D) (Jewelry Box Antiques)

1860s-1880s beads, 8mm matte finished jet on chain.
Price: $165

(C) (Camille Grace)

1860s-1870s locket and bookchain, gold filled, locket has mosaic bird, 1-1/8" x 2"; chain 3/8" x 18" l.
Price: $750

(C) (W. Baldwin)

1860s-1880s locket and bookchain, yellow gold, 1-1/4" x 2-1/8", chain 20" l.
Price: $2,200

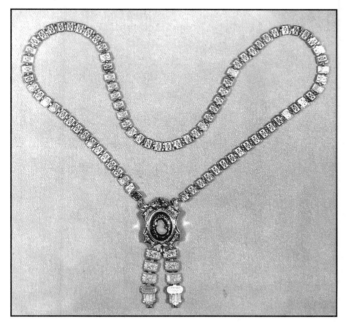

(C) (Jeanenne Bell)

1860s-1880s bookchain necklace, gold filled with stone cameo drop, 1" x 1-1/4", chain 19" l. **Price: $475**

(C) (Jeanenne Bell)

1860s-1880s bookchain necklace, gold over brass bookchain with small stone cameo, 7/8" x 1-1/2" drop.

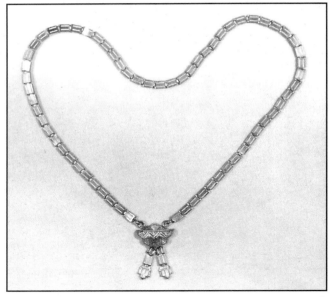

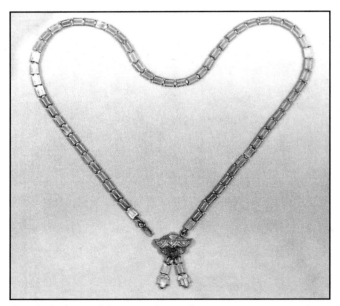

(C) (Jeanenne Bell)

1860s-1880s bookchain necklace, gold over brass, flat links 1/8", drop 3/4" x 1-1/4". **Price: $325**

Bookchain necklace unclasped.

(C) (Jeanenne Bell)

Necklace shown unclasped.

1860s-1870s, necklace, gold filled with 19" original chain, drop is 1-5/8" x 2". Note chain is at top left side of drop. **Price: $395**

1860s-1870s necklace, gutta-percha, chain lengths graduate from 1" to 5/8", drop 1-3/4" x 3". A fine example of the massive style. **Price: $250**

1860s-1870s necklace, yellow gold filled woven chain 8.53mm wide, 20" long, hand carved stone cameo drop. **Price: $695**

1860s-1880s necklace, yellow gold filled bookchain necklace design, chain 18" long, locket 1-1/4" x 7/8". **Price: $650**

1860s-1880s necklace, gold filled on black ribbon, 32" l. **Price: $165**

Late 19th century, Etruscan revival gold and enamel fringe necklace, C & A Giulian, composed of loop-in-loop chain work and hung with rose shaped pendants, highlighted by blue and green enamel, in fitted velvet case, signed on terminals and clasp (some minor damage to chain, one pendant missing, some gold granules missing on clasp). **Price: $50,000**

(D) (Jewelry Box Antiques)

1860s-1880s necklace, yellow gold filled with turquoise and pearl drop, 24" l. **Price: $495**

(C) (W. Baldwin)

1860s-1880s necklace, gold with cabochon garnet, drop 1-1/8", chain 61" l.
Price: $1,210

(C) (W. Baldwin)

1860s-1880s necklace, 14K gold, onyx, pearls and enameling, chain 18" l, drop 1-3/8" x 1-1/2". **Price: $900**

1860s necklace, jet segments, 1-1/2"
x 1-1/4" ea., 18" l.   **Price: $300**

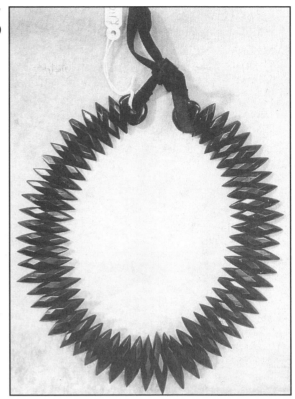

(D) (Jowsey & Roe, Whitby, England)

(D) (Jewelry Box Antiques)

1860s-1880s necklace drop, gold over brass with Venetian glass inset, note granulation, 1" x 1/2". **Price: $195**

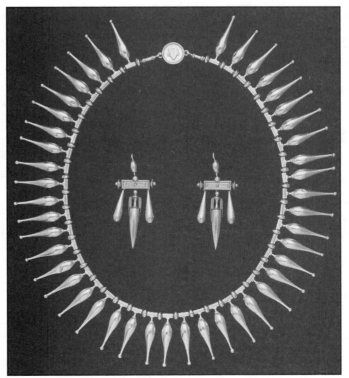

(A) (Photo courtesy of Sotheby's London 7-28-83)

1875-1890s necklace and earrings, gold Hellenistic style
with fringe of pod motif, £2,090.   **Price: $3,720**

1875 Necklace, gold micro-mosaic beetle, gold chain, Italian. **Price: $1,210**

Necklaces: Jet (1) (outer necklace) round granulated, 27" l. **Price: $225**

Jet (2) (center) faceted strand, 19" l. **Price: $165**

Jet (3) (inside center) round, faceted and carved elongated strand, 18" l. **Price: $245**

Pendants

(D) (Camille Grace)

1860s-1880s pendant, 1-1/2" x 2-1/4", petra dura, 1-1/2" x 1-7/8". **Price: $995**

(A) (Photo courtesy of Sotheby's New York 10-5-83)

1875s-1890s, pendant/brooch gold with tinted crystal intaglio of a stag on a cliff (slightly damaged), reverse has glazed compartment. **Price: $495**

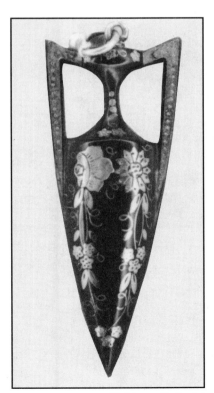

(C) (Norma Benjamin)

1840s pendant, pique.

Price: $425

(A) (Photo courtesy Phillips, London 9-20-83)

Pendant, gold centered with old cut diamond, oval Cambridge blue enamel surrounded by rose diamonds and half pearls, fitted case, £1,600. **Price: $2,848**

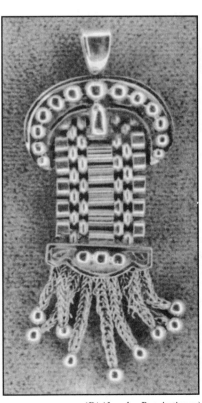

(D) (Jewelry Box Antiques)

1860s-1870s pendant, 14K yellow gold with tassel motif, 1-1/2" x 1/2". **Price: $345**

117

1850s-1870s pendant, gold with oval sard-onyx cameo of Roman maiden. **Price: $935**

1860s-1870s, pendant/brooch, gold with sardonyx cameo, "The Triumph of Love." **Price: $1,540**

1850s-1870s, pendant/brooch, gold with sard-onyx cameo of Hagar and Ishmael (some dam-age), Spaulding & Co. **Price: $990**

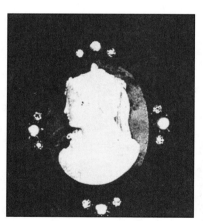

Pendant/brooch, last quarter of 19th century, gold with hard stone cameo of Elizabethan lady. Embellished with 4 pearls and 8 old mine diamonds, reverse has glazed compart-ment and hinged pendant loop, "Tiffany & Co." **Price: $2,530**

(A) (Photo courtesy of Phillips, London 9-20-83)

1860s pendant, gold with enameled plaque encircled with diamonds, reverse has hinged compartment. £950.

Price: $1,691

(A) (Photo courtesy of Sotheby's, London 4-14-83)

1865 pendant, gold centered with blue sapphire and pearls, signed "E R" by Ernesto Rinzi, this has a long slide chain (not shown), £2,200.

Price: $3,916

(D) (Jowsey & Roe, Whitby, England)

1860s-1880s pendant drop, jet frame, 2-1/8" x 2".

Price: $130

1860s-1880s pendant, 1-1/2" x 2-1/4", petra dura 1-1/2" x 1-7/8", one of pair.

Price: $995

Pendant, gold and enameled box panels set with sapphires, emeralds, garnets, and rubies with pearl and diamond solitaire center and pearl drops. Earrings (not shown) en suite (later fittings), each piece is signed "C. G." in oval cartouches, Carlo Guilliano. £5,200.   **Price: $9,256**

(A) (Photo courtesy of Phillips, London 6-21-83)

(A) (Photo courtesy of Phillips, London 4-26-83)

Victorian pendant, gold with diamonds, reverse has compartment for picture or hair. £600.   **Price: $1,058**

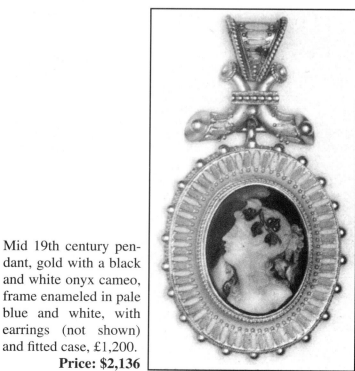

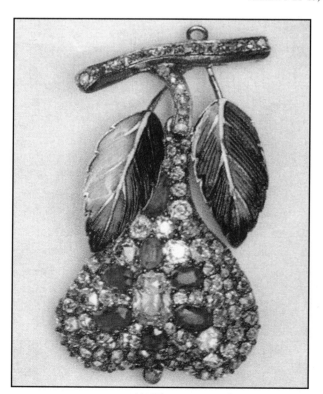

Mid 19th century pendant, gold with a black and white onyx cameo, frame enameled in pale blue and white, with earrings (not shown) and fitted case, £1,200.   **Price: $2,136**

(A) (Photo courtesy Phillips, London 9-20-83)

(A) (Photo courtesy of Phillips, London)

Mid-Victorian pendant, gold with pave set cushion-shaped rubies and diamonds in pear design. The enameled leaves and diamond-set branch are detachable, £7,000.   **Price: $12,460**

Rings

(D) (Jewelry Box Antiques)

1860s-1880s baby ring, 10K gold.
Price: $95

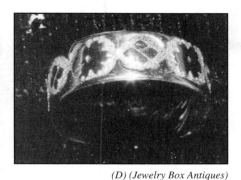

(D) (Jewelry Box Antiques)

1860s-1870s child's ring, 14K gold, "Hettie" engraved inside.
Price: $115

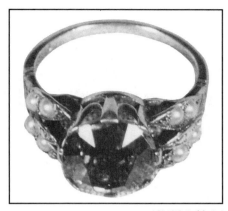

(C) (W. Baldwin)

1860s-1880s ring, 9K amethyst and pearl.
Price: $525

(D) (Camille Grace)

1860s-1870s ring, 18K shell cameo, massive mounting, cameo 1" x 1-1/4". **Price: $545**

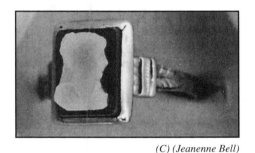

(C) (Jeanenne Bell)

1840s-1860s ring, 11K yellow gold set with hand-carved stone cameo.
Price: $47

(D) (Lucille and Sam Mundorff)

1860s-1880s ring, gold cornelian intaglio. **Price: $425**

(D) (Jewelry Box Antiques)

Ring, 18K yellow gold plaque with woven hair, band engraved, "Ann." **Price: $295**

(D) (Camille Grace)

1870s-1880s ring, 10K cornelian intaglio, 1-1/4" dia. **Price: $425**

1870s-1885 ring, gold filled, 1/4" wide. **Price: $45**

Code in Front of Name

(A) Auction House - Auction Price

(C) Collector - Collector Asking Price

(D) Dealer - Dealer's Asking Price

121

(C) (W. Baldwin)

1860s-1880s ring, gold, amethyst and pearl, head 3/4" x 1-1/8".
Price: $825

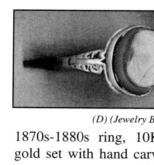

(D) (Jewelry Box Antiques)

1870s-1880s ring, 10K yellow gold set with hand carved stone cameo.
Price: $295

(D) (Jewelry Box Antiques)

1860s-1880s ring, 12K yellow gold set with quartz.
Price: $325

(C) (Jeanenne Bell)

1860s ring, 14K yellow gold centered with oval amethyst with incised carving of a flower inset with gold and rose-cut diamonds, the mounting is embellished with taille d' epergne enameling.
Price: $1,500

(D) (Jewelry Box Antiques)

1860s-1880s ring, 18K yellow gold hollow band with table worked hair inside, engraved with "A.B." inside.
Price: $375

(D) (Jewelry Box Antiques)

1860s-1880s ring, 14K yellow gold initial "A".
Price: $395

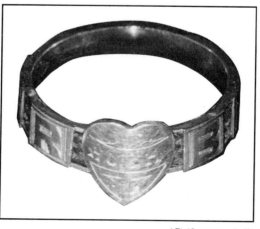

(C) (Jeanenne Bell)

1870s-1880s ring, 9K gold with hair band, engraved "Hugh," blocks spell "Brother," memorial piece, 3/8" wide.
Price: $395

(D) (Jewelry Box Antiques)

1880s ring, 14K yellow gold set with hand carved stone cameo.
Price: $249

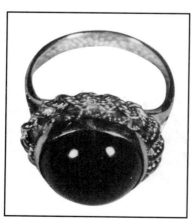

(C) (W. Baldwin)

1860s-1880s ring, gold, cabochon garnet, head 5/8".
Price: $445

Watches & Watch Accessories

(D) (Jewelry Box Antiques)

1860s-1870s watch, sterling silver open face English key, wind key set. **Price: $450**

(D) (Jewelry Box Antiques)

1870s-1880 watch, sterling case, A.W. Watch Co., Waltham, Mass, key wind, key set, movement mkd, "A.W. Watch Co." **Price: $395**

(D) (Jewelry Box Antiques)

1871 watch, yellow gold filled, 6 size hunting case, American Waltham. **Price: $425**

(D) (Jewelry Box Antiques)

1880s watch, gold filled hunting case with movement by Tavannes Watch Co., size 16. **Price: $400**

(D) (Jewelry Box Antiques)

1880s watch, sterling silver, enameled flowers on face, key wind, key set, 1-1/2" dia.
Price: $395

(C) (Anne Noblitt)

1879 watch, 14K gold hunting case, engraved "Josei from John," Dec. 25, 1879, mint condition.
Price: $1,200

(A) (Photo courtesy of Sotheby's New York)

1880s chatelaine watch, gold with enameled scenes depicting themes of love and music in pearl set bezels, gilt oval cylinder movement, 5" l.
Price: $3,300

(D) (Jewelry Box Antiques)

1880s watch, sterling case, key wind-key set movement, beautifully engraved case.
Price: $395

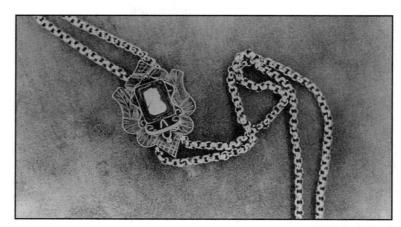

(C) (Jackie Palmer)

1860s slide chain, 8K yellow gold with hand-carved stone cameo in yellow gold filled setting.
Price: $995

124

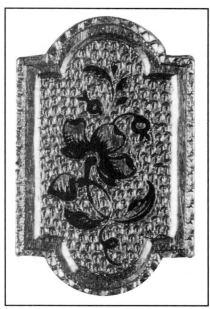

1860s-1870s slide, gold with enameling, 9/16" x 7/8".
Price: $395

1880s-1890s cigar cutter fob, sterling, 1/2" x 1-3/8".
Price: $195

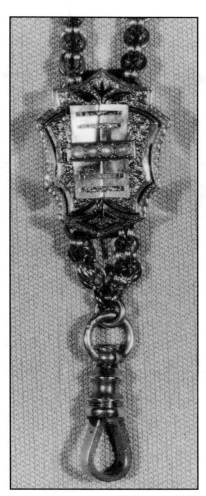

1860s-1870s slide chain, 18K heavy chain 64" l; slide with enameling and pearls, 3/4" x 1".
Price: $2,600

1860s slide and chain, gold top slide with enameling and stone cameo; chain is new gold filled, 52" l.
Price: $525

1860s-1880s Victorian chain, silver over brass, some gold ornamentation. Note anchor, 5" l.
Price: $125

1860s-1870s watch chain, gold over brass with some gold; drop has Ambro type 1/4" wide, drop 1" dia. **Price: $245**

1860s-1880s watch chain, gilt brass fittings, hairwork in 3 patterns, 3/8" x 15" l. **Price: $110**

1860s-1880s watch chain, gilt brass fittings, light brown hairwork, masonic fob, hand engraved and enameled 13" l.
Price: $175

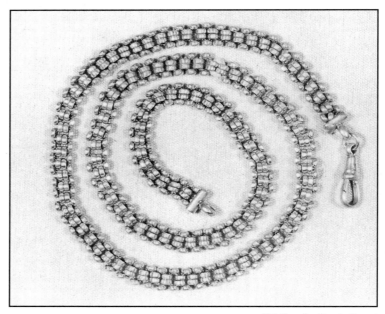

1870s-1890s watch chain, gold filled, makes nice neck chain for today, 1/4" x 10-1/2". **Price: $145**

1870s-1890s watch chain, silver with tassel, 8-1/2" l.

Price: $150

1880s-1890s watch chain, gold over brass fittings, hairwork chain with locket fob, probably American locket, 7/8" x 1-1/8"; chain 10-1/2".   **Price: $195**

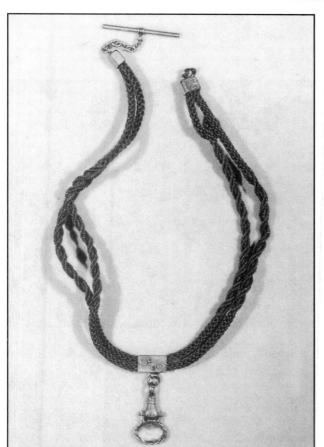

Watch chain, gold over brass fittings, double length of hairwork in 3 patterns. Note fob with hand holding amethyst, 3/8"x 18".   **Price: $225**

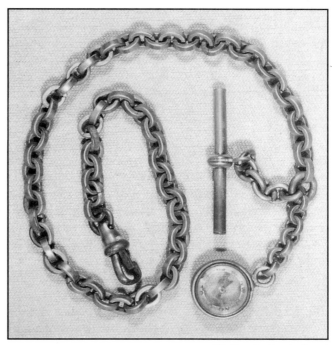

Watch chain and fob, silver over brass with compass fob, 12-1/2" l, compass 1/2" dia.   **Price: $145**

(D) (Jewelry Box Antiques)

1880s-1890s watch pin, gold filled, 1-7/8" x 1-1/2".
Price: $145

(D) (Jewelry Box Antiques)

1880s-1900s watch pin, gold filled. 7/8" x 1". **Price: $125**

(A) (Butterfield and Butterfield, 03/10/98)

Top Left: Circa 1910 Swiss gold hunting cased pocket watch. Case: 14K yellow gold, circular, hinged 4 bodied; dial: white enamel, black Roman numerals, sunk auxiliary seconds dial, gold "Spade" hands; movement: gilt, 16 jewels, lever escapement, cut bimetallic screwed balance wheel, Breguet balance spring. Signed J. Calame Robert on case and dial. Diameter 52mm, accompanied by a 14K yellow gold chain.
Price: $1,610

(A) (Butterfield and Butterfield, 03/10/98)

Bottom: Circa 1900 Mathey Swiss gold chronograph minute repeating hunting cased pocket watch. Case: 14K yellow gold, circular, hinged 4 bodied; dial: white enamel, black Roman numerals, sunk auxiliary sec-

onds dial, chronograph auxiliary dials for seconds, outer tachometer, yellow "Spade" hands, movement: nickeled, highly jeweled, lever escapement, cut bi-metallic screwed balance wheel, Breguet balance spring. Signed E. Mathey on case and dial, diameter 55mm. **Price: $4,029**

(A) (Butterfield and Butterfield, 03/10/98)

Top Right: Circa 1860 Glasgow silver pocket watch. Case: silver, circular, hinged 3 bodied, dial: engine turned silver with applied yellow gold, applied pink Roman numerals, auxiliary seconds dial, blued steel "Spade" hands, movement: key wind, key set, fusee, gilt, jeweled, cut bimetallic screwed balance wheel, flat balance spring, signed R. Stewart Glasgow on movement, diameter 50mm. **Price: $632**

(C) (Jeanenne Bell)

1850s-1880s fob, gold filled fittings, open weave hairwork, finished on one side only, 5/8" x 7/8".
Price: $150

(D) (June O'Donnel)

1880s fob, yellow gold filled with cornelian stone intaglio cameo on black ribbon, 5" x 1-1/2". **Price: $110**

Code in Front of Name

(A) Auction House - Auction Price
(C) Collector - Collector Asking Price
(D) Dealer - Dealer's Asking Price

(D) (Jewelry Box Antiques)

1886 pocket watch, 18K yellow gold boxed hinged case 6S, lever set. **Price: $795**

Sets

1870s-1880s brooch and earrings, gold filled mtg., crepe stone pin, 1-3/4" x 1/4"; earrings 3/8" x 3/4".
Price: $895

Demi parure pendant & earrings, circa 1870s, pierced with a six-pointed star within a diamond crescent motif, (2 stones missing) £3,080. **Price: $5,480**

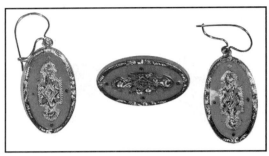

1860s-1880s brooch and earrings, gold filled with "Robin's Egg Blue" enameling, earrings were originally colored buttons and have been converted with 14K wire, all pins are 1" x 5/8". **Price: $375**

1850s-1870s brooch and earrings, 14K hairwork pin 1-3/4" x 5/8"; earrings 5/8" dia.
Price: $800

Assembled suite of antique black jewelry comprising a carved onyx disk within an arched scroll frame of black enamel, suspending three black onyx drops, mounted in yellow gold, and a pair of ear pendants, each designed as an arched black enameled yellow gold plaque, suspending an onyx drop (with notarized statement and bill of sale) (2). Formerly the property of Mrs. Abraham Lincoln. **Price: $18,400**

Pietra-dura suite, brooch and earrings have floral mosaic center. **Price: $1,500**

Victorian micro-mosaic neck-lace and earrings, floral motif on a hollow rope chain, 17" l.
Price: $3,000

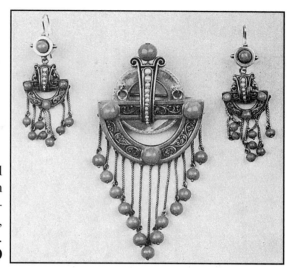

(A) (Photo courtesy of Skinner, Inc., Boston, Mass 12-4-90)

Victorian gold and coral suite, suite composed of pin and earrings set in 14K yellow gold with half pearls, highlighted by black enamel.
Price: $1,200

(A) (Photo courtesy of Skinner, Inc. Boston, Mass 9-25-90)

(A) (Photo courtesy of Sotheby Park Bernet & Co., London 12-15-83)

Demi-parure pendant and ear-rings, circa last quarter of the 19th century, gold with enam-eling, seed pearls and rose dia-monds (slightly imperfect), £1,210.
Price: $2,155

(D) (Jewelry Box Antiques)

1860s pendant and earrings, 14K yellow gold set with lava cameo, pendant 2-1/2" x 1-5/8"; earrings 1-1/4"x 1".
Price: $2,875

(D) (Jewelry Box Antiques)

1880s brooch and earrings, 14K yellow gold with coral flower pin, 2-1/4" x 1-3/4"; earrings 1-1/2" l. **Price: $575**

(A) (Photo courtesy of Skinner, Inc., Boston, Mass 12-4-90)

Victorian bar pin and earrings, set with turquoise and half pearls, approx. 15 ct.
Price: $500

Miscellaneous

(D) (Jewelry Box Antiques)

1870s-1890s chatelaine, gold filled with note pad, 7-1/2" long, pin 2-1/2" x 4". **Price: $895**

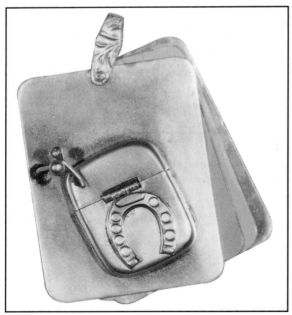

(D) (Jewelry Box Antiques)

1885-1910s notecase, silver plated, front and back slide apart to reveal horn pages, note coin holder on top with horseshoe motif, 2" x 2-1/2". **Price: $275**

1870s-1880s pencil, gold filled with black enameling, 2-1/2" l. **Price: $95**

(D) (Jewelry Box Antiques)

1871 pencil, pat. date, gold filled mother-of-pearl, 1/4" dia., 2-1/2" l. **Price: $95**

(D) (Lucille and Sam Mundorff)

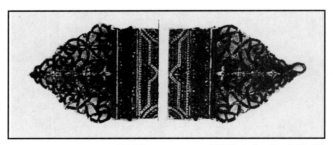

(A) (Photo courtesy of Phillips, London 6-21-83)

Clips, gold (converted from a buckle), black and white enameling, signed "C.G." on both sections, Carlo Giuliano, £443. **Price: $785**

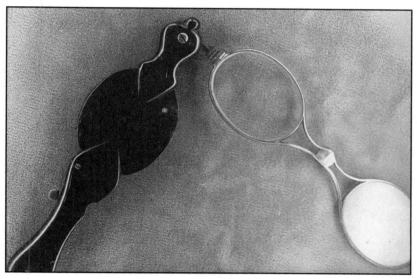

(D) (Jewelry Box Antiques)

1880s lorgnette, tortoise shell (open), 4-3/4" l.   **Price: $485**

(C) (W. Baldwin)

1880s-1890s lorgnette and chain, French hallmark sterling, chain length 61", closed 7/8" x 2-7/8".

Price: $825

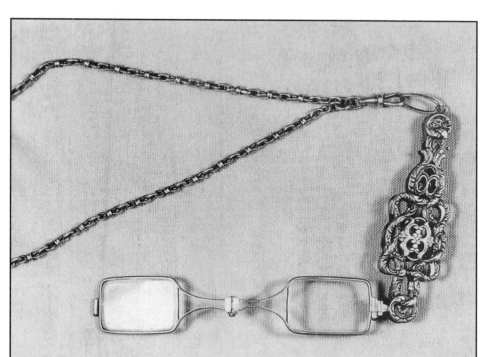

Lorgnette opened.

(C) (Jeanenne Bell)

1860s-1870s jet cameo, surrounded by rose-cut jet, 1-1/4" x 1-1/2".
Price: $450

(D) (Camille Grace)

1880s vinaigrette and slide chain, gold filled, 3/4" x 1", chain 27" l.
Price: $395

(D) (Jewelry Box Antiques)

1860s-1870s slide, gold filled with taille d' epergne enameling, 5/8" x 1-1/4".
Price: $395

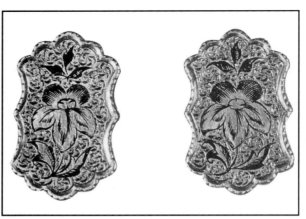

(C) (W. Baldwin)

1860s-1880s collar buttons, gold with black enameling, 5/8" x 1".
Price: $485

Chapter Three: 1890-1917

The American & English Historical Period

In the United States, the years from 1890 to 1919 were filled with extremes and contradictions. The nineties were both gay and naughty. The country was taking on airs of worldliness, but it still had the innocence of youth. America had become the leading industrial nation in the world and its wealth was incomparable. In New York, Society's "400" could boast of more diamonds than most of Europe's royalty. At the same time, others were living in slum tenements. A single room housed as many as nine people.

In April of 1898, Congress declared war on Spain. It was described by some as, "a great little war." Many people began to feel it was the country's Christian duty to be imperialistic. It was also a time of social unrest. Union and management waged bloody battles. Cox's army marched to Washington and women demonstrated for the right to vote.

More than ever, women were involved in the world of business. By 1910, there were 386,765 women employed in offices, an increase of 385,835 since 1870. They were also playing the stock market. The first brokerage firm owned by a woman opened on Wall Street in 1869 and was an immediate success. Women could become rich by investing in the market, but they still could not vote.

In addition to making money, women were also making headlines. Nellie Bly, a reporter for the New York World, captured the country's attention as she set out to beat Jules Verne's fictional record of traveling around the world in eighty days. All Americans followed her travels via her newspaper accounts. She traveled 24,899 miles in seventy-three days, thus beating the record. This stunt, staged by Joseph Pulitzer to increase newspaper sales, also succeeded in proving the world was growing smaller, and women's abilities were getting larger.

The bicycle was the plaything of the nineties. Men, women, and children of all ages spent every possible minute riding the many varieties available. The demand was so great that companies in totally unrelated businesses began to manufacture bicycles. The Chester Frost & Company, wholesale jewelry manufacturers, included bicycles in their 1896 catalogue, "The bicycle is no longer simply a luxury or a toy for children and idle men but an article of everyday necessity for thousands." The "biggest seller" weighed twenty-five pounds and sold for $100. Other bicycles were priced from $94 to $120.

Godey's estimated in 1896 that there were 10,000,000 bicycles in the world, and cyclists traveled more than 100,000,000 miles. In Paris, there was a riding school on the Champs Elysees. For four dollars one could attend until "thoroughly proficient." According to *Godey's*, there was even a bicycle ambulance, "The bicycle ambulance is a humanitarian invention for removing sick people; it runs more easily and makes less noise than the regulation vehicle. It has met with instantaneous success in Chicago."

The most revolutionary form of transportation in this time period was the automobile. It began as a novelty for the rich and succeeded in changing the entire country. In 1903, the automobile made its first "cross country" trip. The journey took fifty-two days, but it proved to the world that it could be done. By 1917, a car could be bought for as little as $345 and there were an estimated 4,700,500 on the roads of America. Car salesmen bragged that their product "would outlast a horse by many years, and none had ever died of hoof and mouth disease."[7]

In 1903, the Wright Brothers helped loosen the strings that had bound man to the ground. This first heavier-than-air-flight caused a surge of hope in the hearts of men who had always wanted to ascend into the heavens. Little did they realize that in less than fifteen years this marvelous new machine would be used in a World War. Man was indeed reaching new heights, but hate and greed were still alive and well.

Entertainment was a booming business during these years. In 1893, Thomas Edison invented the Kintoscope. It required a nickel for operation, and by 1905, hundreds of these "nickelodeons" were in use. Records were selling at a brisk pace. The nation was singing, and sheet music sales soared. With the quickening pace of life, it was only natural for music and dance to become more lively. Dancing became very fashionable, and the dance team of Vernon and Irene Castles introduced new steps to the American public.

In 1900, there were over 2,000 theaters in the country and vaudeville acts were on tour. America was entertained by everything from comedy routines to dog acts. There were also top attractions such as Ethel Barrymore, Enrico Caruso, and Harry Houdini. George M. Cohen's talent filled theaters with music and the hearts of people with song.

By 1910, there were ten thousand movie houses in the country. People were entranced by "the bigger than life" stars on the screen. They became emotionally involved with these film stars, and Mary Pickford became "America's Sweetheart."

When the rumblings in Europe erupted into war in 1914, most Americans did not want to get involved. In fact, many believed that the country would not become a part of the struggle. But on April 6, 1917 a Declaration of War was passed by Congress and signed by President Wilson—willing or not, America was in it.

In England, on January 22, 1901 at 6:30 P.M., Queen Victoria died and left a stunned Great Britain behind. Most people could not remember a time in which she had not been their Queen. Even though they had already turned away from Victorian standards, her physical loss was still incomprehensible.

As late as December 1896, *Godey's Magazine* noted: "Queen Victoria has just had her picture taken; it is that of a hale and hearty old lady in the perennial white cap; in spite of rumors as to her abdication, the Queen holds the reins of estate with a firm grip, and seems in no haste to hand them over to the still jolly and giddy Prince of Wales."

This attitude toward Edward was very prevalent. Throughout his childhood he had shown little ability for his lessons. His parents regarded him as a slow and incapable student. Conscious of the position that would someday be his, they pushed him in his studies and structured his every waking hour.

When he came of age, it was little wonder that he rebelled. He filled his life with things he wanted and sought pleasure at every opportunity. This lifestyle caused Victoria much distress and displeasure.

She was more than embarrassed when he was required to appear in court as part of a divorce proceeding.

In 1863, Edward married Princess Alexandra, the King of Denmark's lovely daughter. Victoria hoped that marriage might settle him down, but it did not. Edward continued his womanizing, and Alexandra learned to live with it.

When Edward finally became King at age fifty nine (59), he surprised everyone with his abilities. He spoke several languages fluently and was interested in International Affairs. On his visits to India, Ireland, and Russia he displayed an innate ability to grasp existing situations. Still it was hard to overcome the image which had been his label since childhood.

King Edward loved wealth and used money as the standard by which he judged people. The nouveau rich were quickly accepted into British society much to the dismay of the gentility. His short reign was filled with the pursuit of pleasure. Some people went to the extreme in this pursuit. It is indicative of this time period that the phrase "if you can't be good-be careful," from the 1912 production of "The Girl in the Taxi" became popular.

The rich middle class was satisfied and complacent while a feeling of unrest and dissatisfaction was prevalent among the poor and working people. Britain had its share of labor disputes and women suffragettes, but for the most part the upper class lived a self-centered existence. They felt Britain's place in the world was established and invincible.

In 1910, Edward's short reign ended. It was also the end of an era of supremacy for Great Britain. Never again would she be the great world power and ruler of the seas. By 1914, she was drawn into the war—the world and Britain would never be the same.

The 1893 Columbian Exposition

Throughout the nineteenth century, expositions and exhibitions played a unique role in the development of art and industry. In 1893, Chicago was the host city for the World's Columbia Exposition. The event was planned to celebrate the 400th Anniversary of the Discovery of America. Countries from all over the world were represented. The visitor was given a mini-tour of the world past and present. The architecture of the "Magic City" had an old world look. A source of "wonderment and admiration", it was described as a "composite of the most exquisite architecture of the Moors and the symmetrical and utilitarian construction of the present."[8] This sentiment was shared by many and resulted in scores of public buildings being built in this style in the succeeding years.

With a 50-cent admission ticket, the visitor could tour the buildings, view the exhibitions, and marvel at the canals complete with gondolas from Venice. The Midway was an exciting place where everyday people could mingle with visitors from all over the world. Belly dancers from Egypt, Dahoney Cannibals from Africa, East India jugglers, and natives from Java were just a few of the "people attractions." The Egyptian dancers received an unusual amount of attention. The writer of the Magic City described the dance as, "a suggestively lascivious contorting of the abdominal muscles, which is extremely ungraceful and almost shockingly disgusting."

The real star of the show was the new and exciting "electricity." "A more wonderful, magical sight was never seen than that revealed by the marvelous displays of electrical apparatus, machinery and devices made in the Electric Building."[9] The *Columbian Exposition Album* included this description:

> The interior of the Electricity Building, either by day or night, but especially at the latter time was a place to conjure by. Crackling sparks - lightning in the miniature - flew from buzzing dynamos. Luminous balls of ever-changing colors chased one another along cornices, up pillars, and round corners; mysterious automatic wands traced iridescent words and erased them again with a magic touch; and the voices of far-off singers were heard as if near by, echoed from the Atlantic Coast along conducting wires. It was a wonderland, the enchanted throne room of Electra.

This great new power was also bringing new wonders for everyday use. The *Popular Science Monthly* was very enthusiastic about these new possibilities:

> The greatest novelty in cooking appliances at the fair is unquestionably the apparatus for cooking by electricity. - The electric current is conducted into plates of enamel, where it meets with resistance and is converted into heat. These plates were attached to specially constructed ovens, boilers, griddles, flatirons, etc. An ordinary stew pan, coffee or tea pot, or steam cooker may be heated on the 'disk heater'. An outfit of articles necessary for a private house cost $60 or $77.50 if a heater for a kitchen boiler is included.

In less than twenty years, the electric range was a popular household appliance. The marvelous power of electricity was benefiting the average working man.

Although the Centennial Exposition included a Women's Building, the Columbian Exposition had "the first full, complete representation ever accorded to women."[10] Miss Sophia Hayden of Boston designed the building and supervised its construction. Statuary ornaments were by Miss Alice Rideout of California. The interior decorations and art works were also the work of women. The library was filled with books written by the fairer sex. A model nursery provided a play room and attendants to care for children. Thousands of women made use of this "infant checkroom" while they visited the sights of the fair.

A good overall view of the grounds could be seen from the Intramural Railway. Its elevated tracks followed the boundary lines of the Fairgrounds. Of course it was operated by electricity. Another means of transportation was the moving sidewalk. "The charge was only five cents, and this permitted the patron to ride thereon as long as he desired, but notwithstanding the cheapness and comfort, the enterprise was not very liberally patronized."[11] That was probably because the moving sidewalk went only 2,500 feet down a long pier and back. Who wanted to look at a lake when there were so many more interesting sights to see?

Visitors to the fair were exposed to brilliant displays of jewelry, and American jewelers were well represented. Tiffany and Gorham even had their own pavilions. There were displays by twenty-nine jewelry manufacturers from New England. They were joined by other companies from all over the world who were showing their finest pieces. Tray after tray of rings, chains, bracelets, earrings, and watches provided a spectacle of delight. The Venetian Glass Works had their own building. Thirty Venetian artists could be seen at work making mosaics, etchings, and blown glass items. The jewelry was not only an attractive addition to the wardrobe, but it also provided a nice souvenir of the fair.

Another interesting attraction was the World's Congress of Beauties. This building had forty ladies from forty nations on display. The men came to gaze upon the beautiful women. The ladies came to see the marvelous costumes made by the famous Worth.

One of the most visited attractions of the fair was the Byzantine Chapel designed by L. C. Tiffany. It provided a beautiful setting in which to highlight his talents for working with stain glass, mosaics, and metal. The public was curious to see his designs, which were considered very new.

The exposition was a huge success—more than twenty-seven million people paid the price of admission to see the wondrous sights. It was a memorable experience that not only affected the architecture of the country, but also announced to the world that the United States had, "come of age."

Fashions in Clothing & Jewelry

The "fin de siecle" (end of the century) mood that enveloped the country created a desire for the dramatic in dress and jewelry. Designers endeavored to make the most of this by designing fashions that were exciting and risqué. Dress that accentuated the figure came into fashion. The princess-style dress was revived even though the dressmakers hated the time involved to fit it properly.

The figure was definitely gaining a new importance in fashion. As early as 1909, an under-endowed lady could improve her bust by wearing, "Nature's Rival Air Form-a corset waist, buoyant and light, that gives instantly the natural, well-rounded bust of beautiful women." The Sahlin Company offered the slender woman, "a perfect form and corset combined." It was advertised to be "the only garment that, without padding or interlining, produces the stylish high bust, straight waist and long hip." For the woman with a figure problem, another advertiser cited the new styles, "demand the Princess Chic Figure Shaper." They

claimed it would give, "better results in figure shaping than other new corsets, at a trifle of their cost."

The apparatus used for shapely figures did not always mix well with the new inventions. *Godey's* July 1896 issue reported this conflict:

> Electricity and corsets are apparently inimical. One of the professors in the Girls High School in Oakland, California discovered that the steels in the young women's corsets seriously affected the electrical apparatus and rendered experiments uncertain; health waists, which did not contain steels, made no disturbance. A galvanometer is placed at the door which immediately indicated the wearers of the obnoxious stays.

Accessories were becoming more daring, "Gloves with tiny purses in the palm for containing car fare are not strikingly new," commented *Godey's Magazine* in July, 1886. "The stocking, however, with a small pocket inserted on the outer portion of the knee is quite fin de siecle. This receptacle is supposed to hold the watch or such jewelry as one is not wearing. On silk stockings these pockets are elaborated with embroidery." This was quite daring since the skirt had to be lifted in order to deposit the treasure.

Also very much in fashion was the wicked look of the snake. The *Ladies' Home Journal* in October 1891 reported, "A wiggling gold serpent having overlapping scales of various hues, forms one of the latest queen chains. The tail terminates the swivel for the watch, while the head holds suspended in its wicked looking jaws a struggling bird of pearls and rubies."

Even with the sinister element, clothing and accessories had a light, delicate look. Bodices were soft and designers wasted no time in creating a profusion of lace pins. The *Ladies' Home Journal* described several in a 1891 article, "Novelties in Jewelry":

> Some enterprising jeweler has invented a lace pin that, owing to its uniqueness and ingenuity, will fill the hearts of the novelty-seeking class with ecstasy. It represents an enamel rose bud at the end of a twig on which a single green leaf is suspended. When this leaf is compressed, the petals of the rose fall open and disclose a photograph circled with rubies, diamonds, and sapphires.
>
> An oddity that cannot fail to inspire comment, is a lace pin representing a vulture about to seize a fluttering bird from its nest. The vulture is of rich gold with an oblong opal inserted in its back, while its victim is of diamonds and emeralds.
>
> Two variegated love birds circled by a laurel wreath in which small diamonds nestle, constitutes a lace pin that will be seen this autumn.

Hats were an intricate part of any wardrobe. They were designed in a variety of styles. Russian turbans and English box turbans, "with crowns matching the suits and bordered with fur or feather ranching" were popular. The October 1896

Midsummer Calling Gowns, August, 1902.

issue of *Godey's* stated, "Oceans of plumes will be greatly worn. Creme felt hats with trimmings of the same color are stylish for evening wear. Dainty capotes of bright-hued velvet studded with gems or embroidered in gold are the proper thing for the theater."

Royalty still exerted an influence on fashion. As late as 1891, Queen Victoria's approval affected a fashion's acceptance. The *Ladies' Home Journal* confirmed this in its fashion suggestions for October, "Long sleeves will continue in fashion during the winter, and the women who like delicate lace ruffles falling down over their hands and making them look so small, may indulge in this fancy, and not only have the knowledge that they are in good taste, but also that it is a fashion approved by the Queen of England."

Because Alexandra was attractive, she influenced fashion even before she became Queen. High necklines and collars complemented her long, graceful neck. Realizing this, she wore them frequently. This started a fashion that prompted a 1896 *Godey's Magazine* to note, "High neck dressing is in the rage just now. A neck band of velvet or ribbon about two and a half inches being the regulation depth. In order to increase the height, a pleating of silk or ribbon, growing narrower in front and extremely high and flaring at the back, is sewn on the inside of the band."

For evening, Alexandra favored choker type necklaces or "dog collars." Soon women all over England, Europe, and America were wearing them. Pearls were another of her favorites. This made them even more desirable to the general public.

Chatelaines had gone out of style in the 1860s, but Alexandra revived the fashion by wearing one. In 1887, the *Young Ladies' Journal* felt it necessary to explain to the younger generation what a chatelaine was, "The chatelaine consists of an ornamental hook to fasten to the waistband, from which suspends five chains, each upholding some article necessary to the worktable for instance, a thimble-holder, a pair of scissors made so as to fasten in their points when not wanted, a pincushion and a yard measure. In some models the latter are exchanged for a silver pencil-case, and a scent-bottle, or a tiny notebook, while some ladies prefer a silver whistle or a circle for suspending a bunch of keys." By 1891, chatelaines were beginning to show signs of the Art Nouveau influence. The October issue of the *Ladies' Home Journal* described one, "For a chatelaine holder, a silver albatross with outstretched wings, from the feathers of which many fancy chains depend, will undoubtedly meet with approval among those of artistic taste."

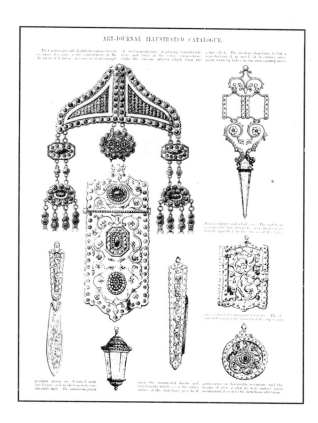

King Edward was an avid sportsman. His horses won the English Derby on three occasions, and this was a constant source of pride. His passion for racing caused the horseshoe to become a decorative motif. Cuff links, fobs, pins, and brooches were just a few of the items that were either made in this shape or carried its motif.

Even with all these influences the American woman felt that Royalty was losing its glamour. In 1902, the Delinator complained, "Queen Alexandra follows fashion at a distance and seeks rather the appropriate and the beautiful rather than the gorgeous."

Stars of the theater also played an increasingly important role in the evolution of fashion. An article in the *Young Ladies' Journal* explained how new styles came into existence:

The theater is where new models are introduced. When a play is being rehearsed, the principal actress has long consultations as to the dress and coiffure she is to wear with her modiste and couturier. Together they invent models suited to the role and person of the actress, and generally get up something very striking and infinitely becoming. Ladies who see an actress look extremely pretty with a certain bonnet on stage, of course wish to have a similar coiffure. They run to the modiste who is the happy inventor of the new model and ask for a similar one, and thus it is that bonnet gets to be the great vogue of the season. Such is the history of the Jane Hading copote, in which the charming actress obtained such an immense success in "La Contesse Sarah"; and also the eccentric hat known by Francillion, the fame of which dates from Alexander Dumas' popular play at La Comedie Francaise.

The increase in women's activities led to changes in the wardrobe. Bicycling was a favorite pastime, and clothing materials were chosen with this fact in mind. In 1896, *Godey's* stated, "For Cycling, the stitched alphines (a hat) of English cloth or of felt are greatly used; they stand any amount of wear and tear and are very comfortable. Young girls are wearing cycling costumes of white pique or mohair. The former possesses the advantage of laundering easily, the latter are only suitable for certain occasions, such as a tea, or for wear at fashionable summer resorts."

McCall's Magazine, June, 1909.

Magazines were filled with articles on cycling. Everything from the proper way of mounting a cycle to their care and maintenance was discussed. Some people even tried to improve on it. These new ideas were not always appreciated as a note in the 1896 *Godey's* illustrated, "A woman has applied for a patent curtain screen for women bicyclists who desire to conceal their identity from public gazes. Verily the way of feminine cyclist is hard enough without interposing further difficulties. Fancy a woman with such an awkward arrangement flapping about her having the courage to wheel at all."

With the hands busily engaged in keeping the cycle on the road, coin purses were attached to a chain and worn around the neck. Watches and lorgnettes were also worn in this manner. It is interesting to note that chains were rather long, so long that when sitting, the attached articles usually rested in the lap.

The whistle bracelet was another popular bicycling accessory. It was a "protective ornament" for women who took long rides by themselves. The shrill whistle could be heard for a distance of two miles. It was used to summon help in case of an emergency.

Golf became a popular sport among women in the 1890s. *Godey's Magazine* was quite adamant about the proper costume for this sport:

> The fancy suits sold in the shops are quite unsuitable for resisting the wear and tear which the inveterate golfer must inevitably encounter. She must not be afraid of a little rain or modicum of mud and should wear thick laced boots either black or tan, with broad low heels, or shoes with leather or cloth legging reaching to her knees. A suit of stout Scotch tweed or English homespun in small checks or mixed colorings is the best choice; it is made with a rather short and well-fitted skirt, a Norfolk or Eaton jacket, or an open fronted coat; a stiff shirt or a shirt waist is worn beneath, and an alpine or tam of the same material as the gloves, covers the head. A covent coat or a silk-lined golf cape is necessary to put on after finishing the game, as one is always heated.

One wonders how they could have played at all.

By 1910, there were 386,765 women working in offices. As this number increased, it became apparent that working women had a unique set of clothing problems. In June of 1909 *McCalls' Magazine* published an article by Miss Pearl Merwin titled "Practical Dress for the Business Woman." She recognized that women who work really did not have time to shop for clothes. She sympathized with the many problems, but took a firm stand on the importance of proper business attire:

> Clothes for business wear should be simple and modest, almost to the point of severity. Therefore, the tailored gown should be the business woman's standby.

The question of trimmings, in the way of laces, ribbons or handwork of any kind is almost eliminated. Suits of a mannish type, with straight skirts of walking length, semi-fitting with notched collars, lapels and pockets are the safeguards for business women. The perfectly plain, tailored shirt waist is the proper thing in the way of a third garment, and should be worn with a line collar and a bow of lace, or of the beautiful and fancy designs now so much in vogue.

Miss Merwin also gave pointers on the proper head gear, shoes, and gloves. On the subject of jewelry she was very firm:

Much jewelry is in bad taste for office and business wear. One, two or three pieces inconspicuously worn are about enough; but when it comes to having the fingers loaded and numbers of showy 'beauty pins' and beads and cheap brooches and loud and fancy hair combs, etc., it denotes not only poor taste and judgment, but rather a weak character as well.

The business women or isolated farm wives could keep abreast of the latest fashions by looking through mail order catalogues. The Montgomery Ward Company and Sears Roebuck Company had catalogues that could fulfill any woman's dreams. In 1909, Macy's published a 450 page *Spring and Summer Catalogue* that was mailed to thousands of homes. Everything from suits to bathtubs were ordered through the mail.

In 1913, Carmen Lowery, the author's grandmother, age fourteen (14), ordered a ring from a mail order catalogue. Although it cost only 32¢, she can still remember the thrill of wearing it to town. Samuel Noblitt, the author's grandfather, remembered that, "a pretty little ring could be ordered from the Gay Lyn Company for only 20¢." He was known to have ordered several before his courting days were over.

Women who did not work outside the home were bombarded by advertisements to sell products to their friends and neighbors. Most of these companies offered jewelry as an incentive. A choice of a "heavily plated chain bracelet with lock and key (similar to the one pictured on page 151), or a solid gold shell belcher birthday ring" was given for selling twelve, 12¢ packages of "Imperishable Perfume." Another perfume company offered "a gold shell ring and a silver chain bracelet with lock and key warranted for five years" for selling ten packs of "Rosebud Perfume" at 10¢ each. If a lady wanted a "beautifully engraved gold filled watch," she had only to sell 100 gold filled "ladies beauty pins" at 5¢

each. *McCall's Magazine* encouraged women to "raise clubs" by selling subscriptions. Each subscription was given a premium. Watches, opera glasses, and rings were given according to the number sold. For example, a Waltham gold filled hunting case watch was free with 48 subscriptions, but even one subscription entitled the seller to a gold filled ring set with a genuine opal. These offers enabled many women to wear jewelry who did not have the money to buy it.

In June 1909, *McCalls' Magazine* had an article entitled "Jewelry for the Prospective Bride." This article is especially important because it introduced earrings with screw backs:

Earrings are very fashionable once more, and the sort most used are the long drop varieties, although the pear hoop earrings shown in one of our illustrations are also new and very becoming. All the latest varieties of earrings are made with a little screw to fasten on each side of the lobe of the ear, so that it is not necessary to have the ears pierced. Very beautiful are the amethyst drop earrings made in this style and also earrings of black and white pearls. Bracelets this year are worn over the transparent lace sleeves as well as the bare arm.

The article pictures two bracelets that were reported to be "revivals from the days of our grandmothers."

(see previous chapter)
Frank Leslie's Illustrated News, Feb. 23, 1878.

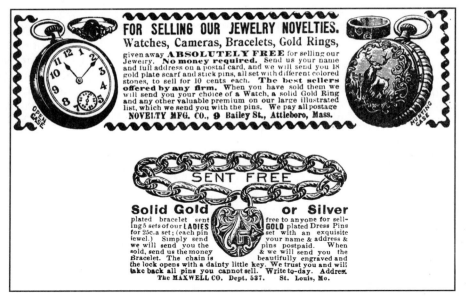
McCall's, March, 1900.

To a trained eye these would never be confused with any other period than the early 1900s. One was a "wide bracelet with knobs of turquoise matrix set in a filigree gold setting," and the other was, "a lovely cameo design." A most charming amethyst and baroque pearl pendant necklace was pictured, and it was noted that "amethyst jewelry of all sorts is extremely fashionable at present."

Opals had lost their unearned reputation for being unlucky. They were being used in the newest designs. "During the last few years a reaction has taken place and American women are accepting the magic gem," an article in the August 1886 edition of *Godey's Magazine* commented. "Many superb designs are seen at the jewelers, one of the latest being a golden eagle with outstretched wings, thickly studded with opals, the edges being encrusted with tiny scintillant diamonds. The shimmering changeful fire of the opal renders it suitable for articles of jewelry to be worn in the evenings, the light glinting upon the translucent hues of the lovely gem in a most fascinating manner. There are striking designs of butterflies, dragon flies and beetles, in opals associated with emeralds and diamonds. These stones admirably express the brilliant beauty of the insects."

New stones were being used. "Like canines, every stone has its day," noted the *Ladies' Home Journal* in 1891, "At present, the Alexandrite appears to be in the ascendancy. This jewel comes from Siberia, and is of a beautiful dark green transparent color, which under any artificial light changes to that of pigeon blood ruby. The Alexandrite is cut like a diamond and is being used by the leading jewelers for lace pins, bracelets and other ornaments."

It was not long before the automobile began to influence fashion. A dustcoat with a belted or buttoned waist was a necessity. As early as 1902, the Marvin Smith Company of Chicago, Illinois listed several "automobile styles ladies' rain coats," and "ladies and misses automobile Mackintoshes," in their catalogue. Scarves that covered the hat and tied under the chin were essential for women, and goggles were a "must."

The hobble skirt became popular between 1910 and 1915. It was a straight skirt that became narrow at the hem line. Walking was difficult, because only small steps were possible. Women felt very sleek and sophisticated in them, so they endured the inconvenience in order to be fashionable.

The sleek look was also becoming fashionable in jewelry. The effects of the Cubist art movement and the geometric machine designs were seen in the straight lines and rectangular shapes being used in jewelry motifs. Safety match holders like the one on page 239 were displayed in catalogues along with those embellished with curlicues and flowers of the late eighteen hundreds. A 1916 catalogue lists such innovative items as a sterling cigarette making case with separate parts for tobacco papers and matches ($12.50); a sterling cigarette case with an engine turned front bordered in blue enamel ($12.50); and a sterling combination pocket knife and screw pencil ($3.75).

The same catalogue included sterling silver articles for women. A vanity case (a compact with space for powder puff, coin holder, mirror, and cards) with an engine turned front and a plain back, was $16.50. A hand engraved one was only $10. This tends to prove that the engine turned design was more desirable.

Throughout this time period, brooches continued to have a very delicate, light look. They were frequently decorated with enameling and pearls. Bar pins and circle brooches were also very fashionable. The jewelry from this time has a charm all its own.

Art Nouveau

The Art Nouveau style was a rare, exotic flower that bloomed for a tantalizingly brief time in the garden of art and design. Seeds for this new style had been gathered from many times and places. The roots can be traced back to the mid-eighteen hundreds when the "naturalistic school" was producing designs based on nature. In his book "The Analysis of Ornament," Ralph Wornum wrote "one particular feature of the school is, that it often substitutes the ornament itself for the thing to be ornamented." This is exactly what the Art Nouveau designers did (i.e., the Metro Lamp Post in Paris).

More seeds were planted at the International Exhibition of 1862 in London. The Japanese exhibited their wares here for the first time and attracted much attention. After the exhibition the goods were sold. Many of the items were purchased by a store in which Arthur Lazenby Liberty was employed. Liberty was to play an important part in the style that would come to be known as Art Nouveau.

The 1876 Centennial Exposition in Philadelphia contributed to the style when it invited the Japanese to build a house on the grounds, to host a Japanese bazaar. This provided the American public an opportunity to view, at first hand, the ancient arts of the Orient. They were fascinated by the superb skill and craftsmanship that went into these works of art. The designs were so different that the Americans were intrigued.

William Morris further nourished the style with his Arts and Crafts movement. His emphasis on handcrafting and the importance of designers and craftsmen working together played an important part in the new movement.

But it took the social climate and mood of the late 1880s for the style to emerge. The fin de siecle (end of the century) had put the world on a psychological edge. There was an almost unreal feeling, perhaps from being suspended from the end of one century to the beginning of another. (A one foot in the boat and the other on the shore sort of thing.) This feeling was expressed by the impressionist artist of the day. If the mood of the country could have been painted, it would have definitely been pastel—soft and hazy.

At the same time, some people were more daring. Maybe it was because of all the nineteenth century and the promise of what the new century might bring. People were confident and ready for anything; the time was ripe for Art Nouveau.

The French took the best from the past—the naturalistic designs of the 1850s, the free flowing lines and enameling techniques from the Orient, the pride in craftsmanship of the Arts and Craft's

movement, the sensuousness of the fin de siecle, and combined them in their own inimitable way and viola—Art Nouveau!

Since Art Nouveau was a decorative period style, its influence was felt in all phases of design. Henri de Toulouse-Lautrec painted posters in this style. Antonio Gaudi (Spain) and Victor Horta (Belgium) designed buildings in the new style, furniture and accessory designers also used the new motifs.

Art Nouveau had an important influence on the jewelry designers of the period. It provided a form of expression for them which seemed to be unlimited. All the forces of nature could be captured in the free flowing asymmetrical lines.

One of the foremost Art Nouveau designers was Rene Jules Lalique (1860-1945). He was one of the few designers who was also a trained jeweler. In 1885, he acquired a fully equipped workshop. Business was good, and by 1900, he was able to move to a larger location. That same year his works were exhibited at the Exposition Universalle in Paris. It was a lucky year for him. All his work on display at the Exposition was bought by Colouste Gulbenkian, a millionaire from Germany. More attention was drawn to his work when Sarah Bernhardt became his patron. She commissioned him to make two pieces of jewelry for her, and his reputation was made! Since she was considered the greatest actress of the time, her clothing and jewelry were highly publicized. This kept his name in the limelight and assured his place in posterity.

Because this new style was art—an expression of the designer—materials were of much less importance than the skill involved in its design and execution. Consequently, jewelry was made using materials such as horn, ivory, tortoise shell, and carved glass. Lalique used the dramatic and exotic as motifs. Orchids, irises, snakes, dragonflies, and sensuous women's heads are some of the motifs he made popular. The stones he used reflect the mood of the work. They consisted of opals, moonstones, and a variety of semiprecious stones. His pieces were highlighted by beautiful enameling techniques.

In England, William Morris (1834-1896) had long been an exponent of craftsmanship. He studied at Oxford and was an artist and poet. In 1851, he visited the Crystal Palace Exhibition in London and was appalled by the machine-made goods that everyone else thought so marvelous. He felt that industry was ugly and that it dehumanized men by taking away their creativeness.

Fascinated by the Middle Ages, he wanted to return to the handmade methods of producing jewelry, furniture, and accessories. In 1861, he founded "Morris and Company." Here he made the famous Morris chair and sold many handmade items. He helped found the Arts and Craft's Exhibition Society in 1886, which provided a showcase for the work of its members. Morris believed that there should be no distinction between designer and the craftsman, and that the best art was achieved when artists worked in partnership. Morris died in 1896, but his ideas lived on in the minds of his fellow artists.

C. R. Ashbee (1836-1942) was a famous name in English Art Nouveau jewelry. Greatly influenced by the philosophy of William Morris, he did much to foster craftsmanship in his country. In 1887, he founded the School and Guild of Handicrafts.

Though most of his work was done in gold and silver, he kept the Art Nouveau tradition of using moonstones and blister pearls. Many fine examples of Ashbee's work can be seen at the Victoria and Albert Museum, including his famous Peacock necklace.

Liberty and Company in London, England had a most important influence on the Art Nouveau style. Before anyone had ever used the term "Art Nouveau," the style was being offered by this company. In fact, the Art Nouveau style was known as "stile Liberty" in Italy for quite some time. A. L. Liberty had always been intrigued by the designs of the orient. He had been employed by Farmer and Rogers when they purchased part of the Japanese exhibit from the International Exhibition of 1862. When he opened his own shop in 1876, it was devoted exclusively to goods from India, Japan, and other parts of the Orient. The aesthetics patronized his shop, and it became a dominant force on the fashion scene. During the Art Nouveau period, Liberty and Company had its own group of jewelry designers. Their work helped further the popularity of jewelry in this design.

In the United States, Louis Comfort Tiffany was the proponent of the Art Nouveau style. At an early age he decided to be an artist. He studied with George Inness, and in 1867, was allowed to enter a painting in the National Academy of Design Exhibition. Elated by this accomplishment, he decided to go to Paris to study. During his two years of study, and the years of travel that followed, his philosophy of art changed. He decided to expand his interests and in 1878, he formed his own company. Louis C. Tiffany and Company specialized in interior design and did both commercial and residential work. Their most prestigious commission was to redecorate parts of the White House.

In 1880, L.C. Tiffany joined his father's business as Director of Design. His job was to design jewelry, and he had a separate floor in which to display his creations. Because of his father's wealth, he never had to worry about the cost of his items. He would spend any amount of money to achieve the effect he desired. Although he wanted his work to be used and enjoyed by all people, the costs involved in manufacturing made this impossible. When he died in 1932, he had spent $11,881,000 of the $13,125,000 that had been left to him by his father.

Samuel Bing was the man responsible for the application of the name Art Nouveau to the style. He was a dealer in Japanese art and became interested in the new style of work. In 1895, he opened a shop "L' Art Nouveau" at 22 Rue de Provence in Paris. He gathered work from all the designers in the new style—jewelry by Lalique and glass by Tiffany—and offered them for sale. So successful was his business that its name became synonymous with the style.

Characteristic motifs of Art Nouveau designs are flowing lines, exotic flowers, asymmetry, plant shapes, sinister looking reptiles, and women with mystical faces and long flowing hair. Materials used were varied. Many of them had little intrinsic value. Horn, copper, tortoise shell, ivory, carved glass, and shells were some of the most popular. Near colorless stones such as opals and moonstones were popular. All types of pearls were used. Semiprecious stones were more favored by the designers than diamonds.

Art Nouveau jewelry is extremely popular at the present time. Because of this many pieces are being reproduced, be sure to buy from a reputable dealer who will guarantee the authenticity of the piece.

Enameling

It is not surprising that the Art Nouveau jewelry designers made use of ancient enameling techniques. The scope and range of enameling could produce an endless variety of effects. One enamel could be applied on top of another to create the varied, flowing colors so indicative of the period. Colors could be opaque or transparent. The possibilities were unlimited, and enamel's durability made it suitable for everyday use.

Enamel is a glass-like mixture of silica, quartz, borax, feldspar, and lead. Metallic oxides are added to produce the desired color. These materials are ground into a fine powder and applied to the article being embellished.

Firing at a temperature of about 1700 degrees Fahrenheit is required to melt the mixture and bond it to the article. Care must be taken since the melting point of the article should be higher than that of the enameling mixture. Each color is fired separately. The color with highest melting points is fired first. Those requiring progressively less heat are fired in succession. The methods of enameling are named according to the method used to prepare the article being decorated. The most popular of these are cloisonné, clampleve, basse-taille, and plique-a-jour.

For cloisonné (Kloy-zoe-NAY) (partition), a design is drawn on the article and traced with fine gold wire. This wire forms partitions into which the enamel mixture is poured. Since powdered enamel tends to shrink when fired, several firings are sometimes necessary for each color. After all colors are fired, the enameling is polished-off even with the top of the wire.

Champleve (Shomp-leh-VAY) (to cut out) is an enameling technique in which the designs are cut out from the background of the metal. The metal between these cut out areas becomes an intricate part of the design. The hollowed areas are filled with enamel and fired in succession of hardness. After firing is completed, polishing is required to finish the piece.

In Basse-taille (Bahs-TAH-ye) (shallow cut) the designs are cut and engraved in the metal. But instead of just filling these depressions, the entire piece is covered with a transparent enamel. Many beautiful designs can be achieved using this method because the color varies with the depth of the design.

Plique-a-jour (Pleek-ah-ZHOOR) is an enameling method that was used to full advantage by the Art Nouveau designers. It is an especially delicate method in that the enameling has no backing-only sides. To achieve this feat the enameling mixture is used in a molasses type form. Sometimes a thin metal or mica backing is used and removed after firing. Cellini used a layer of clay to back his pieces while firing. Whatever material is used, the results are quite lovely. The enameling has the effect of stained glass or gem stones. These translucent enamels are seen at fullest advantage when held to the light.

Taille e' epergne (TAH-ye de A-purn), an ancient form of enameling, was popular in the mid-nineteenth century. After a design was deeply engraved or cut into a metal, it was filled with powdered enamel. The piece was then fired and polished. Although any color could be used in taille d' epergne, the Victorians favored black or blue.

Niello (nye-EL-oh) is considered a form of enameling even though it is not a "true enamel." A mixture of sulphur, lead, copper, or silver is used instead of the powdered glass enamel. After the design is engraved into the metal, the niello mixture is applied. The piece is fired and then polished to remove the niello from all but the incised portion of the design. All niello is black; it is easy to distinguish from black enameling because it lacks sheen. Instead it has a metallic-like luster. Good examples of niello are found in the Siamese jewelry of the 1950s.

The metals used in enameling were as varied as the methods. For champleve and cloisonné, copper and bronze were often used. Gold and silver provided an excellent base for all enameling techniques. Although the metal used is of prime consideration when determining value, the execution of design and the clarity of colors are of the utmost importance. A piece well done in copper using several enameling techniques can sometimes be more valuable than one in gold using one color and technique.

Enameled jewelry is highly collectible. People who are aware of the time, effort, and talent that combine to create these tiny works of art appreciate and treasure them. Although little enameling is being done today in the United States, many lovely pins made in the early 1900s are still available at moderate prices. If you are interested in collecting enamels of this period, now is the time to buy.

Popular Stones & Materials

Amber

Amber beads were popular during the 1890-1917 period and continued to be through the 1920s. According to Marilyn Roos, an amber dealer, it was a different form from what we see today. The inclusions and air bubbles were considered unattractive so the amber was melted to remove them before forming the beads. Sometimes the beads even had a celluloid core.

Amber is a fossilized tree resin. Over fifty million years ago trees taller than the Redwoods of today grew along the shores of the Baltic Sea. The Glacier Age caused them to be swept into the sea. There they solidified under ice and pressure. Scientists believe that the trees probably had a fungus of some type because the resin was so loose it even surrounded dew drops. Amber often has insects, petals of flowers, seeds and bark locked inside. These add to the value of the gem.

One of the oldest gems known to man, amber has been revered through the ages. The Greeks called it "lectron," which is the root word for electricity. Ancient man wore it for protection against disease. As recently as the 1920s, doctors melted amber and mixed it with honey to make a remedy for throat ailments. People even believed that wearing an amber necklace would cure a goiter.

Although light yellow (honey colored) is the color most associated with the name, it can also be brown or red (cherry amber). Color varies according to the depth of water into which the tree fell. Amber can be translucent, opaque, or a mixture of both.

The "feel" of amber is very distinct. The best way to become acquainted with it is to actually handle a piece. It is so lightweight that long beautiful strands can be worn with ease.

Amber is not only a lovely accessory, but it can be a good investment. It can be worn with a feeling of safety no longer associated with diamonds. When buying amber, as with any fine gem, always deal with a reputable source. To insure the beautiful luster of amber take care to protect it from hairspray and perfume. A bath in warm water and gentle detergent will keep it sparkling clean.

Celluloid, glass, and plastic have all been used to imitate amber. Tests to determine the authenticity of a piece can be found in the "Is it Real?" section of this book.

Celluloid

A marvelous new material made it possible for people of modest means to have combs, bracelets, necklaces, and brooches that looked much more expensive than they actually were. Celluloid, the trade name given this material by its inventor John Wesley Hyatt in 1869, was widely used in the 1890-1917 period. Celluloid is an artificial plastic made from pyroxylin and camphor. Combs that looked like tortoise, bracelets and necklaces that could pass for ivory, and pins of every description were made from it.

In December 1896, *Godey's Magazine* included an article on gifts for Christmas. It recognized the affordability of celluloid items:

> Much less expensive are the neat celluloid goods, either silver mounted or adorned with a small miniature or cameo head; here again twenty-five cents to a dollar will purchase much that is attractive in the way of trinket sets, little fancy boxes, trays, pocket combs, brushes, and mirrors.

Because celluloid was highly flammable, its use in jewelry manufacturing was discontinued when safer plastics became available. Since celluloid jewelry was made for a limited time, it stands to reason that these pieces will become more collectible and increase in value. At the present time, however, good bargains can still be found.

Pearls

Pearls were a favorite of Queen Alexandra, and women throughout the ages have prized them. A visit to most any art museum will evidence this fact with portrait after portrait of women wearing pearls with pride. They were used for necklaces, bracelets, earrings, and rings and were sometimes even sewn onto dresses for decoration.

Pearls are formed in mollusks. They begin when a tiny irritant enters the oyster. It reacts by secreting a substance call nacre (NAY-kur) to surround the intruder. The gradual building up of this substance creates the pearl.

The Oriental pearl is the most desirable of pearls. It does not necessarily come from the Orient but derives its name from the luster associated with pearls from that region. They are always formed by nature in sea water. The ones of best quality are found in the Persian Gulf.

Fresh water pearls are found in rivers all over the world. Between 1896 and 1899 pearls valued at over a half million dollars were found in the White

River in Arkansas. Pearls are also found in edible clams and oysters, but these usually lack the luster of the more valuable ones.

Pearls come in many shapes and sizes. When a pearl becomes attached to the wall of a shell and forms a flat back, it is called a button pearl. Blister pearls are another malformation, and the name provides an apt description. Blister pearls and button pearls are quite lovely when set in earrings, brooches, and rings. Another malformed pearl is known as the Baroque pearl. It was perfect for the Art Nouveau jewelry designs and made the ideal appendage for the lavalieres that were so popular during this same time period.

The round pearl is the most desirable and hence the most valuable. It is ideally suited for the popular "string of pearls." Small round pearls that weigh less than a grain are called seed pearls.

Pearls come in a variety of colors: pink, cream, white gold, orange, and black. The color depends on the type of mollusk and the water in which it is found. Black pearls, which are really grey, are the most valuable.

Shapes, colors, and weights are all factors in determining the value of a pearl. Blemishes or any irregularities diminish the value. A perfect pearl is always allowed one blemish, because it can be drilled in that spot. It takes many years to collect a perfectly matched string of pearls. Consequently, they can be most expensive. Prior to the perfecting of cultured pearls, they were more costly than diamonds. Mrs. George Gould, one of the "Society 400", owned a necklace assembled for her by Tiffany's. It was valued at more than a million dollars.

Cultured pearls are real pearls that man has helped nature develop. As early as 1883, Mr. K. Mikimoto was able to produce semispherical ones. It took many more years of experiments and the help of several men to perfect the round cultured pearl.

To produce a cultured pearl an irritant is placed inside the oyster. The natural reaction occurs, and the pearl is formed, but this takes many years. To hasten the process a round Mother of Pearl bead is now used as an irritant. Even with this head start, it takes from three to seven years to produce a cultured pearl.

There are many types of imitation pearls. The most common is a glass ball covered with essence d' orient, a liquid made from fish scales. Plastic is also used to imitate pearls, but it does such a poor job that it usually fools no one.

There are international laws and agreements concerning various aspects of the pearl industry. It is against the law to sell an imitation pearl as a natural pearl. Even cultured pearls must be so designated.

There is no other gem quite like a pearl. To keep this rare beauty, special attention is required. Because elements in the air cause deterioration, the average life span is only 100 to 150 years. That is not to say that in that length of time they will turn to dust; only that they will no longer have their inner sheen. To lengthen the life span, always take care not to expose them to perfume or hair spray. Never clean them with a commercial jewelry cleanser unless it specifies "safe for pearls." A gentle wiping with a soft cloth after wearing will prolong the luster and insure another generation the joy of wearing them. By all means do wear and enjoy them.

Moonstones

The moonstone was a popular stone in the 1890-1917 period. It filled the designer's need for a stone with little color, and its moonish glow added a mystical touch to any piece it adorned.

The moonstone is a type of translucent feldspar. It was so named because of the blue white sheen that seems to glow from within. Some moonstones are colorless; others have a pearly look. They are even found as moonstone cat's eye.

Since the stone is a symbol of the moon, it had romantic associations. Like the moon it symbolized love, romance, and passion. Many felt that it had powers of persuasion in these areas. Consequently, it was a favorite stone to give a sweetheart. The moonstone is one of the June birthstones, but it is seldom used today.

Peridot

King Edward VII considered the peridot his good luck stone. His preference made it popular throughout his reign. Because of its olive green color, the mineralogical name for peridot is olivine, although it is not uncommon to find yellow-green, or even brownish peridots.

Peridots have been mined for over 3,500 years on the small island of St. John in the Red Sea. Other mines are located in Burma, Bohemia, Norway, Australia, Brazil, and South Africa. In the United States, peridots are found in Arizona, New Mexico, and Hawaii.

Because peridots are fairly soft and tend to be brittle, they are not too popular with today's jewelry designers. But a table or emerald cut stone mounted in yellow gold is quite beautiful. The magical properties ascribed to the peridot include the powers to overcome timidness. It must work because most Leo's never seem to have this problem.

Bracelets

(D) (Jewelry Box Antiques)

1890-1910 baby bracelet, silver, 1/4" wide. **Price: $95**

(C) (Jeanenne Bell)

1880-1910 bangle bracelet, gold filled, beautifully engraved, 1/4" wide. **Price: $295**

(C) (Amanda Bell)

1890-1910 bangle bracelet, gold filled for child or small lady. **Price: $160**

(D) (Jewelry Box Antiques)

1890-1915 bangle bracelet, gold filled with faceted pink stone, enameled leaves and 1 pearl, 1/4" x 2-3/4". **Price: $165**

(D) (Jewelry Box Antiques)

1890-1910 bangle, yellow gold filled, hinged. **Price: $270**

(C) (Emogene Livingston)

1890-1900s bangle, hinged, nicely embossed. **Price: $290**

(D) (Jewelry Box Antiques)

1880s bracelet, yellow gold filled crossover style with multicolored gold decoration, plaque measures approx. 7/8" x 1". **Price: $275**

1880s-1890s bracelet, gold and pearls with painted miniature plaques. **Price: $425**

(C) (Pat Horton)

1880s-1890s bracelet, yellow gold filled hinged bangle, approx. 7/8" wide. **Price: $325**

(D) (Jewelry Box Antiques)

1890s-1910s bracelet, 10K yellow gold bangle with pearls and coral and diamonds. **Price: $1,195**

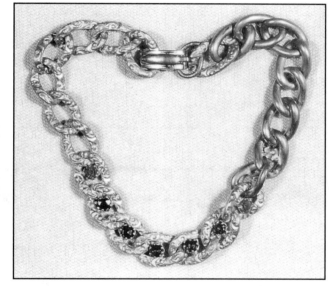

(D) (Jewelry Box Antiques)

1890s-1910s bracelet, gold filled with green stone, turned so that front and back of chain can be viewed, note clasp not original. 7" l. **Price: $50**

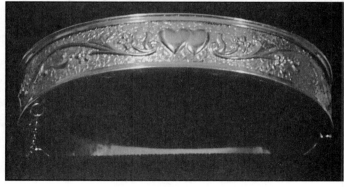

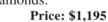

(D) (Jewelry Box Antiques)

1890s-1910s bracelet, gold filled, 1/2" wide. **Price: $240**

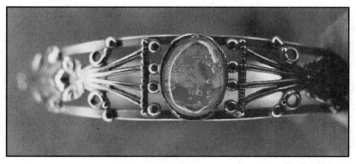

(C) (Pat Horton)

1890s-1910s bracelet, hinged bangle with rose quartz colored glass cabochon. **Price: $295**

1890-1917 bracelet, gold filled curb bracelet with heart lock and key (really works), 1-3/4" l. **Price: $195** (See page 142)

1890-1917 bracelet, gold filled mesh with locket, note adjustable snap catch, locket 7/8" dia., bracelet 1/2" x 7-1/2" l. **Price: $135**

1905 bracelet, gold hinged bangle set with cat's eye and diamonds, £935. **Price: $1,665**

1897 bracelet, gold, made to commemorate the victory of the race horse "Royal Flush," winner of the Diamond Stakes in the Jubilee year 1897. Center has an enameled plaque of Queen Victoria surrounded by diamonds with a locket below. Flanked by four "playing cards," £1,900. **Price: $3,385**

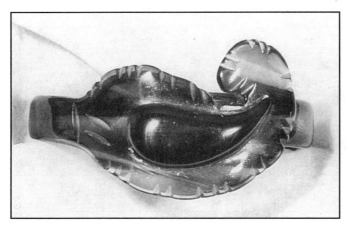

1910-1925 bracelet, celluloid imitation tortoise, 1/2" wide. **Price: $95**

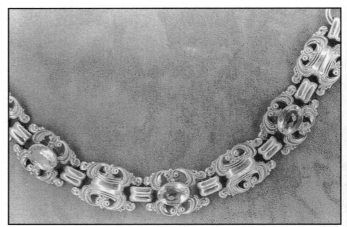

Early 1900s bracelet, yellow gold filled with aqua blue paste stones, approx. 7-3/5" l. **Price: $195**

Bracelet, Art Nouveau, 14K yellow gold composed of 11 repousse slides, each has a lady's head set with a small single cut diamond, American, circa 1900. **Price: $2,200**

1902 bracelet, gold over brass, Queen Victoria on one side of charm; King Edward VII on reverse, coin commemorates King Edward's coronation.

Price: $265

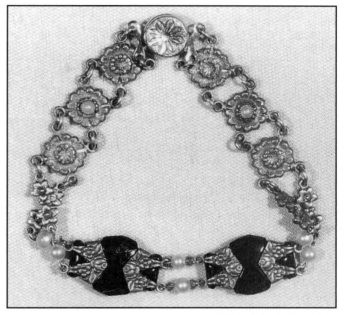

1910s-1920s bracelet, silver over copper with faceted onyx and 3mm faux pearls, has a snap catch, 1/2" w x 7" l. **Price: $115**

Bracelet, Arts and Crafts, set with amazonite cabochons, green-stained chalcedony, rubies, marcasites and amethysts, 20cm long, by Sibyl Dunlop, £200. **Price: $355**

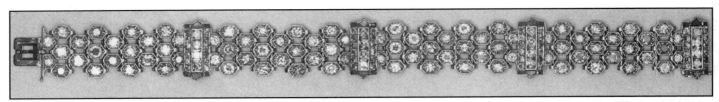

Bracelet, Edwardian gold flexible with diamond set box links, divided by French-cut diamond and calibre emerald baton, £3,400. **Price: $6,055**

1910-1917 bracelet, silver over brass with red molded glass stones, 1" w x 7-1/2" l. **Price: $50**

Bracelet, pat. 1905, yellow gold filled with green and pink gold, locket on top, expansion band 3/8" wide, mkd. "AAG Co." **Price: $125**

Bracelet, Edwardian platinum, set with assorted old mine and rose diamonds, centering a four-strand ruby bead bracelet. **Price: $5,500**

1900 enamel bracelet Tiffany & Co., a center limogé enamel plaque of a peasant woman set in a 14K yellow gold frame flanked by two diamonds. **Price: $2,000**

Charm bracelet, Art Nouveau, made with 7 pins and hat pin tops, all sterling except one. **Price: $1,050**

Victorian tri-color gold bracelet, 14K gold with applied butterfly and floral motif. **Price: $1,600**

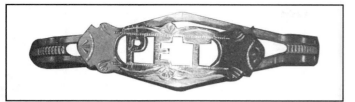

1880-1900 child's bracelet, yellow gold filled, adjustable.
Price: $125

1880-1910 child's bracelet, yellow gold filled, flat adjustable band, engraved, 1/4".
Price: $95

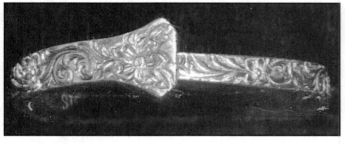

1880-1890 child's bracelet, sterling bangle, hand engraved.
Price: $135

1890-1910 child's bracelet, sterling bangle with 2 hearts, 3/16".
Price: $125

1890-1910 jointed bracelet, gold filled with amethyst stone, 5/8" wide.
Price: $295

1890-1917 jointed bracelet, gold filled, mkd. "A. C. Co.," 1/2" to 1" wide with amethyst stone.
Price: $295

1890-1910 jointed bracelet, gold filled, lion has pink stone eyes and brilliant in mouth, 3/4" x 1" wide.
Price: $325

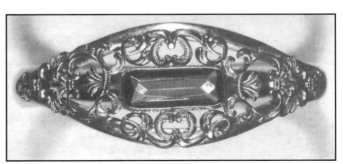

Jointed bracelet patd. Oct 6, 1908, gold filled, mkd. "S. O. B. Co.," topaz-colored stone, 3/8" to 1" wide.
Price: $275

(D) (Camille Grace)

1900-1915 jointed bracelet, gold filled with cameo, 1" x 1-1/4". **Price: $340**

(D) (Camille Grace)

1900-1915 jointed bracelet, gold filled with plaque for engraving, 3/8" x 1" wide. **Price: $265**

(D) (Camille Grace)

1900-1915 jointed bracelet, gold filled with topaz-colored stone, 1/2" x 1-3/8" wide. **Price: $285**

(D) (Camille Grace)

1890-1910 gold filled, lion has ruby eyes and peridot in mouth, 3/8" x 1" wide. **Price: $325**

(A) (Photo courtesy of Sotheby's, New York 10-6-83)

Bracelet, Art Nouveau, gold and enamel, Arnould, France. **Price: $1,540**

Brooches & Pins

(D) (Jewelry Box Antiques)

Circa 1890s-1910 brooch, gold over brass with Venetian mosaic in two colors of green and yellow, approx. 1" x 1". **Price: $85**

(C) (W. Baldwin)

1890-1910 brooch, silver with amethyst and seed pearls, 1-5/8". **Price: $295**

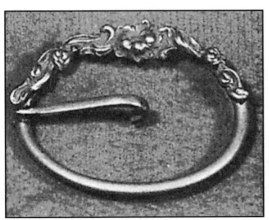

(D) (Jewelry Box Antiques)

1880-1900 brooch, gold filled, 2-3/4" x 2". **Price: $125**

(D) (Jewelry Box Antiques)

Circa 1890s-1910 brooch, painting on porcelain with brass back, approx. 1-1/2" x 2". **Price: $95**

(A) (Photo courtesy of Phillips, London 11-24-83)

Brooch, Art Nouveau, gold with enameling and pearls, Russian maker's mark "A.B.," with male head and "56," £140. **Price: $250**

(Photo courtesy of Phillips, London 11-24-83)

Brooch, "900" owl motif with enameling in brown, violet and yellow, green paste eyes, plique-a-jour wings, holding a pearl, 4.50cm, dragonfly maker's mark, £250. **Price: $445**

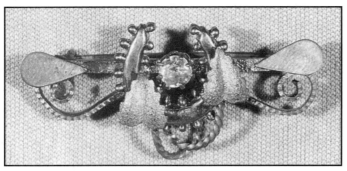

1880-1910 brooch, gold over brass with brilliant, note horseshoe style, 2" x 1". **Price: $60**

1885-1910 brooch, 14K yellow gold with 2 diamonds, 1-1/8" x 1". **Price: $995**

1889-1890s brooch, black enamel over silver mtg., jet flower with seed pearls, 1-1/2" x 2-1/8". **Price: $225**

1880-1910 brooch, gold over brass, star design with imitation pearls and topaz-colored stone. **Price: $60**

1885-1910 brooch, Art Nouveau, 2-1/4" dia. **Price: $995**

1890-1910 brooch, 10K yellow gold with 17 pearls in crescent shape, 1-3/4". **Price: $240**

(C) (Silvia Goldman)

1890-1910 brooch, 14K yellow gold starburst set with diamonds and pearls. **Price: $2,200**

(D) (Jewelry Box Antiques)

1890-1910 brooch, gold on copper with typical Art Nouveau head and brilliant, 1-3/4" l. **Price: $155**

(D) (Jewelry Box Antiques)

1890-1910 brooch, gold filled, 3-1/2" x 1/2". **Price: $95**

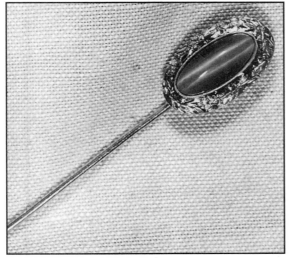

(C) (W. Baldwin)

1890-1910 brooch, gold and tiger eye, 1-3/4" x 3/4". **Price: $95**

(D) (Camille Grace)

1890-1910 brooch, gold filled with 4 moonstones, 1-1/2" x 1-1/4". **Price: $125**

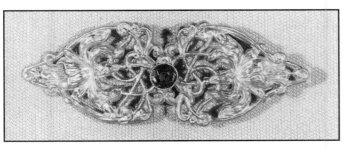

(D) (Jewelry Box Antiques)

1890-1910 brooch, gold filled with blue stone, 2-1/2" x 1". **Price: $70**

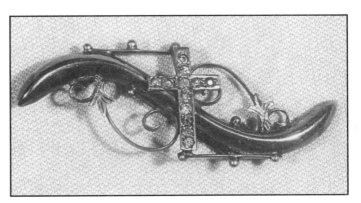

(D) (Jewelry Box Antiques)

1890-1910 brooch, gold filled with some gold and rose cut stones in the cross, 2" x 3/4". **Price: $95**

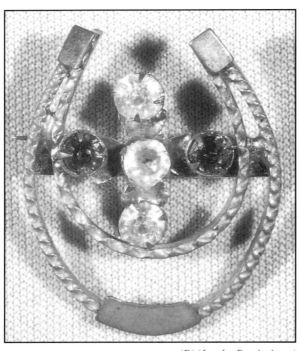

1890-1910 brooch, gold over brass with brilliant and green glass "stones," horseshoe design, 1" x 1-1/4". **Price: $50**

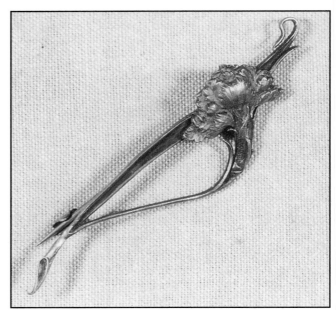

1890-1910 brooch, gold over silver, 3/4" x 2-3/4". **Price: $95**

1890-1910 brooch, silver over brass with faceted purple stone, 3" x 2-1/8". **Price: $95**

1890-1910 brooch, yellow gold filled painted on porcelain of castle, approx. 1-3/4" x 1-1/2". **Price: $170**

(D) (Camille Grace)

1890-1915 brooch, sterling, enameled iris cloisonné and basse-taille, white background with flowers in 3 shades of blue, yellow, and white, 1-1/4" x 1".

Price: $195

(D) (Camille Grace)

1890-1917 brooch sterling, cloisonné and basse-taille enameling, blue background and yellow center, white flowers with green stems. 1-1/2" dia.

Price: $225

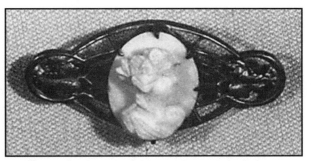

(D) (Jewelry Box Antiques)

1890-1915 brooch, gold over brass, coral cameo, 1-5/8" x 3/4".

Price: $150

(D) (Jewelry Box Antiques)

1890-1915 brooch, gold over brass with coral-colored "stone," 2" x 2".

Price: $95

(D) (Jewelry Box Antiques)

1890s brooch, gold filled with rose cut garnet, 1-3/8" x 1".

Price: $95

159

1890s brooch, gold with onyx and pearl, 1" dia.

Price: $195

Brooch, 18K gold, circular with translucent red, green, and blue enamels, 2.5" dia., stamped "H.G.M.," falcon mark, (rare H. G. Murphy) £350.

Price: $625

1900 brooch, gold and silver buckle motif with pale blue enamel set with 14 old mine diamonds, outer rim bordered by rose cut diamonds and seed pearls.

Price: $3,850

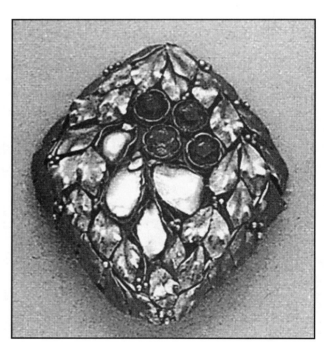

1900 brooch, Arts and Crafts movement, gold with 4 round pink tourmalines and 4 freshwater pearls.

Price: $990

(A) (Photo courtesy of Sotheby's, London 4-14-83)

1900 brooch, gold and silver set with half-pearls and rose cut diamonds, £352. **Price: $625**

(A) (Photo courtesy of Phillips Blenstock House 12-15-83)

Brooch, Art Nouveau, 900 silver, hammer texture with 3 Swiss lapis beads, 3.50cm across, marked with L. B. monogram, £55. **Price: $100**

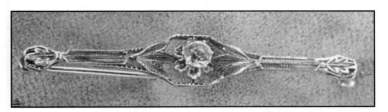

(D) (Jewelry Box Antiques)

1912 brooch, 10K yellow gold set with round brilliant cut crystal. **Price: $195**

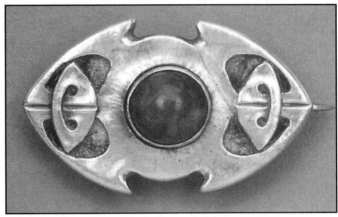

(A) (Photo courtesy of Phillips Blenstock House 12-15-83)

1903 brooch, silver with marble cabochon center and green/blue enamels, "Liberty & Co.," £140. **Price: $250**

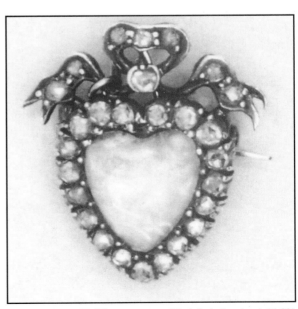

(A) (Photo courtesy of Sotheby's, London 4-14-83)

1900 brooch, heart motif with opal and diamonds, £385. **Price: $685**

Brooch, Art Nouveau, copper, probably was originally silver plated, 2-1/4" x 2". **Price: $225**

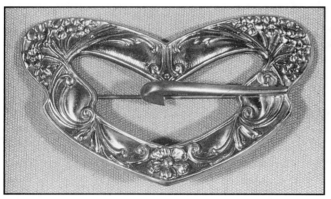

Brooch, Art Nouveau, mkd. "Sterling top. W. B. Co.," two punched stars in back, 3" x 2". **Price: $245**

Brooch, Art Nouveau, gold with oval turquoise, £90. **Price: $160**

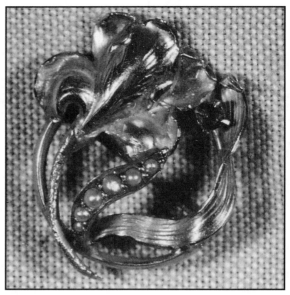

Brooch, Art Nouveau, gold, sapphire and pearls, 7/8" x 7/8". **Price: $245**

Brooch, Art Nouveau, mkd. sterling front, star punch trademark. 1" x 1-1/4". **Price: $225**

Brooch, Art Nouveau, silver over copper,
1-3/8" x 2". **Price: $225**

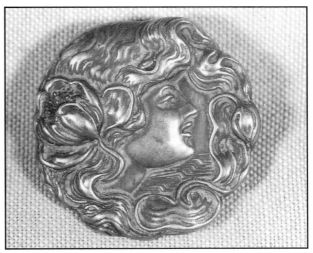

Brooch, Art Nouveau, mkd. "Sterling top. German
silver on back." 1-1/8" dia. **Price: $285**

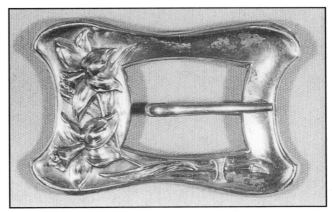

Brooch, Art Nouveau, mkd. "Sterling top. "W.B.
Co.," star punch, 3" x 2". **Price: $225**

Brooch, Art Nouveau, sterling front, star
punch back, replacement pin, 1" x 1-3/8".
Price: $225

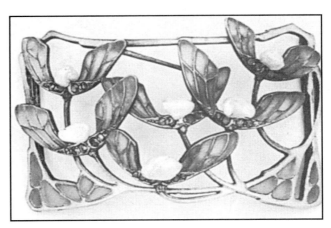

Brooch, Art Nouveau, silver set with rubies and
freshwater pearls, plique-a-jour enameling, £750.
Price: $1,335

Brooch, Art Nouveau, yellow gold, 7/8" x 7/8".

Price: $365

Early 1900s brooch, gold filled, shell cameo, 1-1/2" x 2". **Price: $295**

Early 1900s brooch, celluloid cameo, hook for pin is also celluloid, 1-1/2" x 2". **Price: $50**

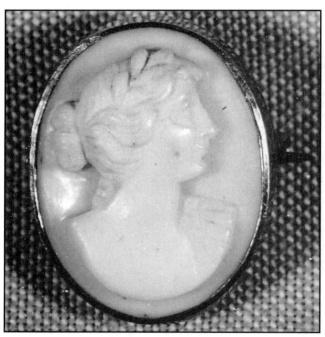

Early 1900s brooch, 10K yellow gold mtg. coral cameo, 3/4" x 7/8". **Price: $325**

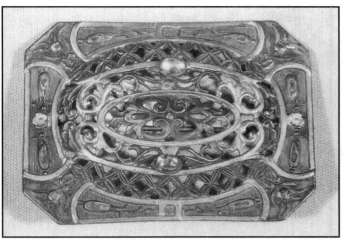

Early 1900s brooch, gold over brass with glass peridots, 2-3/4" x 2". **Price: $125**

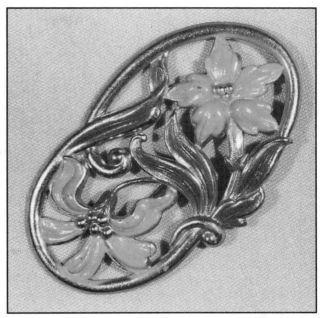

Early 1900s brooch, gold over brass with orchid enameled flowers with green emerald leaves, 2-3/4" x 1-5/8". **Price: $95**

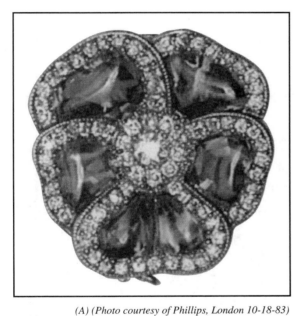

(A) (Photo courtesy of Phillips, London 10-18-83)

Brooch, Edwardian, gold pansy with shaped amethysts edged by small diamonds, £1,700. **Price: $3,025**

(A) (Photo courtesy of Phillips, London 4-26-83)

Brooch, Edwardian, gold set with cushion-shaped mixed cut sapphire, £700. **Price: $1,245**

(A) (Photo courtesy of Phillips, London 10-18-83)

Brooch, Edwardian, gold set with aquamarine and pearls, £3,000. **Price: $5,340**

Brooch, Edwardian, gold set with emeralds and diamonds, £3,000. **Price: $5,340**

Late 19th century brooch, gold crescent centered with a sapphire (approx. 1.25 cts). Further embellished with 4 sapphires and several old cut European cut diamonds. **Price: $3,500**

1880s-1900s brooch, silver, 2-1/8" x 1-1/2". **Price: $185**

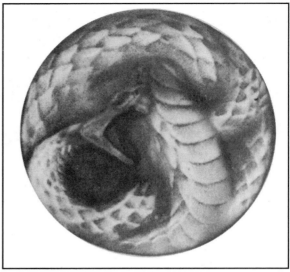

Brooch, gilt metal, snake motif in high-relief molded glass, 4cm, stamped "RL" & "Lalique," £700. **Price: $1,245**

Brooch, Arts and Crafts, with moonstone, "In the manner of Gaskin." £40. **Price: $70**

Brooch, unusual enameled with female dancer .6cm high, signed on reverse "May Patridge," entitled "Flame," £400. **Price: $715**

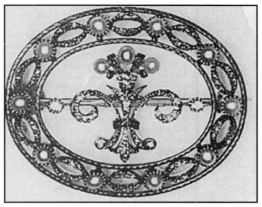

Edwardian brooch, gold with enameled frame set with pearls, rose diamonds and demantoid garnet, fitted case, £1,300.
Price: $2,315

1880s-1910 brooch/pendant, 14K yellow gold mtg., shell cameo with 2" diamonds, 1-3/4" x 2-1/4".
Price: $995

1890s-1910 brooch/pendant, 14K with center diamond and seed pearls, 1-3/4" dia.
Price: $650

Brooch/pendant 1900-1917, 10K yellow gold mtg., shell cameo, 1-1/4" x 1-1/2".
Price: $495

1900-1917 brooch/pendant, 10K yellow gold mtg., coral cameo, 1" x 1-1/4".
Price: $525

167

Brooch/pendant 1900-1917, 10K yellow gold mtg., shell cameo, 1-1/4" x 1-1/2".
Price: $495

Early 1900s brooch/pendant, 14K yellow gold mtg., stone cameo surrounded by pearls, done in Victorian style, 1-1/4" x 1-1/2". **Price: $2,400**

Early 1900s brooch/pendant, 10K yellow gold mtg., shell cameo. **Price: $545**

Brooch/pendant, 1908-1917, 10K yellow gold, shell cameo, 1-7/8" x 2-1/2". **Price: $595**

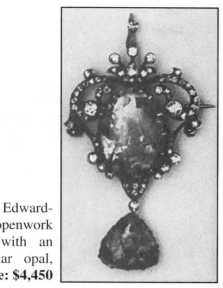

Brooch/pendant, Edwardian, a diamond openwork setting mounted with an oval and triangular opal, £2,500. **Price: $4,450**

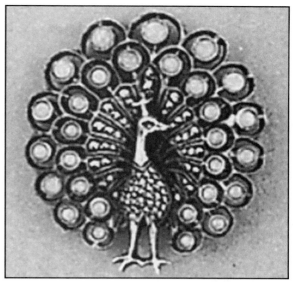

Brooch, 925 silver, peacock feathers set with marcasites and opal cabochons, 4cm high, stamped "TF," (Theodor Fahrner) £95.
Price: $169

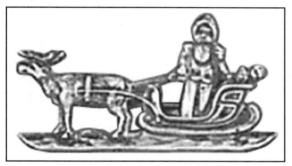

Brooch, 1911 silver, Santa with sleigh and reindeer, 4.5cm l., marked "F.H.M.," £20.
Price: $35

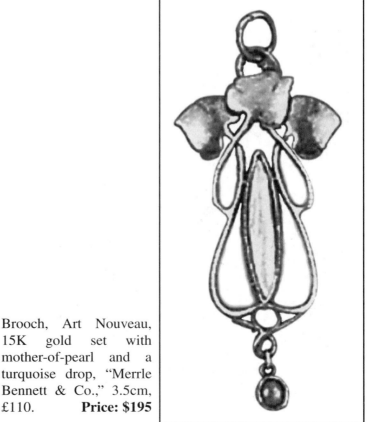

Brooch, Art Nouveau, 15K gold set with mother-of-pearl and a turquoise drop, "Merrle Bennett & Co.," 3.5cm, £110. **Price: $195**

Brooch, Art Nouveau, 9K gold centered with turquoise, embellished with seed pearls and a pearl drop, £50. **Price: $90**

(A) (7-28-83)

1875-1900 brooch, centered with insect set with a cushion-shaped sapphire and rose and cushion-shaped diamonds. The crescent is set with half-pearls between single pearl terminals, £605.
Price: $1,075

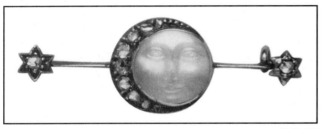

(A) (7-28-83)

1880-1890s brooch, gold with man in the moon carved in moonstone, crescent set with rose diamonds, £550.
Price: $980

(A) (7-28-83)

1875-90 brooch, caduceus set with cushion-shaped rubies and sapphires and rose and cushion-shaped diamonds. £715.
Price: $1,275

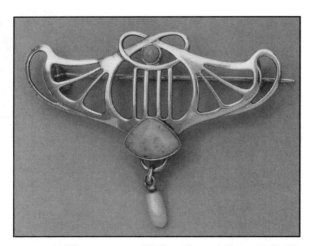

(A) (Photo courtesy of Phillips Blenstock House 12-15-83)

Brooch, Art Nouveau, 9K gold with turquoise cabochon, 4cm across, £70.
Price: $125

(A) (Photo courtesy of Phillips, London 11-24-83)

Brooch Arts and Crafts, centered with a moonstone cabochon, 5cm dia., £40.
Price: $70

1900-1920 bar pin, 10K white gold with aquamarine-colored stone, 2-1/4" x 1/2". **Price: $245**

"Jabot" pin, gold minaret design, set with four pale chrysoprase plaques, embellished with black and white enamel, and tulip-shaped pearl terminal. Signed "C & A. G." in oval cartouche. Guiliani, £650. **Price: $1,157**

1910-1917 bar pin, 10K gold with diamonds, 2-1/8" l. **Price: $345**

1910-1917 bar pin, 10K yellow and green gold with rubies, 2-1/4" l. **Price: $325**

1910-1920 bar pin, 14K yellow gold with pearls and blue stone, 1-3/4" w. **Price: $395**

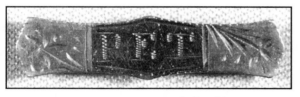

1880s-1990 child's pin, gold top, engraved "PET," 1" x 1-1/4". **Price: $135**

1910-1917 bar pin, 10K yellow gold, 2-1/4". **Price: $195**

1910-1925 pair of pins, 14K white gold filigree with seed pearls. **Price: $450**

1910-1920 bar pin, 14K yellow gold with pearls and ame-thyst, 2-1/2" l. **Price: $295**

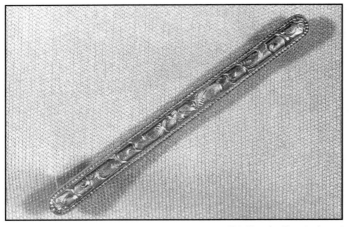

1900-1917 beauty pin, gold filled, mkd. "E. IRA R & Co.," gold top engraved, 1/4" x 2-1/4". **Price: $65**

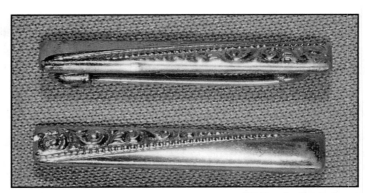

Beauty pins, pat. April 19, 1910, and Oct. 29, 1911, gold filled, 1-1/4" x 1/8". **Price: $68 pair**

1890s-1910 mosaic pin, 9K Roman mosaic, 2" x 3/4". **Price: $475**

Turn-of-the-century clip pin, silver over copper, used to clip on dress and money was pinned inside dress for safe keeping, 1-1/2" x 2-1/2". **Price: $85**

1910 dragon fly pin, 18K yellow gold and platinum containing small round diamonds and blue and green enamel. **Price: $7,750**

Code in Front of Name

(A) Auction House - Auction Price
(C) Collector - Collector Asking Price
(D) Dealer - Dealer's Asking Price

Gold and enamel bar pin and earrings, 14K yellow gold in forget-me-not motif. **Price: $700**

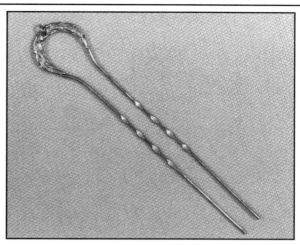

Early 1900s hair pin, gold filled, originally hooked to eyeglasses that rested on the nose. Makes an interesting necklace when attached to neckchain, 2-1/2" l. **Price: $50**

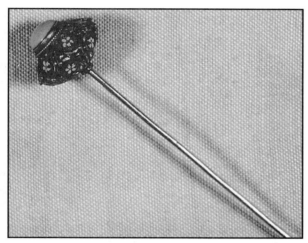

1880-1910 hat pin, 14K gold, Persian turquoise with cloisonné enameling, head 3/4", 6" l.

Price: $245

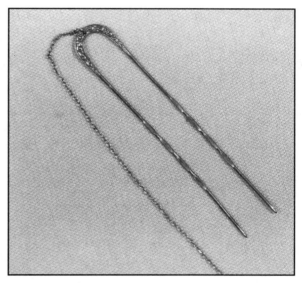

Hair pin same as above, 2-1/2" l. **Price: $40**

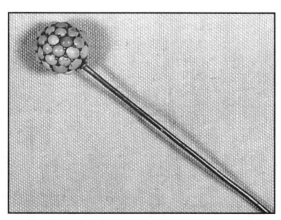

1880-1910 hat pin, gold over brass with Persian turquoise, head 1/2" dia., 6-1/2" l.

Price: $110

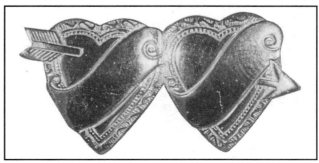

1890-1910 heart pin, gold over brass with popular double heart motif, 1-1/2" x 3/4". **Price: $65**

(D) (Jewelry Box Antiques)

1890-1910 initial pin, initial "B." **Price: $55**

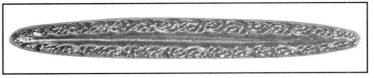

(C) (W. Baldwin)

1890-1915 lace pin, 10K yellow gold, 1-3/4" l. **Price: $165**

(D) (Jewelry Box Antiques)

1880-1900 pin, 14K multi-gold with engraved design, approx. 2" x 3/8". **Price: $295**

(C) (W. Baldwin)

1890-1910 pin, 9K with seed pearls, 1-1/4" l. **Price: $195**

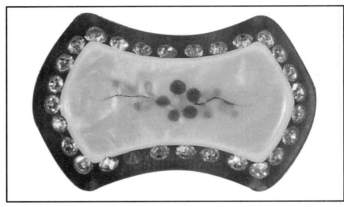

(D) (Jewelry Box Antiques)

1890-1910 pin, celluloid with hand painted flowers surrounded by brilliants. **Price: $40**

(D) (Jewelry Box Antiques)

1880-1890 pin, sterling silver horseshoe, 1-1/4" x 1-1/4". **Price: $125**

(D) (Jewelry Box Antiques)

1890-1910 pin, 14K yellow gold lady's head set with seed pearls, 1" dia. **Price: $295**

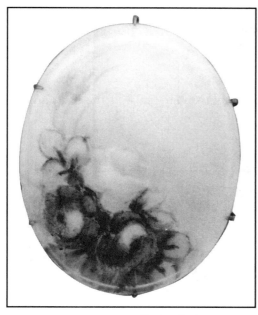

1890-1910 pin, gold over brass frame with paint on porcelain flowers. approx. 2" x 1-5/8". **Price: $80**

1890-1915 pin, yellow gold filled with enameled petals and moonstones, wishbone motif, 1-3/8" x 1". **Price: $95**

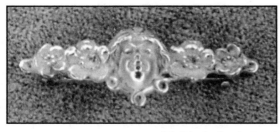

1890s pin, Art Nouveau, gold over brass, approx. 1-1/4" l. **Price: $75**

1890-1910 pin, gold with seed pearls. **Price: $225**

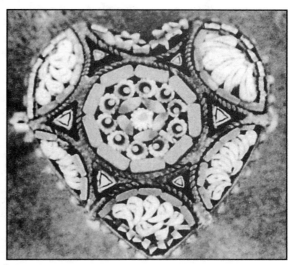

1890-1910 pin, gold over brass mosaic heart, made in Italy, approx. 1" x 1". **Price: $85**

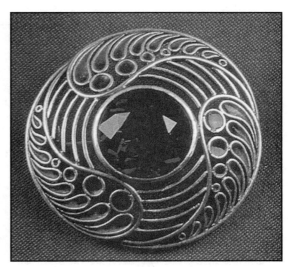

1910 Arts and Crafts plique-a-jour and amethyst pin, signed Tiffany & Co. **Price: $6,440**

1890s pin, bar style. **Price: $65**

1900-1917 pin, copper, enameled cloisonné and basse-taille, 2" x 1". **Price: $165**

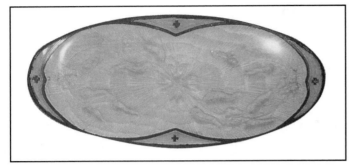

1900s pin, sterling silver set with citrine, made by C.H. Horner. **Price: $250**

Pin, Art Nouveau, gold over brass, head 1" x 1". **Price: $175**

1900-1917 pin, basse-taille in white and soft grey, 3-1/4" x 1/4". **Price: $195**

1900-1917 pin, copper, enameled with robin's egg blue flowers, dark blue and white background, 2-3/4" x 1-1/4". **Price: $95**

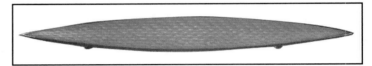

1900-1917 pin, sterling, basse-taille enameling in robin's egg blue, 3" x 1/4". **Price: $135**

1910 pin, 14K yellow gold with engraving, approx. 2" x 3/8". **Price: $195**

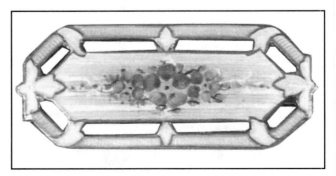

1910-1917 pin, sterling combining several enameling techniques, robin's egg blue and white with dark blue flowers, 1-1/4" x 1/2". **Price: $195**

(C) (W. Baldwin)

1910-1920 pin, 14K amethyst and pearls, 2" l.   **Price: $385**

(D) (June O'Donnell)

Early 1900s pin, sterling silver with enameling, approx.1-1/2" x 1/2".   **Price: $60**

(C) (W. Baldwin)

Early 1900s pin, sterling with peacock eye, used to hold a scarf while riding in an automobile, 7" l.   **Price: $195**

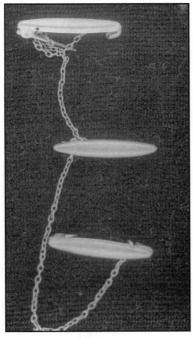

(D) (Jewelry Box Antiques)

1890-1900 pins, 10K yellow gold baby pins, approx. 7/8" x 1/8".   **Price: $125 set**

(D) (June O'Donnell)

Early 1900s pin, ivory, hand painted pansy motif, approx. 1".   **Price: $65**

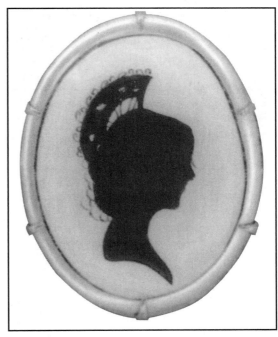

(D) (Jewelry Box Antiques)

Early 1900s pin, base metal frame set with paint on porcelain silhouette, approx. 1-3/4" x 1-3/8".   **Price: $90**

Code in Front of Name

(A) Auction House - Auction Price
(C) Collector - Collector Asking Price
(D) Dealer - Dealer's Asking Price

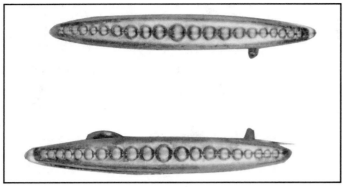

1890-1915 pins, gold filled beauty pins, 1/16" x 1".
Price: $65

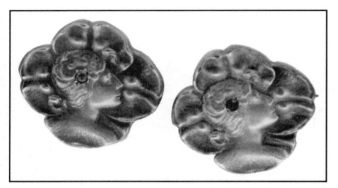

1890s pins, yellow gold filled pair in Art Nouveau style, 3/4" dia.
Price: $165

Pin for glasses (pat'd Feb. 24, 1903) April 26, 1910, gold filled, mkd. "Kitchum & McDonald, N.Y.," 1-1/2" dia.
Price: $40

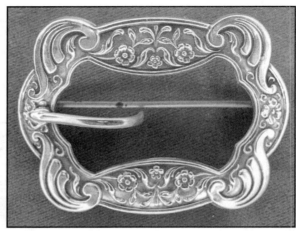

1890-1910 sash buckle pin, sterling silver top, approx. 2-6/16" x 1-7/8".
Price: $195

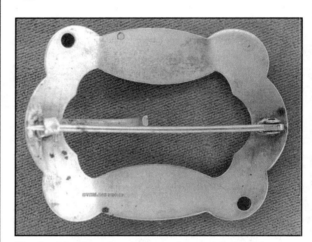

Back side showing hinge, clasp and markings.

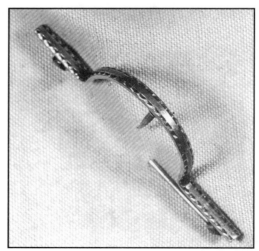

1880-1915 boquet pin, sterling, 2-1/4" w., projects 1".
Price: $185

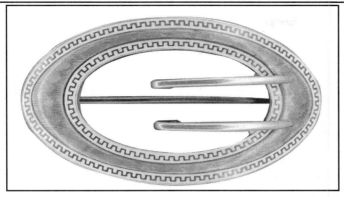

(Jewelry Box Antiques)

1900s sash buckle pin, sterling silver marked "3398-46 Wm. B. Kerr & Co.," with enameling, approx. 2-3/4" x 1-1/2". **Price: $325**

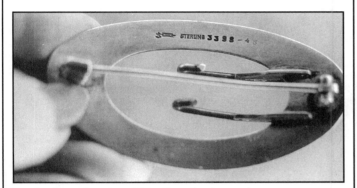

Back view showing "Kerr" maker's mark.

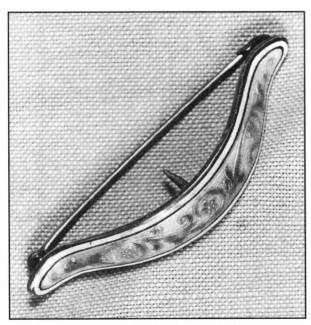

1900-1917 boquet pin, hallmarked silver, enameled, 2". **Price: $245**

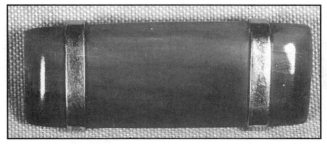

(C) (W. Baldwin)

1890-1910 scarf pin, gold, tiger eye. **Price: $145**

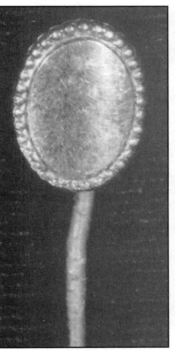

(D) (Jewelry Box Antiques)

(D) (Jewelry Box Antiques)

1890-1910 scarf pin, yellow gold filled, 1/4" x 1/2". **Price: $40**

1890-1910 scarf pin, yellow gold filled, "B" initial, head 1/2" x 3/4". **Price: $50**

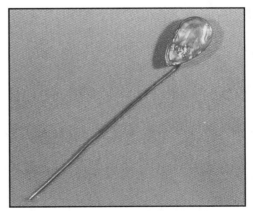

(D) (Jewelry Box Antiques)

1890-1910 scarf pin, sterling, mother-of-pearl. **Price: $55**

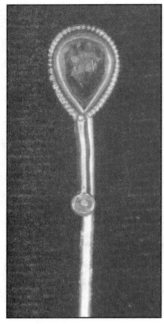

(D) (Jewelry Box Antiques)

1890-1910 scarf pin, yellow gold filled, topaz-colored stone, 1/4" x 5/8".
Price: $50

(D) (Jewelry Box Antiques)

1890-1910 scarf pin yellow gold filled, shield with amethyst stone, 1/2" x 3/4".
Price: $60

(D) (Jewelry Box Antiques)

1890s stickpin, 14K with blue stone and seed pearls, approx. 3/8" x 9/16".
Price: $95

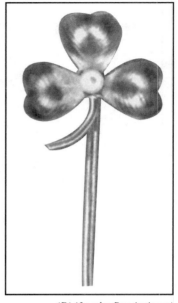

(D) (Jewelry Box Antiques)

1890s stickpin, 14K yellow gold, 3 leaf clover set with pearl.
Price: $145

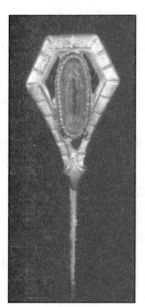

(D) (Jewelry Box Antiques)

1910-1920 scarf pin, yellow gold with ruby-colored stone, 1/4" x 3/4".
Price: $50

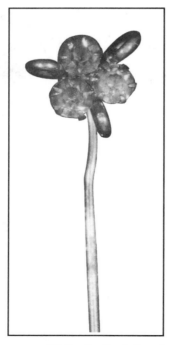

(D) (Jewelry Box Antiques)

Early 1900s scarf pin, yellow gold filled with 3 blue stones, head 1/2".
Price: $60

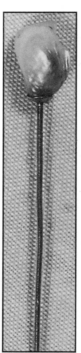

1890-1910 scarf pin, gold with Baroque pearl, 3" l.
Price: $165

(C) (W. Baldwin)

1890-1910 stick pin, 14K yellow gold set with moonstone, worn by Paul Newman in the movie "Mr. & Mrs. Bridge."
Price: $225

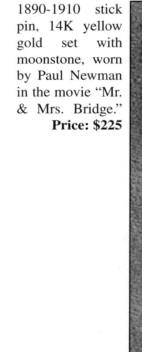

(C) (Michael Marshall)

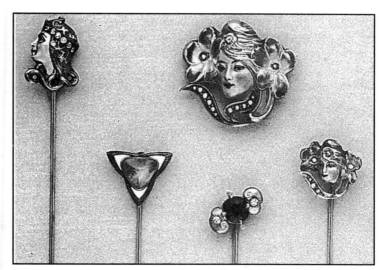

1900 stick pins and brooch, 14K diamond and garnet stickpin signed "Tiffany & Co."; a gold enamel and moonstone stickpin, two gold and diamond stick pins with woman's face and a gold enamel, seed pearl and diamond brooch of a woman's face accented with enamel. **Price: $1,760**

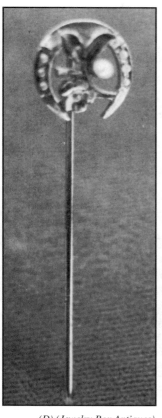

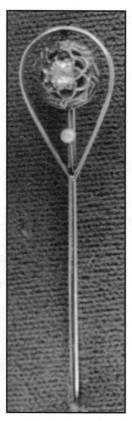

(D) (Jewelry Box Antiques)

(D) (Jewelry Box Antiques)

1890-1910 stickpin, 14K yellow gold set with .07 ct. diamond and seed pearl, approx. 3/4" x 3/8". **Price: $130**

1890s stickpin, 14K with blue stone and seed pearls, approx. 3/8" x 9/16". **Price: $95**

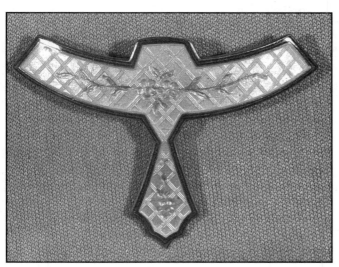

(D) (Camille Grace)

1890-1917 scarf pin, hallmarked sterling with enameling, pink flowers on white background, 2-1/8" x 1-5/8". **Price: $245**

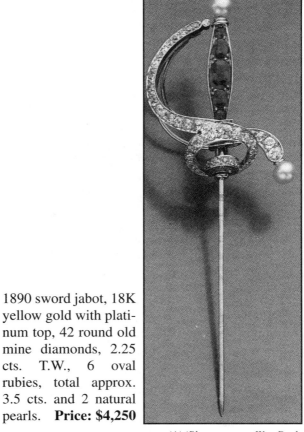

1890 sword jabot, 18K yellow gold with platinum top, 42 round old mine diamonds, 2.25 cts. T.W., 6 oval rubies, total approx. 3.5 cts. and 2 natural pearls. **Price: $4,250**

(A) (Photo courtesy of Skinner, Inc., Boston, Mass 12-4-90)

Victorian enamel portrait pin, 14K yellow gold (minor lead repair). **Price: $400**

(C) (Anne Noblitt)

1890s-1910 initial pin, gold over brass, 1-3/8" x 1-1/8", initial "N." **Price: $55**

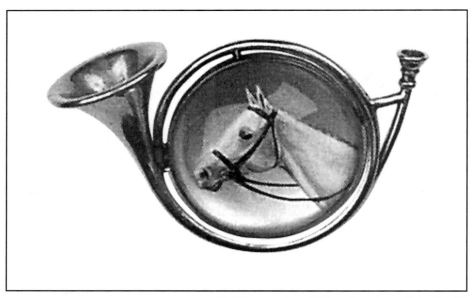

(A) (Photo courtesy of Skinner, Inc., Boston Mass 12-4-90)

Reverse painted crystal intaglio pin, 14K yellow gold. **Price: $1,600**

Crosses

(D) (Jewelry Box Antiques)

1890-1910 cross, gold over copper with seed pearls, 5/8" x 1", on new gold filled chain.

Price: $75

(D) (Jewelry Box Antiques)

1890-1910 cross, gutta-percha on new gold filled chain, 1-3/8" x 2-5/8".

Price: $155

(D) (Lucille and Sam Mandorff)

1880-1910 cross, gold over brass, has Apostles' Creed inside, 1-1/4" x 2".

Price: $175

Code in Front of Name

(A) Auction House - Auction Price
(C) Collector - Collector Asking Price
(D) Dealer - Dealer's Asking Price

Cross, Art Nouveau, gold filled, 1-3/8" x 2-1/4". **Price: $165**

(D) (Jewelry Box Antiques)

Cuff Links

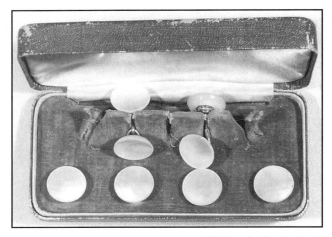

(D) (Jewelry Box Antiques)

1890-1910 cuff link set, gold filled, mother-of-pearl, cuff links and collar button made by Kremitz Co., original box, 5/8" dia. **Price: $135**

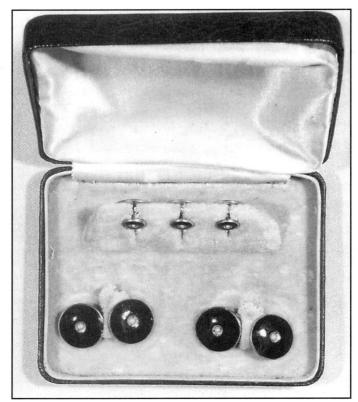

(D) (Jewelry Box Antiques)

Early 1900s cuff link set, sterling with black enameling and pearls, links 5/8" dia. **Price: $195**

(C) (W. Baldwin)

1890-1910 cuff links, 14K gold, sinister looking heads, 5/8" x 5/8". **Price: $345**

(D) (Jewelry Box Antiques)

1890-1910 cuff links, gold filled with imitation opals, mkd. "Lambourne & Co., Birmingham, England." **Price: $110**

(D) (Jewelry Box Antiques)

1890-1910 cuff links, gold filled, mkd. "HA & Co.," note mermaid with flowing hair, 1/2" x 7/8".
Price: $125

(D) (Jewelry Box Antiques)

Early 1900s cuff links, yellow & green gold finish with red cabochon stones, approx. 1" x 3/8".
Price: $95

(A) (Photo courtesy of Sotheby's, New York 10-5-83)

1910 cuff link dream set, 4 buttons and 3 studs of platinum, mother-of-pearl and 11 old mine cut diamonds (approx. .50 cts), 14K gold backs and posts.
Price: $1,045

Earrings

1900 earrings, 14K yellow gold with purple and white enamel, each one has an old European cut diamond set in the center.
Price: $1,045

(A) (Photo courtesy of Sotheby's, New York 10-6-83)

1890s earrings, brass beads 1-1/4" dia., originally buttons.
Price: $295

(D) (Jewelry Box Antiques)

Code in Front of Name

(A) Auction House - Auction Price
(C) Collector - Collector Asking Price
(D) Dealer - Dealer's Asking Price

(D) (Jewelry Box Antiques)

1890-1910 earrings, molded amber glass and gold filled, new 14K wires, 3/4" x 1".
Price: $95

Lavalieres

(D) (Jewelry Box Antiques)

1890-1910 lavaliere, 14K yellow gold with amethyst on original chain, 3/8" x 5/8". **Price: $295**

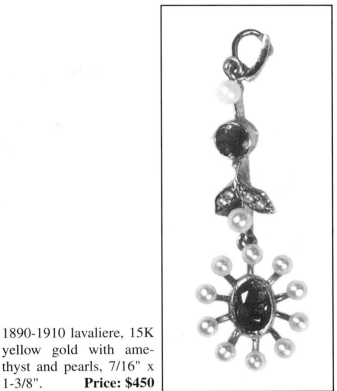

1890-1910 lavaliere, 15K yellow gold with amethyst and pearls, 7/16" x 1-3/8". **Price: $450**

(C) (W. Baldwin)

(D) (Jewelry Box Antiques)

1890-1910 lavaliere, 18K gold with paste stones, 3/8" x 1-1/2" on new 14K chain. **Price: $195**

(C) (Jeanenne Bell)

1890-1910 lavaliere, Art Nouveau, 14K gold with peridot and seed pearls, 1-1/4" x 2" on new 14K chain. **Price: $595**

1890-1915 lavaliere, 14K yellow gold with enameling and pearls, 25" chain also has pearl pendant, 5/8" x 1-3/4".
Price: $565

(D) (Camille Grace)

1890-1917 lavaliere, 10K yellow gold drop on 14K chain, sapphire and pearls, 1/2" x 1-1/8".
Price: $295

(D) (Camille Grace)

(D) (Jewelry Box Antiques)

1890-1917 lavaliere, 14K yellow gold with green gold flowers, small diamond in buttercup mtg., new 14K chain, drop 1" x 1". **Price: $345**

(A) (Photo courtesy of Sotheby's, New York 10-5-83)

1900 lavaliere, 14K gold with diamonds, seed pearls and 2 pear-shaped sapphires (approx. 1.25 cts).
Price: $715

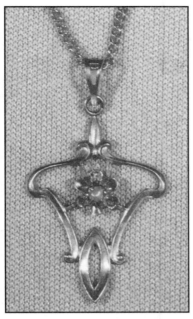

1900-1917 lavaliere, 14K yellow gold with amethyst and pearl, 11/16" x 2".
Price: $345

Lavaliere, Art Nouveau, 10K gold with seed pearls, 3/4" x 1-1/2".
Price: $225

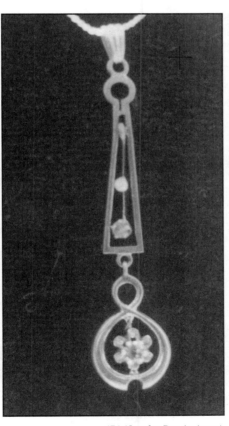

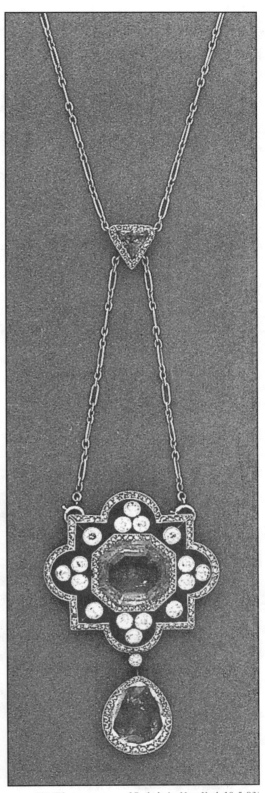

1890-1910 lavaliere, 14K yellow gold set with diamond and freshwater pearl, approx. 1-1/2" l; chain approx. 19" l. **Price: $350**

1890-1910 lavaliere, 10K & 14K yellow gold set with blue sapphires, approx. 3-7/8" x 3/4". **Price: $240**

1910 lavaliere, platinum set with 1 octagonal-shaped emerald and 1 pear-shaped emerald and embellished with numerous rose cut diamonds and 16 collet set European cut diamonds. **Price: $9,350**

Lockets

1890-1910 locket, gold filled with seed pearls set in cross, 1-1/2" dia., mkd. HAC Co.

Price: $165

1880-1910 locket, yellow gold filled, 2" x 2-5/8". **Price: $115**

Circa 1890s-1910 locket, heart shape on original chain, approx. 1-7/8" x 1-7/8". Chain is approx. 24" long. **Price: $160**

1885-1910 locket, gold filled. **Price: $165**

(D) (Camille Grace)

1885-1910 locket, gold filled, mkd. "W & H Co.," girl blowing bubbles, 1-1/4" dia. **Price: $275**

(D) (Jewelry Box Antiques)

1890-1900 locket, gold filled with rose cut clear stone, mkd. "Hayden Mfg. Co. 11499," 1-1/2". **Price: $115**

(D) (Camille Grace)

1890-1900 locket, gold filled, enameled, 3/4" x 1". **Price: $225**

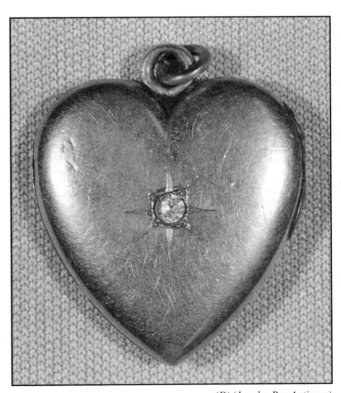

(D) (Jewelry Box Antiques)

1890-1900 locket, yellow gold filled with brilliant stone, 5/8" x 1-1/8" heart. **Price: $85**

1890-1910 locket, 1/4 gold shell marked "W & H Co.," 1" dia. **Price: $145**

1890-1910 locket, 18K, these initial lockets were very popular, 1-1/2". **Price: $395**

1890-1910 locket, gold filled 3-1/2 mm opal, 3/4" dia. **Price: $95**

1890-1910 locket, gold filled mkd. "E. IRA. R.," initials both sides, 1-3/8" dia. **Price: $95**

(D) (Jewelry Box Antiques)

Locket, gold filled mkd. "S.B. & Co.," 1/2" x 1".
Price: $95

(D) (Camille Grace)

1910-1920 locket, chain silver with enameling, pale green background trimmed in black; pink roses. **Price: $265**

(D) (Camille Grace)

1890-1910 locket, gold filled with 9 brilliants, 1-1/4" dia. **Price: $295**

(D) (Jewelry Box Antiques)

1890-1910 locket, gold filled, 1" dia. **Price: $95**

(D) (Camille Grace)

1890-1910 locket, gold filled, 1-1/4" dia.

Price: $165

(D) (Jewelry Box Antiques)

1890-1910 locket, gold filled, 3/4" sq.   **Price: $95**

(D) (Jewelry Box Antiques)

1890-1910 locket, gold filled, initial "B," 1" dia.

Price: $95

(D) (Camille Grace)

1890-1910 locket, gold filled, mkd. "Austen & Stone," with red stones and seed pearls, 1-1/4" dia.

Price: $95

1890-1910 locket, gold filled, mkd. "B & B Sun Bonnet Girl," 1-1/8" dia. **Price: $165**

1890-1910 locket, gold filled, mkd. "J. G. F. Co.," bust of lady, 1-3/8" dia. **Price: $285**

1890-1910 locket, gold filled, note bats and moon, 3 brilliants, 1-1/8" dia. **Price: $195**

1890-1910 locket, gold filled, obviously some never had their initials inscribed, 5/8" x 1-3/8". **Price: $85**

1890-1910 locket, gold over brass with engraved flowers, 1-3/8" dia.　　　**Price: $115**

1890-1910 locket, gold, 1" dia.　　　**Price: $245**

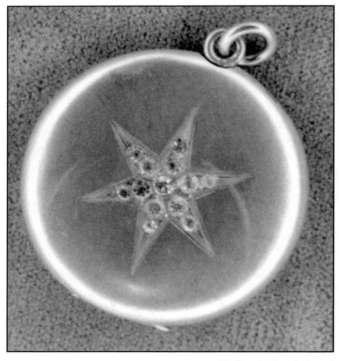

1890-1910 locket, yellow gold filled with seed pearls.
Price: $150

1890-1910 locket, yellow gold filled, 3/4" dia.
Price: $95

1890-1910 locket, yellow gold filled, girl with stars, 1-1/4" dia. **Price: $285**

1890-1910 locket, yellow gold filled, girl's head and clover, 1" dia. **Price: $245**

1890-1914 locket, gold shell, mkd. "Elgin American Mfg. Co.," body of yellow gold, flowers of pink, green, and yellow gold, 1-3/8" dia. **Price: $195**

1890-1915 locket, gold filled with alternating white and green stones, 1" dia. original chain 18".

Price: $85

(D) (Jewelry Box Antiques)

1890s locket, 14K with 4 small diamonds, 1-1/8"
dia. **Price: $495**

(D) (Camille Grace)

1900-1910 locket, gold filled with enameled
flowers, 3/4" dia. **Price: $185**

(D) (Jewelry Box Antiques)

1905 locket, sterling silver hallmark. **Price: $150**

(C) (Jeanenne Bell)

1906-1914 locket, gold filled, given to Kate
Hawkins Hooper (author's grandmother) by her
husband W. E. Hooper, value to author
$1,000,000, another just like it... **Price: $165**

(A) (Photo courtesy of Sotheby's, New York 10-6-83)

Locket, Art Nouveau,14K gold with 1 small old European cut diamond, reverse has monogram.
Price: $1,650

(D) (Jewelry Box Antiques)

Locket, Art Nouveau, yellow gold filled with brilliant, 1-1/4" dia. on old gold filled chain.
Price: $245

(D) (Jewelry Box Antiques)

Early 1900s locket, gold over brass with red "stone," 1-1/4" dia.
Price: $75

(D) (Camille Grace)

Engraved 9-19-1908 locket, gold filled, two girls—one has turquoise around neck; the other has clear stone around her neck, 1-1/2" dia.
Price: $285

(D) (Camille Grace)

1885-1914 locket, gold filled, mkd. "Lady Fair." 1-1/4" dia.　　**Price: $195**

(D) (Jewelry Box Antiques)

1880-1910 locket and fob, gold filled, 1" x 1-1/8".
Price: $95

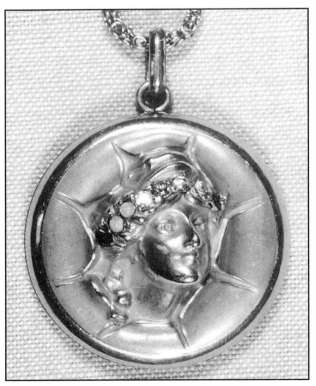

(D) (Camille Grace)

1885-1910 locket and chain, gold filled with 4 diamonds, 2 opals, and 2 garnets, 1-1/4" dia., chain 16" l.　　**Price: $395**

(D) (Jewelry Box Antiques)

1890s-1910 locket and fob, gold over brass, mkd. "W & H Co.," 1" x 1-1/4".　　**Price: $60**

(D) (Jewelry Box Antiques)

1890s locket and fob, gold gilt over brass, 2-1/2mm opal, 1" x 1-3/8". **Price: $95**

(A) (Photo courtesy of Phillips, London 7-7-83)

Pendant/locket, sterling with green and white enameling, front slides to reveal mirrors within. Maker's mark for F. Mahla of Pforzheim, £130. **Price: $240**

(D) (Jewelry Box Antiques)

1890-1910 locket/fob, gold over brass, mkd. "B. B. Co.," note Swaka, a decorative motif that can be traced to the Egyptians, 1" x 1-1/4". **Price: $95**

(D) (Jewelry Box Antiques)

Locket, inscribed "Dec. 23, 1903," gold shell, 1-1/8" dia., mkd. "S O B & Co." **Price: $95**

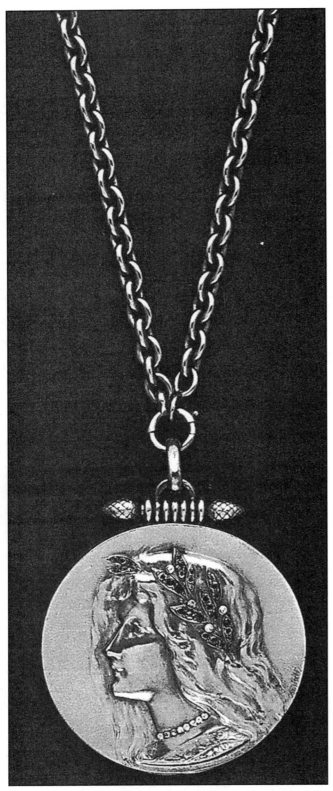

(A) (Photo courtesy of Sotheby's, New York 10-5-83)

1900 locket/pendant, gold with lady's head wreath set with 30 small round emeralds and 4 small round diamonds. Her necklace is set with 8 single cut diamonds, completed by a heavy link chain.

Price: $4,675

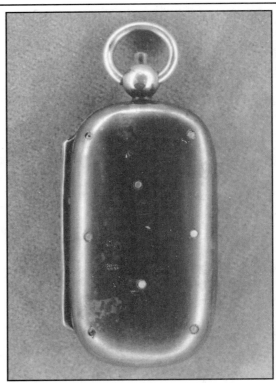

(D) (Jewelry Box Antiques)

1890s money locket, German silver set with turquoise and a yellow gold bale, 3" x 1-1/4" overall.   **Price: $225**

Money locket shown open.

Necklaces

(A) (Photo courtesy Wm. Doyle Galleries, New York 12-7-89)

Art Nouveau peridot, freshwater pearl and gold pendant necklace, 14K yellow gold with kite and pear-shaped peridots and freshwater pearls. **Price: $2,800**

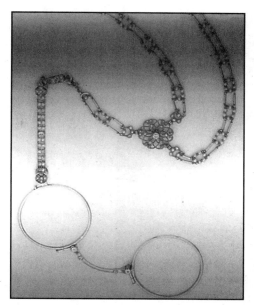

(A) (Butterfield and Butterfield 05/22/97)

Edwardian diamond, cultured pearl, platinum, gold lorgnette pendant-necklace, opens to reveal one pair of round spectacles, the handle enhanced by European and single-cut diamonds weighing a total of approximately 1.05 cts. suspended by a fancy link chain enhanced by cultured pearls accented by single, European, and rose-cut diamonds, all in platinum. The total diamond weight is approximately 1.20 cts., (damage, evidence of repair). **Price: $10,925**

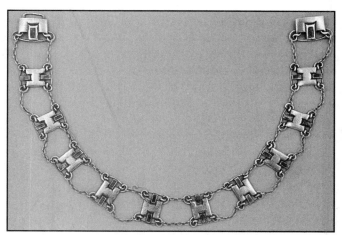

(A) (Photo courtesy of Phillips, London 11-24-83)

1902 necklace, silver "Cymric" with blue enameled panels, probably designed by Archibald Knox, 44cm, Liberty and Co., £280. **Price: $500**

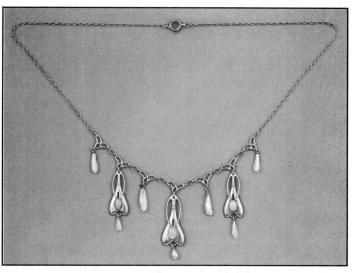

(A) (Photo courtesy of Phillips, London 11-24-83)

Necklace, Art Nouveau, 9K gold with opal cabochon and freshwater pearls, 44cm l., £340. **Price: $605**

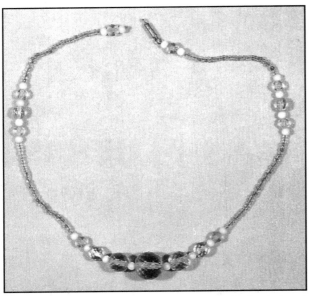

(D) (Jewelry Box Antiques)

1900-1910 pink glass faceted beads with clear and white, 16" l.   **Price: $60**

(A) (Photo courtesy of Sotheby Parke Bernet & Co. London 11-24-83)

1900 long chain, gold chain set at intervals with engraved ivory beads set with cabochon sapphires, rubies, and amethyst (some missing), £825.

Price: $1,470

Necklace, Art Nouveau "950" set with mother-of-pearl and amethyst, stamped M.B. & Co. £110.   **Price: $195**

(A) (Photo courtesy of Phillips, London 7-7-83)

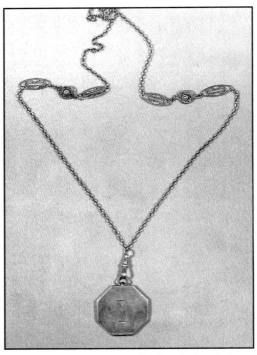

1910-1917, chain and locket sterling, octagonal locket, chain 44" l., locket 1-1/2".

Price: $295

(D) (Jewelry Box Antiques)

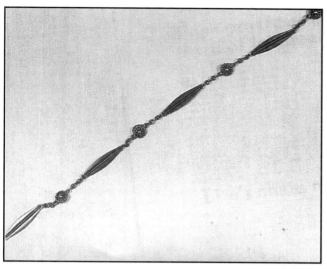

1890-1910 neckchain, gun-metal, 59-1/2" l.

Price: $145

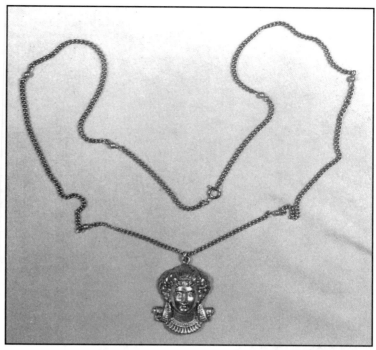

1880-1910 necklace, silver over copper, lady's head on original chain, grey imitation pearls, head 1-1/4" x 1-5/8"; chain 25" l.

Price: $95

1880-1917 necklace, sterling with amethyst, chain 20" l.; drop 1" x 2-1/4".

Price: $285

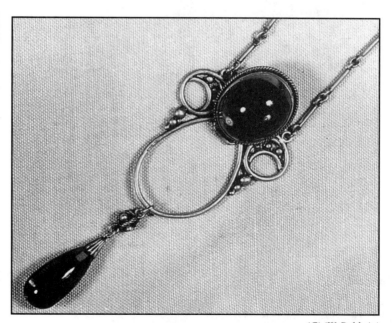

1880-1910 necklace, silver with amethyst stones, chain 16", drop 1-1/2" x 3".

Price: $345

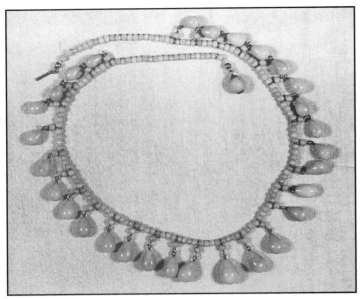

(C) (W. Baldwin)

1890-1910 necklace, coral and gold, 17" l. **Price: $825**

(D) (Jewelry Box Antiques)

1900-1920 necklace, gold filled with pink faceted glass "stone," drop 5/8" l., chain 16" l. **Price: $58**

(A) (Photo courtesy of Sotheby's, New York 12-7-83)

Necklace, Art Nouveau, gold grape motif of fresh-water pearls with emerald pink and green leaves. **Price: $1,870**

(D) (Jewelry Box Antiques)

1910-1920 necklace, silver over brass, crystal drops on 16" long chain, barrel clasp. **Price: $125**

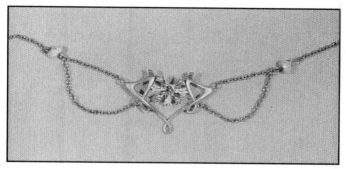

Necklace, Art Nouveau, gold over brass, 2 baroque pearls and seed pearls, and small topaz, drop 1-3/8" x 1". **Price: $185**

1900-1920 pressed cut amber beads, 18" l, 5/8" dia. **Price: $225**

Necklace "950" with faceted amethyst, 42cm l., Merrle Bennett & Co., £120. **Price: $215**

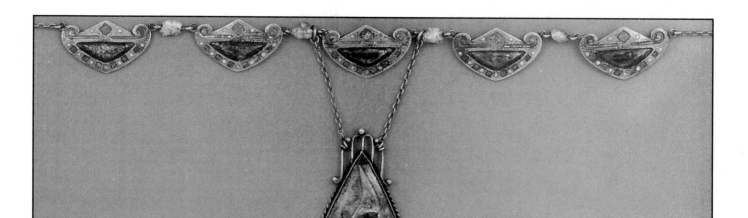

Necklace, Arts and Crafts, enameled panels in green, blue and orange, Baroque pearl, £300. **Price: $535**

1890s necklace and earrings, 14K with brilliant, pendant 5/8" x 1-1/4"; earrings 3/4" l.
Price: $425

(C) (Jeanenne Bell)

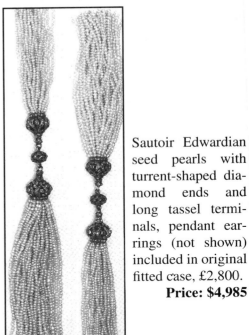

Sautoir Edwardian seed pearls with turrent-shaped diamond ends and long tassel terminals, pendant earrings (not shown) included in original fitted case, £2,800.
Price: $4,985

(A) (Photo courtesy of Phillips, London 6-21-83)

(A) (Photo courtesy of Phillips, London 11-24-83)

Necklace, Arts and Crafts, blister pearls, in the manner of Edgar Simpson, £240.
Price: $430

(A) (Butterfield and Butterfield 03/10/98)

Aquamarine, diamond, seed pearl, platinum necklace; Featuring pear-shaped aquamarines measuring approximately 14.50 x 7.80 x 5.40 to 10.00 x 6.30 x 4.20mm, enhanced by round-cut aquamarines measuring approximately 5.10 x 3.70mm, accented by seed pearls, further accented by European-cut diamonds, (two seed pearls missing, seed pearls not tested for origin). Approximately 15-1/2 inches.
Price: $5,465

Pendants

(A) (Photo courtesy of Sotheby's New York 10-5-83)

Late 19th century pendant/brooch, gold centered with a carved moonstone head of a warrior surrounded by old European cut diamonds and seed pearls, T. B. Starr. **Price: $2,420**

(A) (Photo courtesy of Southeby's, London 6-29-99)

Circa 1910 pendant/brooch, carved opal, sapphires and diamonds. £1,400. **Price: $2,300**

Pendant, Arts and Crafts, moonstone and mother-of-pearl, 5.50cm l., by Gaskin, £440. **Price: $785**

(A) (Photo courtesy Phillips, London 11-24-83)

(D) (Jewelry Box Antiques)

1880-1900 pendant, 18K yellow gold with genuine amethyst and pearls, 1-1/4" x 1-1/2".

Price: $595

(A) (Photo courtesy of Phillips, London 11-24-83)

Pendant, gold moth with opal cabochon body and plique-a-jour wings, pearl drop, 9cm w., stamped "Jules," £190. **Price: $340**

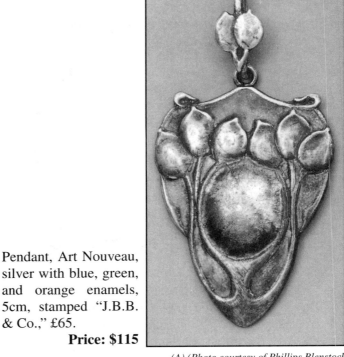

Pendant, Art Nouveau, silver with blue, green, and orange enamels, 5cm, stamped "J.B.B. & Co.," £65.

Price: $115

(A) (Photo courtesy of Phillips Blenstock House 12-15-83)

(D) (Jewelry Box Antiques)

(A) (Photo courtesy of Phillips, London 4-26-83)

Pendant, Edwardian, gold set with diamonds on a fine link chain, case, £1,400. **Price: $2,490**

1880-1890 pendant, gold over brass with 1" dia. faceted amethyst-colored stone worn on black silk cord, 3" x 3-1/2". **Price: $85**

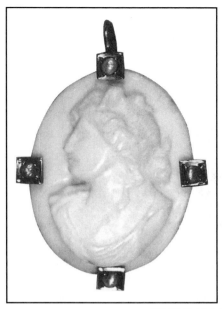

1890-1910 pendant, 14K yellow gold with 4 seed pearls and coral cameo, 7/8" x 1-1/8". **Price: $365**

(C) (W. Baldwin)

(A) (Photo courtesy of Phillips Blenstock House 12-15-83)

1904 pendant, 9K gold with enameled scene, stamped "W.H.H.," £120. **Price: $215**

(D) (Jewelry Box Antiques)

1910-1917 pendant, gold filled with pearl, 1/2" x 1-1/8". **Price: $95**

(A) (Photo courtesy of Phillips, London 7-7-83)

Pendant, "950" with mother-of-pearl half pearls and translucent blue enamel, boasts mother-of-pearl drop, German, probably designed by Otto Prutsher, maker's mark for Heinrich Levinger of Pforzheim, £180. **Price: $320**

(D) (Lucille and Sam Mundorff)

1915-1917 pendant, 10K mother-of-pearl with feathers make bird design, 1-1/2" dia. **Price: $245**

Back side showing peacock.

(C) (Mignon Stufflebam)

1916 pendant, 10K gold, enameling and feathers on mother-of-pearl background, covered with beveled glass, 1-1/4" dia. **Price: $195**

Pendant, opposite side.

Pendant, Art Nouveau, gold and plique-a-jour, maiden's headband set with rose cut diamonds, diamond and pearl drop, 4cm, £400. **Price: $710**

1900 pendant/brooch, gold set with black opals and 6 old European cut diamonds (approx. 1.25 cts).

Price: $2,090

Pendant, "950" with faceted amethysts, M.B. & Co. £120. **Price: $215**

Early 1900s pendant, sterling silver, heart motif, opens to reveal slots for coins. **Price: $295**

Pendant, Edwardian gold with 5 rose cut diamonds, two sapphires and pearls, £850.   **Price: $1,515**

Pendant, Edwardian, yellow gold with blue sapphire and diamond, fitted case, £2,800.

Price: $4,985

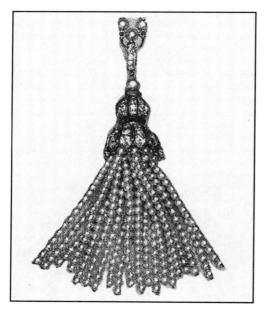

Pendant, Edwardian, pearl tassel pendant with diamond cap, calibre emerald hoops and diamond triangular drops, necklace set at intervals with pearls. Also has a longer, similarly set necklace en suite, £4,200.   **Price: $7,475**

Pendant, Edwardian, gold with a pear shaped aquamarine within a frame embellished with old rose cut diamonds, £650.   **Price: $1,160**

Pendant, Edwardian, gold with brilliant cut diamonds and emeralds, given to the Swedish opera singer Arvid Odmann by his admirers, £2,100. **Price: $3,785**

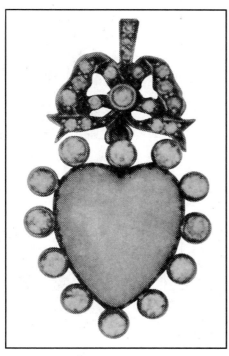

Pendant, late Victorian heart-shaped opal, embellished with old cut diamonds, £850. **Price: $1,515**

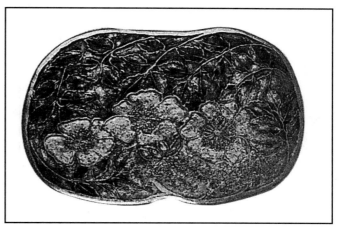

Pendant, late Victorian, gold and silver set with old cut brilliants and matching diamond drops and diamond pendant loop, fitted case, £3,200. **Price: $5,695**

Pendant, Edwardian, opals and diamond, £950. **Price: $1,690**

215

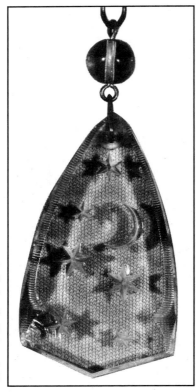

Pendant necklace, 1890 dusty rose glass pendant on dusty rose silk cord, note crescent and stars pendant, 1-1/4" x 3" drop; cord 42" l. **Price: $165**

(D) (Jewelry Box Antiques)

(A) (Photo courtesy of Sotheby's, New York 10-6-83)

Pendant/brooch, Art Nouveau, 18K yellow gold with green enamel, woman's headband set with small old European cut diamonds. **Price: $1,045**

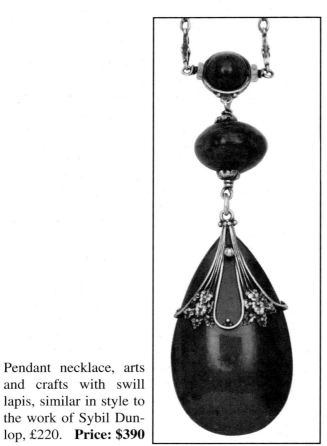

Pendant necklace, arts and crafts with swill lapis, similar in style to the work of Sybil Dunlop, £220. **Price: $390**

(A) (Photo courtesy of Phillips, London 7-7-83)

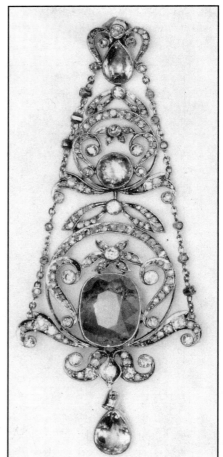

Pendant, Edwardian, rose-diamond framework set with oval and pear-shaped pink tourmalines, £1,300. **Price: $2,315**

(A) (Photo courtesy of Phillips, London 1-24-84)

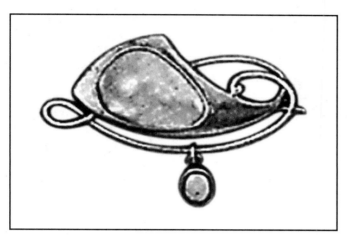

(A) (Photo courtesy of Phillips, London 7-7-83)

Pendant, 9K gold with mother-of-pearl center and a turquoise drop, 5cm, Merrle Bennett & Co., £120.
Price: $230

(A) (Photo courtesy Phillips, London 11-24-83)

Pendant, "950" with mother-of-pearl and faceted chrysolite, 3.50cm, M.B. & Co., £85.   **Price: $150**

(D) (Jewelry Box Antiques)

1890 pendant note pad, sterling silver, measuring approx. 1-1/4" x 2-1/2".
Price: $295

Note pad open to show celluloid pages.

Pendant, Arts and Crafts, enameled shield-shaped, 4.50cm attributed to C. R. Ashbee, £220.
Price: $390

Pendant/locket, gold with blue and green enamels, glass front and back. "Probably designed by Archibald Knox," 3.25cm, Liberty & Co., £130. **Price: $230**

Pendant, silver with enameling, 7 cm, "M. B. & Co.", £70. **Price: $125**

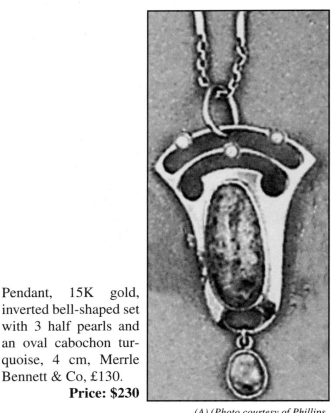

Pendant, 15K gold, inverted bell-shaped set with 3 half pearls and an oval cabochon turquoise, 4 cm, Merrle Bennett & Co, £130.
Price: $230

1860 pendant, gold with royal blue enameling and diamonds, £1870. **Price: $3,330**

1900 pendant necklace, platinum, pear-shaped rubies each approx. .50 cts., assorted small round rose diamonds and platinum chain necklace. **Price: $9,000**

1908-1917 pendant necklace, 14K yellow gold mtg. coral cameo with 17" chain, 7/8" x 1". **Price: $545**

Rings

(D) (Jewelry Box Antiques)

1890 ring, 14K crossover style set with rose cut garnets.
Price: $295

(A) (Photo courtesy Wm. Doyle Galleries, New York 12-12-90)

Edwardian diamond ring, 1910 platinum, centered by one European cut diamond, approx. 2.25 cts., within a filigree field of 26 single cut diamonds, further enhanced with sapphire bands. **Price: $6,500**

(A) (Photo courtesy Wm. Doyle Galleries, New York 12-12-90)

Edwardian diamond ring, platinum filigree mounting, centered by an old mine round diamond, approx. 1.10 cts., within a surround of 10 assorted small round diamonds, total approx. .35 cts. **Price: $2,600**

(A) (Photo courtesy of Sotheby's New York 4-10-84)

Late 19th century ring, gold rectangular head set with a checkerboard pattern of 22 calibre cut rubies and 23 old European cut diamonds (approx. 55 cts). **Price: $1,760**

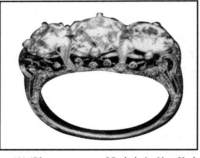

(A) (Photo courtesy of Sotheby's, New York 10-5-83)

1915 ring, platinum centered with 1 old European cut diamond (approx. 1.50 cts) and flanked by 2 old European cut diamonds (approx. 1.60 cts). Further embellished with old European and single cut diamonds (several missing). **Price: $3,300**

(D) (Jewelry Box Antiques)

1880s-1890s ring, 14K yellow gold, opal and ruby cigar band. **Price: $240**

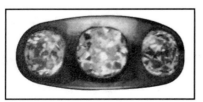

(A) (Photo courtesy of Sotheby's, New York 10-5-83)

1900s ring, gold gypsy mounting centered with 1 old European cut diamond (approx. .50 cts) flanked by 2 old European cut diamonds (approx. .40 cts). **Price: $715**

(D) (Jewelry Box Antiques)

1880-1900 ring, 10K yellow gold set with 3 oval moonstones. **Price: $280**

(A) (Photo courtesy of Skinner, Inc., Boston, Mass. 12-4-90)

Right: diamond and ruby ring, 18 diamonds and 5 graduated rubies, 14K yellow gold. **Price: $700**
Left: emerald and diamond ring on round cabochon cut emerald, surrounded by round diamonds in an engraved platinum mounting. **Price: $700**

(D) (Jewelry Box Antiques)

1890-1900 ring, 14K yellow gold belcher-style mounting set with original amethyst-colored garnet, glass doublet.
Price: $295

(D) (Jewelry Box Antiques)

1890s-1900s ring, 14K yellow gold set with amethyst and seed pearls. **Price: $295**

(D) (Jewelry Box Antiques)

Early 1900s ring, 10K yellow gold baby's signet. **Price: $95**

(D) (Jewelry Box Antiques)

1890-1910 ring, 10K yellow gold signet style with initials, approx. 1/2" x 7/16". **Price: $170**

(D) (Jewelry Box Antiques)

1890-1910 ring, 14K yellow gold belcher garnet/glass doublet.
Price: $295

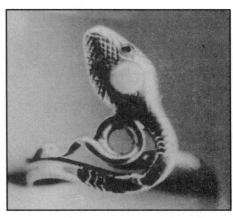

(C) (Antiques Image)

1890-1910 ring, 14K yellow gold "snake" set with opal and garnet.
Price: $395

(D) (Jewelry Box Antiques)

1890-1910 ring, 14K yellow gold horseshoe set with seed pearls.
Price: $295

(D) (Jewelry Box Antiques)

1890-1910 ring, 14K yellow gold set with citrine, approx. 5/16".
Price: $295

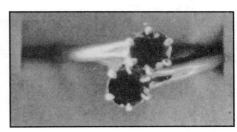

(D) (Jewelry Box Antiques)

1890-1910 ring, 14K yellow gold set with garnet and green glass doublets.
Price: $230

(D) (Jewelry Box Antiques)

1890-1910 ring, gold filled yellow gold with 14 pearls and 4 garnets, head 3/4" x 1/4". **Price: $65**

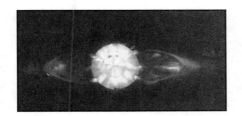

(D) (Jewelry Box Antiques)

1890-1910 ring, gold filled, claw mtg. with rose cut brilliant.
Price: $65

(C) (Eucivia Alvarado)

1890s ring, 10K yellow gold crossover garnet/glass doublet.
Price: $280

(D) (Jewelry Box Antiques)

1890s ring, 10K yellow gold gypsy mounting set with opals. **Price: $225**

(D) (Jewelry Box Antiques)

1890s ring, 10K yellow gold gypsy mounting with three opals. **Price: $295**

(D) (Jewelry Box Antiques)

1890s ring, 14K yellow gold set with .12ct. diamond. **Price: $475**

(D) (Jewelry Box Antiques)

1890s ring, 14K yellow gold set with bloodstone. **Price: $325**

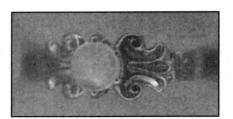

(C) (Jennifer Hill)

1890s ring, 14K yellow gold set with hand carved moonstone. **Price: $425**

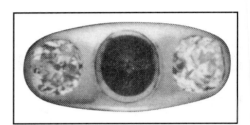

(A) (Photo courtesy of Sotheby's, New York 10-5-83)

1900s ring, 14K gold gypsy mounting centered with 1 old European cut diamond (approx. .90 cts.), flanked by 2 old European cut diamonds (approx. 1.20 cts.), signed "S. Sons." **Price: $1,650**

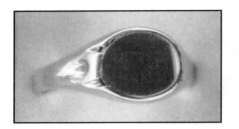

(C) (Amanda Bell)

1890s ring, 14K yellow gold signet "locket ring," head approx. 14.58mm x 10.23mm. **Price: $600**

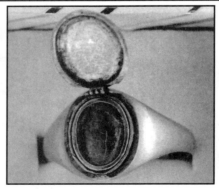

Ring, shown with locket open.

(A) (Photo courtesy of Sotheby's, New York 10-5-83)

1900 ring, 18K gold centered with an 8.3mm natural pearl flanked by 1 old European cut diamond (approx. 1.75 cts) and another old European cut diamond (approx.1.90 cts). **Price: $6,875**

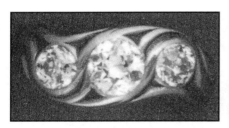

(A) (Photo courtesy of Sotheby's, New York 10-5-83)

1900s ring, Art Nouveau gold asymmetrical band centered with one old European cut diamond (approx. .85 cts) flanked by 2 old European cut diamonds (approx. .90 cts). **Price: $1,870**

(D) (Jewelry Box Antiques)

1905-1920 ring, 10K yellow gold signet ring with engraving, approx. 7/16" x 3/8". **Price: $195**

(D) (Jewelry Box Antiques)

1910-1920 ring, mkd. "sterling," 1/4" wide. **Price: $50**

(D) (Jewelry Box Antiques)

Early 1900s ring, 14K yellow gold set with coral and seed pearls. **Price: $495**

Ring, side view.

(D) (Jewelry Box Antiques)

Early 1900s ring, 10K yellow gold child's signet. **Price: $110**

(D) (Jewelry Box Antiques)

1905-1912 ring, 14K yellow gold coronet mounting set with cabochon cornelian. **Price: $325**

Ring shown lying flat.

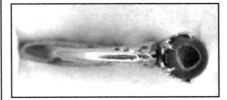

(A) (Photo courtesy of Sotheby's, New York 10-5-83)

1915 ring, platinum-centered with one briolette diamond in an open work panel embellished with single cut diamonds and several calibre cut emeralds. **Price: $2,310**

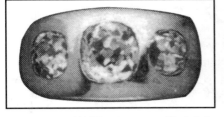

(A) (Photo courtesy of Sotheby's, New York 10-5-83)

1917 ring, platinum band centered with 1 cabochon emerald (approx. .80 cts), flanked by 2 old European cut diamonds (approx. .90 cts). **Price: $1,870**

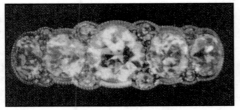

(A) (Photo courtesy of Sotheby's, New York 10-5-83)

1900s ring, platinum top-half set with 1 old European cut diamond (1 ct), 4 old European cut diamonds (approx. 1.80 cts) and spaced by 8 small old European cut diamonds, gold shank. **Price: $2,090**

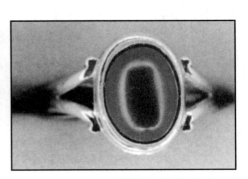

(D) (Jewelry Box Antiques)

Early 1900s ring, 10K yellow gold set with oval jade stone approx. 9.6mm x 7.3mm. **Price: $245**

Watches & Watch Accessories

(A) (Photo courtesy of Wm. Doyle Galleries 12-83)

1915 diamond and black onyx lapel watch and pin, the platinum pin containing forty-two round diamonds approx. total 6.00 cts., and the watch containing one hundred round diamonds approx. total 3.00 cts., and three round diamonds approx. total .90 ct., signed Cartier. **Price: $9,000**

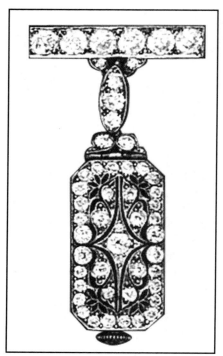

Platinum lapel watch, with 52 round diamonds weighing approx. 2.75 cts., Tiffany & Co. **Price: $1,980**

(A) (Photo courtesy of Sotheby's, New York 9-14-83)

(C) (Anne Noblitt)

1911 watch, gold filled hunting case. Elgin with beautiful white and pink enameled dial, gold hands, chain is gold filled with pat. date, "Sept. 22, 1903." **Price: $595**

(A) (Photo courtesy of Wm. Doyle Galleries New York 9-21-83)

1890-1910 lapel watch and pin, yellow gold and silver with rose cut diamonds. **Price: $2,700**

Late 19th century lapel watch and pin, gold with enamel, dial is white with blue Arabic numerals. **Price: $715**

1889 watch, yellow gold filled hunting case, U.S. Watch Co., approx. 1-3/4" dia. **Price: $495**

1895 watch, gold filled case, size 16 Elgin movement. **Price: $295**

1890s watch, yellow gold fob watch, back pavé set with old cut diamonds, bezel is also set with diamonds. Bow brooch set with diamonds and centered with collet set ruby, £3,250. **Price: $5,785**

1890-1900 watch, 9K gold, English hallmark, O.F. with beautifully enameled back, O size. **Price: $750**

Watch, picture of back of watch.

(D) (Jewelry Box Antiques)

1890-1910 watch hunting case, yellow gold filled, 6S.   **Price: $395**

Watch shown closed.

(D) (Jewelry Box Antiques)

1900 watch, 14K yellow gold hunting case 6S, 16 jewel Elgin, approx. 1-1/2" dia.   **Price: $1,150**

Front of watch.

1900 watch, 14K yellow gold hunting case, 6S, 15 jewel Elgin. **Price: $1,075**

(D) (Jewelry Box Antiques)

Back view of watch.

Late 1800s watch, 18K yellow gold, open face, key set and wind with fancy hands, approx. 1-5/16".

Price: $695

(D) (Jewelry Box Antiques)

Back side of watch.

(C) (W. Baldwin)

1899 watch, gold filled hunting case, 11 jewels with 3 diamond chips, O's on braided neck cord.   **Price: $450**

(D) (Jewelry Box Antiques)

1907 watch, yellow gold filled, open face Elgin, 15 jewels, approx. 2" dia.   **Price: $395**

1890-1910 watch chain, gold filled, lion's head has pink stone eyes.   **Price: $145**

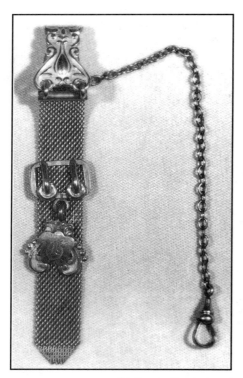

(D) (Jewelry Box Antiques)

1890-1910 watch chain, gold filled, mkd. "FM Co. Belt Buckle Fob."   **Price: $125**

(C) (Lela Reed)

1890-1915 watch chain, gold filled mesh with fob. Fob 3/4" dia.; chain 1/2" x 4" l.   **Price: $125**

(A) (Photo courtesy of Sotheby's, New York 4-10-84)

1914 wristwatch, 18K gold, ladies' half hunting case with 15K flexible bracelet. 1" dia.   **Price: $1,045**

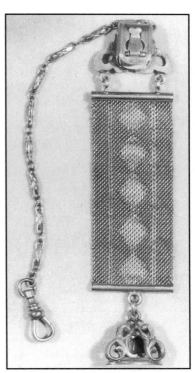

(C) (Lela Reed)

1880-1910 watch chain with locket fob, gold filled, chain 8-1/2" l.; locket 7/8" x 1-1/4".   **Price: $95**

(D) (Jewelry Box Antiques)

Watch chain, pat'd June 17 and Aug. 12, 1902, gold filled with citrine in fob, picture of chain's back showing the mechanism, chain 5-1/2" l.
Price: $125

(D) (Jewelry Box Antiques)

1890-1910 watch chain, gold over copper, note lady's head, 6-1/2" l.
Price: $185

(D) (Jewelry Box Antiques)

1890-1920 watch chain, woven ribbon chain with gold filled slide and swivel, wooden T bar, 1/4" x 8-1/4".
Price: $30

(A) (Photo courtesy of Sotheby's, New York 4-10-83)

1919 wristwatch, 14K gold and enamel rectangular man's "Lady Waltham," 1-3/4" l.   **Price: $880**

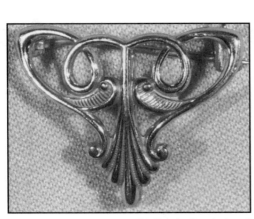

1910-1920 watch pin, gold filled, 1" x 1".   **Price: $125**

(D) (Jewelry Box Antiques)

(D) (Jewelry Box Antiques)

1900-1917 watch chain with locket fob, gold filled, mkd. "S & BL Co."   **Price: $110**

1890-1910 watch fob ribbon, with gold-filled fob. Watch attached to swivel was kept in vest pocket and ribbon and fob hung out, 6-1/2" l. **Price: $40**

(C) (Lela Reed)

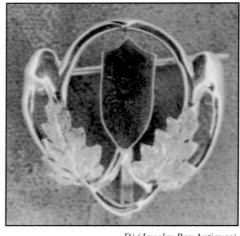

D) (Jewelry Box Antiques)

1890-1910 watch pin, 14K yellow gold multicolor gold leaves motif, approx. 1" x 7/8". **Price: $225**

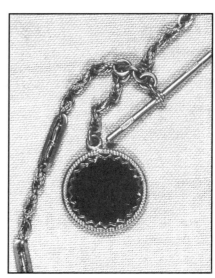

(C) (W. Baldwin)

1890-1915 watch chain, 9K cornelian intaglio, chain 14", fob 7/8" dia. **Price: $475**

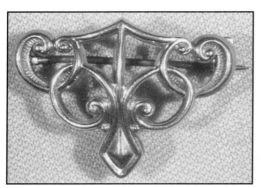

(D) (Jewelry Box Antiques)

1890-1910 watch pin, gold filled, 1" x 1". **Price: $125**

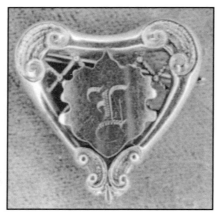

(D) (Jewelry Box Antiques)

1890-1910 watch pin, yellow gold filled with initials, approx. 1" x 1". **Price: $125**

(C) (W. Baldwin)

1885-1910 watch pin, gold filled, 1" dia. **Price: $195**

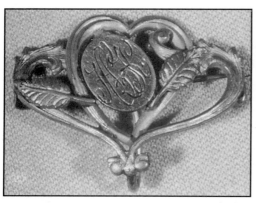

(D) (Jewelry Box Antiques)

1890-1910 watch pin, gold filled green and pink gold, 1-1/4" x 1". **Price: $135**

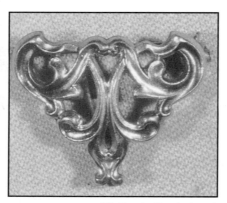

(D) (Jewelry Box Antiques)

1890-1910 watch pin, gold filled, 7/8" x 3/4". **Price: $125**

(D) (Jewelry Box Antiques)

1890-1910 fob, gold filled with "topaz" stone. **Price: $85**

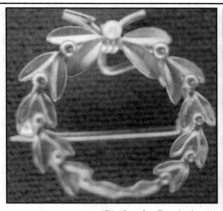
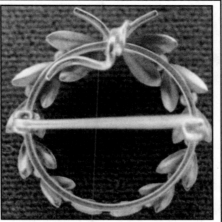

1890-1910 watch pin, 14K yellow gold leaf motif with pearl, approx. 13/16" x 7/8". **Price: $225**

Watch pin's back with hook for watch.

1900-1920 watch pin, gold filled, 1" x 3/4". **Price: $125**

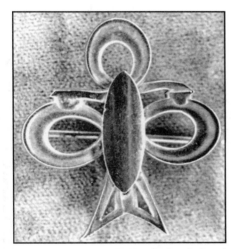

1890s-1910 watch pin, yellow gold filled, approx. 1-1/8" x 1-1/16". **Price: $125**

Watch pin, Art Nouveau, 14K yellow gold with enameled face and pearls, 1-5/16" x 1-3/16". **Price: $850**

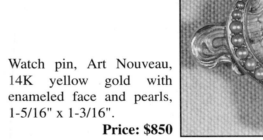

Circa 1910, Henry Capt, Geneve, fine gent's yellow gold split-second chronograph, moon phase, perpetual calendar, minute repeating pocket watch. Case: 18K yellow circular, hinged 4-bodied, case back is personalized with initials. Dial: white enamel, black Arabic numerals, auxiliary seconds dial, aperture for day, date, month, moon phase, auxiliary dials for 30 minutes, yellow "Spade" hands. Movement: rhodiumed, highly jeweled, lever escapement, cut bi-metallic screwed balance wheel, Breguet balance spring. Signed Henry Capt on case, dial and movement. Diameter 53 mm. **Price: $19,550**

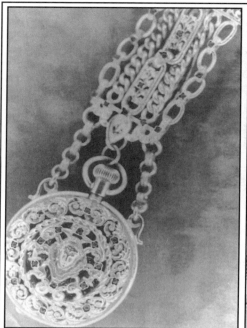

(A) (Photo courtesy of Wm. Doyle Galleries 9-21-83)

Late 19th century pendant/watch and brooch, 18K yellow gold with enamel miniature, Patek Philippe movement, fitted box. **Price: $2,000**

(C) (Cindy Stokes)

1880-1900 chatelaine/watch, yellow gold filled with red and blue stones and open face pocket watch, approx. 6-1/2" l. x 1-1/2" w. Watch is approx. 1-5/8" dia. **Price: $900**

Back view of watch.

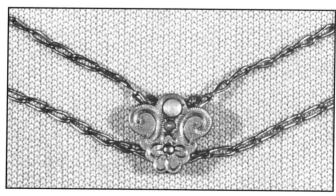

(D) (Jewelry Box Antiques)

1890-1910 slide chain, yellow gold filled, slide has 2 opals and 1 ruby, chain 52" l. **Price: $295**

(D) (Jewelry Box Antiques)

1890-1917 slide chain, yellow gold filled chain with 10K slide, chain 19", slide has garnet and 4 seed pearls. **Price: $295**

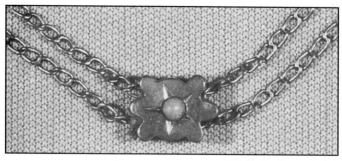

(D) (Jewelry Box Antiques)

1890-1910 slide chain, gold filled, slide has genuine opal, chain 48" l. **Price: $295**

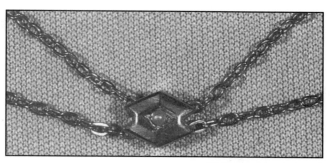

(D) (Jewelry Box Antiques)

1890-1915 slide chain, gold filled, slide with pearl, chain 52" l. **Price: $285**

(A) (Photo courtesy of Sotheby's New York 4-10-84)

1910 pendant/watch, platinum and gold open face watch with translucent blue guilloche enameling centered with a rose diamond, the back rim is set with calibre cut emeralds. The front of the dial is bordered with rose cut diamonds. The piece is suspended from a black ribbon sautior with platinum and rose cut diamond ornaments. Dial is signed "Cartier," and the sautior is signed "Cartier Paris." **Price: $5,500**

(D) (Jewelry Box Antiques)

1905 fob, hallmarked sterling, note garter surrounding dart, target, 1" dia. **Price: $85**

(D) (Jewelry Box Antiques)

Fob, hallmarked sterling, 1901 in England. Originally worn on watch chain, this makes an interesting piece to wear on a chain around the neck, 1-1/4" x 1-3/4". **Price: $95**

(D) (Jewelry Box Antiques)

1880s-1890s fob, 14K yellow gold, approx. 1-1/2" x 1". **Price: $250**

(D) (Jewelry Box Antiques)

1890s fob, 14K fittings with hand-carved lava skull, approx. 3/4". **Price: $295**

1900 pendant/watch & chain, platinum with diamonds and enameling, Majestic Watch Co., 18 jewel movement, necklace spaced with 33 collet-set old European cut diamonds (approx. 2.50 cts), signed "Cartier."
Price: $7,150

(A) (Photo courtesy of Sotheby's, New York 10-5-83)

(C) (Jeanenne Bell)

1880-1890 chatelaine, silver, pin 3-1/2" x 1-1/2"; note pad 1-7/8" x 2-1/2" with celluloid pages noting days of week; key wind watch. **Price: $825**

(A) (Photo courtesy of Sotheby's, New York 10-6-83)

1890s pendant/watch with brooch, 14K yellow gold with 1 pear-shaped ruby and several old European cut diamonds. **Price: $990**

(C) (W. Baldwin)

Fob, Art Nouveau, gold filled, 1-1/4" x 2". **Price: $145**

(C) (W. Baldwin)

1890-1910 slide chain, 14K chain and slide, 1 opal, chain 48" l. **Price: $895**

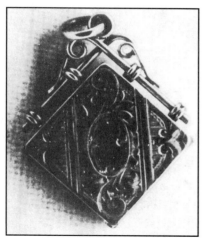

(D) (Jewelry Box Antiques)

1890-1910 fob locket, 14K yellow gold, approx. 1-1/8" x 1".
Price: $295

(D) (Jewelry Box Antiques)

1890-1910 fob, Art Nouveau influences, gold filled with blue, aqua, and garnet stones, 7/8" x 2-3/4".
Price: $155

(D) (Jewelry Box Antiques)

Fob, hallmarked sterling, initial section is 9K gold, 1-1/4" x 1-3/4".
Price: $95

(D) (Jewelry Box Antiques)

1890-1917 slide chain, yellow gold filled, heavy rope chain 48" l., slide has fleur-de-lis motif.
Price: $280

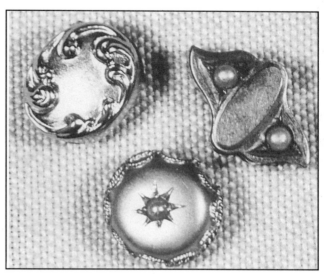

(C) (W. Baldwin)

1890-1917 three slides, gold, average 3/8".
Price: $250 ea.

Miscellaneous

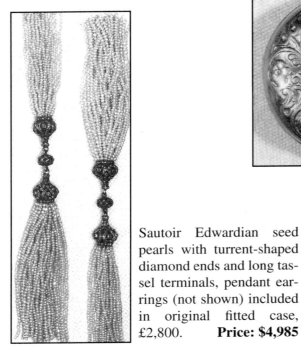

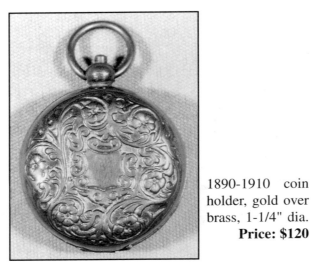

1890-1910 coin holder, gold over brass, 1-1/4" dia. **Price: $120**

Sautoir Edwardian seed pearls with turrent-shaped diamond ends and long tassel terminals, pendant earrings (not shown) included in original fitted case, £2,800. **Price: $4,985**

Belt buckle, Art Nouveau, silver over brass, 3" x 2". **Price: $245**

Art Nouveau, gold lorgnette, 14K yellow gold. **Price: $1,000**

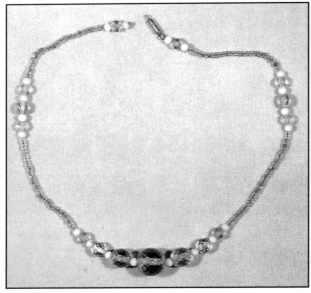

1900-1910 pink glass faceted beads with clear and white, 16" l. **Price: $60**

1900-1920 pressed cut amber beads, 18" l, 5/8" dia. **Price: $225**

(D) (Camille Grace)

Belt buckle dated June 25, 1901, silver, 1-3/4" x 1-1/2". **Price: $120**

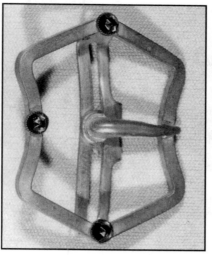

(D) (Jewelry Box Antiques)

1890-1910 buckle, gold over brass with 3 rose cut amethyst color "stones," only 1/2 of buckle.
Price: $15

(D) (Camille Grace)

Buckle pendant, Art Nouveau, mkd. "sterling," originally part of a belt buckle, makes a handsome pendant. 2-3/8" x 3". **Price: $195**

(D) (Jewelry Box Antiques)

1880-1910 card case, silver, beautifully engraved, 2-1/2" x 3-3/4".
Price: $345

(D) (Jewelry Box Antiques)

Chatelaine note pad, Art Nouveau, silver over brass, pad 1-3/4" x 2-3/4".
Price: $365

(C) (W. Baldwin)

1900-1917 compact, sterling, mkd. "Elgin American" on mesh chain, overall length 7-3/4", compact 1-5/8" x 2". **Price: $195**

(D) (Jewelry Box Antiques)

1890-1910 charms, sterling.
Price: $18-$32 ea.

Code in Front of Name

**(A) Auction House -
   Auction Price**
**(C) Collector -
   Collector Asking Price**
**(D) Dealer - Dealer's
   Asking Price**

Early 1900s compact, 14K yellow gold, all hand engraved, approx. 2-1/2" x 3-1/2". **Price: $6,500**

1900 clip, Art Nouveau, gold woman's profile set with several old European cut diamonds. **Price: $880**

1890-1910 eyeglasses, tortoise shell frame, glass, 1-3/8" dia., 3-1/4" l., opened 5". **Price: $125**

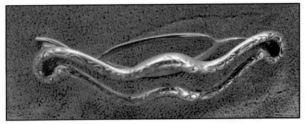

1912 barrette, 12K yellow gold with engraving, approx. 1-3/4" x 3/8". **Price: $180**

1890s lorgnette, sterling silver to wear on a chain around the neck, approx. 2" x 3-3/4". **Price: $26**

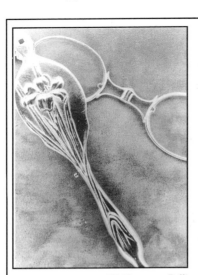

Lorgnette shown open.

1890s lorgnette, yellow gold filled. **Price: $450**

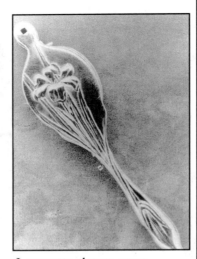

Lorgnette shown open.

(D) (Jewelry Box Antiques)

1910-1920 match case, silver plated, mkd. "Brun Mill Co., Made in U.S.A." Can be worn on a cord around neck or on a watch chain, 1-3/4" x 2-1/2".
Price: $85

(C) (Lucille and Sam Mundorff)

1880-1910 match safe, German silver, 1-3/4" x 2-3/4".
Price: $195

(D) (Jewelry Box Antiques)

1880-1910 match safe, silver over brass, 1-3/4" x 3".
Price: $85

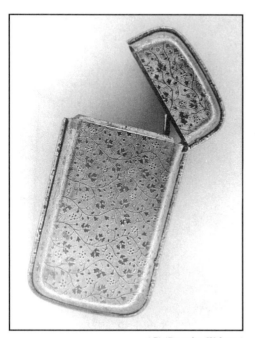

(C) (Douglas Webster)

1880s-1890s match safe, brass, approx. 3" x 1-1/2" x 1/2".
Price: $95

(C) (W. Baldwin)

1890-1910 match safe, sterling, Art Nouveau, 1-5/8" x 2-1/2".
Price: $325

(D) (Jewelry Box Antiques)

Money holder and original chain, pat. 1903, silver over brass, popular for lady bicyclist rider, 1-1/4" dia., original sterling chain.
Price: $260

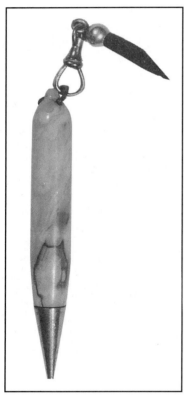

1890-1910 pencil on silk
cord, 1/2" dia. x 2-3/4" l.
Price: $40

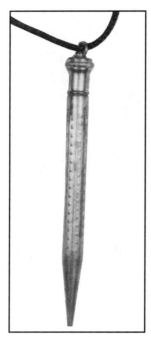

Early 1900s pencil,
gold over brass with
cord, pencil 4" l.
Price: $40

1880-1910 pencil, sil-
ver, hand engraved
monogram and sham-
rocks, 3/8" d x 2-3/4" l.
Price: $60

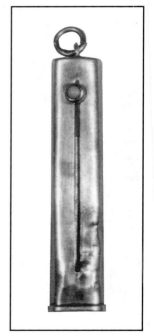

1903 pencil, English
hallmark, sterling, tur-
quoise stone is
punched to reveal
pencil. Worn on cord
around the neck or as
a fob, 1/2" x 2-1/4".
Price: $50

1915 powder box and lipstick case, 14K gold with platinum and diamond medallions. Embellished with translucent deep green enamel over a guilloche ground,
Tiffany & Co. **Price: $1,320**

Early 1900s, fountain pen mkd. "Engle
Pencil Co., N.Y. U.S.A. #26." A nice piece
to hang from silk cord or neck chain, has
14K gold tip, 1/4" dia. x 3-1/2" l.
Price: $45

240

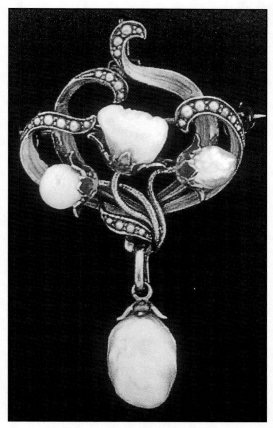

(A) (Photo courtesy of Butterfield and Butterfield, 12/09/98)

14K gold brooch by Bippart, Griscom and Osborn, featuring freshwater and seed pearls set in a floral design, accented with enamel, "torch" maker's mark.

Price: $1,725

(A) (Photo courtesy of Butterfield and Butterfield, 12/09/98)

Diamond, turquoise, gold pendant-locket with longchain suspending one circular pendant-locket, highlighted by an applied cluster center one European-cut diamond, encircled by turquoise cabochons, enhanced by European-cut diamonds, set on an applied yellow and rose gold initial motif, together with one openwork fancy link longchain, all 14K gold, gross weight approx. 103.00 grams, approx. 68 inches.

Price: $1,380

(A) (Photo courtesy of Butterfield and Butterfield, 03/10/98)

Circa 1904, Waltham USA lady's gold, diamond, and ruby pendant watch. Case: 14K yellow gold, circular, hinged 4 bodied, back of case set with 3 European-cut diamonds and one ruby. Dial: gold tone, blue Arabic numerals, blued steel "Louis XVI" hands. Movement: ruby, 15 jewels, lever escapement, cut bi-metallic screwed balance wheel, Breguet balance spring, signed Waltham on dial and movement, diameter 29mm. Watch is suspended from a 14K yellow gold diamond, ruby lapel brooch.

Price: $2,590

Circa 1900 Swiss gold ball pendant watch. Case: 18K yellow gold sphere with raised gold decoration. Dial: white enamel, blue and red Arabic numerals, blued steel "Spade" hands. Movement: wind by turning bezel, set by depressing pin and turning bezel, gilt, jeweled, lever escapement, cut bi-metallic screwed balance wheel, flat balance spring, diameter 17mm.

Price: $1,035

Circa 1770 Vauchez Paris multicolor gold pocket watch. Case: 18K multicolor circular, hinged. Dial: white enamel, black Roman numerals, gold "Louis XVI" hands. Movement: gilt, verge escapement, nonmetallic balance wheel, flat balance spring. Signed "Vauchez" on dial and movement, diameter 38mm.

Price: $1,265

Lady's Art Deco diamond wristwatch, cream-colored dial of rectangular outline, with black Arabic chapters and hands, within a platinum case, enhanced by a diamond bezel, attached to a diamond and simulated sapphire enhanced bracelet, with ribbon attachment, size adjustable, dial, movement Glycine, with fitted case, containing 140 round-cut diamonds.

Price: $4,370

(A) (Photo courtesy of Christie's East, NY, 12/09/98)

(A) (Photo courtesy of Butterfield and Butterfield, 10/30/98)

Pair of Art Deco diamond, black onyx, platinum earrings, Linz. Each black onyx long hexagonal-shaped drop decorated with an applied floral motif highlighted by one marquise-cut diamond, enhanced by European and single-cut diamonds, the drop surmounted by European-cut diamonds applied to a hexagonal and square-shaped black onyx surround; total diamond weight is approx. 3.40 cts., signed Linz.

Price: $13,800

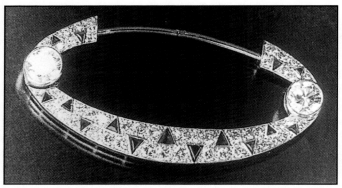

(A) (Photo courtesy of Christie's East, NY, 12/09/98)

Art Deco diamond and simulated sapphire brooch of oval outline, set with diamonds and triangular-cut simulated sapphires, with two circular-cut diamonds gauged at approximately 0.75 ct., mounted in platinum with French hallmarks, Mauboussin, containing 48 circular-cut diamonds.

Price: $7,475

(A) (Photo courtesy of Christie's East, NY, 12/09/98)

Diamond brooch, rectangular outline, designed with openwork foliate, set with diamonds and French-cut simulated sapphires, the central old mine-cut diamond gauged at approximately 0.95 ct., mounted in white gold topped yellow gold (repair evident); containing 90 rose, old mine, old European round and circular-cut diamonds.

Price: $4,020

(A) (Photo courtesy of Christie's East, NY, 12/09/98)

Pair of Art Deco diamond and ruby ear clips. Each designed with a floret enhanced with diamonds and rubies, suspending a modified lozenge of openwork design, set with diamonds and rubies mounted in platinum, containing 6 round and circular-cut diamonds. **Price: $2,990**

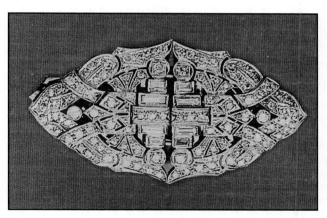

(A) (Photo courtesy of Christie's East, NY, 10/20/98)

Art Deco diamond double clip brooch, each of shield-shaped outline and openwork design, entirely set with diamonds, mounted in platinum, containing 8 baguette and 102 old-mine, old European and round-cut diamonds. **Price: $3,450**

(D) (Jewelry Box Antiques)

Circa 1920s-1930s necklace, 14K white gold die-struck filigree with etched crystal centered with diamond chain, approx. 18" l, drop approx. 1-1/4" x 3/4". **Price: $1,195**

(D) (Jewelry Box Antiques)

Circa 1920s-1930s ring, 14K white gold die-struck filigree set with approx. .65 ct. T.W. of diamonds. **Price: $1,195**
Right: Side view of ring.

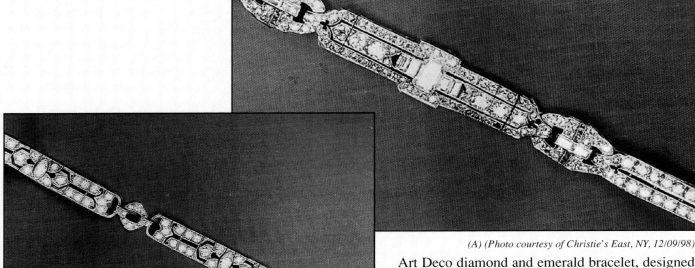

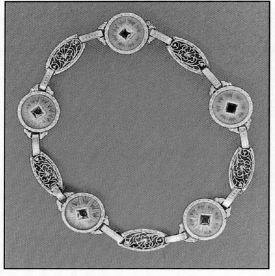

Art Deco diamond bracelet designed as three modified rectangular panels entirely set with diamonds, with diamond enhanced oval spacers, mounted in platinum, containing 3 marquise, and 102 round and circular-cut diamonds. **Price: $5,520**

Art Deco diamond and emerald bracelet, designed as a modified line bracelet, entirely set with diamonds, with emerald accents, mounted in platinum (several diamonds missing), 7-1/4" containing 9 rectangular and 176 round and circular-cut diamonds. **Price: $8,625**

Circa 1920s-1930s bracelet, 14K white gold filigree with Lalique-style etched crystals set with blue sapphire. **Price: $1,295**

Circa 1920s-1930s bracelet, 14K white gold with Lalique-style crystals centered with diamonds. Top plaque approx. 1/2" by 3/4", center drop approx. 1-3/8" by 1", chain approx. 16" l. **Price: $1,295**

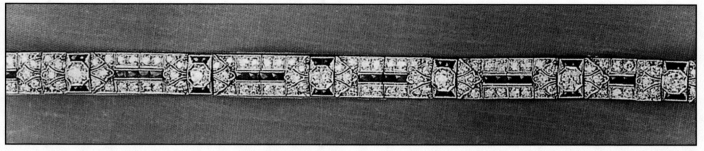

(A) (Photo courtesy of Christie's East, NY, 02/12/98)

Art Deco diamond and simulated sapphire bracelet set with old European and circular-cut diamonds, enhanced by French-cut simulated sapphires, mounted in platinum, containing 114 diamonds. **Price: $5,175**

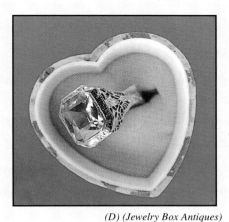

(D) (Jewelry Box Antiques)

Circa 1920s-1930s ring, 14K white gold die-struck filigree with approx. 5.24 cts. Aquamarine. **Price: $995**

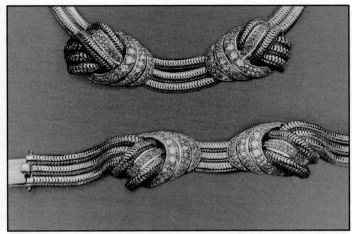

(A) (Photo courtesy of Christie's East, NY, 10/20/98)

(A) (Photo courtesy of Christie's East, NY, 10/20/98)

Retro ruby, moonstone and yellow gold flower brooch, designed as a flower sprig, the petals set with cabochon moonstones with ruby accents, the pistil set with a cabochon ruby, mounted in 14K rose and yellow gold.
Price: $2,760

Suite of Retro yellow gold and diamond jewelry comprising a necklace or yellow tubular snake links, highlighted by two scrolled terminals of pavè set diamonds, 14-1/4", and a bracelet, en suite, 6-1/2" containing 296 round and circular-cut diamonds. **Price: $12,650**

(A) (Photo courtesy of Christie's East, NY, 10/20/98)

Retro sapphire and diamond brooch designed as a stylized flower head, centering a cluster of cabochon sapphires, within a yellow gold sculpted circular frame embellished by diamonds, Trabert, Hoeffer, & Maubousin, containing 12 circular-cut diamonds.   **Price: $2,530**

(A) (Photo courtesy of Christie's East, NY, 06/11/98)

Pair of Retro sapphire and yellow gold brooch clips, each modified rectangular outline, centering invisible set rectangular-cut sapphires, flanked by yellow gold scrolls, the top accented by circular-cut sapphire accents, mounted in 18K yellow gold (with French hallmarks).

Price: $21,850

(A) (Photo courtesy of Christie's East, NY, 02/12/98)

Retro diamond and sapphire brooch bracelet designed as a fixed bangle bracelet, centering a scrolled terminal detaching into a brooch, enhanced by baguette and cabochon-cut sapphires and a pavé set diamond, mounted in 14K yellow gold, Cartier 2175; containing 24 circular-cut diamonds.   **Price: $3,910**

(D) (Jewelry Box Antiques)

Circa 1940s pin, 10K yellow gold, flower motif, approx. 2" x 2".   **Price: $295**

Left: Retro aquamarine, diamond and ruby brooch designed with a floral motif of circular and fancy-cut aquamarines, offset by circular-cut diamonds and rubies, emanating a spray of yellow and rose gold scrolls, containing 19 old mine and old European-cut diamonds.   **Price: $1,840**

Right: Retro aquamarine, ruby and diamond brooch designed as sprays of sculpted rose and yellow gold scrolls, offset by an old European-cut diamond, weighing approx. 1.28 cts., and a rectangular-cut aquamarine, gauged at approx. 40.00 cts., embellished by diamonds and circular-cut rubies (one ruby missing), containing 41 old European, round and circular-cut diamonds.   **Price: $2,070**

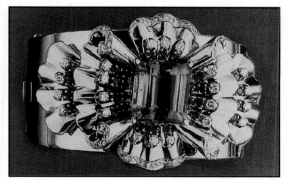

Retro aquamarine, diamond and ruby brooch bracelet designed as a stylized 14K yellow gold bow, centering a rectangular-cut aquamarine, gauged at approx. 24.40 cts., within a diamond and ruby surround, mounted in platinum-topped yellow gold; and a detachable 14K yellow gold hinged bangle bracelet, 7"; containing 22 circular and 40 round-cut diamonds.   **Price: $3,680**

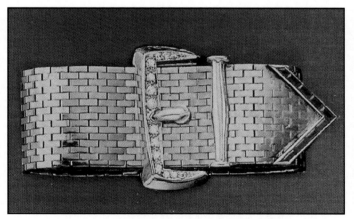

Retro diamond, ruby and gold buckle bracelet designed as a 14K yellow gold brick link bracelet terminating with rectangular-cut rubies, the clasp designed as a diamond enhanced buckle, 8-3/4", containing 14 circular-cut diamonds.   **Price: $2,300**

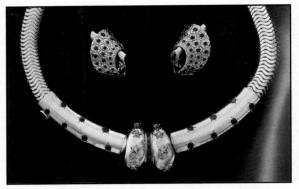

Pair of ruby, 18K gold earrings, signed "Van Cleef & Arpels," reference #6709. Accompanied by a signed Van Cleef & Arpels pouch. **Price: $3,450**

Retro diamond, ruby, 14K gold necklace, gross weight is approx. 125.30 grams, having white-plated accents. **Price: $1,725**

Retro aqua, diamond, ruby, 18K cocktail ring featuring square-cut aquas, ranging from 2-3mm, accented by single-cut diamonds, weighing a total of approx. 1.50 cttw, accented by calibre-cut and cabochon rubies, stones set in platinum. **Price: $1,725**

Diamond, emerald, platinum, cocktail ring, featuring calibre-cut emeralds, highlighted by old mine-cut and single-cut diamonds. **Price: $1,495**

Circa 1950 Swiss lady's multicolor gold, diamond, integral bracelet wristwatch. Case: 14K yellow, white and pink gold, textured bezel set with diamonds and green stones, hinged. Dial: silvered, blued steel "Baton" hands. Movement: nickled, 17 jewels, lever escapement, monometallic screwed balance wheel, flat balance spring. Bracelet: 14K pink gold hinged bangle, safety clasp. Signed "Adler" on dial, width of bezel: 14mm. **Price: $1,265**

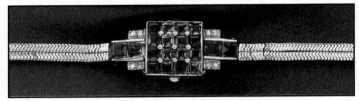

Circa 1950 Swiss lady's gold, amethyst, and diamond covered integral bracelet wristwatch. Case: 14K yellow gold with plated pink accents, cover set with amethyst. Dial: copper color, black Arabic numerals, blued steel hands. Movement: nickled, 17 jewels. Bracelet: 14K yellow gold with plated pink accents, integral double serpent link, safety clasp. Signed "Lucien Piccard" on dial and movement, signed "Paul Ditisheim Solvin" on case. **Price: $747**

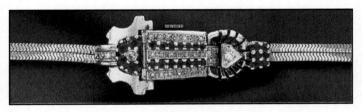

Circa 1940, Bulova Swiss lady's Retro white gold, diamond, ruby-hinged wristwatch. Case: 14K pink gold having plated white accents, hinged cover and lugs set with single and European-cut diamonds and rubies. Dial: pink, black Roman numerals, blued steel hands. Movement: caliber 5AB, nickled, 17 jewels. Bracelet: 14K pink gold with plated white accents, integral serpent link, safety clasp, overall length is 6-1/2", stamped 14K. Signed "Bulova" on dial and movement, width of bezel: 14mm. **Price: $1,265**

Chapter Four: 1920-1930

The American Historical Period

The twenties were years of action and reaction. The word used most to describe this decade is "roaring," but "scandalous," "shocking," and "flaming" are also apt adjectives. The world had survived the war, and a feeling of recklessness prevailed.

When the Eighteenth Amendment made alcohol illegal, it became fashionable to break the law. Speakeasies sprang up overnight, and with them came a new devil-may-care society. The forbidden, the sinister, and the shocking had more allure than ever before. It did not take long for organized crime to become involved in bootlegging. Al Capone and his business associates made headlines. Instead of watching this fiasco with disdain and disgust, many Americans were fascinated and sometimes even envious. The country's values were turned upside down, and the glitter of money was on top of the heap.

"Business" was the by-word of the twenties. Organizations that combined business lunches with service projects flourished. The Lions, Rotary, and Kiwanis Clubs grew at a phenomenal rate. They managed to provide many charitable services that shed a positive light on business. Christianity and free enterprise were combined to everyone's advantage.

In August of 1920, women won the right to vote. This long awaited victory had an emotionally liberating effect, especially on the younger generation. They felt that they were on an equal par with men and should be entitled to all the privileges. They went to barber shops and had their long hair bobbed. Girdles were discarded and dresses were shortened. Lips were painted. If men could smoke and drink, so could they. The emphasis was on youth, and it was indeed flaming.

This reckless craze was also expressed in the popular dances. The loose and uninhibited steps of the Charleston and the Black Bottom were performed across the nation. Dance marathons became the rage, and couples danced for days and sometimes weeks to win the prizes these contests offered.

Automobiles had an increasing effect on the American way of life. Fifteen million new cars were registered between 1920 and 1929. As production rose, the prices declined. By 1924, a Tin Lizzie could be bought for as little as $290. With 470,000 people employed by the automobile industry, the car was becoming a way of life. People who did not even own a bathtub took pride in their new automobile. Travel for pleasure became common. The Sunday drive began to have an effect on church attendance. The older generation was appalled at the freedom the automobile afforded the youth. It initiated a new form of courtship, and condemnation from the pulpit had no influence on its popularity. The older generation was convinced that the world was on the road to hell.

Another innovation was changing the home life—the radio. It had been toyed with by amateurs for a number of years, but when KDKA started broadcasting in November of 1920, the commercial and entertainment value was quickly recognized. Radio manufacturers stepped up production, and sales climbed to almost two million dollars in that year. By 1928, the *Montgomery Ward Company Catalogue* offered nine pages of radios and radio equipment. Table model prices ranged from $85.75 for a six tube, one dial, battery operated set, complete with speakers to $146 for an eight tube, one dial model that included antenna equipment and a drum speaker. The more expensive model plugged into a light socket and promised "no more fussing with batteries, hydrometers, acids, water, and equipment."

All the new owners needed to do was "plug into the light socket, connect antenna, ground the wire and tune in." Radio tables with matching benches, priced at $9.67, $11.35, and $12.95 were also available. If the customer wanted a handsome cabinet model, it was available in a variety of styles:

Spanish ($162.25), Tudor ($196.75), and the High-boy ($203). Of course all items could be purchased for a few dollars more on the Easy Payment Plan.

All the companies were offering merchandise on the deferred payment plan. Why wait to own a new car or radio when for only a few dollars down and a few dollars a month it could be enjoyed now? More and more people adopted this philosophy even though it added to the cost of the item. It was so easy to take advantage of these Easy Payment Plans that many homes were completely furnished on credit.

With the work day reduced to eight hours, there was more time for attending movies and sporting events, listening to the radio, or reading. New magazines were started, and the number of professional authors increased from 7,000 in 1920, to 12,000 by 1930.

Movie attendance continued to increase. Going to the movies at least once a week became an intricate part of life for millions. Movie palaces were built to provide a voluptuous atmosphere for viewing the Kings and Queens of Hollywood. Viewers felt as if they knew the stars personally. When Valentino died in 1926, over 100,000 stood in line to pay their last respects.

Radio and newspapers had a positive effect on sports. Professional players had an opportunity to become instant celebrities. It was a short step from the sports' arena to Hollywood. Babe Ruth, Jack Dempsey, and Gene Tunney were but a few of the many who capitalized on their fame by making movies.

What the country needed was a national hero. When C.A. Lindbergh took off from Roosevelt Field, New York, the flight was covered by radio and newspapers, even though his chances of reaching his destination were slim. America went wild with jubilation when thirty-three and one-half hours later he arrived in Paris, tired and triumphant. He was welcomed home with hero's honors including a ticker tape parade in New York City.

Everybody loves success stories. After hearing how average people made fortunes in the stock market, the general public was eager to try its luck. Housewives shaved money from their household allowance to invest. Instead of putting the money into savings' accounts, people bought stocks, hoping to make their fortune. But on October 24, 1929, the bubble burst. The market went under, carrying with it the hopes, dreams, and fortunes of thousands of people.

The thirties began on a somber note. After the gaiety of the twenties, it was a nightmare. Alan Jenkins described it in his book *The Thirties*, "This was the depression, the slump, deeper than anyone could have imagined, after the Twenties bull market and the 1929 crash; the first middle class poverty that American had ever known, the worst years America went through not excluding two world wars."

In the weeks following the crash, there was hope that conditions would improve. The president refused to admit to the nation just how bad things really were. When it became apparent that the economy was not improving, but actually getting worse, the country realized that something had to be done. Government leaders were adamantly against Americans being put on the "dole," but no one had any ideas about what could be done to relieve the situation.

Then came F.D. Roosevelt and his "new deal." No one really knew what this new deal was, but almost anything would be better than the one they had. Roosevelt won the election by a landslide vote. True to his word, he immediately began to implement new government programs. These programs became known to the people by their initials. The N.R.A. regulated working hours and wages; the C.C.C. employed young men to work in areas of conservation; the P.W.A. financed the programs of the W.P.A. People were employed to do everything from building bridges to entertaining. The nation was working its way out of the economic crisis. Roosevelt's new deal was the right deal.

During this time of economic uncertainty, the radio offered a delightful form of escape. By tuning in Amos n' Andy, people could forget their troubles and laugh. Other comedy favorites were George Burns and Gracie Allen, Fibber McGee and Molly, Edger Bergen and Charlie McCarthy, Jack Benny and Bob Hope. The Lux Radio Theater brought drama into the living room. For those who loved music, there was Kate Smith. In the mind's eye, the listener visualized the performers. These mental pictures became so real that it was sometimes quite a shock to be confronted with an actual photograph of the star.

By 1935, there were more than thirty million radios. The *Sears Roebuck Catalogue* for that year shows that prices had dropped. It pictured, "The most advanced battery operated radio in the world: complete with tubes, batteries, and antenna for only $39.95." It boasted that this radio had a weather band and worldwide reception. A smaller AC-DC table model was priced at $18.95, and an AC electric radio in a beautiful cabinet was only $31.50. These new low prices made it possible for more and more homes to have this wonderful form of amusement. The radio was changing the living habits of America. Schedules were altered to assure time to listen to favorite programs.

Movies were more popular than ever. A double feature complete with newsreel was only a dime, a small price for being transported into a make believe word of glamour, sophistication, and adventure. Stars such as Joan Crawford, Greta Garbo, Jean Harlow, and Mae West were the epitome of sex appeal and glamour. Clark Gable, James Cagney, Robert Taylor, and Tyrone Power caused hearts all over the country to skip a beat whenever they appeared on the screen. Fred Astaire, Ginger Rogers, Bing Crosby, Judy Garland, Mickey Rooney, and Shirley Temple sang and danced their way into the hearts of America.

In a society sadly in need of money, the rich held a fascination all their own. Playboys and debutantes were big news. Papers were filled with descriptions of coming out parties and social events for these select few. The December 27, 1937 issue of *Life* magazine included the article "A Day in the Life of a Debutante." Through a series of photographs the readers were taken through a typical day that began with breakfast in bed and included exciting activities such as sitting for society page photographs, selecting her coming-out dress (a mere $300), and checking off names of eligible bachelors in Juliana Cuttings' famous book. "Because her party was small," stated the article, "with only 300 guests and costing $5,000, only a fraction of the Cutting list was used." A popular definition of a debutante was, "A bare back with lots of 'green backs'."

In the latter years of the decade, a new sound played to a new beat emerged. The sound was big band, and the beat was swing. The new pied pipers were Benny Goodman, Glenn Miller, Jimmy Dorsey, and Artie Shaw. With this new style came jive talk and jitterbugging—a new generation had emerged.

By the end of the decade, America had a new hope, technology. People felt that through science, engineering, and technology the world would become a better place in which to live. DuPont was developing new materials such as nylon and polyethylene. Laboratories were experimenting with sulphur drugs and antibodies. In 1939, The World's Fair opened in New York. It was filled with displays that pointed to a future bright with hope.

Fashions in Clothing & Jewelry

The fashions of the twenties were as erratic as the times. Everything was fast-paced and changing, and this was reflected by the fluctuating styles. Hem lines yo-yoed up and down, waistlines disappeared and then reappeared at the hip line, hairstyles went from long to short and then back to shoulder length—all this in ten short years!

After the war, women experienced an exhilarating feeling of liberation. This feeling was expressed most profoundly by the clothing they wore. Fashion took on a boyish look. The bust was ignored, the figure was sublimated, and dresses became short sacks. By 1925, the hem line was at the knee and sometimes even above it. Hair was cropped off in what was commonly referred to as a "bob." In some styles the back was cut short, but a little length was left at the side to be plastered to the cheek in "spit curls." Cloche hats snugly fit the head so these wisps of hair were the only proof that any existed.

Girls who adhered to the modern styles were known as "flappers." An amusing description of a "Flapper Jane" appeared in the September 9, 1925 edition of *The New Republic Magazine*:

Jane isn't wearing much, this summer. If you'd like to know exactly, it is; one dress, one step-in, two stocking, two shoes. A step-in, if you are 99 and 44/100 percent ignorant, is underwear - one piece, light, exceedingly brief but roomy. Her dress, as you can't possibly help knowing if you have even one good eye and get around at all outside the Old People's Home, is also brief. It is cut low where it might be high, and vice versa. The skirt comes just an inch below her knee, overlapping by a faint fraction her soiled and twisted stockings. The idea is that when she walks in a bit of breeze, you shall now and then observe the knee (which is not rouged - that's just newspaper talk) but always in an accidental Venus-surprised-at-the-bath sort of way. This is a bit of coyness which hardly fits in with Jane's general character.

Jane's haircut is also abbreviated. She wears of course the newest thing in bobs even closer than last year's shingle. It leaves her just about no hair at all in the back, and 20 percent more than that in the front about as much as is being worn this season by a cellist (male)' less than a pianist, and much much less than a violinist. Because of this new style, one can confirm a rumor heard last year: Jane has ears. The corset is as dead as the dodo's grandfather; no feeble Publicity pipings by the manufactures, or calling it a "clasp around" will enable it, as Jane says, to 'do a Lazarus.' The petticoat is even more defunct. Not even a snicker can be raised by telling Jane that once the nation was shattered to its foundation by the shadow-skirt. The brassiere has been abandoned, since 1924. While stockings are usually worn, they are not a sine-qua - nothing doing. In hot weather Jane reserves the right to discard them, just as all the chorus girls did in 1923. As stockings are only a frantic, successful attempt to duplicate the color and texture of Jane's own sunburned slim legs, few but expert boulevardiers can tell the difference.

These which I have described are Jane's clothes, but they are not merely a flapper uniform. They are the style of 1925, Eastern Seaboard. These things and none other are being worn by ladies who are three times Jane's age, and look ten years older; by those twice her age who look a hundred years older. Their use is so universal that in our larger cities the baggage transfer company's one and all declare they are being forced into bankruptcy. Ladies who used to go away for the summer with six trunks can now pack twenty dainty costumes in a bag.

Many people shared this disdain for modern attire. The *Literary Digest* of November 21, 1925, informed that "admittance to the audience with the Pope was recently denied to 32 women and girls, because they were not properly clothed." The Hebrew Union of Orthodox Congregations also passed a "resolution condemning the scant garb of women." These had little effect on fashions. They were worn until they were no longer amusing.

The arts were having an increasingly important effect on design. The popularity of the Russian Ballet had brought with it a profusion of bright colors. Art movements such as Cubism, Favasium, and Futurism influenced fabric designs making geometric prints popular.

Jewelry was used to compliment the dress and soften the effect that short hair had on the features. Dangling earrings, long ropes of beads, and a multitude of bracelets all added to the razzle-dazzle of the outfit. Everything that glittered or dangled captured the imagination. Crystal and rhinestones became fashionable.

There were necklaces to adorn any neckline. Beads combining crystal and jet were dramatic and therefore, fashionable. An illustrated jewelry catalogue for 1923 lists "fine faceted novelty beads" in a choice of imitation jet, blue sapphire and crystal rondel, imitation jet with crystal rondel, transparent ruby, and aquamarine with crystals. The beads were 34 inches long, and the tassels added another four inches. Prices ranged from $1.50 to $3. Today they would cost from $68 to $125.

Amber beads were popular. A twenty-inch necklace of genuine amber in a "clear light color" was priced at only $9, but a twenty-four inch Bakelite bead necklace in the "old amber color" was the same price. Evidently the new Bakelite was highly desirable.

There was an infinite variety of jewelry on the market. An article in *Country Life*, December 1926, comments on this:

Ten years ago the conventional jeweled pin at the height of fashion was the straight bar pin, for it was best suited to the need of the softer blouse and of the frocks which often had V necklines flanked by turned-back collars. Now we see more circles and ovals and use of pearls, as a plain pearl necklace is correct with almost any simple daytime dress. Also, the small plain hat has created the need for jeweled hat ornaments, which were not necessary when hats had more trimming, such as feathers and flowers.

It may also be supposed that this restraint imposed on jewels for daytime by wearing of sports clothes has had something to do with the elaborateness of jewels worn for the late afternoon and evening. We see in the holiday displays more wide jeweled bracelets than those of slender one-stone width, and when the latter are worn they are most often worn in numbers.

Doubtless, too, the prosperity of the present time has something to do with the great variety seen in jewelry. To harken back to the history of civilization, we find always in periods of prosperity jewelry becomes more varied and more specialized in its uses, for people can afford different types for different needs.

By 1927, women were beginning to tire of the masculine look. When Lavin unveiled her new designs for feminine dresses made of soft materials, they were a welcome change. Greta Garbo also had a softening influence. Her starring role in "The Woman of Affairs" caused women to wear slouch hats and to let their hair grow longer.

Designers began to have an impact on clothing for the average woman. Madeline Veornet, Leanne Lavin, and Coco Channel were designers whose creations were known and admired by American women. Reproductions of Channel's jewelry collection adorned her creations. Designers were branching out into all fields of personal adornment. *The Deliniator* of April 1928 makes this growing influence quite clear:

But what have the dressmakers to do with jewelry? Nothing-any more than they have to do with perfume, or powders, gloves or shoes, or hats, bags, flowers or lingerie; but all these — and a great many things besides-they now make and sell because they have found that everything that a woman puts on or uses on her body while she is wearing one of their gowns, enormously affects the chic of the gown. That is why women who buy a Vionnet gown want Vionnet lingerie; or any woman who buys Lanvin sports suit wants the hat that goes with it; or any woman who believes Channel can make a smart gown is equally convinced she can make the smart perfume to accompany it. And now, when she buys her dress, she buys, at the same time and place, the jewels to complete it.

Since the dressmakers have thus summarily taken the designing of jewelry into their own hands, two expected developments have taken place; first, the jewels bear a much closer relation to the gown than formerly; and second, they are not genuine.

Once-not so long ago-no lady worthy of the name would have been caught dead or alive, wearing imitation jewelry. Today even the ladies who have their safety vaults full of genuine stones, have also their complete regalis of imitation jewelry-jewelry so gargantuan and blatant that there is not the smallest pretense that it is genuine. Indeed, that is just where the fun and the chic of the new jewelry comes in. It doesn't consist in a string of pearls so tiny and so meticulously perfect that they really might be real, but in a yard or so of "emeralds" of a size that no real emeralds ever could be; or a yard of "diamond" bracelets up the arm such as the Empress of all the Russians never had. That's the new jewelry!

And all this the dressmakers of Paris have brought about. They have made their perfumes the smartest in the world, beating the perfumers at their own game; and now they bid fair to beat the jewelers at theirs. For no jeweler in the world, not all the Cartiers and Tiffany combined, could turn out jewelry of the stupendous proportions that ladies demand today. After all, there is only one Culliman in all the world, and today thousands of women are clamoring for their Culliman.

Designers created special jewelry for "bathing costumes." There were "painted and waterproofed wooden balls for necklaces, bracelets and earrings!" The article stated, "some people will wear them and no doubt look excessively chic."

It took awhile for this new Paris trend to combine jewelry and clothing designs to filter down to the average woman. However, by 1936, the concept was so highly accepted that the Sears, Roebuck Catalogue featured dresses that came complete with accessories. A "hand smocked dress with matching bracelet and clips" was advertised as the "fashion of the hour", and cost a mere $3.98. The bracelet was described as a "lovely carved bracelet." The clips were of the same color and material. Another "4 star jubilee feature" was a "satin back crepe dress of cleanse with handmade scroll trim." A "stunning pin, bracelet and buckle" came with it. The advertisement stated they were "beautifully carved." They were all most likely made of Bakelite.

A look at a Montgomery Ward's fall 1928-29 catalog gives some interesting insight regarding the average American woman's dress on the eve of the stock market crash. The "featured fashions" were direct from New York and Paris. Hem lines had already begun to drop below the knee. Silhouettes were long with an accent on the hip line. Silk crepe, canton crepe, and silk georgette were popular materials. They came in intriguing colors such as maroon glacé (cocoa), Monet (bright) blue, English (dark) green, Chianti (deep) red, and Claret red. The most expensive dress in the catalog was $24.98. Many styles ranged in price from $9.98 to $15.98. There were even a few dressy dresses in the $5.98 to $6.98 price range.

Wrap coats with fur trim were in fashion. They were all shown with side buttons at the hip line. Raccoon coats were popular. *Montgomery Wards' Catalogue* described them as "the youthful raccoon fur coat which you see on every college campus and at every sports or social gathering of the fall and winter." The price was $265.

The 1928-29 Montgomery Ward catalogue included twenty pages of jewelry. The "latest novelties in necklaces" were crystal, peach, topaz, or sapphire colored stones; a 16" length of composition beads inter strung with gilt beads and a central ornament (1" x 1-1/4") in either sapphire blue, amber, rose, or light green colored glass (98 cents); and "to complete the smart outfit-indestructible pearls, a full 56" long (98 cents).

Pearls were by far the most popular necklace in the 1920s. The perfecting of the cultured pearl caused the price of oriental pearls to decline, but not enough to enable the average working girl to buy them. For her there were the "reproduction" or "indestructible" pearls. The *Montgomery Wards' Catalogue* pictured them in many prices and sizes. A strand of pearls with "a beautiful opalescent hue, carefully matched in color and perfectly graduated in size" was guaranteed not to break, crack, peel, or discolor and was priced at only $9.95. For the more budget-minded customer a 24" length of imported French pearls was priced at $.98.

Pearls were always considered to be in good taste. An essential accessory for a woman's wardrobe, they were worn with both day and evening dresses. The 60" rope was advertised to be "a favorite with our customers." Other standard lengths were 15", 18", 24", and 30".

Many new rhinestone ornaments were pictured in the catalogue. A rhinestone flexible bracelet about 5/8" x 6-1/2" with a white metal back was $1. An oval cameo pin about 1-1/2" x 1-3/4" with three rhinestones on each side was $.79. Belt buckles and shoe ornaments in the modern style were the most pictured rhinestone ornaments.

Synthetic stones were highly advertised. The man-made sapphires and rubies were set in 10, 14, and 18 Karat filigree mountings. Let this be a warning, a stone can be in a lovely 18K gold mounting obviously made in the twenties and still be synthetic. They were advertised to have "all the brilliance, all the hardness of genuine mined stones—the same rich color and the same sparkling luster." Prices ranged from $4.98 to $13.75.

Birthstones were very popular. Most were placed in white gold filigree rings, but they were also available in lavalieres and pins. A filigree "birth month bar pin" in 10K white gold with a "small round stone" was priced at $1.98. Today it would bring 20 to 50 times that. Almost all the birth month jewelry was in white gold because it resembled platinum, which was so popular at the time.

The dramatic look of onyx in a white gold mounting made it a favorite for rings. They were available in 14K gold and usually included a diamond set in the onyx. One ring pictured in this combination was "enhanced by the decorative raised pierced setting that holds the diamond ($12.75)." A more Deco-looking dinner ring described as an "artistic 14K white solid gold ring with genuine black onyx and genuine diamond with an oval-cut center" was priced at $6.98. Again, it would easily be worth 40 times that amount today.

Styles in wedding rings were changing. The gold wedding band had been replaced by one of platinum engraved with orange blossom flowers. For the first time, matching wedding and engagement rings were available. The *J. R. Woods & Sons Catalogue* for 1927 states, "This usually appeals to the prospective bridegroom and insures the sale to him of the wedding ring. Many times the wedding ring can be picked out at the same time as the engagement ring and laid away until just before the marriage. Also at the time it is quite possible to tell the customer about the returning custom of men's wedding rings which should match the brides. Wide-awake jewelers often make three sales instead on one."

By 1928, these wide-awake jewelry companies were combining the wedding ring and the engagement ring into a bridal set. The *Montgomery Wards' Catalogue* pictured four priced from $29.85 (an 18K white gold engraved band, matching engagement ring set with a one-eighth carat diamond) to $166.35 (a solid platinum set that had a 3/8 carat diamond).

In the twenties, the emphasis was on youth. The easiest way to hide the years was to cover them with cosmetics. Elizabeth Arden and Helena Rubenstein capitalized on the craze and became leaders in the industry. Lips were painted a la Clara Bow. Powder and rouge became necessities. "In the year 1929, every American woman bought more than one pound of powder and eight rouge compacts. There were 1,500 brands of face cream and 2,500 different perfumes."[12]

Catalogues pictured "smart new compacts." They were available in round, rectangular, and octagonal shapes, and each had its own little chain handle. The white metal cases were engraved and most had enameled plaques. Inside the compact was a mirror and a place for powder and rouge. Refills could be purchased in most stores.

By looking through the *1931-32 Montgomery Ward Catalogue*, it is very apparent that something had happened to the economy. Prices had dropped drastically! The most expensive dress "direct from the New York opening" was only $3.94. Quite a difference when compared to the $24.98 price in the 1928-29 catalogue.

The catalogue also pictured longer dresses. Throughout the decade, the hemline gradually lowered. In 1931, it was at mid-calf; by the fall of 1933, it had dropped to between the calf of the leg and the ankle.

The biggest influence on fashion in the thirties was Hollywood. People escaped their problems for a few hours by going to the movies. There they were exposed to the newest in fashion, bigger than life on the silver screen. In 1933, Adrian, a fashion designer for Hollywood, stated, "Motion Pictures are becoming the Paris of America. There, when women see the stars in pictures, they can see them as their fashion guides."[13]

Clothing retailers were quick to realize the tremendous influence that the stars had on the American women. The *1931-32 Montgomery Ward Catalogue* featured, "styles worn at Hollywood First Nights." Next to their lovely, "Sun Down frock of luxurious silk canton crepe with graceful shoulder bows of transparent velvet" ($4.74), was a picture of Claudette Colbert, "exotic Paramount star" and an invitation to see her in her newest film "Death Takes a Holiday." With coats advertised to be Hollywoods' favorite was a picture of Helen Twelvetrees, also a Paramount star. Another advertisement assured that, "Hollywood favors smartly tailored sports coats." It featured Marlene Dietrich as "Paramount Pictures tailored queen. See her in 'Song of Songs'."

The *1935-36 Sears Roebuck Catalogue* featured, "autograph fashions worn in Hollywood by the stars." The advertisement for a "lovely smocked dress ($3.98)" claimed to be "a fashion in the wardrobe of the exquisite Hollywood star, Adrienne Ames. Each dress bears her autograph label." In the section that advertised collars, stars such as Ann Southern and Marion Nixon were shown wearing their "autograph fashions." The hat section pictured six hats ($1.69 - $1.98) modeled by their namesake stars. Who could resist the urge to buy one after seeing now smart it looked on the star?

Movie fashions became big business. An article about the Modern Merchandising Bureau in New York City appeared in the January 1937 issue of *Fortune Magazine*. It explained that:

> The work of the bureau consists of providing retail shops with models of hats and dresses worn by the stars of current films, but it is a good deal more complicated than it sounds. First of all, the bureau has to study the stills of coming attractions and figure out what styles are going to be popular. Then it has to arrange with a manufacturer to have them made up before the picture is released. And finally it has to supply retail shops with advertising that mentions the movie from which the model was taken and the theater at which it is playing.

In April of 1937, *National Business* published "A 12,000 Mile Style Parade," by Edgar Lloyd Hampton. He commented on the fact that Hollywood was the "world's style capital" and that young American designers were creating movie fashions that were changing the clothing habits of the nation.

First on the list we might mention the sex dress (that close fitting gown which caused so many automobile accidents back around 1930.) It established a vogue for the tight fitting dress and influenced the styles of the entire world. To a yet greater degree, has the movie influenced the youthful styles of clothes, and for 'girls of every age.'

A specific example of a definitely-created new style was the High-Tie which they put around Clara Bow's waist a dozen years ago, sweeping the flappers of that period into an entirely new vogue. Paris later modified this tie into a narrow girdle involving the waistline of everything from a street suit to an evening gown, and the world forthwith adopted it as its own.

Another example, and it caused our ultra-fashionables to shudder when it appeared upon our streets, around 1924, was a little hat which the younger movie stars wore pushed back against their foreheads. Yet within a year, the smartest thing in the Paris fashion plates was a hat cut close across the forehead and pushed clear back against the hairline.

Slacks were a Los Angeles invention. To create demand, the manufacturer put them on beautiful movie stars, with the studios cooperation, and gave the photographs to the press. As one manufacturer laughingly put it, "They looked so darned cute that every woman wanted them."

The word "chic" became the byword of the 1930's. It was used to describe anything that was "in." "Chic" was the ultimate compliment. Glamorous, swanky, slinky, and stunning were other adjectives that vividly described the mood staged by Hollywood.

Glamourous Jean Harlow was the envy of women everywhere. She made the slink bias cut dress popular. It was worn to proms, weddings, and coming-out parties. Women loved the chance to be feminine again. Backs were rediscovered, and dresses with "intriguing open spaces" in the back became fashion news.

In 1935, Helen Koues wrote this fashion report for *Good Housekeeping Magazine:*

> Our new silhouette again shows full skirts over smooth hips for day and evening wear. Full sleeves for the day, with loose-backed fingertip coats, fitted short coats, and capes - long capes to the floor, short capes to the hips - all with the simplicity that is both feminine and new. Sailor hats are with us again. And

taffeta for morning, noon, and night in patterns varying from tiny strawberries to great modern splashes of color. The evening clothes were never lovelier, never more feminine; ruffles, great sashes, taffetas, and nets; or the scarves of the mysterious East find occidental use. And so women once again, although she flies a plane or runs a motor, goes back to feminine wiles and Furbelaws; but she remains attuned in action to a swiftly moving world in which she plays an ever increasing part in the affairs of men.

The Exposition des Arts Decoratifs in Paris placed an emphasis on modern style that evolved into the Neo-modern School of Dress Designers. According to an article in *The Deliniator* of October 1936, they created clothes that were "logical and inevitable for modern life" and gave them "arresting perfection by harmony, line and fabric." Alix Schiaparelli, Robert Piquet, and Marcel Rochas were named as creators in the new school. Several of their designs for Butterick Patterns were illustrated. One of the dresses had a "swinging hemline fourteen inches off the floor, broad shoulders and a slim waistline." It featured the "new, young, alert silhouette" that was popular. A long dress with "sculptural lines that follow the supple body of the modern woman" was pictured. Its "glistening cire satin falls in the unbelted princess line and the bodice is slit and clasped together with a bowknot clip," stated the article. The coat featured was described as having "princess lines to follow the structure of your body to the waistline and then flare away from your long slender legs." (Did they assume that all women had long slender legs?) The "fullness of the sleeves and wide reverse" were said to "give breadth to the top of the coat above the belted waistline."

Because the economy was depressed and money was tight, the important part jewelry could play in revitalizing on old outfit was stressed. Even though the *1931-32 Montgomery Ward Catalogue* featured fewer dresses and lower prices than in 1928-29, their jewelry section had been expanded. A new dress might cost two or three dollars, but an old one could be dressed up with a new 56" length of "unbreakable imitation pearls" for only 29 cents.

The emphasis was on costume jewelry. Evidently Montgomery Ward had a high concept of costume jewelry. Their 1931-32 catalogue advertised that "the smartest and most attractive of new costume jewelry creations" was made of genuine rock crystals combined with "sparkling genuine diamond centers." The "richness and beauty" of the stones were "further enhanced by the delicate tracery of pierced designs." These Lalique type jewels were set in both 10 and 14 Karat white gold. The 14K pendant was $21.75; a 14K ring $14.85; and a 10K bracelet was $16.50. Today these pieces would cost at least 50 times that amount.

For those who could not afford diamonds, the new smart silver jewelry with real "stones" provided a flashy look. The "real stones" were "genuine marcasites," and their glitter provided the glamorous look dictated by Hollywood designers. The jewelry had a slightly heavier look than that of the previous decade. The long dangling rectangular earrings and necklaces were definitely in the style now referred to as—Art Deco. A necklace on a 15" chain with ear drops and bracelet to match, made of sterling silver and set with marcasites, was priced at $4.48.

Marcasites were also used to surround other stones. Genuine Chrysoprase (jade green), genuine onyx (black), and genuine cornelians (burnt orange) were set in sterling silver and "studded with sparkling real marcasites." These were very popular, and a good many examples are still in existence today. A complete set consisting of a necklace, ear drops, bracelet, and gold ring sold for $7.98. Today, the same set would cost in excess of $450.

If a piece of jewelry was done in the new modern style, this fact was always brought to the attention of prospective buyers. "Another example of pleasing modernism in genuine stone set jewelry" was the "hand-carved genuine stones linked with a washed gold sterling silver chain." They were available in a choice of Rose Quartz, Amethyst Quartz, and Jade. The pendants sold for $2.48, and the bracelets were $5.98. Throughout the decade, the term modernistic was used to describe the styles now referred to as Art Deco.

Not everything was designed in the modernistic style. Several pieces of jewelry listed as "the kind grandmother wore," were illustrated in the 1935-36 Sears Roebuck catalog. The advertisement stated, "Antique designs are new again. Modernized into up-to-the minute accessories. Natural gold color metal with just a trace of black enameling outlining the engraved designs will give a rich added touch to most any costume and has the appearance of much more expensive jewelry." These modernized antique designs could be ordered in bracelets, dress clips, brooches, or button earrings. They could never be mistaken for Victorian pieces. Even with the black enameling they still looked very Deco.

In the September 1934 issue of Country Gentleman, Ruth Hogeland noted that "the quaint old Victorian fashions of using lovely slim ladylike hands with frilled cuffs as ornaments has reached to the costume jewelry field. Now we have beautifully carved composition ones in white or bright colors, serving as clips. They come singly or in pairs." The materials and colors used for these pieces assure that they will never be mistaken for Victorian.

Rhinestones continued to be popular throughout this time period. The *1935-36 Sears, Roebuck Catalogue* called them the "most necessary, useful costume accessories for the fall and winter season." They offered "the newest creations direct from the leading New York Stylists." The designs were "reproduced from high-priced models," and the rhinestones were "set in white platinum-like metal" that was "rhodium finished to prevent tarnishing." Another advertisement made it quite clear that "rhinestones can be worn with any costume-for daytime or evening."

The *Sears, Roebuck Fall and Winter Catalogue* for 1936-37 noted:

> Nothing adds to the costume more than a rhinestone ornament. Adding a brilliant buckle or clip to a dress gives it an entirely new appearance. Sears offers the newest styles, most modern designs, copied from expensive Paris creations. Only the finest rhinestones are used. They are set in highly polished metal mountings, closely resembling platinum.

A flexible bracelet, button earrings, a belt buckle, and dress clips were illustrated. Each piece was $.95. Rhinestones were truly the jewelry for the masses.

"Massiveness is an important note in jewelry," stated an article in *Collier's* for November 11, 1933. "A bracelet set with great square-cut topazes may be echoed by two square topazes that make a ring heavy as a mans. Clips, worn singly or in pairs, to ornament a hat, a bag, or to drape a neckline, are larger than ever."

Clips were a very versatile accessory. They could be worn on the dress, hat, or hand bag. Consequently, they became a necessity for the well-groomed woman. *The Independent Woman* stated in November 1937, "Clips are always good. Newest are the large gold ones, either plain or set with jumbo-sized chunks of bright stones. These clips need not be expensive-just so long as the effect is good."

Costume jewelry designs are indeed an indicator of what has captured the minds, hearts, and imagination of the people. In the 1920s, the discovery of King Tut's tomb made it fashionable to wear jewelry bearing his likeness. Many Egyptian motifs were incorporated into Art Deco designs. When Franklin D. Roosevelt became president of the United States, he and his family became the favorite subject for newspaper and magazine articles. Even his Scotch Terrier, "Fala," was photographed. By 1935 women were wearing pins in the shape of a Scottie. The *Sears Roebuck Catalogue* for that year featured three variations of the "Scottie Dog Pin": one about 2" long with a black carved head in a choice of dull gold or silver color (48¢); another was a "carved design on pressed wood" in an "Ivory-Tan color, size

1-3/4" x 1-1/2" (10¢); the third was enameled in natural colors, size 1-1/2" x 1" (19¢).

Women were intrigued by things from the Orient. Lounging pajamas with an oriental look were worn for entertaining at home. Jewelry made in China, and stones imported from the Orient became very fashionable.

The economy had an effect on ring designs. Smaller diamonds were placed in illusion settings to give them a larger look. In the twenties, wedding bands were often encircled with diamonds, but in the thirties the diamonds were only set across the top. *Business Week*, September 10, 1938, said that diamond imports had been small because jewelers were selling from stock. The article was optimistic because:

> Jewelers are luring the customers back into their shops again with other come-ons. Feminine fashion this year is of course, the jeweler's delight. The ladies are supposed to wear their hair pulled up on their heads this year, and this exposed a large expanse of neck and ear for the jewelers to cover. They're concentrating on such pre-1900 items as pendant, earrings, big necklaces, jeweled combs, barrettes, hairclips, and even (God forbid) tiaras. Gold jewelry set in semiprecious stones, which haven't been around in a number of years, is back on their shelves, and so is flower jewelry.

Art Deco

There is much discussion and confusion concerning Art Deco. Generally it is a term applied to a decorative style of the twenties and thirties. But the term was never used during the time in which the style was popular, thus adding to the confusion.

Perhaps the confusion as to what constitutes Art Deco can be attributed to the many varied influences that combined to produce the style. The Russian Ballet, Cubism, King Tut, the Bauhaus and the Paris Exposition all contributed to the collage that became known as Art Deco.

As in most period styles, the seeds of the style were sewn in the previous decade. When Dieghilev's Russian Ballet Company made its 1910 debut performance in Paris, it won the hearts and imagination of all Europe. The bold colors in the scenery and costumes designed by Leon Balst signaled a liberation of color for the "pastel" world. By the twenties, his bright emerald greens, vivid reds, and shimmering blues (along with his stenciled patterns and luxurious fabrics) had become incorporated into all fields of fashion and design.

Through the set designs of the Ballet Russes, many people were exposed for the first time to "modern art." Cubism and its offspring, orphism, neoplastecism, fauvism, and futurism provided the geometric lines and abstract designs for Art Deco

style. The new art expressed a psychology of design for people living in a modern world filled with action and speed.

When Howard Carter discovered the opening to a tomb in Egypt on November 26, 1922, little did he realize the impact it would have on modern fashion. When the discovery was officially announced three days later, it was publicized throughout the world. Never had there been such a discovery! Newspapers were filled with descriptions of the many ancient objects made of gold. The riches of the young King were almost beyond belief.

By the time the burial chamber was opened in February 1923, King Tut and his world had already influenced fashion and design. Women were wearing Tut hats and jewelry bearing his likeness. Stones used in King Tut's jewelry, lapis lazuli, cornelian, chalcedony became popular. Egyptian motifs such as the falcon, vulture, and scarab were seen on everything from belt buckles to pendants. At first these unusual materials and designs were used in copies of the ancient articles, but it was not long before they were assimilated into the Art Deco style.

Art Deco takes its name from the International Exposition des Arts Decoratifs which was held in Paris in 1925. Nations from all over the world were invited to participate with the stipulation that they submit only those exhibitions executed in new modern designs. Any designs based on styles of the past or that incorporated those styles were strictly forbidden.

The November 1925 *International Studio Magazine* reported on the exhibit. Their opening paragraph gives an insight to the style of the exposition:

> When Cezanne uttered his historic dictum that all form could be reduced to the cone, the cylinder, and the cube, the cornerstone was laid for a movement which had its fullest expression in the International Exposition des Arts Decoratifs in Paris. Cezanne's esthetique, the credo of modern art, was developed simultaneously with the age of scientific research and the glorification of the machine. Both of these are determining factors in the development that we substituted the philosophy of the angle for the curve, that we came to see that the intersection of two planes might be as beautiful as the relation of two colors, and the beauty was as existent in mere mass and proportion as in ornamented shapes. It is due to this that we have learned that designs whose inspirations are the clean lines of the machine may be quite as beautiful as those deriving from animal, human or flower forms. To have absorbed consciously or not this esthetique is a necessary perquisite to an enjoyment and appreciation of the new note for which the International Exposition des Arts Decoratifs stood sponsor.

For hundreds of years, sources from the past had provided inspiration for designs. The time had come for something new.

> Gone are the time-honored motives of the lotus and the fleur-de-lis, the Doric column and the Gothic arch. In their place we are asked to see as beautiful and decorative, angles and geometric designs; instead of ornamentation, flat surfaces and proportioned masses. Gone is all carving and superimposed decoration; interest and variety must depend upon the application of color and flat design, or the quality of beauty existing in the unadorned material.[14]

The exposition also provided tangible evidence of the many influences on modern design. "In the modern decor there are evidences of the Wiener Werksteade, Munich Succession, Swedish and Polish peasant art, English Pre-Raphaelitism and French Cubism," stated the International Studio. It described the exposition as "looking like nothing so much as a Picasso abstraction."

The article acknowledged the importance of the Exposition and stated:

> With the Exposition des Art Decoratifs, a new style is established to take its place with the historic periods. To the Renaissance, the Jacobean, the Georgian, the Rococo and the Colonial is added the Modern. It can no longer be said to be in a state of experimentation representing isolated examples by the more venturesome of the designers. It is a concerted movement representing the fruit of many minds and many years' experience. For the first time there is revealed to the public the spirit and achievement of the whole modern decorative art movement, in the form of architecture, interior decoration, furniture, the arts of the silversmith, the jeweler, the worker in metals, and the designers of textiles and wallpapers.

The exposition became the focal point for the new modernistic designs. They gained world acknowledgment. In the years that followed, the style became more defined.

Knowledge of all these varied influences on the Art Deco style shatters the veil of confusion and makes it easy to identify. Today, almost anything done in the Art Deco style is very collectible. Because of this demand, jewelry can be quite expensive. That is not to say that bargains cannot be found. They can, especially in costume jewelry.

Popular Stones & Materials

Emerald

Emeralds have been popular since before the time of Cleopatra, but their rich green color made them especially desirable for the jewelry of the 1920s and 30s. The gem is at its best when used in the rectangular or square step cut that is also known as the emerald cut. It was well suited to the geometrical shape of Art Deco jewelry designs.

The emerald is part of the beryl group of colored stones. Prized for its medium light to medium dark green color, in larger sizes it is sometimes more expensive than a diamond of the same size. All genuine emeralds have inclusions referred to by gemologists as a "jardin." Often stones of the most desirable color also contain the most inclusions. These are more desirable than a pale stone with little "jardin."

The most beautiful emeralds come from Columbia. They are so esteemed that the finest emeralds from any location are known as Columbian emeralds. Other deposits are mined in Brazil, Rhodesia, Australia, South Africa, and India. In the United States, emeralds are found in North Carolina, Maine, and Connecticut.

Man has always been fascinated by the emerald. In ancient times it was believed that gazing at an emerald would restore eyesight. Many wore it because they believed it would heighten intelligence and help them to save money. Today, it is a favorite birth stone for people born in May, hopefully bringing them success and love.

Ruby

Rubies both genuine and synthetic were widely used in the 1920s and 1930s. Their bold red color helped create the dramatic effect that was so much in demand. The ruby is part of the corundum group of colored stones. To be termed a ruby, it must have a transparent red or purplish red hue. The lighter red stones are known as pink sapphires. "Pigeon's blood" red is the most desirable color and is identifiable by a slight blue cast in the pure red stone. These and other rubies are known as Burmese, regardless of where they were mined. Ruby deposits are found in Burma, Thailand, Ceylon, and Africa. In the United States, they are mined in Montana and North Carolina.

Biblical references attest to the high value placed on the ruby throughout the ages. A large ruby is sometimes more valuable than a diamond of comparable size. The ruby's hardness makes it a practical stone with a multitude of uses.

Fortunate is the person born in July, because the ruby is the birthstone for that month. Wisdom, wealth, and health are but a few of the many blessings that are believed to belong to the wearer of this lovely gem.

Marcasites

In the 1920s and 1930s, the average woman could add glitter and glamour to her life by wearing marcasites. Their reflective sparkles adorned pins, earrings, necklaces, bracelets, clips, and buckles.

The "stone" known as marcasite is actually pyrite (PIE-rite). There is a mineral named marcasite, and, although it is similar in appearance, it is not suitable for jewelry. This case of mistaken identity is now commonly accepted. The iron sulfite, pyrite is cut into small pointed or rounded facets to create marcasites. Since their luster is metallic, their brilliance comes from light reflecting off the facets.

Marcasites were fashionable substitutes for diamonds as early as the 1700s. They were always mounted in silver as were the diamonds of that period. In the mid 1800s, they once again came into favor. The fashion waned until the glittering mood of the twenties revived it again.

Within the last few years, marcasite jewelry has risen sharply in price. Better marcasites are set in and not just glued. Of course, the metal the "stones" are in and the design of the piece are also factors that greatly influence price. There are many new marcasite pieces on the market. Buying from a reputable dealer who will guarantee in writing the age of the piece, is the best assurance for the new collector.

Ivory

Ivory, one of the oldest materials used for ornamental purposes, has been recognized throughout the history of civilization for its beauty and value. In the 1920s a resurgence of interest in African carvings brought with it a renewed interest in ivory.

As most people know, ivory is the tusk of the African Elephant. But many do not realize that the tusks of the hippopotamus and walrus are also classified as ivory. Elephant ivory is distinguishable by its "cross hatched" or "engine turned" look when viewed under magnification. The other ivories have wavy grain lines. Once the ivory has been carved into bracelets, necklaces, and earrings, it is very hard to distinguish its origin.

The so-called vegetable ivories, the coroze nut from South America and the doum-palm nut from Central Africa, are often mistaken for genuine ivory. They are used to make beads and smaller items. A way to distinguish between vegetable and animal ivory is listed in the "Is it Real?" section of this book.

Ivory tends to yellow with age, but according to expert dealer Edward J. Tripp, this only adds to its value. It can be bleached, but this takes away value and beauty. He also cautions against subjecting ivory to extreme changes in temperature that could cause cracking or splitting. Since ivory is porous and is easy to stain, care should be taken to keep it away from anything that might discolor it.

Bakelite

Jewelry made of bakelite was popular during the 1920s and 1930s. This new plastic was invented in 1909 by Leo Hendrick Baekeland (1863-1944). He came up with the resin while trying to develop a new type of varnish.

Bakelite is a phenolic plastic and can be molded or cast. Jewelry items are molded. The name Bakelite is a trade name for the Bakelite Corporation. The same mixture is known as Durez when made by the Durez Company and other names when manufactured by other companies.

~ *Price Guide 1920-1930* ~

Bracelets

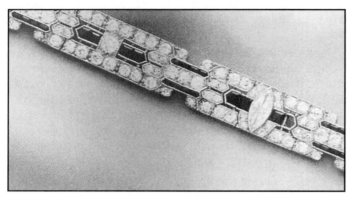

(A) (Butterfield and Butterfield, 10/30/98)

Art Deco diamond, sapphire, synthetic sapphire, platinum bracelet, centering one marquise-cut diamond, enhanced by European-cut diamonds weighting a total of approximately 6.90 cts., further enhanced by single-cut diamonds weighing a total of approximately 1.60 cts., accented by square, shield, and rectangular-shaped natural and synthetic sapphires, set in platinum; total diamond weight is approximately 9.10 cts., measuring approximately seven inches, (evidence of repair, one stone missing). **Price: $11,500**

(C) (Anne Noblitt)

1915-1920s bracelet, silver filigree with topaz stone, 3/8" w. **Price: $195**

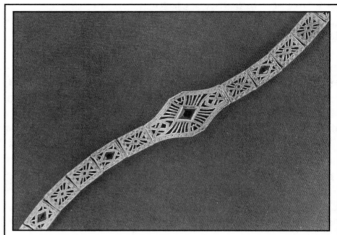

(C) (Carrie Golec)

Circa 1920-1930 bracelet, sterling silver die-struck filigree, set with citrines, made by "Simmons," approx. 1/2" x 7-1/2" l. **Price: $350**

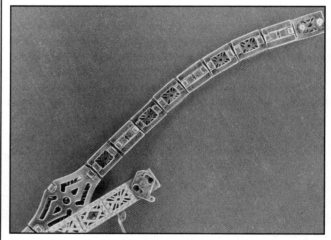

Back of same bracelet showing unusual snap safety clasp patented by "Simmons."

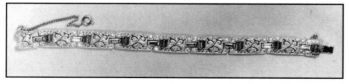

(D) (Jewelry Box Antiques)

1920-1930 bracelet, rh. finished white metal, 1/2" x 7". **Price: $225**

(D) (Jewelry Box Antiques)

1920-1930 bracelet rhinestones set in bow motif, 1" w x 6-3/4" l. **Price: $145**

(D) (Jewelry Box Antiques)

1920s-1930s bracelet, silver over brass clasp, faceted black and crystal beads with opaque glass beads, 7" l. **Price: $30**

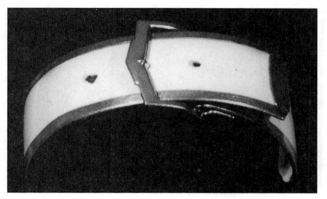

(D) (Jewelry Box Antiques)

1920s bracelet, gold over brass with cream-colored celluloid insert, 3/4" wide. **Price: $50**

(D) (Jewelry Box Antiques)

1920s-1930s bracelet, 10K white gold filigree set with diamond and 2 sapphire baguettes. **Price: $895**

(D) (Jewelry Box Antiques)

1920s-1930s bracelet, 10K white gold filigree set with crystal centered with one .15 ct. diamond. **Price: $1,200**

(D) (Jewelry Box Antiques)

1920s-1930s bracelet, white gold filled with sapphire blue paste stone approx. 1" wide. **Price: $195**

(D) (Jewelry Box Antiques)

1920s bracelet, copper with black enameled ground and pink, green, orange, yellow, and white flowers, 1" x 7". **Price: $85**

(C) (W. Baldwin)

1920s-1930s bracelet, .830 silver, mkd. Georg Jensen, 7/8" w x 7-1/4" l. **Price: $850**

(C) (Silvia Goldman)

1920s-1930s bracelet, 10K white gold filigree set with .53 ct. diamonds and sapphires. **Price: $1,950**

(D) (Jewelry Box Antiques)

1920s bracelet, sterling fittings with 3 rows of imitation pearls strung on sterling chain, 7". **Price: $55**

(C) (W. Baldwin)

1915-1920 child's bracelet, white metal with glass ruby, hinged bangle, 1/4" w. **Price: $60**

(D) (Jewelry Box Antiques)

1920s bracelet, silver with engraved designs, 5/8" x 6-1/2". **Price: $95**

(D) (Jewelry Box Antiques)

1930s gold over brass bracelet, place for 2 pictures, 2" x 1-3/4". **Price: $60**

(D) (Jewelry Box Antiques)

1930 bracelet, silver over brass bangle, 1" w. **Price: $70**

(D) (Jewelry Box Antiques)

1925-1935 bracelet, rhinestones with blue baguette stone, nicely done, 3/8" x 7" l. **Price: $125**

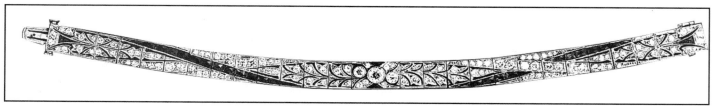

(A) (Photo courtesy of Sotheby's, New York 10-5-83)

1925 bracelet, platinum pierced mounting set with round and old European-cut diamonds and 27 calibre-cut sapphires.
Price: $3,850

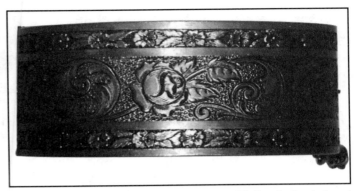

(D) (Jewelry Box Antiques)

1930-1940 bracelet, Bakelite hinged, 1-1/8" w.
Price: $175

(D) (Jewelry Box Antiques)

1930-1940 bracelet, gold over brass, hinged bangle with safety and black enameling, 1" w.   **Price: $95**

(A) (Photo courtesy of Sotheby's, New York 10-19-83)

1925 bracelet, Art Deco, gold and platinum with black enamel and diamonds, Cartier, Paris.
Price: $6,600

(A) (Photo courtesy of Sotheby's, New York 12-7-83)

1937 bracelet, platinum and white gold centered with one large cabochon emerald and Arabic inscription. Buckle motif set with 184 diamonds (approx. 10 cts) and 48 calibre-cut emeralds.   **Price: $14,300**

(D) (Camille Grace)

1930s bracelet, mkd. sterling Germany, marcasites with chrysoprase, 3/4" x 7-3/4".   **Price: $350**

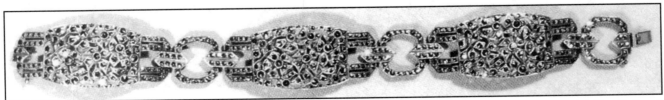

(D) (Camille Grace)

1930s bracelet, silver and marcasites, mkd. "Made in France," 7/8" x 7-1/2".   **Price: $325**

Bracelet, Art Deco, white gold square arched panels set with diamonds and citrine. £3,000. **Price: $5,340**

1920-30s pair of hinged bracelets, white metal with black enameling and silver ornamentation, oval shape, 1" w. **Price: $150**

1930s-1940s bracelet, white metal set with rhinestones, 1" x 7" approx. **Price: $95**

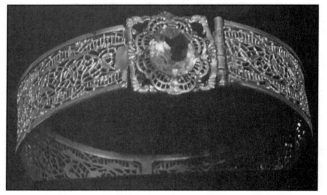

1920s hinged bracelet, silver plate filigree with pink glass "stone," 5/8" w. **Price: $195**

1921 hinged bracelet, English hallmark, sterling, 3/8" w, heavy. **Price: $165**

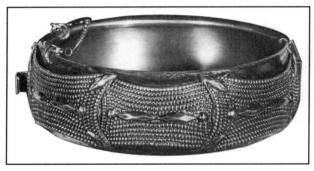

1920s hinged bracelet, gun-metal with imitation cut-steel design, 1" w with safety chain. **Price: $50**

1920-1930 hinged bracelet, gold filled with Wedge-wood-type center, 3/4" w. **Price: $95**

Multicolored stone bracelet, white gold containing lapis, onyx, carnelian, amethyst, citrine, jade and one hundred and thirty six assorted small round diamonds approx. total 5 cts. **Price: $16,000**

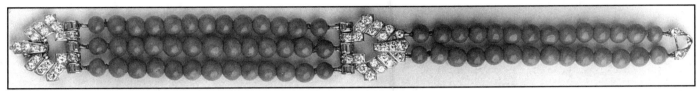

Bracelet, Art Deco, three rows and two rows of coral beads, mitre-shaped diamond divider and clasp, in fitted case by "Cartier," £2,400. **Price: $4,270**

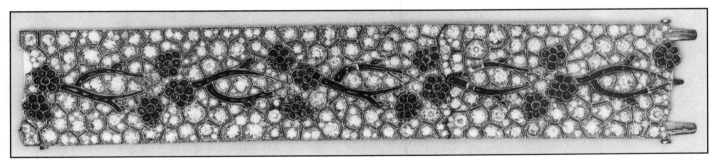

Bracelet, Art Deco, white gold set with numerous brilliants and decorated with green paste cabochons and onyx, £7,800. **Price: $13,885**

Bracelet, Art Deco, gold with center diamond approx. 3.5 cts, panels set with diamonds and "French" cut sapphire batons, £7,000. **Price: $12,460**

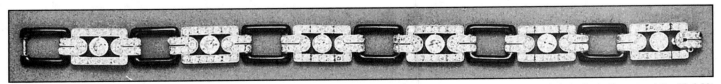

1925 bracelet, gold with black enamel and diamonds, £4,180. **Price: $7,440**

Brooches / Pins

(A) (Butterfield and Butterfield, 10/30/98)

Diamond, sapphire, black onyx, platinum brooch, designed as a ship featuring full, single, baguette, and square-cut diamonds, enhanced by buff-top calibre-cut sapphires, accented by square-shaped black onyx, further accented by black onyx cabochons, completed by triangular-shaped ruby and sapphire flags, set in platinum; total diamond weight is approximately 1.70 cts., (one black onyx cabochon missing). **Price: $5,750**

(D) (Jewelry Box Antiques)

Circa 1920s-1930s brooch, white gold die-struck filigree with approx. .35 cts. TW diamonds, approx. 2-7/8 long. **Price: $750**

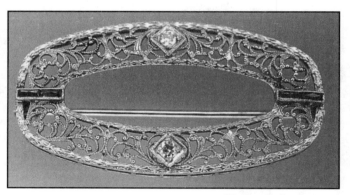

(A) (Photo courtesy of Skinner, Inc., Boston, Mass 9-25-90)

Art Deco-style brooch, Egyptian motif, cabochon-cut sapphire and set with diamonds, emeralds and rubies in 18K. **Price: $1,700**

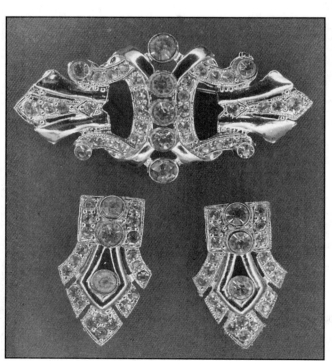

(C) (Anne D. Roberts)

Circa 1930s and 1940s brooch/clip combination white metal set with rhinestones overall, approx. 3-1/4" x 1-3/4." Clips only 1-3/4" x 3/4", clips fit into holes on either side of brooch to form more complete piece. **Price: $250**

(D) (Jewelry Box Antiques)

Circa 1920s-1930s brooch, 14K white gold filigree with diamond and sapphires, approx. 1-1/2" x 3/4". **Price: $595**

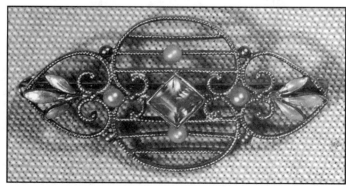

(C) (W. Baldwin)

1915-1920s brooch, 14K yellow gold with peridot and enameling, 1-3/8" x 3/4". **Price: $250**

1920 brooch platinum and gold set with 2 carved jade leaves spaced by scroll motifs embellished with round and single cut diamonds. **Price: $715**

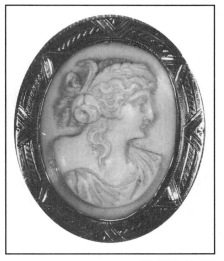

(C) (W. Baldwin)

1915-1920s brooch, 10K yellow gold, pink coral cameo, 1-1/4" x 1-5/8". **Price: $600**

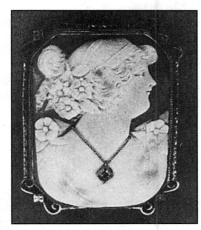

(D) (Jewelry Box Antiques)

1912-1920s cameo, white gold filigree mounting set with hand-carved shell cameo wearing diamond necklace, 1-1/2" x 2" dia. **Price: $800**

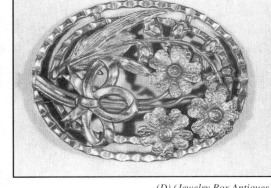

(D) (Jewelry Box Antiques)

1920-1930 brooch, gold over brass, 3" x 2-1/2". **Price: $40**

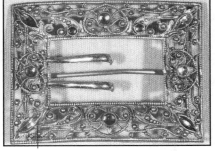

(D) (Jewelry Box Antiques)

1920-1930 brooch, gold over brass with colored "stones," 3-1/2" x 2-3/4". **Price: $60**

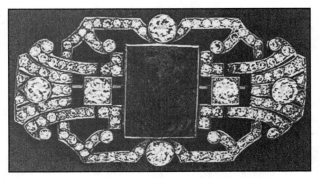

1920 brooch, platinum centered with a lapis lazuli cameo of a soldier with helmet, embellished with old European cut diamonds. **Price: $1,980**

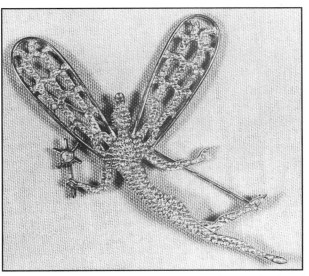

(D) (Camille Grace)

1920s brooch sterling with rhinestones, Tinkerbell, 3-1/8" x 2-1/2". **Price: $195**

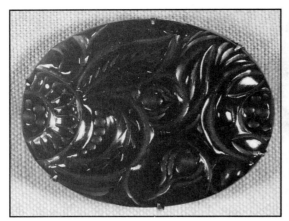

1920s-1930s brooch, mkd. "sterling Germany," chrysoprase stone, 1-5/8" x 1-3/4".
Price: $195

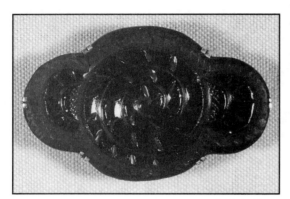

1920-1930 brooch, mkd. "sterling Germany," cornelian, 1-7/8" x 1-1/4".

Price: $245

1920s-1930s brooch, white gold filled set with crystals, 2-3/4" x 1/2".
Price: $95

1920s-1930s brooch, sterling bezel with nicely done shell cameo, 1-1/4" x 1-5/8".
Price: $325

1920s brooch, sterling, Denmark with enameling, 1-1/4" dia.
Price: $225

1920s brooch, gold over brass, Venetian glass mosaic, done in older style, 1-1/2" x 1-1/8".
Price: $115

1930 brooch, platinum mounting alternately set with 6 square-cut sapphires and 9 old European cut diamonds (approx 1.50 cts). Marcus & Co.
Price: $1,540

1930 brooch, platinum "Arc-De-Tri-umphe" motif topped by a half-moon-shaped diamond (approx. 1.50 cts) and further set with a total of approx. 4.20 cts of diamonds, Cartier, Paris. **Price: $10,450**

1920s brooch, mkd. "sterling made in England," glass cover over plastic figure with shining blue background, 1-1/2" dia. **Price: $145**

(D) (Jewelry Box Antiques)

(A) (Photo courtesy of Sotheby's, New York 12-7-83)

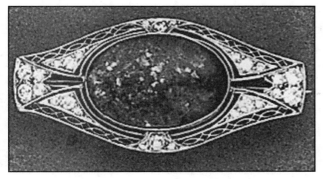

(A) (Photo courtesy of Sotheby's, New York 12-7-83)

1930 brooch, platinum openwork mounting centered with oval black opal (approx. 5.50 cts), embellished with diamonds, Marcus & Co. **Price: $3,850**

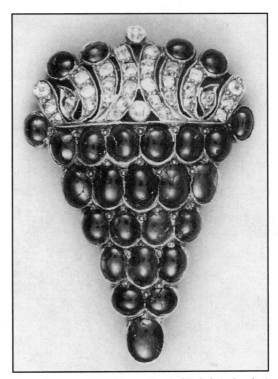

(A) (Photo courtesy of Sotheby's, London)

(A) (Photo courtesy of Sotheby's, New York)

1930 brooch, platinum with oval crystal centered with a carved opal depicting a group of grape harvesters, on each side is a platinum band set with calibre-cut sapphires and old European cut diamonds, Wadderien. **Price: $4,400**

1930 brooch, stylized bunch of grapes set with cabochon rubies and rose-cut and brilliant-cut diamonds, £935. **Price: $1,665**

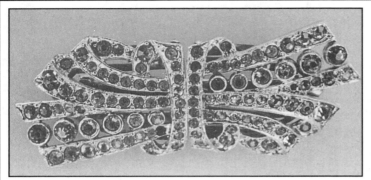

1930s-1940s brooch white metal set with rhinestones, dress clip duet pin, 1" x 2-3/8". **Price: $200**

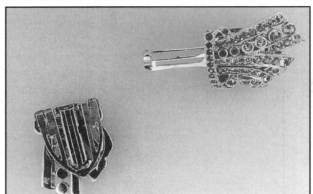

Brooch shown with one dress clip removed to reveal mechanism.

1930s brooch, gold over brass with amethyst-colored glass stones, 2-1/2" x 3". **Price: $85**

1930s brooch, mkd. "sterling silver German," enameled flower with marcasites, 2" x 1-3/4".
Price: $145

1930s brooch, silver over white metal chrysoprase and marcasites, 2" x 1-5/8". **Price: $190**

1930s brooch, silver with marcasites and aquamarine colored stone, 2" x 1". **Price: $245**

(C) (W. Baldwin)

1930s brooch, mkd. sterling, 1-7/8" x 1-1/2".
Price: $225

(D) (Camille Grace)

1930s brooch, sterling, marcasites. **Price: $135**

(C) (W. Baldwin)

1930s brooch sterling, chrysoprase, 1-3/4" dia. **Price: $225**

1930s brooch, silver over base metal, imitation marcasites, 2-1/8" x 1-5/8". **Price: $40**

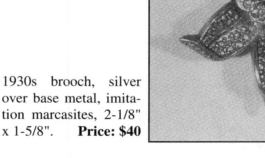

(D) (Jewelry Box Antiques)

(A) (Photo courtesy of Sotheby's, New York 12-7-83)

1930s brooch, Art Deco, platinum set with rubies, sapphires, emeralds, and black onyx. Oriental-style bird on a flowering branch, branches highlighted with black enamel. **Price: $9,350**

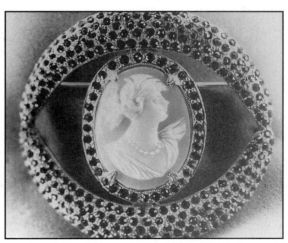

(D) (Jewelry Box Antiques)

1930s brooch, white metal set with brilliant and hand-carved shell cameo, originally was a decorative button, approx. 2-1/2" x 3".
Price: $180

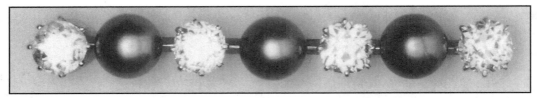

Brooch, Art Deco, black enameled with alternating old brilliant-cut diamonds & black Oriental pearls, £5,500. **Price: $9,790**

Brooch, Art Deco, carved rock crystal vase with a floral bouquet of diamonds, rubies, emeralds and sapphires. Individually numbered, £2,600. **Price: $4,630**

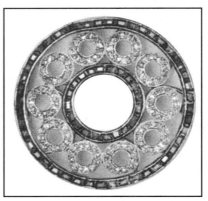

Brooch, Art Deco, gold hoop with emeralds and sapphires with smaller hoops of diamonds in between. £2,000. **Price: $3,560**

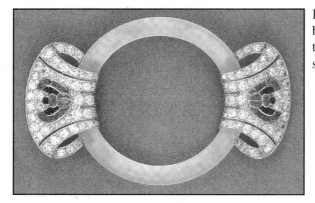

Brooch, Art Deco, platinum with center ring of crystal flanked by pavé set diamond scrolls decorated with Egyptian-style beetle motifs set with rubies, emeralds and black onyx. Fitted box stamped J. Chaumet, Inc., France. **Price: $11,500**

Brooch, Art Deco, white gold pavé set with old cut and rose-cut diamonds, calibre-cut sapphires (some synthetic) set in Grecian key design, £1,900. **Price: $3,380**

1930s brooch and earring set, white metal painted navy blue with blue glass "stones," brooch 2-1/4" x 3"; earrings 5/8" x 1-5/8". **Price: $65**

(D) (Jewelry Box Antiques)

1915-1920s brooch/pendant, 10K yellow and green gold with pink coral cameo, 1-1/2" x 1-3/4".
Price: $600

(D) (Jewelry Box Antiques)

1915-1920s brooch/pendant, 10K yellow gold mtg., shell cameo, 1-1/4" x 1-5/8".
Price: $485

(C) (W. Baldwin)

1915-1920s brooch/pendant, 14K coral cameo, 1-1/2" dia.
Price: $550

(D) (Camille Grace)

1915-1920s brooch/pendant, 14K yellow gold, coral cameo, 1-1/2" x 1-5/8".
Price: $500

(C) (W. Baldwin)

1920 brooch/pendant, 10K yellow gold mtg., shell cameo, 1-3/8" x 1-3/4". **Price: $525**

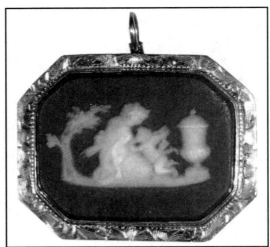

1915-1925 brooch/pendant, 10K Wedgewood, 1-1/8" x 7/8". **Price: $425**

(D) (Camille Grace)

Code in Front of Name

(A) Auction House - Auction Price
(C) Collector - Collector Asking Price
(D) Dealer - Dealer's Asking Price

Brooch/pendant, Art Deco, 1/12 10K gold filled; new gold filled chain, 1" x 1-1/4" overall. **Price: $40**

(D) (Jewelry Box Antiques)

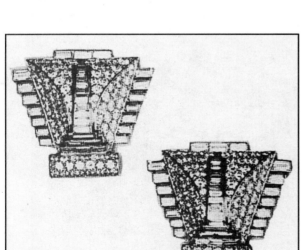

(A) (Photo courtesy Phillips, London 1-24-84)

Double clip brooch, Art Deco, white gold with diamonds by Cartier, £5,400. **Price: $9,610**

Double clip brooch, Art Deco, white gold with circular, step-cut and kite-shaped aquamarines and diamonds. Le Roy et Fils. £1,600. **Price: $2,850**

(A) (Photo courtesy Phillips, London 10-18-83)

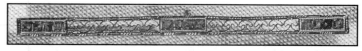

(C) (W. Baldwin)

1915-1920s bar pin, 10K white and yellow gold with synthetic sapphire, 2-1/4". **Price: $195**

(C) (W. Baldwin)

1910-1920s bar pin, 10K yellow and white gold with pearls and peridot, 2-3/8". **Price: $225**

(C) (W. Baldwin)

1920s bar pin, 14K white gold filigree, 2" l. **Price: $225**

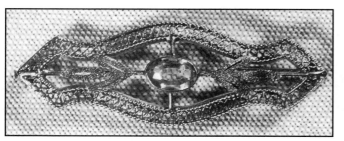

(C) (W. Baldwin)

1915-20s bar pin, 10K yellow gold filigree with pin stone, 1-1/2" x 5/8". **Price: $145**

(C) (W. Baldwin)

1915-1920s bar pin, yellow and white gold filigree with synthetic sapphire, 2-1/2". **Price: $295**

(D) (Jewelry Box Antiques)

1920s bar pin, sterling and brilliants, 2-1/2" x 1/8". **Price: $95**

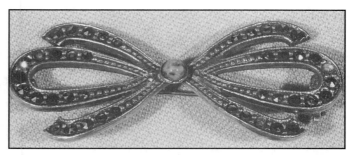

(D) (Jewelry Box Antiques)

1920s-1930s bow pin, silver mtg. with marcasites and turquoise center stone, 1-7/8" x 3/4". **Price: $145**

(D) (Jewelry Box Antiques)

1920s pair of pins, gold over brass mtgs., paintings on porcelain, reflect Florida land boom of the 1920s, 1" dia. **Price: $95**

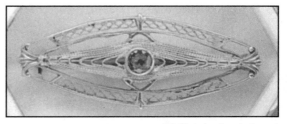

(D) (Jewelry Box Antiques)

1912-1920s pin, 10K yellow gold filigree set with peridot stone, 1-5/16" x 9/16" approx. **Price: $195**

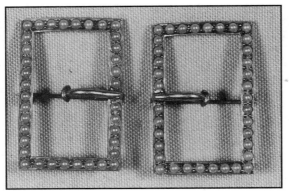

(C) (W. Baldwin)

1915-1930 pair buckle pins, sterling silver with pearls, 1" x 1-3/8". **Price: $110**

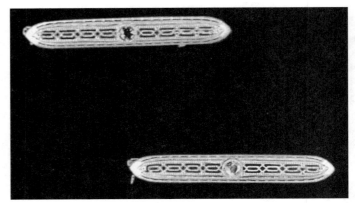

(D) (Jewelry Box Antiques)

1912-1920s pair of beauty pins, 14K white gold top and yellow gold backs, filigree set with blue sapphire, 1-1/8" x 1/8". **Price: $190 pair**

(D) (Jewelry Box Antiques)

1912-1920s pin, white gold filled filigree set with faux pearl and blue sapphire paste stone, 2" x 3/16" approx. **Price: $95**

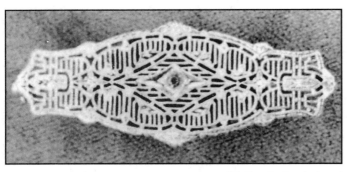

(D) (Jewelry Box Antiques)

1915-1920s pin, sterling silver with paste brilliant, 1-3/4" x 3/4", approx. **Price: $115**

1920-1930 pin, copper over base metal, Egyptian motif, 1-1/4" x 1-1/2". **Price: $30**

(D) (Jewelry Box Antiques)

(D) (Camille Grace)

1920-1930 pin, mkd. "China" with hand-carved cornelian stone, 2-1/8" x 7/8". **Price: $165**

(D) (Camille Grace)

1920s-1930s pin, silver over copper, mkd. "China," hand-carved lapis stone, 2-7/8" x 1-1/4". **Price: $150**

284

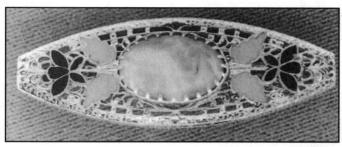

1920s pin, white gold filled filigree with enameling and green paste stone, 1-15/16" x 3/4", approx. **Price: $135**

1925-1930 pin, mkd. 10K, Egyptian motif with marbleized glass scarab and baroque pearls, 2" x 1-1/4". **Price: $245**

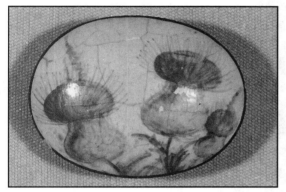

1930-1940 pin, wood, hand-painted, to wear on beach, 2" x 1-1/2". **Price: $40**

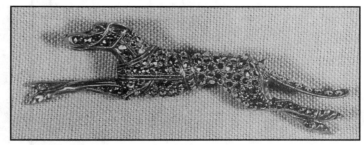

1930s pin, sterling, marcasites, greyhound showing popular speed motif of Deco style, 2-1/4" x 5/8". **Price: $195**

1930s pin, white metal, lizard design with imitation marcasites, red glass eyes, 2-3/4" l. **Price: $60**

Late 1930s pin, sterling, Dutch girl with umbrella, 1-5/8" l. **Price: $95**

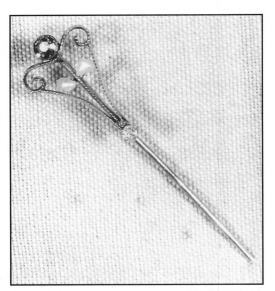

(C) (W. Baldwin)

1905-1920s scarf pin, gold with amethyst, pearl, and 1 diamond. **Price: $145**

(D) (Jewelry Box Antiques)

1920-1930 pin locket, gold over copper with basse-taille enameling, green ground with pink flowers, 1-1/2" x 2-1/2". **Price: $95**

(D) (Jewelry Box Antiques)

1915-1920s scarf pin, white metal with brilliant and dark blue enamel trim. 3/8" dia. **Price: $65**

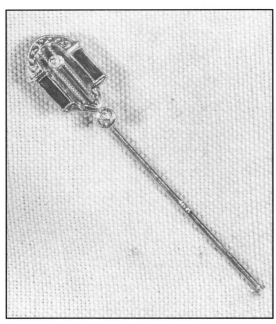

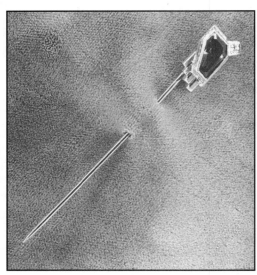

(D) (Jewelry Box Antiques)

1930s stick pin, 14K white gold set with synthetic sapphire and diamonds. **Price: $170**

(C) (W. Baldwin)

1915-1920s scarf pin, white gold, 2 sapphires, 1 diamond. **Price: $175**

Buckles

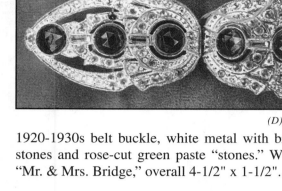

1920-1930s belt buckle, white metal with brilliant-cut rhinestones and rose-cut green paste "stones." Worn in the movie "Mr. & Mrs. Bridge," overall 4-1/2" x 1-1/2".   **Price: $150**

1920-1930 belt buckle, cut-steel with velvet inserts, 2-1/2" x 3".   **Price: $80**

1930s belt buckle, cut-steel, 2-1/2" x 1-7/8".   **Price: $95**

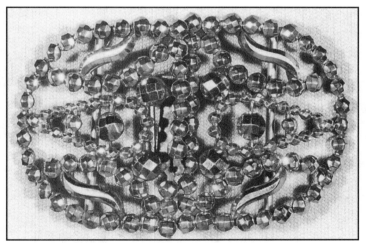

1930s belt buckle, cut-steel, 2-3/4" x 1-3/4".   **Price: $75**

1930 belt buckle, white metal mkd. "B," rhinestones, 2-1/2" x 1-3/4".   **Price: $85**

Earrings

(D) (Jewelry Box Antiques)

1920-1930 earrings, gold filled, mkd. Czechoslovakia, blue molded glass, 1" x 2" l. **Price: $55**

(D) (Jewelry Box Antiques)

1920-1930 earrings, gold over brass filigree with imitation coral flowers, 5/8" x 1-3/4". **Price: $40**

(D) (Jewelry Box Antiques)

1920-1930s earrings, gold over brass with imitation lapis, mkd. Czechoslovakia, 5/8" x 1-3/4" l. **Price: $80**

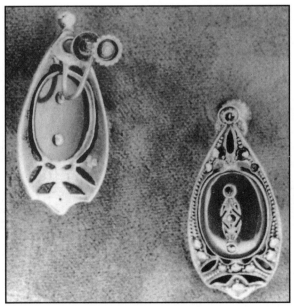

(D) (June O'Donnell)

1920-1930 earrings, sterling silver set with cornelian and marcasites, screw backs, approx. 1/2" x 1/2". **Price: $195**

(D) (Jewelry Box Antiques)

1920-1930s earrings, white metal, butterfly wings, approx. 3/4" x 9/16". **Price: $65**

1920s earrings, Art Deco, silver with marcasites, 1-1/2" l. **Price: $125**

1920s earrings, faceted crystal with new 14K wires, 3/8" x 1/2" l. **Price: $95**

1925 earrings, jade, onyx and diamonds, drops are carved jade, links are composed of rose-cut diamonds. Top hoop is onyx, £495.

Price: $880

1925 earrings, jade, onyx and rose-cut diamonds, £825. **Price: $1,470**

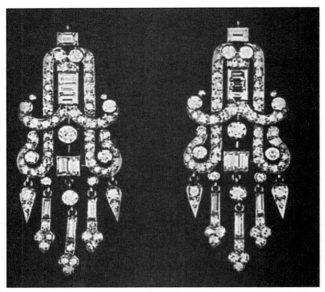

(A) (Photo courtesy of Sotheby's, Parke Bernet & Co.)

1925 earrings, white gold Girandole design, decorated with round and baguette diamonds (lacking fittings), £3,080. **Price: $5,480**

(D) (Jewelry Box Antiques)

1925-1930s earrings, gold filled, blue marbleized glass, 1" x 1-7/8". **Price: $55**

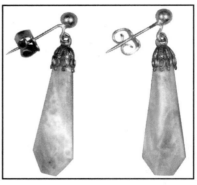

1930s earrings, gold filled mountings with marbleized green glass drops, new gold posts, 1-5/8" l. **Price: $30**

(D) (Jewelry Box Antiques)

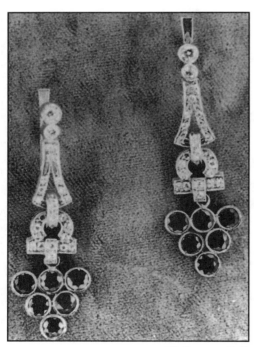

(C) (Jeanenne Bell)

1930s earrings, 14K white and yellow gold set with 3.34 cts. blue sapphire and 1.12 cts. diamonds. **Price: $3,250**

(D) (Jewelry Box Antiques)

1930s earrings, gold-filled mtg., agate drops, new 14K gold posts, 1-7/8" l. **Price: $95**

Lavaliere

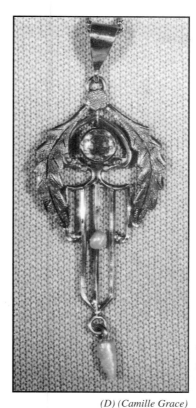

(D) (Camille Grace)

1910-1920s lavaliere, 14K yellow and green gold with rubies and pearls, 1-3/8" x 1-1/2".
Price: $450

1915-1920s lavaliere, 10K white gold with aquamarine and pearls, 5/8" x 1-3/4".
Price: $425

(D) (Camille Grace)

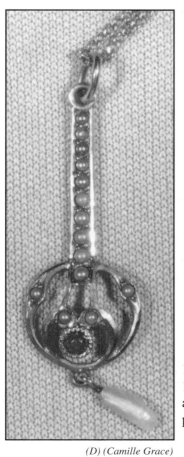

1915-1925 lavaliere, 10K yellow gold with amethyst and seed pearls. 1-1/2" x 1-3/4".
Price: $295

(D) (Camille Grace)

(D) (Jewelry Box Antiques)

1915-1925 lavaliere, 10K yellow gold with sapphire and baroque pearl, original 14" chain, 1-3/8" x 1-1/2".
Price: $280

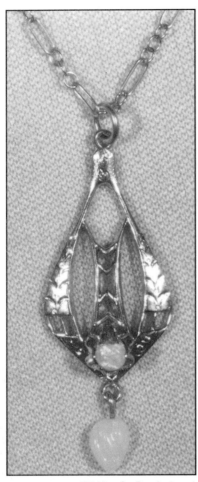

1915-1925 lavaliere, gold filled with genuine opal and baroque pearl on new gold filled chain, 3/8" x 1-1/2". **Price: $125**

(D) (Jewelry Box Antiques)

1920s-1930s lavaliere, 10K yellow gold with peridot, 3/4" dia. **Price: $225**

(D) (Camille Grace)

(A) (Photo courtesy of Sotheby's, New York 10-5-83)

1920 lavaliere, platinum kite-shape mount centered with 1 marquise-shaped diamond (1.20 cts) and 2 old European cut diamonds (approx. 1ct). Also embellished with 9 smaller old European cut diamonds and calibre-cut rubies. **Price: $2,860**

Lockets

(D) (Jewelry Box Antiques)

1915-1920s locket, gold over brass with original black ribbon, 1/4" x 2".
Price: $115

(C) (Anne Noblitt)

1920-1930s locket, gold filled, 2" dia. **Price: $115**

(D) (Jewelry Box Antiques)

(D) (Jewelry Box Antiques)

1920-1930s locket, gold filled, mkd. S.B. & Co., 2 red stones surrounded by clear stones. 1-5/8" dia. **Price: $125**

1930-1940 locket, gold over brass on new gold filled chain, 1" x 1-1/4". **Price: $60**

(D) (Jewelry Box Antiques)

1925-1930s locket, gold filled, mkd. "F & B.," 1" dia. **Price: $115**

(C) (Susan Berstrand)

(D) (Camille Grace)

1930s locket, silver, black enameling on original chain with marcasites, 30" l. **Price: $365**

Circa 1910-1920s locket, sterling silver enameled with a lavender background, dragonfly maker's mark, 1-1/4" dia. **Price: $295**

Necklaces

(D) (Jewelry Box Antiques)

1915-1920s baby necklace, yellow gold filled with new gold filled chain. **Price: $55**

(D) (Jewelry Box Antiques)

Circa 1920s-1930s necklace, 14K white gold, double links with an onyx and diamond drop, chain approx. 18 in. long, drop approx. 1" x 1-1/2". **Price: $1,695**

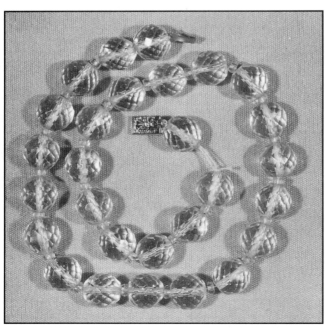

(D) (Jewelry Box Antiques)

1920-1930s beads, faceted crystal beads, 16" l x 1/2" dia. **Price: $145**

(D) (Jewelry Box Antiques)

1920-1930 beads, gold over brass clasp, jet beads, 17" l. **Price: $150**

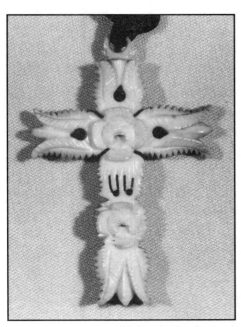

1920-1930 cross, hand-carved ivory on silk cord, 1-3/4" x 2-1/2".

Price: $95

1920s beads, cherry amber graduating from 8mm to 1/2", overall length 23".

Price: $575

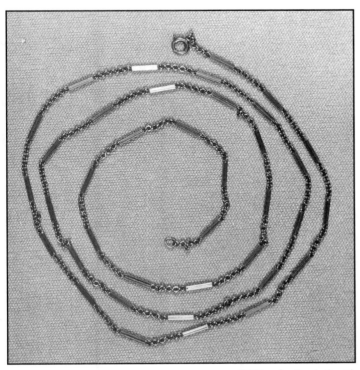

1915-1920s chain, 10K yellow gold (heavy), 25" l.

Price: $245

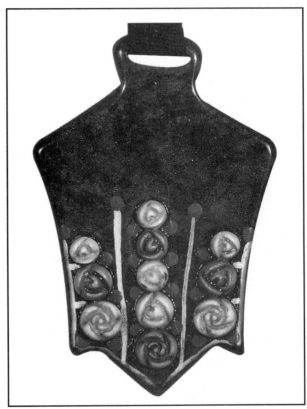

1920s necklace, celluloid, 1/2" x 2-1/2".

Price: $40

1920 necklace, silver filigree with blue stones in drop, chain 16" l, drop 1" x 1-1/2". **Price: $225**

1920s faceted jet and crystal beads, hand knotted, 54" l. **Price: $190**

1915-1920s necklace, 10K white gold with some yellow gold, shell cameo and pearls, 1/2" x 5/8", original chain. **Price: $445**

1920 necklace, platinum openwork set with old European cut diamonds and 2 pear-shaped sapphires (approx. 9 cts). The chain is set with 49 collet-set diamonds (approx. 5 cts), detachable pendant, Black, Star & Frost Co. **Price: $9,000**

1920-1930 necklace, chain with drop of clear plastic with imitation jet cameo of plastic, chain 28" l, drop 2" w x 2-1/2" l. **Price: $95**

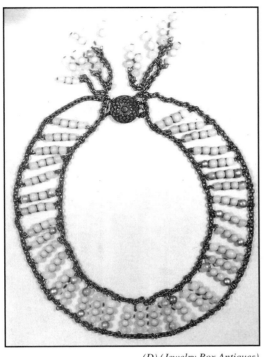

(D) (Jewelry Box Antiques)

1920-1930 necklace, gold over brass with imitation pearls and coral, 1-1/4" w x 16" l.
Price: $60

(D) (Jewelry Box Antiques)

1920-1930 necklace, silver over brass, opaque green "stone" with imitation pearls, 18" l. **Price: $60**

(D) (Jewelry Box Antiques)

1920-1930 necklace, gold over brass with imitation pearls, 32" l.
Price: $40

(D) (Jewelry Box Antiques)

1920-1930 necklace, hand-carved bone, approx. 9-1/2mm. **Price: $70**

1920-1930 necklace, sterling, lapis and marcasites, chain 18" l, drop 7/8" x 2".
Price: $295

(C) (W. Baldwin)

297

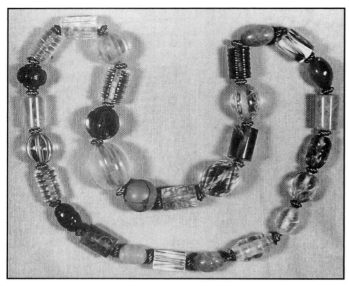

(C) (W. Baldwin)

1920-1930s necklace, beads of cornelian, amethyst, rose quartz, rock crystal, jade, turquoise, Peking glass, hand carved, 21" l. **Price: $525**

Code in Front of Name

(A) Auction House - Auction Price
(C) Collector - Collector Asking Price
(D) Dealer - Dealer's Asking Price

(D) (Jewelry Box Antiques)

1920-1930s necklace, gold filled on 28" gold filled chain, drop 1-1/4" x 2". **Price: $30**

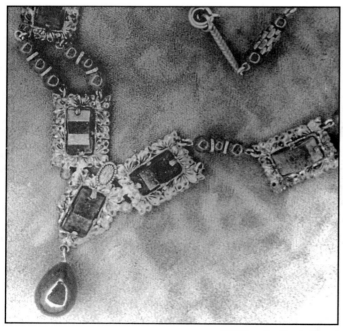

(D) (Jewelry Box Antiques)

1920-1930s necklace, gold over brass with imitation lapis stones, approx. 24" l. **Price: $150**

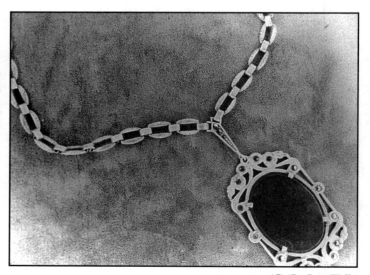

(C) (Dr. Betty Walls)

1920-1930s necklace, sterling silver set with chrysoprase and marcasites on original 16" sterling chain, pendant approx. 2" x 1-1/4". **Price: $245**

(C) (W. Baldwin)

1920s necklace, 10K white and yellow gold with blue stone and pearls, length 15", drop 1-3/8" x 1".
Price: $445

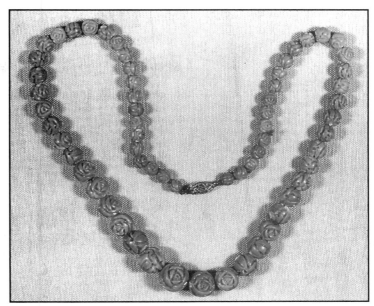

(C) (W. Baldwin)

1920s necklace, 14K clasp, carved coral flower beads, 17" l.
Price: $400

(C) (W. Baldwin)

1920s necklace, crystal drop, 1" x 2", necklace length 18-1/2".
Price: $275

(D) (Jewelry Box Antiques)

1920s necklace, faceted crystal glass drop on silver-plated chain, 16" l.
Price: $185

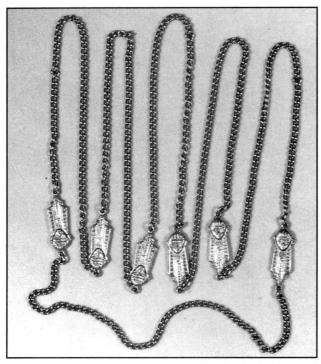

(D) (Jewelry Box Antiques)

1920s necklace, gold over brass chain with 6 King Tuts, chain 52" l, tuts 3/4" x 1-1/8". **Price: $65**

(D) (Jewelry Box Antiques)

1920s necklace, made of carnival glass beads with end tassels, necklace approx. 62" L and approx. 6mm diameter. **Price: $195**

(D) (Jewelry Box Antiques)

1920s necklace, gold over brass with celluloid cameo, 1" x 1-1/4". **Price: $20**

(D) (Jewelry Box Antiques)

1920s necklace, silver chain with celluloid imitation ivory, 18" l. **Price: $30**

(D) (Jewelry Box Antiques)

1920s necklace, silver over brass, glass "stones" with white cameo heads, 15" l.   **Price: $65**

(D) (Jewelry Box Antiques)

1920s necklace, silver over brass, large blue glass drop, some blue enameling, chain 25" l, drop 1-1/4" x 2" l.   **Price: $170**

(C) (Margaret Sorrell)

1920s necklace, sterling filigree on new 16" chain, paste stones, 3/4" x 1-1/2".   **Price: $140**

(D) (Jewelry Box Antiques)

1920s necklace, sterling filigree with black onyx drop, 3/4" x 1-1/8".   **Price: $175**

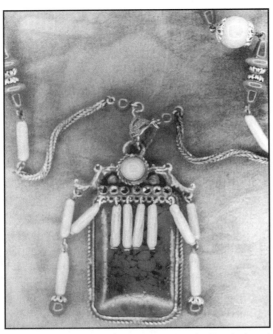

(D) (Jewelry Box Antiques)

1920s necklace, yellow gold filled with clear, pink and blue glass, approx. 18" l with 5 dangles ranging in length from 2-1/2" to 3-1/4". **Price: $190**

(D) (Jewelry Box Antiques)

1925-1930s necklace, jade green Bakelite drop with imitation marcasite on dog, new sterling chain, drop 1-3/4" x 1-1/2" L. **Price: $125**

(D) (Jewelry Box Antiques)

1925-1930s necklace, plastic used to imitate carved ivory, 16" l. **Price: $40**

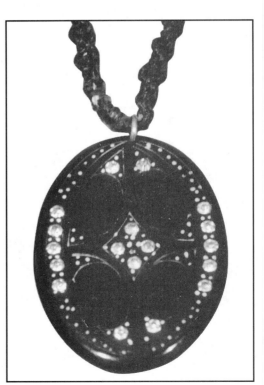

(D) (Jewelry Box Antiques)

1925-1930s necklace, plastic with rhinestones on original hand woven cord; cord 39" l, drop 1-3/8" x 2". **Price: $95**

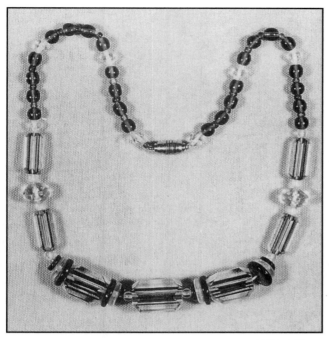

(C) (W. Baldwin)

1928-1930s necklace, glass, amethyst, and crystal, 15" l. **Price: $175**

1930 necklace, Art Deco, 5.3mm-8.4mm jade beads (93) with a carved jade Buddha seated on a lapis base mounted in a platinum and 18K white gold. Further embellished with one oval-shaped cabochon emerald, 3 fancy-shaped carved emeralds and blue enamel.

Price: $7,700

(A) (Photo courtesy of Sotheby's, New York 12-7-83)

(D) (Jewelry Box Antiques)

1930 necklace, oxidized metal with large blue glass "stones," and small ones in colors of pink, green, topaz, and brilliant, 1-1/2" x 2-1/2". **Price: $30**

(C) (Kate Throneberry)

1930 necklace, gold over brass chain with cornelian and pearls, chain 19" l. **Price: $80**

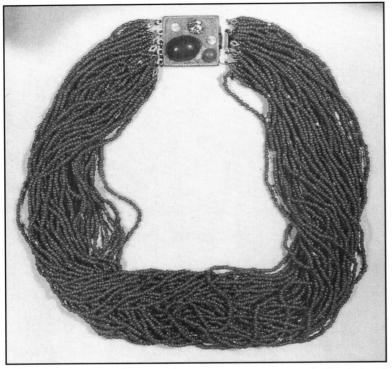

(D) (Jewelry Box Antiques)

1930s necklace, 40 strands of small hand-cut beads, lapis blue color, note clasp, approx. 2" x 18" l. **Price: $125**

(A) (Photo courtesy of Sotheby's, New York 4-10-84)

1930 necklace, platinum chain 56" long decorated with 30 rubies and 29 small diamonds. **Price: $4,125**

Code in Front of Name

(A) Auction House - Auction Price
(C) Collector - Collector Asking Price
(D) Dealer - Dealer's Asking Price

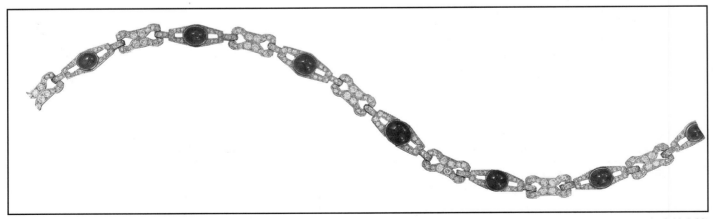

(A) (Photo courtesy of Sotheby's, New York 10-5-83)

1930 necklace, platinum choker set with 9 cabochon rubies (approx. 23 cts) and 316 old European-cut diamonds (approx. 9.15 cts). **Price: $24,000**

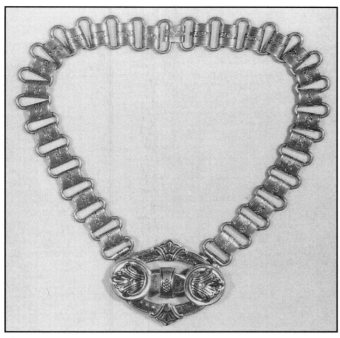

1930s necklace, gold over white metal, place for 2 pictures, chain 16-l/2" x 1-3/4". **Price: $125**

1930s necklace, silver over brass with blue glass and small black rondels strung on wire, overall length 15-1/2" l; drop 1-3/4" x 1-1/4". **Price: $65**

1930s necklace, sterling with hematite and marcasites, chain 15" l, drop. 7/8" x 1-3/4". **Price: $325**

1930s necklace, small hand-cut black bead strands woven together, 3/4" w x 15" l. **Price: $80**

Necklace, Art Deco, plastic with marcasites on original cord complete with slide, cord 35" l, drop 1-1/2" x 3". **Price: $185**

(D) (Jewelry Box Antiques)

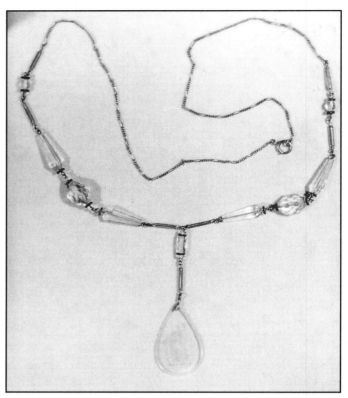

(D) (Jewelry Box Antiques)

1920s pendant necklace, silver over brass chain with clear and green glass, drop had design etched into back, 1" x 1-5/8", overall length 31". **Price: $165**

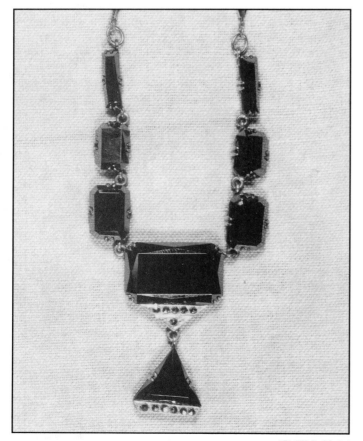

(C) (W. Baldwin)

Necklace, Art Deco, sterling with hematite and marcasites, 16" l, center drop 3/4" x 1-1/2". **Price: $295**

(D) (Camille Grace)

1930s necklace, drop, silver mtg. shell cameo with marcasites, 3/4" x 1". **Price: $285**

306

Pendants

(C) (Kate Throneberry)

1920s necklace pendant, celluloid with colored flowers, 1-3/8" x 1-6/8". **Price: $55**

(D) (Jewelry Box Antiques)

1920-1930s pendant, white metal set with imitation blue sapphire and brilliant, approx. 1-1/4" x 1". **Price: $95**

(D) (Camille Grace)

1930s pendant, mkd. "sterling Germany," marcasites and chrysoprase surrounded by black enamel, 7/8" x 1-1/2" l. **Price: $325**

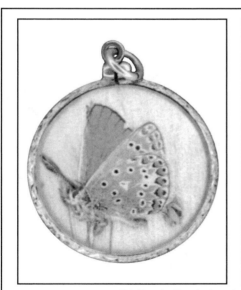

(D) (Jewelry Box Antiques)

1915-1920s pendant, yellow gold filled with butterfly behind glass, approx. 1" dia. **Price: $145**

(C) (Susan J. Berstrand)

1910-1920s perfume bottle pendant, sterling silver with enameling. **Price: $250**

Rings

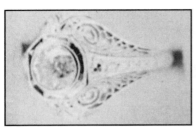

(D) (Jewelry Box Antiques)

1900-1920s ring, platinum filigree set with approx. 1.50 cts total weight of diamonds. **Price: $3,400**

(D) (Jewelry Box Antiques)

Circa 1920s-1930s ring, 14K white gold set with three aquas. **Price: $695**

(D) (Jewelry Box Antiques)

Circa 1920s-1930s ring, 14K white gold set with nevette-shaped ruby.
Price: $425

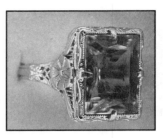

(D) (Jewelry Box Antiques)

Circa 1920s-1930s ring, 14K white gold filigree with green gold and pink gold embellishments, set with amethyst.
Price: $695

(D) (Jewelry Box Antiques)

Circa 1920s-1930s ring, 14K white gold filigree set with synthetic ruby.
Price: $395

(C) (W. Baldwin)

Ring, 14K white gold filigree and almadine garnet. **Price: $495**

(C) (Patricia Horton)

1910-1920s ring, platinum filigree set with approx. 1.37 cts. total weight of diamonds. **Price: $2,450**

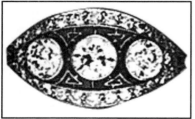

(C) (Barbara Adams)

Circa 1920s-1930s ring, 14K white gold, flip-style. Ring can be worn with shell cameo exposed or flipped over to reveal an onyx and diamond top. **Price: $995**

Ring in process of being flipped.

Same ring with onyx top exposed.

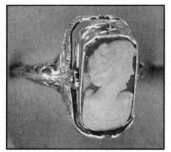

(A) (Photo courtesy of Sotheby's, New York 12-7-83)

1920 ring, platinum mounting set with 3 old European cut diamonds and 27 small old European cut diamonds (1 missing). **Price: $1,320**

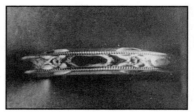

(D) (Jewelry Box Antiques)

1920-1930s ring, 14K white gold band with engraving (old store stock).
Price: $195

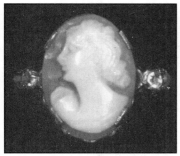

(D) (Jewelry Box Antiques)
1920-1930 ring, 14K R.G.P. shell cameo and 2 white stones, 1/2" x 5/8".
Price: $95

(C) (Denise Johnson)
1920-1930s ring, 14K white gold filigree embellished with yellow gold and set with cabochon-cut lapis.
Price: $595

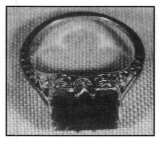

(C) (W. Baldwin)
1920-1930s ring, 14K white gold filigree with synthetic ruby, head 3/8" x 7/16".
Price: $425

(C) (Dr. Betty Wall)
1920-1930s ring, 14K white gold set with blue sapphires and diamonds.
Price: $985

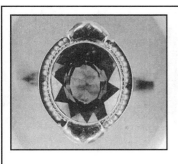

(C) (Jeanenne Bell)
1920-1930s ring, 14K white gold centered with synthetic blue sapphire surrounded with seed pearls strung on gold wire and embellished with blue and orange enameling.
Price: $900

(D) (Jewelry Box Antiques)
1920-1930s ring, 14K white gold set with onyx and diamond.
Price: $325

(D) (Jewelry Box Antiques)
1920-1930s ring, 14K yellow gold filigree set with approx. .17 ct. diamond.
Price: $625

(D) (Jewelry Box Antiques)
1920s ring, 14K white gold band.
Price: $210

(D) (Jewelry Box Antiques)
1920-1930s ring, 18K white gold set with .22 ct diamond.
Price: $525

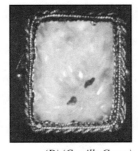

(D) (Camille Grace)
1920-1930s ring, gold over copper, mkd. "China," hand-carved rose quartz, 5/8" x 3/4".
Price: $125

(C) (Jeanenne Bell)
1920-1930s ring, 18K white gold filigree set with diamonds and blue sapphire baguettes shown actual size.
Price: $980

1920-1930s ring, platinum with 1.51 cts. blue sapphire. 1/2" x 1/2" approx. **Price: $2,450**

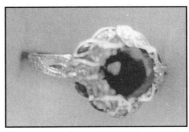

(D) (Jewelry Box Antiques)

(C) (Jeanenne Bell)

1920-1930s ring, 18K white gold set with diamond and blue sapphire baguettes, shown actual size. **Price: $975**

(D) (Camille Grace)

1920-1930s ring, gold over copper. mkd. "China" hand carved, turquoise stone, 7/8" dia. **Price: $125**

(C) (Jennifer Hill)

1920s ring, 10K white gold filigree set with bloodstone intaglio. **Price: $395**

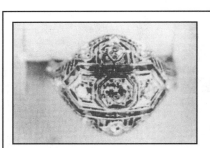

(D) (Jewelry Box Antiques)

1920-1930s ring, platinum set with approx. .50 ct, diamond and embellished with blue sapphire baguettes. **Price: $1,150**

(D) (Jewelry Box Antiques)

1920s ring, 14K white gold filigree set with onyx and diamond. **Price: $365**

(D) (Jewelry Box Antiques)

1920s ring, 14K white gold set with tiger's eye cameo. **Price: $425**

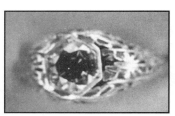

(C) (Silvia Goldman)

1920s ring, 14K white gold set with 1.02 ct. natural brown diamond. **Price: $9,000**

(D) (Jewelry Box Antiques)

1920s ring, 14K white gold set with synthetic ruby, worn in the movie "Mr. & Mrs. Bridge." **Price: $395**

(C) (Silvia Goldman)

1920s ring, 14K white gold filigree with full figure cameo surrounded by seed pearls. **Price: $875**

(D) (Jewelry Box Antiques)

1920s ring, 14K white gold with amethyst. **Price: $340**

(D) (Jewelry Box Antiques)

1920s ring, 14K white gold filigree set with onyx. **Price: $395**

(D) (Jewelry Box Antiques)

1920s ring, 14K yellow gold Buddha ring set with diamonds, rubies and emeralds, approx. 3/4" x 3/16". **Price: $995**

(D) (Jewelry Box Antiques)

1930-1940 ring, 10K yellow gold set with cabochon synthetic ruby, worn in the movie "Mr. & Mrs. Bridge." **Price: $495**

(D) (Jewelry Box Antiques)

1920s ring, 18K white gold filigree set with 2 blue sapphires, 1.56 cts. approx. total weight. **Price: $1,270**

(D) (Jewelry Box antiques)

1920s ring, 18K white gold filigree watch ring with a Bulova movement, 7/8" x 9/16" approx. Side view showing shoulders of ring, open work on the shoulder lifts to used as a winding stem for the watch. All in mint condition. **Price: $995**

(D) (June O'Donnell)

1930-1932 ring, sterling silver set with hematite and marcasites, bought at the Chicago World Fair 1932, Century of Progress International Expo, head approx. 3/4" x 1/2". **Price: $195**

(C) (Janet Radon)

1920s ring, 18K white gold set with 4.38 ct. blue zircon. **Price: $595**

(D) (Jewelry Box Antiques)

1920s ring, white gold filigree set with aquamarine. **Price: $450**

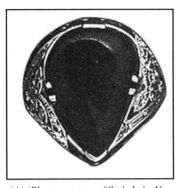

(A) (Photo courtesy of Sotheby's, New York 10-5-83)

1925 ring, platinum centered with 1 cabochon ruby (approx. 14 cts), leaves set with 10 marquise-shaped diamonds, 12 baguettes, 24 single-cut diamonds and 18 calibre-cut rubies (many missing). **Price: $2,530**

1930s ring, 10K yellow gold initial ring set with black onyx and letter "F." **Price: $245**

(D) (Jewelry Box Antiques)

(A) (Photo courtesy of Sotheby's New York 12-7-83)

1930 ring, platinum band of stepped design centered with a row of square cut emeralds bordered by rows of diamonds and emeralds. **Price: $3,850**

(D) (Jewelry Box Antiques)

1930s ring, sterling, hematite surrounded by marcasites, 1" x 1-1/8". **Price: $245**

(D) (June O'Donnell)

1920s ring, sterling silver set with cornelian and marcasites, head approx. 1-1/4" x 3/4". **Price: $165**

(A) (Photo courtesy of Sotheby's, New York 12-7-83)

1930 ring, platinum centered with a row of 7 square cut sapphires bordered by small round diamonds, Marcus & Co. **Price: $2,310**

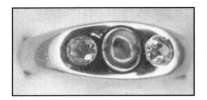

(D) (Jewelry Box Antiques)

1930s ring, 10K yellow gold set with cabochon synthetic blue sapphire and 2 rounded brilliant-cut synthetic cabochon sapphires. **Price: $395**

(D) (Jewelry Box Antiques)

1930s ring, mkd. "sterling Germany," marcasites, 3/4" x 1". **Price: $195**

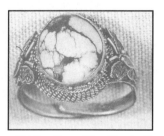

(D) (Lucille and Sam Mundorff)

1930s ring, silver. mkd. "China" with turquoise, 3/4" dia. **Price: $145**

(D) (Jewelry Box Antiques)

Early 1900s ring, platinum set with .65 ct. diamond. **Price: $1,125**

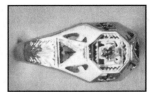

(D) (Jewelry Box Antiques)

1930s ring, 14K yellow gold set with .23 ct. diamond. **Price: $650**

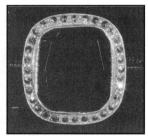

(D) (Jewelry Box Antiques)

1930s ring, mkd. "sterling Germany," onyx with marcasites, head 5/8" x 1". **Price: $245**

(D) (Camille Grace)

1930s ring, sterling with marcasites and enameling, 7/8" x 1-1/4". **Price: $265**

(D) (Jewelry Box Antiques)

1920s ring, 18K white gold filigree set with .15 ct. diamond. **Price: $395**

(D) (Jewelry Box Antiques)

1930s ring, 14K yellow gold set with .23 ct. diamond. **Price: $650**

(D) (Lucille and Sam Mundorff)

1930s ring, silver, marcasites and cornelian, 3/4" x 1-1/8". **Price: $225**

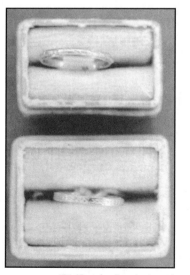

(D) (Jewelry Box Antiques)

1920s rings, 10K white gold baby bands. **Top: $85; Bottom: $95**

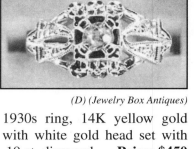

(D) (Jewelry Box Antiques)

1930s ring, 14K yellow gold with white gold head set with .19 ct. diamond. **Price: $450**

(D) (Jewelry Box Antiques)

1930s ring, silver, marcasites, beautifully done, 1/2" x 3/8". **Price: $195**

(D) (Jewelry Box Antiques)

1930s ring, sterling, marcasites, some damage. 1" x 1/2". **Price: $125**

(A) (Photo courtesy of Sotheby's, New York 10-5-83)

Ring, 1935 platinum centered with 1 emerald-cut aquamarine (approx. 40 cts) with 12 round diamonds and 16 calibri-cut synthetic rubies. **Price: $4,400**

312

Watches & Watch Accessories

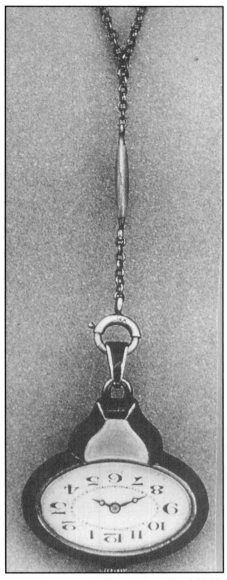

Circa 1920 enamel pendant watch, Swiss silver gilt; case: silver gilt, oval, openface, bezel and back has translucent pink enamel surrounded by black enamel; chain has translucent pink enameled spacers; dial: silver, black Arabic numerals, blued steel "Breguet" hands; movement: nickeled, 15 jewels, lever escapement, cut bi-metallic screwed balance wheel, two adjustments, Breguet balance spring. Signed Aster Watch Co. on both case and movement, width of bezel 29 mm.

Price: $630

Circa 1925 Dudley USA "Masons" gold-filled pocket watch, case: yellow gold-filled, circular, openface, display back; dial: gold tone, black Arabic numerals, auxuliary seconds dial, blued steel "Skeleton" hands; movement: 12 size model #2, nickeled and gilt, 19 jewels, lever escapement, cut bi-metallic screwed balance wheel, Breguet balance spring. Signed Dudley on dial and movement, diameter 44 mm.

Price: $2,590

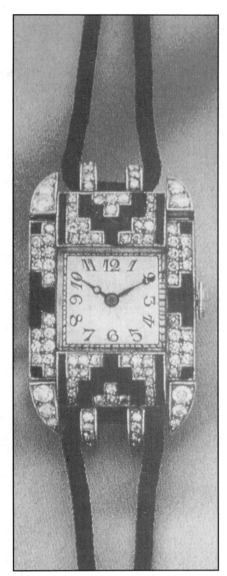

Circa 1920 Swiss lady's platinum, diamond, blue stone, seed pearl integral bracelet wristwatch, case: platinum, bezel set with single, full and European-cut diamonds and blue stones, tonneau, hinged, winding crown with synthetic sapphire terminal; dial: silvered, black Arabic numerals, blued steel Breguet hands; movement: nickeled, highly-jeweled, lever escapement, cut bi-metallic screwed balance wheel, Breguet balance spring; bracelet: 18K white gold, seed pearls, 18K rhodium plated yellow clasp, integral, signed Eszeha on dial, width of bezel 15 mm.

Price: $6,900

1920 watch, gold filled open face 12S, 3 adjustment, 17 jewel, "Gruen Guild," 1-12/16". **Price: $325**

1929 watch, white gold filled open face 12S, 17 jewel, Waltham, 1-7/8". **Price: $295**

Ball watch pendant, platinum and diamond filigree attached with a black cord necklace. **Price: $3,000**

1920s watch band, yellow gold filled filigree, approx. 3/16" x 6". **Price: $95**

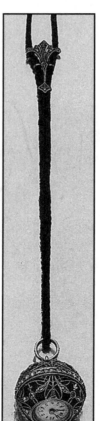

Circa 1920s Swiss lady's Art Deco, platinum, onyx bracelet wristwatch, case: platinum, bezel set with single-cut diamonds and black onyx, rectangular, hinged lugs set with single-cut diamonds; dial: textured silvered, black Arabic numerals, blued steel Breguet hands; movement: gilt, highly jeweled, lever escapement, cut bimetallic screwed balance wheel, Breguet balance spring; bracelet: black cord, width of bezel 20mm. **Price: $8,625**

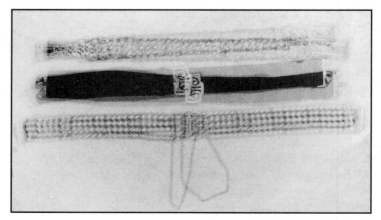

Watch bands, top: pearls and imitation sapphires, pat'd 2-7-22; middle: ribbon watch band; bottom: imitation pearls mkd. 1/10 14K gold filled, pat'd Nov. 9, 1926, FELCO. **Price: $75-$125**

1920s watch chain, white metal, slipped onto belt and allowed watch to fit in pocket, chain 7" l. **Price: $50**

Watch clip, Art Deco, oblong dial with black Roman numerals and asymmetric black enamel border, individually numbered, by "Cartier," £980. **Price: $1,745**

1920 wristwatch, 9K gold octagonal case, Rolex nickel level movement, 15 jewels, white enamel dial with Roman numerals, English hallmarks, 1-1/4" dia. **Price: $1,760**

1920s wristwatch, mkd., rolled plate, white gold, movement mkd. "Solomon Watch Co.," Swiss, 6 jewels, 2 adj. **Price: $265**

1920-1930s wristwatch, yellow gold filled with hand set rhinestones, lid opens to reveal watch, worn in the movie "Mr. & Mrs. Bridge." **Price: $395**

(D) (Jewelry Box Antiques)

1920s wristwatch, sterling case and bracelet, movement marked "ABRA-Watch Co.," Geneva, 6 jewels, 2 adj. **Price: $345**

(D) (Jewelry Box Antiques)

1908-1915 fob, yellow gold filled with black enameling, 1-1/2" x 5/8". **Price: $125**

(D) (Jewelry Box Antiques)

1920s wristwatch, white gold filled. **Price: $425**

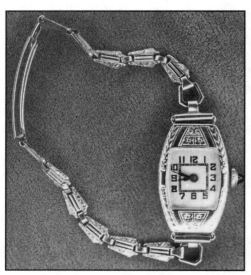

(D) (Jewelry Box Antiques)

1920s wristwatch, white gold filled set with sapphire crown and has original band, worn by Joanne Woodward in movie "Mr. & Mrs. Bridge."**Price: $495**

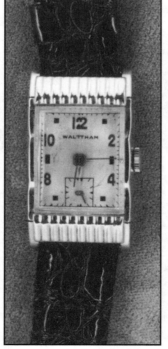

(D) (Jewelry Box Antiques)

1930-1940s wristwatch, yellow gold filled Waltham with fancy dial. **Price: $425**

(D) (Jewelry Box Antiques)

1920s wristwatch, white gold filled. **Price: $345**

(D) (Jewelry Box Antiques)

1930s wristwatch, 14K gold filled case, movement mkd. "Helbrose Watch Co.," 7 jewels, Swiss, celluloid and leather watch band. **Price: $295**

(D) (Jewelry Box Antiques)

1930s wristwatch, white metal mechanical stop watch, Mentor "old store stock," original box.

Price: $325

1935 wristwatch, 18K man's two-toned gold, Bacheron & Constantin, Geneve, circular nickel lever movement #414241, three adjustments, 17 jewels, bi-metallic compensation balance, silvered matte dial with gold Arabic numerals, 14K brickwork strap.

Price: $1,400

(A) (Photo courtesy of Sotheby's, New York 4-10-84)

(A) (Photo courtesy Wm. Doyle Galleries, New York 12-12-90)

(A) (Photo courtesy Phillips, London 6-21-83)

Wristwatch, Art Deco, gold and diamond, signed and numbered, Cartier, fitted case. £5,000.

Price: $8,900

Wristwatch, platinum, signed "Cartier," the 19-jewel movement with 8 adjustments signed "European Watch and Clock Company, Inc."; the case and band set throughout with 25 round full-cut diamonds, and 118 assorted round diamonds, total approx. 2.50 cts., with a rose diamond crown.

Price: $5,125

Wristwatch, Art Deco, white gold set with alternating lines of small brilliant-cut diamonds and French-cut onyx. Matching shoulders on a bracelet set with onyx plaques and diamonds, £2,600.

Price: $4,630

(A) (Photo courtesy Phillips, London 9-20-83)

(A) (Photo courtesy of Sotheby's, New York 4-10-84)

1936 wristwatch, 18K man's Patek Philippe & Co. retailed by Tiffany & Co., nickel lever mount, bi-metallic compensation balance, 18 jewels, 3 adjustments, 1-1/2" long.

Price: $1,650

Pocket travel watch, black enameled case, "Zenith," 6cm, £170. **Price: $305**

Traveling watch, Art Deco with simulated black onyx and marcasite bands, 4cm, £180. **Price: $320**

1929 traveling watch, silver case with black enamel lacquered with bird, 3.50cm, "Le Captive" by Dunhill, £160. **Price: $285**

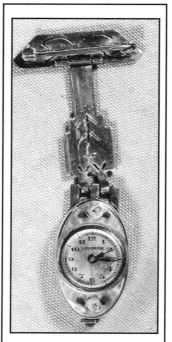

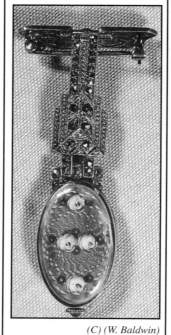

1920-1930s pin watch, .935 silver with marcasites, watch is beautifully enameled with pink flowers, "C. Bucherer," 1-3/16" x 2-3/4". **Price: $1,150**

1930-1940s lapel pin watch, white metal with rhinestones, approx. 3-1/8" x 1". **Price: $425**

Miniature traveling clock, pink guilloche enameling with white enamel dial and rose-cut diamond hands, grey agate base, original case, by "Cartier," £1,200. **Price: $2,135**

Sets

1930s formal cuff-link and studs set, white gold filled set with onyx cuff link and studs, original box. **Price: $175**

(D) (Jewelry Box Antiques)

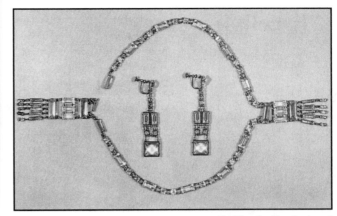

(D) (Jewelry Box Antiques)

1920-1930 necklace and earrings, sterling with lead crystal baguette, one tassel hangs in front and one in back, note clasp location, 23" l; earrings 1/2" x 2-1/2".
Price: $350

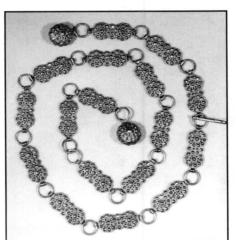

(D) (Jewelry Box Antiques)

1920-1930 necklace, imitation marcasite, 43" l including original ribbon, has matching belt, adjustable, 5/8" x 35" l. **Price: $195 set**

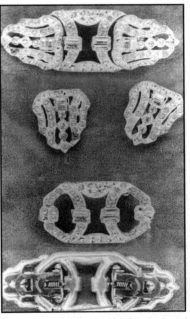

(D) (Jewelry Box Antiques)

1920s-1930s duet brooch, (pin and dress clips), white metal with rhinestones, top view complete; middle view shows dress clips removed from frame, bottom view shows back of assembled pin and dress clips.

Price: $250

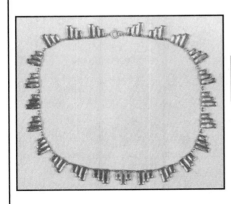

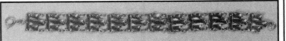

(D) (Jewelry Box Antiques)

Bracelet, Art Deco, 7" l; necklace, silver over brass, mkd. "Czechoslovakia," emerald colored glass baguettes, 1/2" x 16" l.
Price: $125 set

Miscellaneous

(D) (Jewelry Box Antiques)

1920s buckle, Bakelite with enameled metal head, this is 1/2 of buckle, 2-3/4" x 2-1/2".
Price: $75

(A) (Photo courtesy Wm. Doyle Galleries, New York 5-2-90)

1925 Art Deco dress clip, platinum top and white gold base containing four pear shaped rubies approx. 2.0 cts., and fifty-one assorted small round old mine diamonds approx. 1.75 cts. and small calibre rubies.
Price: $4,000

(A) (Photo courtesy of Skinner, Inc., Boston, Mass 12-4-90)

Art Deco platinum dress set with black onyx and centered by pearls.
Price: $1,000

1920s button, white metal and fabric, 2-1/4" dia.
Price: $50

(D) (Jewelry Box Antiques)

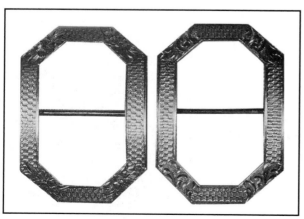

(C) (W. Baldwin)

1920s garter buckles, 14K gold, 1" x 1-1/2".
Price: $165

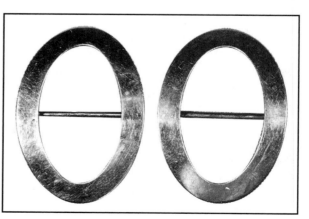

(C) (W. Baldwin)

1920s garter buckles, 14K gold, 1" x 1-1/2".
Price: $165

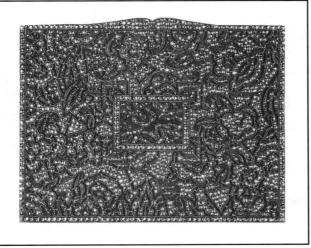

1930s cigarette case, silver with marcasites, 3-3/8" x 2-7/8". **Price: $600**

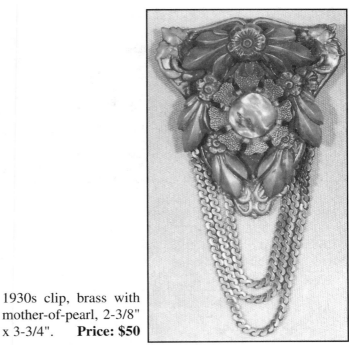

1930s clip, brass with mother-of-pearl, 2-3/8" x 3-3/4". **Price: $50**

1915-1920s necessary, sterling, place for rouge, powder, and coins, 2-3/8" x 3-3/8". **Price: $265**

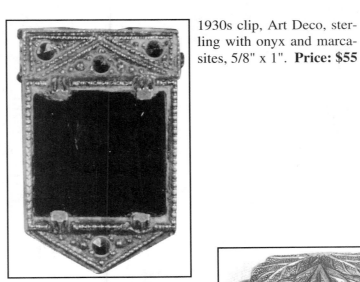

1930s clip, Art Deco, sterling with onyx and marcasites, 5/8" x 1". **Price: $55**

1930s clip, gold over brass leaves and clip with Bakelite grapes, 2" x 2". **Price: $45**

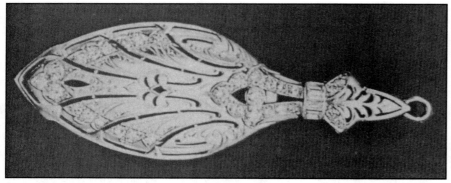

Diamond lorgnette, designed as a modified navette-shaped case enhanced with diamonds, opening to reveal reading spectacles, all suspended from a detachable diamond chain 15-1/2 in., Tiffany & Co., containing four baguette and thirty-six circular-cut diamonds. **Price: $3,450**

1926 compact, Art Deco, silver with enameling, 8.5cm x 6.5cm, £140.
Price: $250

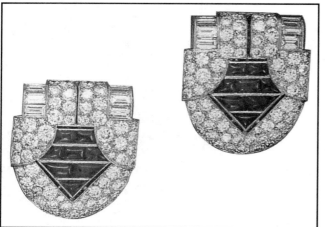

1930s clips, platinum with arrow motif of 16 calibre-cut rubies, further embellished with four baguette diamonds (approx. 2 cts), 12 smaller baguettes and 4 square cut diamonds (totaling approx. 2.20 cts).
Price: $8,800

1930s compact, white metal with soft yellow and black enamel, mkd. "Evans," place for rouge and powder, 2-1/4" dia.
Price: $140

1925-1930s compact, white metal with navy blue enameling, mkd. Evans, 2-3/8" dia.
Price: $95

1925 compact & lipstick case, Art Deco, gold, jade and lapis, Berlioz-Leroy, Paris-Cannes. **Price: $1,980**

(D) (Jewelry Box Antiques)

1920s cufflinks, 14K white gold white with mother-of-pearl and cultured pearl, approx. 1/2". **Price: $395**

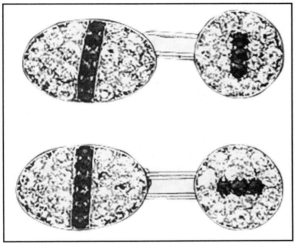

(A) (Photo courtesy of Sotheby's, New York 10-15-83)

1920s cufflinks & 2 studs, gold and platinum set with rubies and old mine diamonds.

Price: $2,310

1920-1930s dress clips, white metal with rhinestones, approx. 1" x 2".
Price: $125 pr.

(D) (Jewelry Box Antiques)

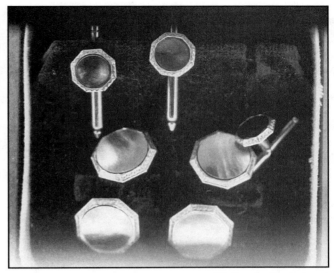

(D) (Jewelry Box Antiques)

1920s cufflinks, white and yellow gold filled, grey mother-of-pearl. **Price: $140**

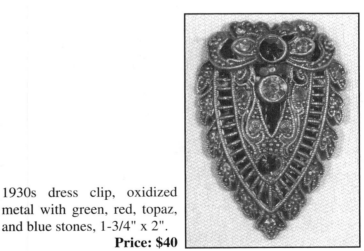

1930s dress clip, oxidized metal with green, red, topaz, and blue stones, 1-3/4" x 2".
Price: $40

(D) (Jewelry Box Antiques)

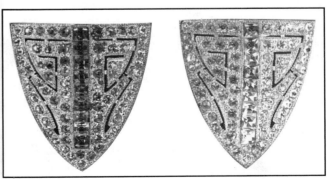

(D) (Jewelry Box Antiques)

1920-1930s dress clips, white metal with foil-backed clear stone, overall 1-1/2" x 1-3/4". **Price of pair: $80**

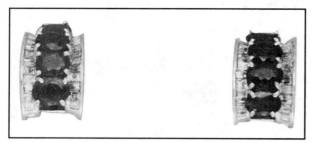

1935 ear-clips, platinum set with 8 oval-shaped rubies (approx. 8 cts) and 40 baguette diamonds (approx. 2 cts). **Price: $5,225**

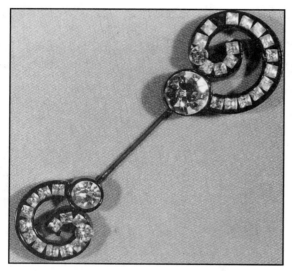

(D) (Jewelry Box Antiques)

1930s hat ornament, plastic with rhinestones, 1" x 3-1/4" l. **Price: $30**

(D) (Jewelry Box Antiques)

1920s glasses and chain, mkd. 1/10, 12K gold filled, chain barrel mkd. "Kitchall McDougal, Montclair, N.J." **Price: $95**

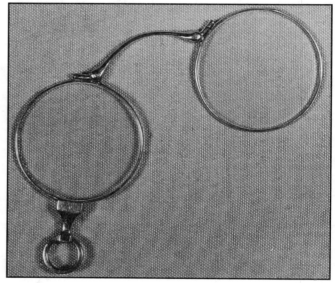

(C) (W. Baldwin)

1915-1925 eyeglass lorgnette, 14K gold, dia. of glass 1-1/2". **Price: $350**

Code in Front of Name

(A) Auction House - Auction Price
(C) Collector - Collector Asking Price
(D) Dealer - Dealer's Asking Price

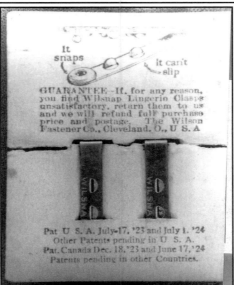

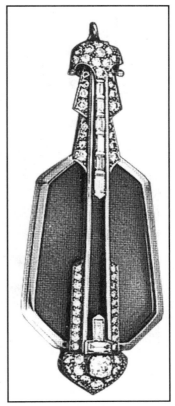

(D) (Jewelry Box Antiques)

1924 lingerie clasp, on original card, pat. date can be of help in circa dating.
Price: $195

1925 lorgnette, Art Deco, platinum
set with diamonds. **Price: $2,475**

*(A) (Photo courtesy of Sotheby's,
New York 12-7-83)*

(D) (Camille Grace)

1920-1930s clip lorgnette, white metal, dress clip lorgnette with rhinestones. **Price: $450**

1930s tie tack, gold over white metal, snake motif, 3/4" dia. **Price: $25**

1920s-1930s strap holder, silver over brass, green enameling on links of chain. **Price: $40**

1920-1930s necessary, beautifully enameled to wear on finger, separate lipstick, 2-1/8" x 2-1/4". **Price: $325**

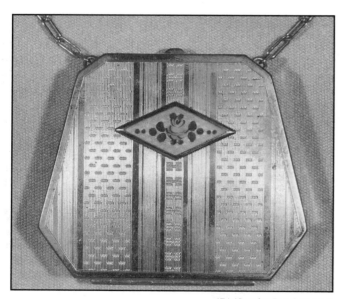

Vanity case and coin holder, one identical to this in 1928-1929 *Montgomery Ward Catalogue*. White metal with enamel plaque, 2-1/2" x 2-1/8". **Price: $125**

1920s vanity case, white metal with enameled plaque, 2-1/8" x 3-1/2". **Price: $125**

Chapter Five: 1940-1950

The American Historical Period

The forties dawned on a world filled with "Wars and rumors of war." Most Americans did not want to become involved in these foreign entanglements. However, as the European situation changed, people began to think that the United States should give aid to Great Britain. Any indecisiveness about involvement was shattered on December 7, 1941 when the Japanese bombed Pearl Harbor. Shocked and indignant, the country united to fight the enemy.

Everyone pulled together to ease the workload created by the war. Ships, planes, guns, shells, and a million other items were needed to win. There was work for everyone. Almost 18 million women worked outside the home. They discovered they could do jobs that had been traditionally assigned to men, and do them well. Many women did volunteer work in blood banks and canteens. Others planted victory gardens and raised a large portion of their food. These activities made them feel like working partners with the men in uniform.

Teenagers gained a more important role in society. With men off to war and women away at work, they were called upon more often. Some were lured away from school at age 14 by high paying factory jobs. In September 1943, *McCalls* magazine published an article about the "4-4 Plan." It told of the success many cities had experienced with a program that encouraged teenagers to attend school four hours and work four hours, "The academic program was arranged for these students so that none of the essentials were omitted...." Teenagers without regular jobs did odd jobs and baby-sitting.

People were earning more money than ever before, but there was little to spend it on. The war had caused shortages in everything from gasoline to sugar. Rationing coupons and points became a part of American life. The slogan "use it up-wear it out-make it do" was enacted daily by people who wanted to do their part in the war effort. Money was

needed to win the war, and the public responded by putting its money into war bonds.

When the war ended August 14, 1945, people celebrated by ringing church bells, kissing strangers, blowing whistles, and partying. At last their friends and loved ones would be coming home. Congress had prepared for the homecoming by passing the G.I. Bill of Rights. This program provided funds to make the Veteran's assimilation back into society easier. Money was made available for going back to school, buying a house, or going into business.

In retrospect, most people would agree that the fifties were indeed fabulous. But what they choose to forget is that these were the years in which America learned to live with fear. Postwar events had shattered all hope of world peace. Only a few months before the new decade began, it was learned that the Russians also possessed "the Bomb." People went on with their lives and continued to dream their dreams, but lurking in the back of their minds was the haunting fear of annihilation.

The American dream of home ownership led to an exodus from the city and into the suburbs. The housing industry mushroomed. Subdivisions seemed to pop up overnight in places where cows once grazed. New schools were built to educate the products of the post war "baby boom." Shopping centers were built to accommodate the needs of these "bedroom" communities.

The American dependency on the automobile continued to grow. Fathers needed a car to get to work, and mothers had to have a way to get the children to dancing lessons and Little League practice. The Sunday drive continued to be popular even though it often included a ride past the latest home-built bomb shelter. The automobile and the suburbs became as much a part of the American way of life as "mom and apple pie."

For the youth of America, the fifties were a great time in which to be alive. Middle class affluence had provided them with money to spend. The record industry boomed. A new rhythm, entirely different from the big band sound, was emerging. It was based on rock, rhythm, and soul.

In the South, white radio stations refused to "air" these records, so the white youth listened to the "colored" stations. They liked what they heard. The songs of Little Richard and Fats Domino were what the new generation wanted. A new dance was needed to fit the new beat. The Bop became popular overnight.

Elvis Presley had this new sound and beat. Teenagers went wild over his records. Within months his music was at the top of the charts. Adults were convinced that the gyrating hips of this new idol would lead teenagers down the wrong path. In fact, many believed that rock and roll was the work of the devil.

In the late 1950s the Hoola Hoop had hips all over America gyrating. Almost everyone who could stand and wiggle, tried it. Literally millions were sold.

Television was creating a whole new life style. Family schedules were centered around favorite T.V. shows. One town even experienced a water shortage when Milton Berle paused for a commercial, because everyone chose this time to go to the bathroom.

Most stations did not start telecasting until late afternoon, but some new T.V. owners were content to look at a test pattern. Shows such as "I Love Lucy," "Your Show of Shows," "Dragnet," "Ed Sullivan," and "Your Hit Parade" were worth the wait. It was new, fun and fabulous!

Fashions In Clothing & Jewelry

The war in Europe had far reaching effects on the fashion industry. With France engaged in the war, American designers had to rely on their own expertise to capture the American woman's fancy. The September 8, 1941, *Time* stated, "U. S., couturiers, last week and this, unveiled for the first time the American woman packaged-in-the-U.S." The styles were not as dramatic or "seductively named" as the ones originating in Paris, but the American designers presented "good wearable, saleable clothing. The chief trends of this ingenuity show in slender skirts with slits or 'back drops' which fall much lower behind than in front; 'front peplums' give fullness to tight skirts; the 'deep armhole cut' and 'soft shoulder'."

The United States' declaration of war brought many changes in the American way of life. A War Production Board was formed to regulate production of goods and insure that war needs would be met. Fashions were designed to use as little material as possible. At the same time, no dramatic changes were made so that last season's clothes would still be fashionable. The Office of Price Administration suggested that the American housewife make this pledge; "I will buy carefully. I will

McCall's, Sept. 1943

328

take good care of the things I have. I will waste nothing." This was quickly paraphrased to "Eat it up. Wear it out. Make it do. Do without." And it became the motto of the war years.

There were shortages in everything from cotton dresses to hosiery. Women used leg make-up instead of nylons. When stores were fortunate enough to receive shipments, there were always more customers than stockings. Bloomingdales in New York solved this problem by allowing customers to buy two pairs of stockings with each War Bond purchased. According to *Business Week*, February 20, 1943, Bloomingdales sold all 3,000 pairs within 40 minutes, and War Bond sales "totaled $39,000."

The jewelry industry was also experiencing its share of shortages. The September 5, 1942 *Business Week* reported: "Sales are at high level, but present bread-and-butter stock can't be replenished. The most serious shortage is metal. The supply of silver plate and of inexpensive jewelry made from base metals is now strictly limited to inventories that manufacturers and retailers have on hand. There will be no more when these are exhausted. Sterling silver has been widely used to replace the baser and scarcer metals." Consequently, if a piece of jewelry is marked 1/20 12K on Sterling or G. F. on S. S., it was probably made during these years.

The War Production Board also limited use of imported silver. "Under the recent W.P.B. crackdown, manufacturers can continue to use up their stocks of imported silver-purchased mostly at around 35¢ an ounce-until October 1. After that they must use domestic silver, which cost over twice as much, or nothing. War industrial requirements will gobble up whatever silver is obtained as a result of arrangement providing for a 45¢ price for good neighbor producers."[15]

The article noted "important shortages other than metals are cultured pearls, imported from Japan and the Dutch East Indies, and high grade imitation stones which have, in the past come chiefly from Central Europe. The bulk of the trade's largest suppliers-watch manufacturers, makers of silverplate and sterling, and the biggest volume producers of costume jewelry already are wholly or partially engaged in war work for which they are particularly suited virtue of highly precision equipment and staffs of skilled metalworkers."[16]

In spite of these limitations, jewelry sales continued to soar. *Business Week*, April 17, 1943, explained it this way: "With the workers unable to spend their bulging bankrolls on automobiles, refrigerators or silk shirts, jewelry sales (including silver, watches, and clocks) last year hit an all time high of $790,000,000 showing a 30% increase over 1941 and considerable gain over the biggest previous year."

The article also told of more restriction placed on metals:

Conservation order M-162 prohibited use of platinum and its counterpart, iridium, used as the hardening agent in platinum alloy. Platinum is needed now as a catalyst in producing nitric and sulfuric acids for munitions plants; it is widely used in chemical, electrochemical, and electrical fields as well as in the dental industry. Platinum clad metals are used to prevent metallic contamination of food and vitamins products in critical stages of processing.

Also out is rhodium (conservation order M-95), which is used to prevent tarnish in silver products and give them a light plating. And manufacturers are restricted in the use of silver itself, WPB's M-199 allows them 50% of the amount used in either 1941 or 1942 whichever was greater. This allowance must be cut even farther, what with silver being used as a substitute for tin in soldering, for nickel plate, copper, and stainless steel in lining chemical vats and aviation and electrical equipment particularly bus bars for conducting current in electrolytic plants.

In short, the use of only two of the jewelers basic materials are wide open-precious stones which can be marketed only in settings of precious metals, and palladium, a platinum metal which the conservative jewelry trade has been reluctant to adopt because it is new to the industry. Deprived of platinum, manufacturers are at last turning to palladium, using unrestricted ruthenium rather than iridium as the hardening agent in its alloy.

Bader and Co. Inc., of Newark, N.J., the world's largest dealer in the platinum metals (palladium, platinum, iridium, ruthenium, osmium) has assured jewelers that palladium is an adequate substitute for platinum, and the International Nickel Co. of Canada, LTD., which produces palladium as a by-product of nickel, is hopefully looking to the jewelry industry to absorb its stockpile, which has long been a drug on the market.

Jewelers, finding no consumer resistance to palladium, show signs of adopting it for postwar marketing of rings, pins, and watches. Consumers cannot distinguish it from platinum, don't mind its being slightly lighter in weight (about the same as a 14 carat yellow gold). The current market value is about 70% that of platinum-OPA's Maximum Price Regulation 309 establishes ceiling at $35 per troy ounce for platinum, $24 for palladium.

Once the palladium backlog is absorbed, current production may not provide a supply sufficient to exclude platinum from an expanding postwar market since platinum is somewhat more plentiful. But now that trade prejudice has been overcome, palladium promised competition for the traditionally treasured white metals.

In September 1944, order L-45 was rescinded eliminating these restrictions on gold and platinum. The jewelers were jubilant! The federal excise tax on jewelry had been raised from 10% to 20% in April, and it was hoped that the easing of restrictions might stimulate sales.

With women performing jobs formally done by men, some basic changes in wardrobes were necessary. The American woman was quick to realize that slacks were the answer. "Starting with the defense industries in England and then hopping the Atlantic, slacks have spread from the purely sports category to all fields of female activity-from air raid work to dressy evening lolling," commented the *New York Times Magazine* in March 1, 1942. "It is not great novelty this year to see women hurrying about Manhattan in them during the week, and on a recent Sunday two East Seventies types were seen tramping up the ultra-bourgeois street, Madison Avenue, in flannel trousers and tennis shoes. The sale of slacks in department stores is estimated to be about ten times greater than it has ever been before at this time of year, and dress designers working on new collections are including all sorts of versions of the pants movement, from something strictly for harems to boy's tights cut off just below the knee."

The April 13, 1942 *Time Magazine* states:

> U.S. women by the millions have renounced skirts in favor of slacks....Not since Mrs. Amelia Bloomer created an international uproar in 1849 by appearing in public in voluminous Turkish trousers had such a feminine trouser sensation swept the country. High-school girls in Brooklyn's big Abraham Lincoln High School struck for the right to wear slacks. In Detroit Mayor Edward Jefferies grudgingly admitted that a female employee of the city, forced by priorities to bicycle to work, might do her job in slacks. Pants made good sense for wartime. Lieutenant Commander Roy R. Darron ordered women employed in the machine shops of the Alameda Naval Air Station in California to wear pants to work.

There was an alternative for the women who did not want to wear pants—culottes. "Thousands of girls nowadays are doing the marketing, going to first-aid classes, garden-club meetings, and their war jobs on two wheels instead of four," noted *Colliers*, May 9, 1942. "Well, fashions usually more or less express the times in which they appear. The bicycle boom means culottes in a big way. They seem the best answer to what-to-wear-while-pedaling."

Clothing sizes were being standardized. During the late 1930s, W.P.A. workers had been used by the Department of Agriculture's Bureau of Home Economics to "measure 147,000 children and 15,000 women."16 Boy's clothes were first to receive the fruits of this effort. Sizes were gauged by height and hip measurement instead of the unsatisfactory yardstick of age. Sears Roebuck was the first to apply the information to women's clothing. In 1943, they came out with "36 different sizes in 6 classifications (ranging from junior scale to stout)."17 Women could find their correct size by measuring their waist, bust, hips, and length.

After the war, women had money to spend—and spend it they did. According to an article in *Colliers*, December 15, 1943:

> American women are crazy over jewelry. They spend a billion three-hundred million a year on it. The young girls are buying tiny jeweled pins to fasten on demure velvet neckbands. One store reports a brisk sale of butterfly cutouts for a suntan, or initials will be cut in the anklet. The dealers say those combs edged with imitation gold, so popular even a year ago for hold back a page-boy bob, don't sell so much anymore; but with fourteen-carat tops, at eighteen dollars a pair for the small ones, they can't be kept in stock. Gold barrettes to hold the hair out of little girl's eyes sell for eleven dollars apiece. Gold bobby pins are seven-fifty a pair-gold snowflakes to screw on, of course, are extra. Sterling silver bicycle clips, at five dollars a pair is another popular item. They're good for holding up sweater sleeves-or clipping in slacks legs for the slim, ballet look.

> To see what the trend is, you don't have to go into fine jewelry shops. All you have to do is to walk into that old copycat, the five-and-ten. There you'll see sophisticated sunbursts, and dome-shaped earrings and bracelets, replicas of the costly gold ones that are popularly studded with chips of turquoise, diamond and ruby. Elegant, not gaudy, is the word.

Costume jewelry became big business. Many designers switched to the costume jewelry industry during the depression. Their expertise caused the industry to blossom.

In 1946, Providence, Rhode Island, was the costume jewelry capital of the United States. Coro Incorporated, with 2,000 employees and sales of $16,000,000, was headquartered here. This undisputed leader in the industry was founded in 1902 as Cohn and Rosenberger. Later, the company was renamed using the first two letters of each name. Coro's high priced line was sold under the name of Corocraft.

Costume jewelry was produced in all price ranges. Trifari, Drussman & Fishel was the style leader. Their jewelry was priced from $10 and up. R.M. Jordan was a leader in the medium priced jewelry: $1 to $20. Monet was known for its tailored jewelry, and Forstner was the leading producer of the popular snake chains.

In December 1946, *Fortune Magazine* noted, "the twenties and early thirties were dominated by modernistic patterns, sleek and severe, while the past half dozen years have seen an inundation of Renaissance elegance and Victorian fancy-scroll motifs, flower sprays, sunbursts, nosegays. This trend is continuing with increasingly delicate designs and a strong return of white finishes after the wartime reign of gold. Paris is featuring invisible mountings and flexibility-which increases the shimmer and may increase the interest."

By 1947, Western Wear started to make the news. The lady responsible for this new attire was Marge Riley. Born in South Dakota, Marge spent time on a ranch in Wyoming. Her love for the west led her to design clothes for herself and later others. In 1948, her shops were doing a "six figure" annual business. She designed clothes for Joanne Dru, Roy Rogers, and Gene Autry. An outfit ranged in price from $370 to $750. Marge's dream was to mass-produce Western Clothes the average person could afford.

Dior created the biggest fashion sensation of the decade when he presented his "New Look" in 1947. Women had grown tired of the narrow skirts and squared shoulders of the war years. Dior offered a new feminine look with long (12" off the floor) full skirts, small waist, and rounded soft shoulders. It was a welcomed change!

Nylon was also a welcomed addition to the wardrobe. It had been on the market in the form of stockings, parachutes, and toothbrushes for years, but new developments in weaves and dyes made it the perfect "wash and wear" fabric. How liberating! No longer was a gal dependent on an iron for that fresh look. Nylon also made the perfect petticoat for the "new look." Stiffened nylon called crinoline became part of every woman's wardrobe in "the fifties."

The jewelry used to compliment this new style was huge. It took on larger proportions, just as it did in the 1860s when skirts were widened. Massive rings were so in style that *Life Magazine* featured a full page on them in April 1952.

Huge earrings were also popular. *Look Magazine*, May 31, 1955, included an article on "Whopper Earrings." The newest styles were "bigger than silver dollars." *Look* jokingly called them "ear muffs-summer style." Large pearl buttons, "gold saucers,"

and bouquets of flowers were a few of the many motifs.

In the mid-fifties, short shorts caused quite an uproar. They were cool, great looking on the right figure, and sure to receive attention. The August 1, 1955 *Newsweek* included this "short" dilemma:

> Some congressman took a dim view of the female knee. A lady who wore shorts in the visitor's gallery, they argued, was hardly a lady. What's more, she impaired the dignity of the House and distracted its members. They asked William (Fishbait) Miller, the doorkeeper, to bar anyone over 10, of the female persuasion who appeared in shorts.

> The Senate, on the other hand-older and perhaps less susceptible-was entirely unconcerned by the spectacle. If a lady, even one over 10, wanted to wear shorts in the Senate gallery, she was welcome to do so.

> Last week, as Washington sweltered in a heat wave well beyond its normally unbearable summer temperature, the unofficial House rule became a 'silly season' issue. Offended and annoyed by the ban on shorts, a number of women complained to their congressmen, who looked into this violation of 'constitutional rights.' They found that the Senate maintained its dignity and its equanimity in the presence of bare knees-and the House rule was rescinded.

By 1956, short shorts had become a permanent part of the fashion scene. Most people wondered "What next?" The question was answered by the chemise. Men could not understand why women would want to wear these "sacks." Jack Nabley of the *Chicago Daily News* called it, "a tent looking for a desert to light on." But women liked them. More importantly (to the manufacturers), they bought them. Even Marilyn Monroe added a few to her wardrobe. "If the sack is truly a crime, as some critics allege, there are some accessories after the fact-accessories such as gloves and hats, and stockings and shoes, costume jewelry and furs," stated the May 5, 1958 *Newsweek*. It also described the proper accessories for the new chemise. The relatively plain style required many accesories. Jewelry was very important. "The chemise hiked sales 10 percent for Coro, Inc., biggest of the fashion jewelry manufacturers. Hot items: Ropes (of heavy beads), bibs (of several parallel strands), bracelets, and chemise-length (from earlobe to shoulder) earrings."[18]

Bracelets

(C) (Cindy Stokes)

1940-1950s bracelet, gold over silver vermeil, 4 hand painted ivory plaques, approx. 1" w x 7" l. **Price: $250**

(C) (Jeanenne Bell)

1940s bracelet, 10K yellow gold with 3 synthetic blue sapphires, 3/8" w x 7" l. **Price: $385**

(D) (Jewelry Box Antiques)

1940s bracelet, gold-filled with silver wings insignia, 5/8" hinged with safety. **Price: $95**

(D) (Jewelry Box Antiques)

1940s bracelet, gold over brass with 3 strands of imitation pearls, clasp 1-1/4" dia. **Price: $30**

(D) (Jewelry Box Antiques)

1940s bracelet, white metal, hinged bangle with safety chain, 1-1/4" w. **Price: $75**

(D) (Jewelry Box Antiques)

1940s bracelet, gold over white metal, hinged bangle with safety, 3/4" w. **Price: $95**

(C) (Peggy Carlson)

1940s bracelet, silver with pig skin inserts, 3/4" x 7-3/4" l.
Price: $125

(D) (Jewelry Box Antiques)

1940s bracelet, yellow gold filled with expandable heart motif, bracelet approx. 1/2" w and heart approx. 7/8".
Price: $125

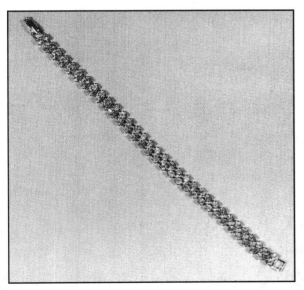

(D) (Jewelry Box Antiques)

1950 bracelet, 2 rows of rhinestones, 6-1/2" l.
Price: $85

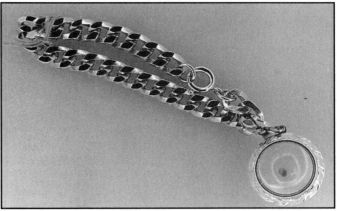

(D) (Jewelry Box Antiques)

1940s bracelet, sterling silver with spring ring latch on "lock."
Price: $160

(D) (Jewelry Box Antiques)

1940s bracelet, yellow gold filled with flower engraving, approx. 5/8" w.
Price: $285

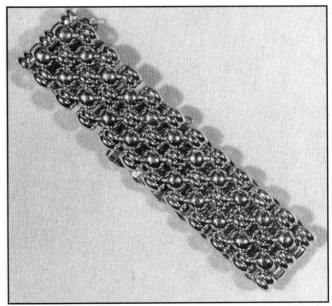

(C) (Jeanenne Bell)

1950s bracelet, mkd. "Made in Switzerland plaque d'ore 20 microns," with safety, 1" w.
Price: $225

Code in Front of Name

(A) Auction House - Auction Price
(C) Collector - Collector Asking Price
(D) Dealer - Dealer's Asking Price

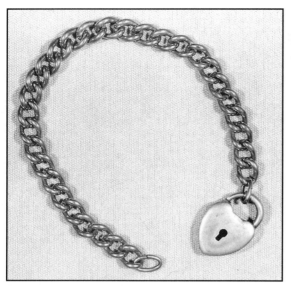

(C) (Peggy Carlson)

Early 1940s bracelet, silver, heart has jump spring opening, note plainness in comparison to the one from the 1890s, 7" l. **Price: $120**

(D) (Jewelry Box Antiques)

1940s slide bracelet, yellow gold filled with multi slide, cameo is hand carved shell, bracelet approx. 1" w x 7-1/2" l. **Price: $275**

(C) (Mary Holloway)

1943-1945 charm bracelet, sterling with 26 sterling charms. **Price: $450**

(D) (Jewelry Box Antiques)

Late 1930-1940s bracelet, plastic section strung on 2 elastic bands, alternating black and amber colors. Design is incised molding from the back and painted blue, green, and gold, 1-1/4" w. **Price: $200**

(C) (Jeanenne Bell)

Late 1940s bracelet, gold filled, mkd. "Coro," each flower has a pearl center, 3/4" x 7-1/2". **Price: $125**

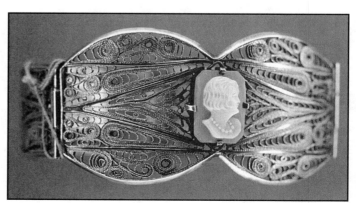

(D) (Jewelry Box Antiques)

Circa 1930s-1940s bracelet, silver open work with hand carved shell cameo, approx. 1-1/2" w. **Price: $290**

(D) (Jewelry Box Antiques)

1940s child's bracelet, sterling with yellow and pink gold, locket 1" dia. mkd. "Lusitern-Sterling 1/12 12K G.F. on Sterling." **Price: $125**

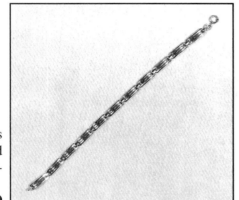

1940s child's bracelet, gold filled on sterling, 6-1/2" l. **Price: $60**

(D) (Jewelry Box Antiques)

(D) (Jewelry Box Antiques)

Circa 1940s bracelet, gold filled with five oval scenic plaques, approx. 1" x 7/8". **Price: $850**

(D) (Jewelry Box Antiques)

Child's bracelet, hallmark sterling, adjustable 1/4" heavy. **Price: $125**

(D) (Jewelry Box Antiques)

1940s child's bracelet, yellow gold filled with pink and green gold, expansion type with locket, locket 3/4"; bracelet 1/2" w. **Price: $125**

(C) (Anne Noblitt)

1940s hinged bangle bracelet, gold filled, beautiful 3/4" w. **Price: $295**

(A) (Butterfield and Butterfield, 03/10/98)

Retro citrine, emerald, diamond, platinum, 14K gold bangle, Trabert & Hoeffer Mauboussin; centering one emerald-cut citrine, enhanced by oval-shaped emerald cabochons, accented by single-cut diamonds, set in platinum. Signed "Trabert & Hoeffer Mauboussin, Reflection Series," accompanied by a signed, Trabert & Hoeffer Mauboussin leather box, approximately 6-1/4". **Price: $5,750**

Brooches & Pins

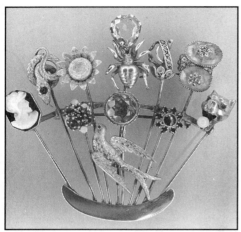

Brooch comprised of 11 stick pins gold, gold-filled and silver, 3-1/4" x 3". **Price: $995**

(D) (Jewelry Box Antiques)

Stick pin brooch, diamond, cultured pearl, seed pearl, opal moonstone, sapphire, garnet, turquoise, silver, low karat gold, 14K gold. (Seed pearls not tested for origin.)
Price: $2,585

(A) (Butterfield and Butterfield, 03/10/98)

(D) (Jewelry Box Antiques)

Circa 1940s brooch, hand-carved shell cameo, scene. **Price: $795**

1940-1950 brooch/pendant, gold filled, transfer on porcelain accentuated by hand painting and surrounded by pearls, 1-3/4" x 2-1/8". **Price: $80**

(D) (Jewelry Box Antiques)

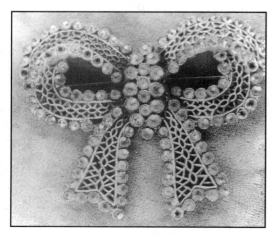

(D) (Jewelry Box Antiques)

1930-1940 brooch, gold over brass set with "paste Topaz stone," approx. 2-1/2" x 2".
Price: $95

1940s brooch/pendant, .925 silver, shell cameo, 1-3/8" x 1-3/4". **Price: $385**

(C) (W. Baldwin)

1940 brooch/pendant, silver over copper mtg. with shell cameo, new 20" sterling chain, cameo 1-1/4" x 1-1/2". **Price: $195**

(D) (Jewelry Box Antiques)

1940-1950s brooch, rhinestones, mkd. "Weiss" 2-5/8" x 1-3/8". **Price: $125**

(C) (Anne Noblitt)

(A) (Photo courtesy of Sotheby's, New York 12-7-83)

1940s brooch, gold maple leaf set with fancy colored sapphires and citrines in shades of green, yellow and burnt orange, Verdura. **Price: $2,860**

1940s brooch, 14K gold with shell cameo, 1-3/8" x 1-3/4". **Price: $495**

(C) (W. Baldwin)

1940s brooch, sterling. This style brooch was advertised in the *"Brecken Book," of Jewelry* in 1947, "Minute design pierced brooch. $5.75," 1-3/4" x 1-1/3". **Price: $125**

(D) (Camille Grace)

(D) (Jewelry Box Antiques)

1940s brooch, gold filled, 1-3/4" x 2-1/4". **Price: $30**

(D) (Camille Grace)

1940s brooch, yellow gold filled with topaz-colored stone, 1-1/4" x 1". **Price: $60**

(D) (June O'Donnell)

1950s brooch, gold metal mkd. Francors, strawberry motif with enameling and set with dark pink paste stones, approx. 3" x 1-3/4".

Price: $225

(D) (Jewelry Box Antiques)

1950s brooch, rhinestones, 2" dia.

Price: $85

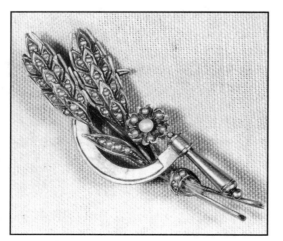

(C) (W. Baldwin)

1940s brooch, gold over silver with pearls, 2-1/2" x 7/8". **Price: $195**

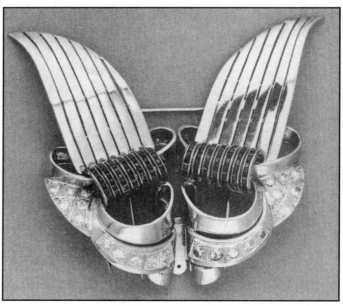

(A) (Photo courtesy of Sotheby's, New York 12-7-83)

1940 double clip brooch, platinum with calibre-cut rubies and old European cut diamonds. **Price: $2,475**

1940s pin with cross, gold over brass, Victorian hand holding cross, hand 1-1/2" x 1/2", cross 3/4" x 1/2", cross should be hanging down. **Price: $50**

(D) (Jewelry Box Antiques)

(D) (Jewelry Box Antiques)

Pin/1940s locket, gold metal "sweetheart pin," pin approx. 1-1/2" x 3/4", locket approx. 1" x 3/4".
Price: $85

(C) (Amanda Bell)

1940s pin, gold-filled, spells "Amanda," these name pins were very popular. A common misconception is that they were made of 10K gold wire; this is not true. The pin measures 2-3/8" x 1/2". **Price: $50**

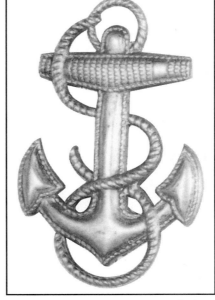

1940s pin, sterling with gold wash, anchor motif, 3/4" x 1-1/4". **Price: $70**

(C) (Peggy Carlson)

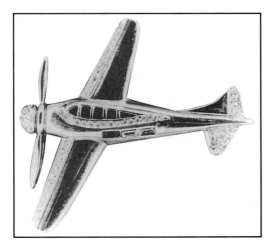

(D) (June O'Donnell)

1940s pin, sterling silver airplane with rhinestones, approx. 2-3/4" x 2-1/2".
Price: $135

1950s pin, black enameled metal, mkd. "Weiss," berries are red stones with green stone tops, 1-1/2" x 1/4".
Price: $70

(D) (Jewelry Box Antiques)

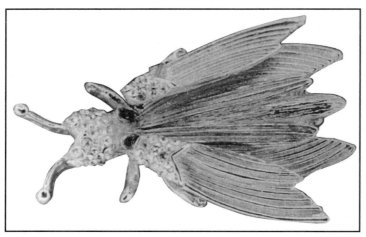

(D) (June O'Donnell)

1940s pin, gold-colored metal, trembler fly motif set with rhinestones and mkd. "Hattie Carnegie," approx. 2" x 1".

Price: $250

Back of pin V-135 showing maker's mark

1940s pin/locket, yellow gold filled with enameled flower, holds 4 photos, approx. 2-1/2" x 1".

Price: $95

(D) (Jewelry Box Antiques)

Pin/locket opened to reveal photos.

Earrings

(D) (Jewelry Box Antiques)

1940-1950 earrings, mkd. "Limoges, France," clip backs. **Price: $65**

(C) (W. Baldwin)

1940s earrings, 14K gold with cabochon garnets, clips 3/4" x 7/8". **Price: $495**

(D) (Jewelry Box Antiques)

1940s earrings, gold over white metal with shell cameos on new 14K gold wires, 3/4" x 1-1/2" l. **Price: $225**

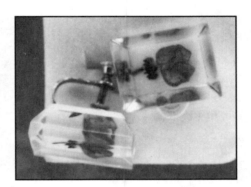

(D) (Jewelry Box Antiques)

1940s earrings, lucite, approx. 1/2" x 3/4". **Price: $70**

(D) (Jewelry Box Antiques)

1940s earrings, gold over sterling mountings, hand-carved cinnabar drops, 1-1/2" l. **Price: $125**

(D) (Jewelry Box Antiques)

1940s earrings, sterling mtgs. with hand-carved ivory in original box, 3/4" x 1". **Price: $150**

(C) (Mary Holloway)

1945 earrings, white metal and rhinestones, 3/4" x 1". **Price: $95**

(C) (Mary Holloway)

1945 earrings, white metal with rhinestones, 1-1/4" x 1-5/8". **Price: $60**

(D) (Jewelry Box Antiques)

1950s earrings, sterling, Siam motif with Niello enameling, 5/8" x 1". **Price: $95**

(C) (Peggy Carlson)

1952 earrings, copper. mkd. "Gert Barkin, New Hope, Pa," 3/4" dia. **Price: $85**

(C) (Mary Holloway)

1940s earrings, early copper with sterling screws, 1" x 1". **Price: $60**

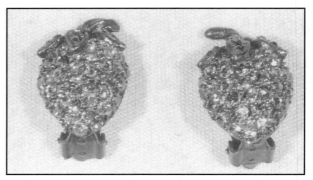

(D) (Jewelry Box Antiques)

Earrings, strawberries. **Price: $70**

(C) (Mary Holloway)

1945 earrings, white metal, antiqued key-hole motif, 1" x 2". **Price: $75**

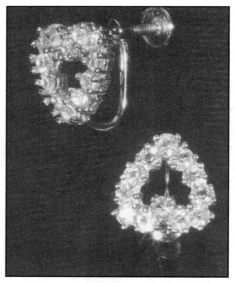

(D) (Jewelry Box Antiques)

1950s earrings, sterling, rhinestones, in original box, 1/2" x 1".

Price: $125

Lockets

1940s locket, yellow gold over brass, 7/8" x 1". **Price: $50**

1940s locket, 1/20 12K G.F. mother-of-pearl top with gold cross, original box and chain.
Price: $60

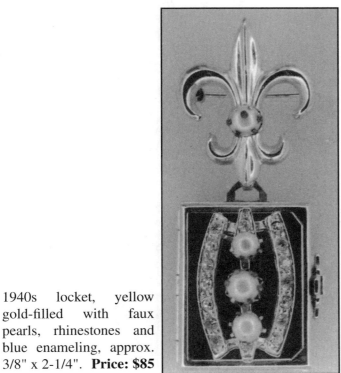

1940s locket, yellow gold-filled with faux pearls, rhinestones and blue enameling, approx. 3/8" x 2-1/4". **Price: $85**

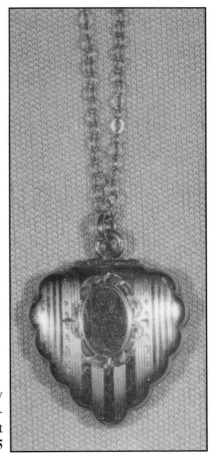

1940s locket, yellow gold-filled, on original 18" chain, mint condition. **Price: $75**

343

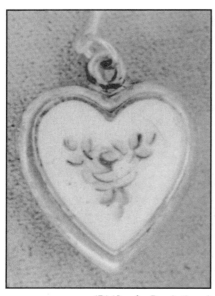

1930-1940s locket, yellow gold filled heart shape with enameling, approx. 3/4" x 3/4".
Price: $80

(D) (Jewelry Box Antiques)

1940s locket, yellow gold-filled heart, 3/4" x 1". **Price: $55**

(D) (Jewelry Box Antiques)

1940s locket, yellow gold-filled heart, 1" x 1-1/4". **Price: $60**

(D) (Jewelry Box Antiques)

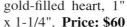

1940s locket, yellow gold-filled heart, 3/4" x 1". **Price: $70**

(D) (Jewelry Box Antiques)

1940s locket, gold over sterling heart with military insignia on mother-of-pearl, new gold filled chain, locket 5/8" x 1".
Price: $60

(D) (Jewelry Box Antiques)

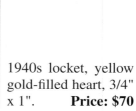

1940s locket, yellow gold-filled with faux pearls, rhinestones and blue enameling, approx. 3/8" x 2-1/4". **Price: $85**

(D) (Jewelry Box Antiques)

Necklaces

(D) (Jewelry Box Antiques)

1940s cross necklace, yellow gold filled with green gold leaves, cross approx. 1-1/2" x 1", chain 18" l.
Price: $80

(D) (Jewelry Box Antiques)

1940s cross necklace, mkd. "1/20 12K G.F. on sterling," original box and chain, cross 3/4" x 1-1/8". **Price: $65**

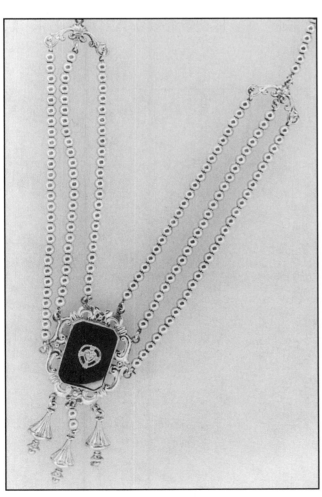

(D) (Jewelry Box Antiques)

1930-1940s necklace, yellow gold filled set with onyx and brilliant, approx. 18" l. **Price: $165**

(D) (Jewelry Box Antiques)

1940-1950s necklace, rhinestones, mkd. "D'vera, N.Y."
Price: $95

345

1940s necklace, gold over brass, chain 28" l, drop onyx and pearl 1-1/4" x 1-7/8".

Price: $95

1940s necklace, gold on copper, drop has green marble-ized stone with imitation amethyst and pearls, drop 1-3/4" x 2-1/4".

Price: $60

1940s necklace, 10K yellow, pink, and green gold with aquamarine stone on original chain, drop 3/4" x 1-1/4".

Price: $395

1950s necklace, silver over brass, rhinestones, mkd. "Garne Jewelry."

Price: $80

(D) (Jewelry Box Antiques)

Necklace, sterling with rhinestones, Arlene Francis made this motif famous when she wore it on T.V. show "What's My Line?" **Price: $95**

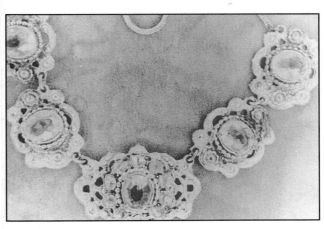

(D) (Jewelry Box Antiques)

1940s necklace, yellow metal set with yellow paste stones, 16" overall, 5 plaques ranging from 1-1/8" x 7/8" to 1-3/4" x 1-1/4" (has matching bracelet). **Price: $170**

1940s necklace, rhinestones. **Price: $95**

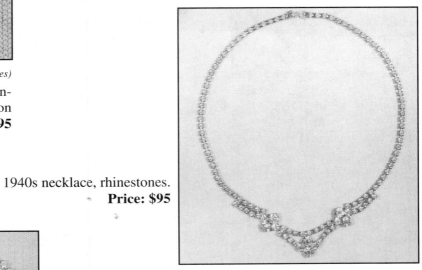

(D) (Jewelry Box Antiques)

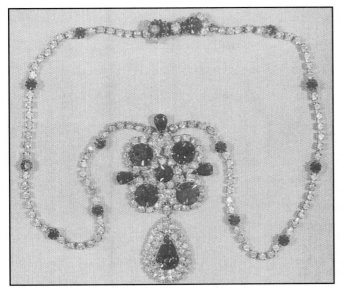

(D) (Jewelry Box Antiques)

1950s necklace, rhinestones and imitation blue sapphires, each stone nicely set. **Price: $345**

1950s necklace, rhinestones, 14" l. **Price: $80**

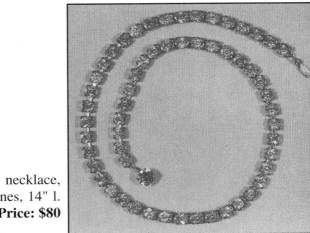

(D) (Jewelry Box Antiques)

Rings

(D) (Jewelry Box Antiques)

1930-1940s ring, 14K yellow gold with white gold head set with .19 ct diamonds. **Price: $495**

(D) (Jewelry Box Antiques)

Circa 1940s ring, 14K yellow gold, Retro Modern style, set with three garnets. **Price: $295**

(D) (Jewelry Box Antiques)

1940-1950s ring, 10K yellow gold oval onyx with diamond.
Price: $325

(D) (Jewelry Box Antiques)

Circa 1940s ring, 14K pink, yellow and green gold, set with blue zircon. **Price: $475**

(C) (Nancy Fargo)

1940-1950s ring, 14K white gold set with synthetic Alexandrite-like sapphire, approx. 9/16" x 1/4".
Price: $295

(D) (Jewelry Box Antiques)

Ring, 10K yellow gold with jade, 15/16" x 7/16".
Price: $380

(D) (Jewelry Box Antiques)

Circa 1940s ring, 14K yellow gold, Retro Modern style, set with cultured pearl. **Price: $330**

(D) (Jewelry Box Antiques)

1940s ring, 10K yellow gold set with opal and 2 synthetic rubies, approx. 7.2mm. **Price: $235**

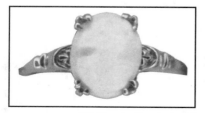

(D) (Jewelry Box Antiques)

1940s ring, 10K yellow gold cameo. **Price: $295**

(D) (Jewelry Box Antiques)

1940s ring, 10K yellow gold with hand carved shell cameo.
Price: $395

(A) (Photo courtesy of Sotheby's New York 12-7-83)

1940s ring, gold with 8 round fancy greenish to brownish grey-yellow natural color diamonds, 16 calibre-cut cabochon rubies and 18 round and single cut diamonds. **Price: $2,750**

1940s ring, 14K yellow gold band. **Price: $195**

1940s ring, 14K yellow gold with synthetic rubies.

Price: $235

1940s ring, 14K yellow gold set with aquamarine, 3.22 cts approx.

Price: $695

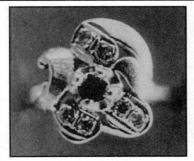

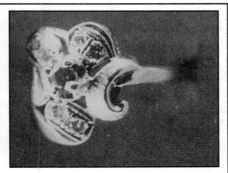

1940s ring, 14K pink and white gold set with blue sapphire and diamonds.

Price: $1,050

Side view of ring.

Watches & Watch Accessories

1940s watch pin, gold over sterling, 2-1/2" x 3/4".   **Price: $115**

1946 money clip watch, gold with watch, 5/50cm x 4cm, Cartier, engraved "Douglas Fairbanks for Alan P.P.W. May 46." £140.
Price: $250

1943-1944 watch chain, made of coins from Australia, New Zealand, 7-1/2" l.
Price: $125

1937 gentleman's wristwatch, Patek Phillipe & Co., 18K yellow gold with 18 jewel movement.
Price: $5,000

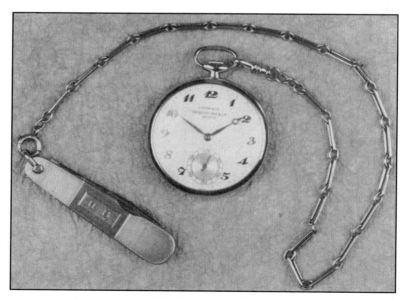

1948 open-face pocket watch, Patek Phillipe & Co., 18K yellow gold with 18 jewel nickel movement, in original box, with 14K yellow gold watch chain and pen knife.   **Price: $1,500**

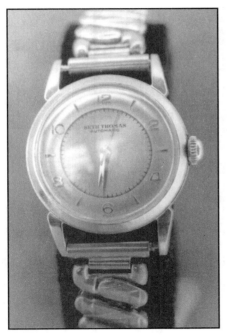

1950s wristwatch, yellow gold filled, Seth Thomas, approx. 1-1/4".
Price: $395

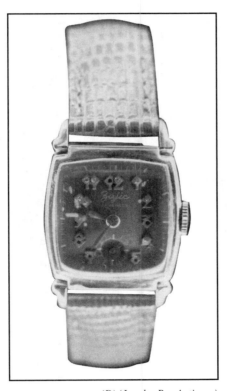

1940s wristwatch yellow gold filled, Lord Elgin.　**Price: $395**

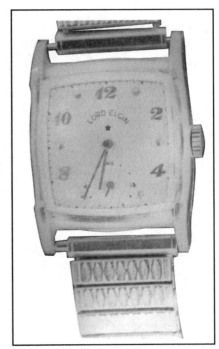

1940s wristwatch yellow gold filled, Lord Elgin.　**Price: $395**

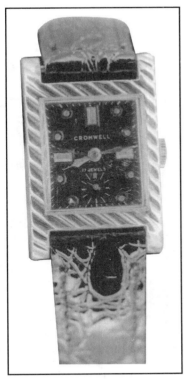

1930-1940s wristwatch, yellow gold filled, Cronewell, 17 jewel with black dial.
Price: $425

1930s wristwatch, yellow gold filled "Gruen Veri-thin," 1" x 1" approx.　**Price: $465**

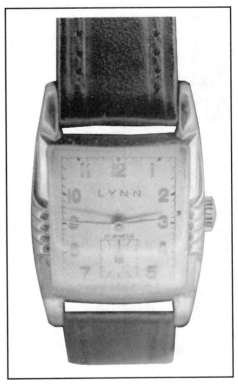

1930-1940s wristwatch, 10K rolled gold plated, Monarch Watch Co., 17 jewel, dial marked Lynn.　**Price: $425**

1940s wristwatch, 14K yellow gold, movement mkd. "Hamilton-911," 17 jewels.
Price: $395

1940s wristwatch, yellow gold filled, Bulova excellency. **Price: $350**

1950s wristwatch, 14K yellow gold, Kingston, mkd. Hamilton, 17 jewels.
Price: $575

1940s wristwatch, 10K yellow gold Benrus.
Price: $380

1940s wristwatch, 18K gold, Patek Phillipe & Co., Geneve, nickel lever movement, 18 jewels, adjusted to 5 positions, mono-metallic compensation balance, silvered and matte dial, Arabic and baton numerals, dial and movement signed, 1-3/8"dia.
Price: $990

1940s wristwatch, yellow gold filled mkd. "Wittnauer Watch Co.," 17 jewel.
Price: $395

1940s wristwatch, white gold filled Geneva deluxe set with rhinestones, dial approx. 5/8" x 5/8". **Price: $225**

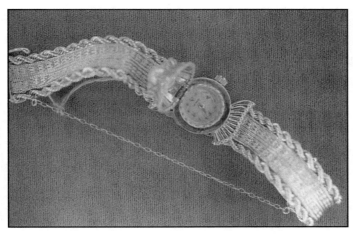

1950s wristwatch, platinum and diamond man's Patek Phillippe & Co., Geneve, nickel lever movement, mono-metallic compensated balance, 5 adjustments, silvered dial applied with calibre and brilliant cut diamonds.
Price: $1,980

(D) (Jewelry Box Antiques)

1940s watch, 14K yellow gold with diamonds and pearl cover, "Lafemone" approx. 9/16" w. **Price: $2,800**

(A) (Photo courtesy of Sotheby's, New York 4-10-84)

(A) (Photo courtesy of Sotheby's, New York 4-10-84)

1940s wristwatch, 18K rectangular man's Patek Phillippe & Co., Geneve, tonneau nickel lever movement, 3 adjustments, 18 jewels, signed Tiffany on movement and case, 18K brickwork strap, 1-3/4" dia.

Price: $3,025

(A) (Photo courtesy of Sotheby's, New York 4-10-83)

1950s wristwatch, man's 18K gold square case with 14K link strap, Patek Phillippe & Co. movement #959431, nickel lever, mono-metallic compensation balance, silvered matte dial applied with gold baton numerals.

Price: $1,210

(D) (Jewelry Box Antiques)

1950s wristwatch, 14K yellow gold, Kingston, mkd. "Hamilton.," 17 jewels.

Price: $495

Sets

1940s brooch and compact, mkd. "Sterling by Cini," compact 4" dia.; brooch 2-1/2" x 2-3/4". **Price: $450**

(D) (Lucille and Sam Mundorff)

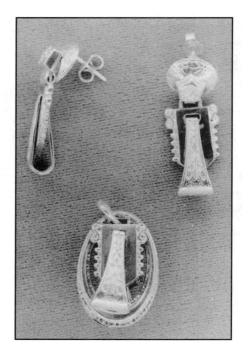

(D) (Jewelry Box Antiques)

1940s pendant/earrings, yellow gold filled copy of a Victorian design, pendant 1-1/16" x 10/16"; earrings 1-5/16" x 1/2". **Price: $135**

Early 1940s pin and earrings, plastic with design incised in molding in back and painted, pin 1-1/8" x 1/2", earrings 3/4" x 3/4". **Price of set: $125**

(C) (Peggy Carlson)

(C) (Mary Holloway)

1949-1952 brooch and earrings, white metal with rhinestones, brooch 2" dia.; clip earrings 1" x 1". **Price: $125**

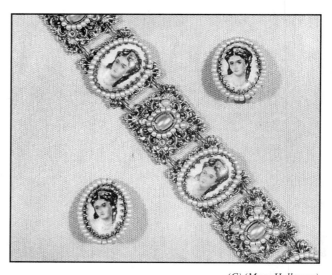

(C) (Mary Holloway)

1940s bracelet and earrings, yellow gold over brass, transfer on porcelain accentuated with hand painted details, pearls strung on wire, bracelet 1" x 7"; earrings 3/4" x 1". **Price of set: $125**

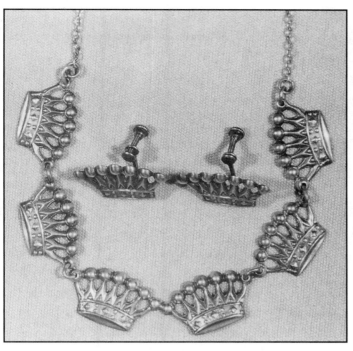

(C) (Peggy Carlson)

1940s necklace and earrings, copper with enameling.
Price: $125

(D) (Jewelry Box Antiques)

1940-1950s necklace and earrings, sterling, crowns each marked "sterling," 7/8" x 5/8". **Price: $145**

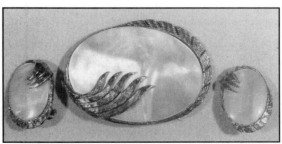

1940s-1950s pin and earrings, gold filled with mother-of-pearl, pin 2-3/8" x 1-7/8", earrings 7/8" x 1-1/4". **Price: $80**

(C) (Anne Noblitt)

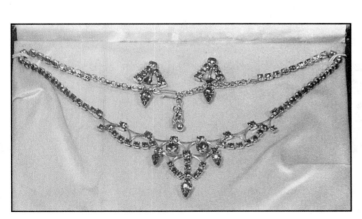

(D) (Jewelry Box Antiques)

1950s necklace and earrings, silver finished white metal with amethyst-color stones, original box with original price of $5. **Price: $165**

(D) (Jewelry Box Antiques)

1940s-1950s necklace and earrings, gold over white metal, mkd. "Leo Glass," topaz-colored "stone," original box, original price $38. **Price: $85**

(D) (June O'Donnell)

1930-1940s pin/earrings, sterling silver duette set by Coro Craft, set with rhinestones.

Price: $350

Closer look at pin.

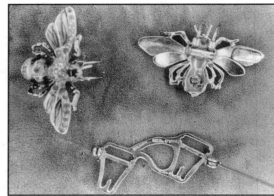

Pin apart to show front.

(C) (Peggy Carlson)

Late 1950s bracelet, mkd. "Sterling England," 6 old masters, each 5/8" x 1", original box states, "This bracelet is hand painted in oils," bracelet 7" l.

Price: $195

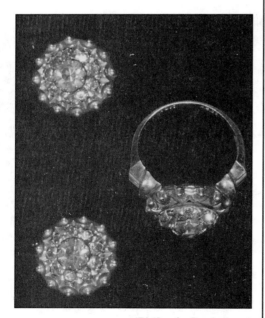

(D) (Jewelry Box Antiques)

1940s ring and earrings, 10K gold with aquamarine-colored stone, 5/8".

Price: $395

(D) (Jewelry Box Antiques)

Brooch/pendant 1-7/8" x 2-3/8".

Price: $195

Miscellaneous

(D) (Camille Grace)

1940s cigarette case, gold over brass, mkd. "Evans," top is mother-of-pearl with enameling, 3" x 4".   **Price: $195**

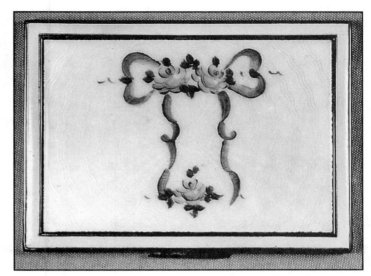

(D) (Camille Grace)

1940s cigarette case, mkd. "Evans," beautifully enameled, 4-3/8" x 3-1/4".   **Price: $195**

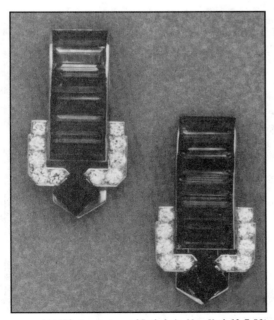

(A) (Photo courtesy of Sotheby's, New York 12-7-83)

1940s clips, gold and platinum set with 12 emerald cut citrines, 20 square cut citrines and 20 round diamonds, Cartier, London.   **Price: $4,400**

(C) (Mary Holloway)

1957 cross 1/20 12K gold filled, 1" x 1-3/4".   **Price: $50**

357

(D) (Jewelry Box Antiques)

1950s cross, 14K yellow gold, (dated Dec. 25, 1953) 1-1/4" x 3/4".
Price: $125

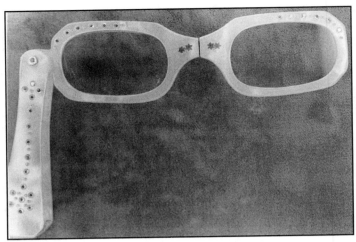

(D) (Jewelry Box Antiques)

1950s eyeglasses, lucite studded with rhinestones, approx. 1-1/8" x 3" closed.
Price: $95

(D) (Jewelry Box Antiques)

1940s pendant/charm, 14K yellow gold with flower motif set with cabochon amethyst and pink sapphire, approx. 3/8".
Price: $590

(D) (Jewelry Box Antiques)

1930s perfume pendant, white metal with enameled flowers motif, approx. 1-1/2" x 1".
Price: $135

Chapter Six: 1940s Retro

The Retro Modern Style

The 1940-1950s time period had a variety of jewelry styles. Just as the 1890-1910 period had Arts and Crafts, Art Nouveau and Edwardian all at the same time, the 1940-1950s had designs inspired by romantic Victorian pieces, and a new style that is now referred to as Retro Modern.

Since styles do tend to overlap, it is interesting to see jewelry of white gold filigree and the Victorian romantic style pictured along the side of Retro Modern pieces. In illustration "A", one can see how dramatically different the Retro pieces are from the romantic revival cameo's and chatelaine pin locket. In illustrations "B" and "C" from the 1942 L & C Mayers Co., there is a sharp contrast between the Retro pins and filigree ones. The same is true with the bracelets in illustrations "D" and "E" from the same catalog.

As early as 1932, a subtle change of style was showing up in jewelry catalogs. By the late 1930s, the style now known as Retro Modern was very much in evidence. The new designs based on nature were stylized and rendered with shiny finishes on pink, green, yellow, and rose gold. These designs had a more dimensional look than the proceeding period.

Retro Modern is not a period style. It was not reflected in architectural styles or in the decorative arts other than jewelry. But it is a definite, recognizable style for jewelry design from the late 1930s throughout the 1940s. It is not as sleek and streamlined as Art Deco. Many of the pieces have polished curves. The cone definitely replaced the geometric cube of Art Deco.

Rubies were often set in the rose gold which was so popular. Many pieces had several colors

COSTUME AND SPORT JEWELRY

Effective New Styles. Well Made and Beautifully Finished. Good Color. Hand Set Simulated Stones. Attractive Gift Boxes.

PRICES SUBJECT TO CATALOG DISCOUNTS. SEE PAGE 1.

Unless ordered on Dealer or Company Purchase Forms specifying that articles are to be resold, prices on this page are subject to a 10% Federal Excise Tax.

GOLD FILLED EARRINGS

A—DJ 3008 .... $3.80
1/20-12 Kt. rose gold filled. Deep color simulated garnets. Bright finish petals.

B—DJ 3009 .... $4.50
1/20-12 Kt. rose and green gold filled. Fine color simulated blue green zircon. Newest design.

Illustrations actual size.

DJ 3011 2 Pc. Set in Gift Box; Yellow Gold Filled, 2 Genuine Zircons......$15.50
1/20-10 Kt. yellow gold filled LaValliere and bracelet. 2 genuine zircons, good color blue-green. Artistic floral ornaments in softly blended rose and green gold filled. Bracelet has safety chain; LaValliere, 16 in. chain. Neat gift box.

CHATELAINE PIN AND LOCKET

DJ 3010 .... $8.00
1/20-10 Kt. yellow gold filled. Satin finish, two tone, hand engraved floral effect. Detachable locket, holds two photos, can be worn on a chain. Bow knot chatelaine pin with safety catch suitable for attaching lapel watches.

DJ 3012 .... $4.00
1/20-12 Kt. yellow gold filled brooch. Softly blended rose and green gold filled flower and leaf motif. 2 simulated blue-green zircons. Safety catch. Matches bracelet DJ 3005.

DJ 3013 .... $10.00
1/20-12 Kt. yellow gold filled brooch. Genuine carnelian cameo, hand carved. Safety catch.

DJ 3014 .... $7.20
1/20-12 Kt. yellow gold filled locket. Genuine hand carved carnelian cameo. Hidden locket holds 2 photos. 18 in. chain.

DJ 3015 .... $5.20
1/20-12 Kt. yellow gold filled brooch. Genuine carnelian cameo, hand carved. Safety catch.

DJ 3016 .... $4.80
1/20-12 Kt. yellow gold filled. 2 tone decoration. Simulated blue-green zircon.

SPORT, IDENTIFICATION BRACELETS, ANKLETS AND TAGS

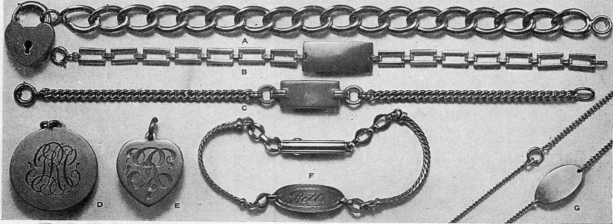

(Tags Shown May Be Attached to Any Bracelet.)

A—SLAVE BRACELET
DJ 3017 1/20-12 Kt. Yellow Gold.........$6.00
Good weight, bright finish slave links and padlock clasp.

B—IDENTIFICATION BRACELET
DJ 3018 10 Kt. Yellow Gold.............$14.80
Medium weight, bright finish. Tailored design.

C—IDENTIFICATION BRACELET
DJ 3019 1/20-12 Kt. Yellow Gold Filled...$4.20
Good weight, bright finish, curb chain.

BRACELET TAGS

D—DJ 3020 .... $2.50
1/20-12 Kt. yellow gold filled, bright finish, heavy weight. May be attached to any bracelet. (Monogram #300 illustrated $1.00 list extra.)

E—DJ 3021 .... $3.00
1/20-12 Kt. yellow gold filled, bright finish, heavy weight. May be attached to any bracelet. (Monogram #320 $1.50 list extra.)

(Prices for Engraving Listed Separately)

F—IDENTIFICATION BRACELET
DJ 3022 .... $6.00
Simmons quality yellow gold filled, good weight. Bright finish. Ratchet clasp. Length 7 inches. (Style 304 Engraving, .80 list, extra.)

G—ANKLETS
DJ 3023 10 Kt. Yellow Gold.............$7.50
DJ 3024 Sterling Silver 1.60
Medium weight, bright finish. Curb chain. Length, 9 inches.

═══ L. & C. MAYERS CO. FIFTH AVE., NEW YORK ═══

III

Illustration A.

GOLD BROOCHES AND PINS

14 Kt. and 10 Kt. White and Yellow Gold, Effective New Styles, Well Made and Splendidly Finished. Fine Quality Blue White Diamonds, Faceted and Full Polished. Choice Quality Colored Stones and Cultured Pearls. Safety Catches. Attractive Gift Boxes. Illustrations Actual Size.

PRICES SUBJECT TO CATALOG DISCOUNTS. SEE PAGE 1.

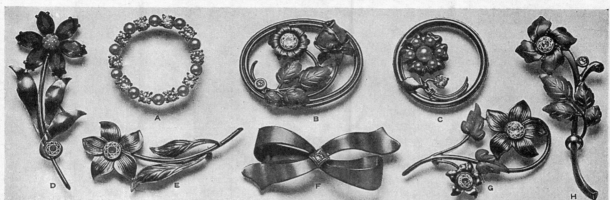

A—DJ 2785 14 Kt...........$72.50
Yellow gold circle pin, good wgt. 10 genuine zircons, fine color blue-green, alternate with 10 lustrous full-cultured pearls.

B—DJ 2786 14 Kt...........$63.50
Yellow gold, heavy wgt. Modulated and engraved flowers and leaves. Genuine blue-green zircon; fine blue white full-cut diamond.

C—DJ 2787 14 Kt...........$35.80
Yellow gold circle pin; heavy weight, bright finish. 1 large and 6 smaller full-cultured pearls. Genuine blue-green zircon.

D—DJ 2788 14 Kt...........$69.50
Yellow gold flower pin; heavy weight, bright finish. 6 fine deep-color genuine amethyst petals; genuine opal center.

E—DJ 2789 10 Kt...........£14.00
Yellow gold flower pin; light weight, bright finish. Engraved and modulated leaves and flower. Simulated amethyst center.

F—DJ 2790 14 Kt...........$61.50
Rose and green gold bow knot pin; good weight, beautifully modeled. Fine blue white full-cut diamond.

G—DJ 2791 10 Kt...........$23.80
Yellow gold spray pin; medium weight, bright finish. Engraved and modulated. 2 genuine blue-green zircons.

H—DJ 2792 14 Kt...........$58.00
Yellow gold spray pin; good weight. Beautifully modeled and hand engraved. Genuine zircon, fine color blue-green. Fine full-cut diamond.

DJ 2793 14 Kt.....................$56.60
Rose and yellow gold, heavy weight, bright finish. Beautifully styled, modulated design. Large genuine zircon, deep blue-green.

DJ 2794 14 Kt.....................$127.50
White gold, beautifully pierced and chased. 1 large full-cut, and 6 smaller fine blue white diamonds.

DJ 2795 14 Kt.....................$112.00
Yellow gold, good weight, bright finish. Large genuine zircon, very deep blue-green. 2 fine blue white full-cut diamonds.

DJ 2796 10 Kt.....................$24.50
Rose and green gold bow knot pin; good weight, beautifully modeled. Genuine zircon, good color blue-green.

DJ 2797 14 Kt.........$39.50
Yellow gold, good weight, bright finish. Modeled rose gold bow knot. Fine full-cut diamond.

DJ 2798 10 Kt.........$53.00
Yellow gold, good weight, bright finish. Beautifully hand made. 5 genuine zircons, deep blue-green.

DJ 2799 10 Kt.........$24.50
Yellow gold, medium weight. Neatly pierced and modeled bow-knot design. Genuine zircon, fine color blue-green.

DJ 2800 10 Kt.....................$25.00
Yellow gold, medium weight. Daintily pierced and chased floral design. Fine blue white diamond.

DJ 2801 14 Kt.....................$35.00
Yellow gold, good weight, bright finish. Beautifully pierced design. 3 genuine zircons, deep blue-green.

DJ 2802 14 Kt.............$31.50
White gold, good weight. Daintily pierced filigree. Fine blue white full-cut diamond. Excellent value.

DJ 2803 10 Kt.............$21.00
White gold, good weight. Neatly pierced and chased filigree. Fine blue white diamond.

DJ 2804 10 Kt.....$25.00
Yellow gold; rose and green gold flower on genuine black onyx. Fine white diamond.

DJ 2805 10 Kt.........$17.00
Yellow gold, medium weight; neatly pierced. Genuine zircon, good color blue-green.

DJ 2806 10 Kt.....$15.00
Rose and green gold; good weight, bright finish. Genuine blue-green zircon.

DJ 2807 10 Kt.........$10.50
Yellow gold, medium weight. Daintily pierced and chased. Simulated blue sapphire.

DJ 2808 10 Kt.........$22.50
Yellow gold, medium weight, bright finish. 3 genuine amethyst of fine color.

L.&C.MAYERS CO. FIFTH AVE., NEW YORK

100

Illustration B.

GOLD BRACELETS

14 Kt. and 10 Kt. White and Yellow Gold. Exquisite Designs, Well Made and Beautifully Finished. Fine Quality Blue White Diamonds, Faceted and Full Polished. Attractive Gift Boxes. Illustrations Actual Size.

OTHER FINE GOLD BRACELETS SHOWN ON PAGES 96 AND 97.

PRICES SUBJECT TO CATALOG DISCOUNTS. SEE PAGE 1.

Unless ordered on Dealer or Company Purchase Forms specifying that articles are to be resold, prices on this page are subject to a 10% Federal Excise Tax.

DJ 2768 14 Kt. White Gold; 17 Fine Blue White Diamonds.......................$320.00
DJ 2769 14 Kt. White Gold; 5 Fine Blue White Diamonds........................ 125.00
Fine quality blue white diamonds. 14 Kt. white gold flexible links; good weight, beautifully pierced and chased.

DJ 2770 14 Kt. Yellow Gold; 10 Fine Blue White Diamonds.....................$185.00
10 fine quality blue white diamonds set in centers of exquisitely designed flower links. 14 Kt. yellow gold; good weight, bright finish.

All Our Diamonds are Fine Quality Blue White, Faceted and Full Polished. Make This Your Standard.

DJ 2771 14 Kt. White Gold; Fine Blue White Diamond.........................$50.00
DJ 2772 14 Kt. Yellow Gold; Fine Blue White Diamond......................... 50.00
Fine quality blue white diamond. 14 Kt. gold flexible links, neatly pierced and chased; good weight, bright finish.

DJ 2773 14 Kt. Yellow Gold; 3 Genuine Blue Sapphires...........................$42.00
3 light blue genuine sapphires in beautifully made flowers. 14 Kt. yellow gold links; good weight, bright finish; hand engraved green gold leaves.

DJ 2774 14 Kt. Rose and Green Gold..$33.50
14 Kt. rose gold effectively designed scroll links; 14 Kt. green gold connecting links. Good weight, bright finish. Stylish modern bracelet.

DJ 2775 10 Kt. Yellow Gold; Fine Blue White Diamond...........................$40.50
Fine quality blue white diamond. 10 Kt. yellow gold flexible links; daintily pierced and chased. Light weight, bright finish.

DJ 2776 10 Kt. Yellow Gold; Fine Diamond in Genuine Black Onyx................$34.50
Fine blue white diamond in center of genuine black onyx. 10 Kt. yellow gold neatly pierced links; light weight, bright finish.

L. & C. MAYERS CO. FIFTH AVE., NEW YORK

Illustration C.

of gold incorporated into the design. Lady's bracelet watches became very popular. The lids covering the dials were often encrusted with rubies and diamonds. Many watch dials were also finished in a rose or red-gold.

One reason that yellow gold became popular again in the 1940s was because the government restricted the use of platinum. It was needed in munitions plants. The War Production Board had limited the use of silver, consequently "gold filled" was the available material for costume jewelry.

After Dior came out with the "New Look" in 1947, jewelry took on much larger proportions. I had the pleasure of being the jewelry consultant for the movie, "Mr. & Mrs. Bridge," starring Joanne Woodward and Paul Newman. We used jewelry from the 1920s, 1930s and 1940s to accessorize the costumes. When I brought out Retro Modern pieces for the 1940s scenes, the costume designer said, "They look so modern!" Indeed they do, but when you think about it, so many of our clothing's styles are the same as they were then. Shoulder pads are a good example.

Retro Modern style jewelry has become very much in demand in the last few years. As the demand increases, so will the prices. Many good examples of Retro Modern are included in this section. I placed them together so you can get a "feel" for the design and the elements that came together to form this style.

Bracelets

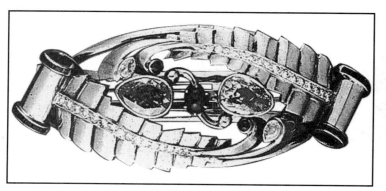

(A) (Photo courtesy of Sotheby's, New York 10-5-83)

1940 bracelet, pink and yellow gold bangle centered with 1 pear-shaped diamond (approx. 2.25 cts) and 1 pear-shaped diamond (approx. 1.80 cts). Embellished with 2 small pear-shaped diamonds and numerous small round diamonds and calibre-cut rubies. **Price: $3,685**

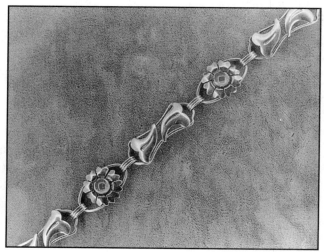

(D) (Jewelry Box Antiques)

1932-1945 bracelet, gold over silver with 2 pink cabochon stones, approx. 6-1/4" l. **Price: $125**

(D) (Jewelry Box Antiques)

1932-1945 bracelet, 10K pink and green gold set with cultured pearls, approx. 1/2" w. **Price: $430**

1937 bracelet, 14K gold bangle with bell-shaped clip (detachable) set with 1 square-shaped ruby, 26 calibre-cut rubies and 26 single cut diamonds, by Cartier. **Price: $4,400**

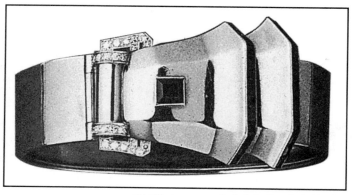

(A) (Photo courtesy Sotheby's, New York 10-6-83)

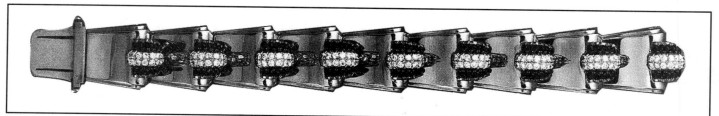

(A) (Photo courtesy of Sotheby's, New York 12-7-83)

1938 bracelet, 18K pink gold with 144 ruby cabochons and 135 round diamonds (approx. 5 cts total). **Price: $8,250**

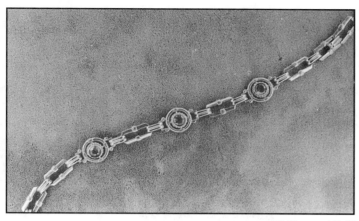

1940s bracelet, 10K yellow gold set with synthetic blue sapphires, approx. 1/4" w x 7" l.   **Price: $425**

1945 bracelet, 14K yellow gold with pink gold cornucopia with yellow gold leaves, centrally set with 1 marquise-shaped diamond, 1 old mine yellow diamond, 4 small round diamonds, 1 round yellow diamond and numerous round and calibre-cut sapphires and rubies, missing watch movement.   **Price: $1,430**

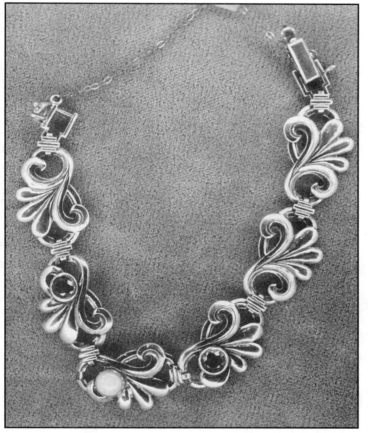

Retro Modern bracelet, gold filled on sterling set with 2 synthetic blue sapphires and 1 opal.   **Price: $295**

1940s bracelet, sterling marked "Truant sterling," blue "stones" are plastic. 3/4" w x 7-1/2" l.

Price: $125

Brooches & Pins

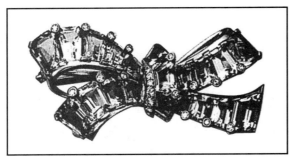

(A) (Photo courtesy Wm. Doyle Galleries, New York 5-2-90)

1940 bow brooch, set with twenty fancy-cut aquamarines, total approx. 50.00 cts, embellished with twenty-one small round diamonds, total approx. .50 cts. **Price: $9,000**

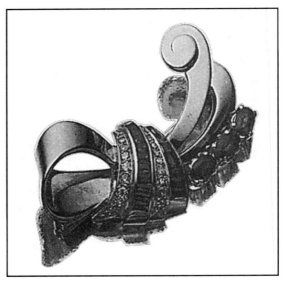

(A) (Photo courtesy Wm. Doyle Galleries, New York 9-19-90)

1940 brooch, 14K yellow gold and platinum with bands of thirty round full-cut diamonds, total approx. 1.00 cts. and assorted square-cut garnets. **Price: $4,500**

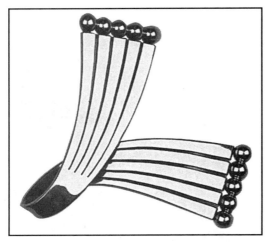

(A) (Photo courtesy Skinner, Inc., Boston, Mass 12-4-90)

1940s brooch, 14K yellow gold.
Price: $650

(A) (Photo courtesy Wm. Doyle Galleries, New York 12-7-89)

1940 two-tone gold, ruby, aquamarine and diamond scroll brooch, 18K yellow and red gold. **Price: $9,000**

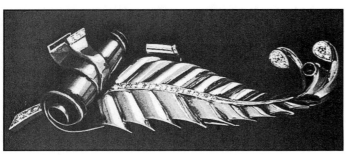

(A) (Photo courtesy of Sotheby's, New York 10-5-83)

1940 brooch, yellow and pink gold leaf motif embellished with rubies and diamonds. **Price: $1,320**

1940s brooches, pink gold studded with 124 round and single cut diamonds (approx. 4 cts) and 8 round and oval-shaped cabochon rubies.
Price: $1,650

1940 gold, diamond, and ruby scroll brooch, 18K yellow gold and platinum, set with cabochon rubies and pavé diamond, signed "Reflection, Trabert and Hoeffer, Mauboussin."
Price: $2,900

1940s brooch mkd. "1/20 12K G.F. Iskin Jewelry," pink, yellow, green gold with a shining finish, blue stones, original box.
Price: $125

(D) (Jewelry Box Antiques)

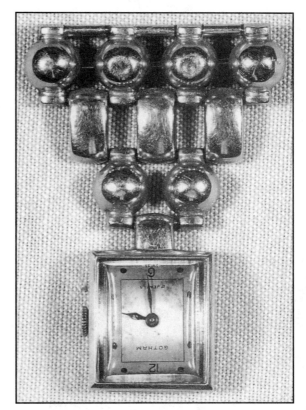

(C) (W. Baldwin)

1930s pin watch, 14K Gotham Swiss watch, 1-1/2" x 2-1/8".
Price: $1,200

(C) (Paul & Sally Ficken)

1932-1945 Retro Modern pin watch, yellow gold filled, worn by Joanne Woodward in the movie "Mr & Mrs. Bridge."
Price: $495

1930s pin, mkd. "sterling Denmark," attributed to Georg Jenson, a Danish sculptor, 1-1/8" x 7/8".
Price: $225

1932-1945 pin, sterling silver flower motif, approx. 3" x 1-3/4". **Price: $135**

1940s Retro Modern pin, yellow and pink gold filled with blue synthetic stone, approx. 1" dia. **Price: $95**

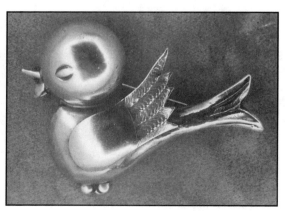

1940s Retro Modern pin, Mexican silver, bird-shaped, 2-1/4" x 1-3/4". **Price: $85**

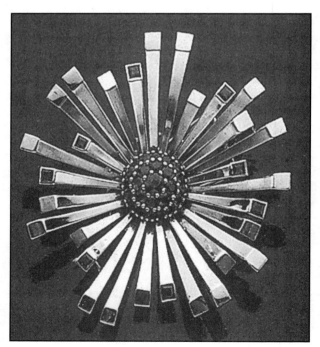

1950 star burst pin, 14K yellow gold with blue sapphire star and round and square sapphires.
Price: $1,100

*(A) (Photo courtesy Skinner, Inc., Boston, Mass
9-25-90)*

1940s gold, ruby and diamond bow pin, 14K yellow gold set with eight diamonds, approx. .50 ct, and 12 rubies approx. 1.00 ct.   **Price: $1,200**

(D) (Jewelry Box Antiques)

Retro Modern pin, gold filled with faux pearls, citrine paste and foil "stones," worn in the movie "Mr. & Mrs. Bridge," 3 x 4" overall.   **Price: $145**

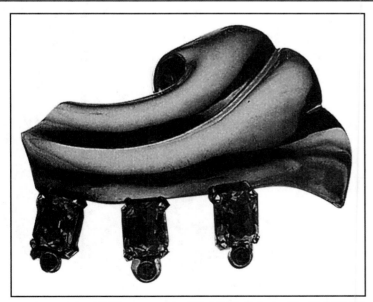

(A) (Photos courtesy of Wm. Doyle Galleries, New York 5-2-90)

1940 gold pins, (above) with three faceted citrines and three cabochon rubies, (right) designed as a two-toned grape cluster and leaf.   **Price: $1,400**

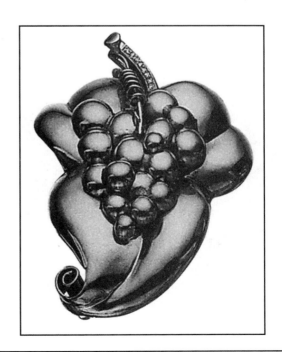

Clips

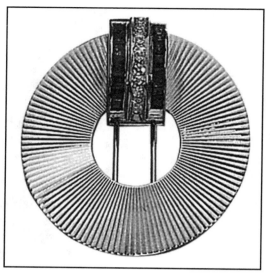

(A) (Photo courtesy Wm. Doyle Galleries, New York 9-19-90)

Clip, 14K red gold with six round single-cut diamonds, total approx. .10 cts and fourteen square-cut rubies, approx. 9.5 dwt. **Price: $800**

(A) (Photo courtesy Wm. Doyle Galleries, New York 12-12-90)

Retro-style clips, 18K yellow gold and platinum with 18 round and 8 baguette-cut rubies, and 28 round full-cut diamonds, total approx. .75 cts.

Price: $2,750

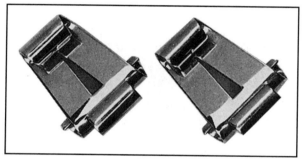

(A) (Photo courtesy of Skinner, Inc., Boston, Mass 12-4-90)

1940s dress clips, 14K yellow gold with scroll design, 15 dwt. **Price: $1,000**

Dress clips, 14K yellow gold with 8 round diamonds and 22 square calibre blue sapphires, total approx. 17.5 dwt. **Price: $3,750**

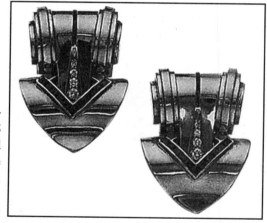

(A) (Photo courtesy of Wm. Doyle Galleries, New York 12-12-90)

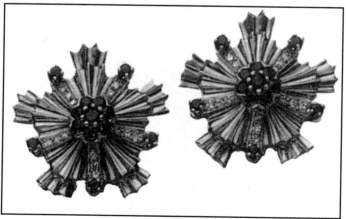

(A) (Photo courtesy Wm. Doyle Galleries, New York 5-2-90)

1945-Retro ear clips, 14K yellow gold centered by ruby clusters with thirty diamonds, total approx. .50 cts, signed "Tiffany and Company." **Price: $4,000**

(A) (Photo courtesy Wm. Doyle Galleries, New York 12-7-89)

1940 pair of gold, ruby, and diamond scroll ear clips, 18K yellow and white gold, pavé diamond and borders by cabochon rubies. **Price: $3,250**

Rings

(D) (Jewelry Box Antiques)

1930-1940s ring, 14K yellow gold set with .30 ct. diamonds, worn in the movie "Mr. & Mrs. Bridge."

Price: $945

(D) (Jewelry Box Antiques)

1932-1945 Retro Modern ring, 14K yellow gold set with diamond and synthetic sapphire. **Price: $895**

(C) (Dorothy Richards)

1932-1945 ring, 14K yellow gold, Tiffany moonstone and sapphires (Mkd. Tiffany & Co.). **Price: $1,500**

(D) (Jewelry Box Antiques)

1932-1945 Retro Modern ring,14K yellow gold set with .30 diamond and .40 ruby. **Price: $1,995**

(D) (Jewelry Box Antiques)

1940s Retro Modern ring, 10K yellow gold style, set with .72 cts., amethyst. **Price: $295**

(A) (Photo courtesy Wm. Doyle Galleries, New York 9-20-89)

1940 gold and diamond ring, 14K red gold enhanced by full-cut diamonds. **Price: $1,400**

Watches

1940s watch pin, gold filled with pink and green gold with glossy finish, 1-1/2" x 1". **Price: $85**

(D) (Jewelry Box Antiques)

(A) (Photo courtesy Wm. Doyle Galleries, New York 9-20-89)

1940s lady's diamond and platinum bracelet watch, platinum, decorated with a diamond arrow motif, brushed platinum bracelet. **Price: $1,500**

Retro Modern wristwatch, 14K yellow gold buckle motif set with diamonds and blue sapphires. When sides are pressed buckle opens and reveals an "Omega" watch. **Price: $3,995**

(D) (Jewelry Box Antiques)

1940 bracelet watch, 18K yellow gold, a stepped disk, a matte gold with face, flexible gold snake chain bracelet, signed "Gubelin." **Price: $2,300**

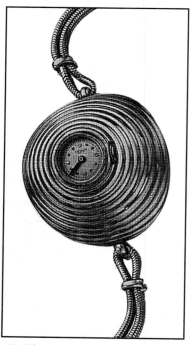

(A) (Photo courtesy Wm. Doyle Galleries, New York 12-7-89)

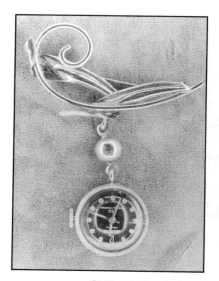

(D) (Jewelry Box Antiques)

1940s lapel watch, yellow gold filled "old store stock" with dark red dial, approx. 2-1/2" l. **Price: $395**

(D) (Jewelry Box Antiques)

1940s pendant watch, pink gold-filled monarch on Retro bow pin. **Price: $395**

(D) (Jewelry Box Antiques)

1940s lapel watch, yellow gold filled, Marcel Boucher, brown dial. approx. 3-1/2" x 1-3/4". **Price: $395**

Sets

(A) (Photo courtesy of Sotheby's, New York 12-7-83)

1940s clip and earrings, 18K pink gold, the brooch has 10 round diamonds and 14 round cabochon rubies, the ear-clips have 18 round diamonds and 20 round cabochon rubies. **Price: $1,430**

(A) (Photo courtesy of Sotheby's, New York 10-5-83)

1945 bracelet and earrings, 14K yellow gold-hinged bracelet had detachable center set with rubies and diamonds, matching ear-clips, Trabert & Hoeffer, Mauboussion. **Price: $2,420**

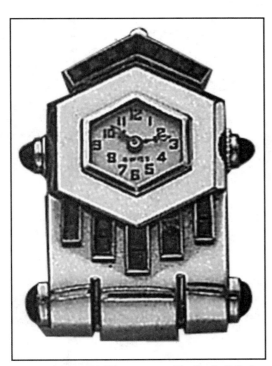

(A) (Photo courtesy Wm. Doyle Galleries, New York 12-12-90)

Clip watch and purse clasp combination, platinum, signed on the 17 jewel movement Ebel, and set with bands of calibre rubies, signed on the back "Van Cleef and Arpels, Inc., from France." **Price: $3,000**

(D) (Jewelry Box Antiques)

Retro Modern pin and earrings, yellow gold filled on sterling set with pink "stones," worn in the movie "Mr. and Mrs. Bridge," 3" x 1-3/4" overall. **Price: $195**

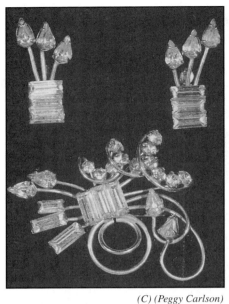

1940s pin and earrings, 1/20 12K G.F. M & S Co., pin: 1-3/8" x 1-1/4"; earrings: 1/2" x 1".
Price: $150

(C) (Peggy Carlson)

(D) (Jewelry Box Antiques)

1940s necklace and bracelet, mkd. "1/20 12K on sterling," amethyst stones, original box with price tag marked $18.95. **Price: $255**

(D) (Jewelry Box Antiques)

1940s necklace and bracelet, mkd. "Pr. St. Co. 1/20 12K G.F," original box tagged "Nancy Lee," red stones, original price $24.00. **Price: $195**

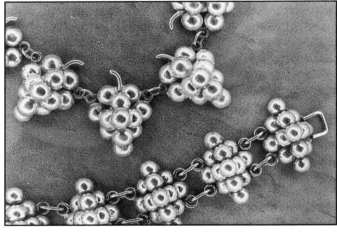

(D) (Jewelry Box Antiques)

1940s necklace and bracelet, sterling silver "Barrera." **Price: $450**

(D) (Jewelry Box Antiques)

1940s pin and earrings, mkd. "1/20 12K G.F. Art," original box, pin can be worn as a necklace, earrings have screw backs.
Price: $145

(A) (Photo courtesy Wm. Doyle Galleries, New York 9-21-83)

1940s clips and earrings, 14K yellow gold set with sapphires and citrines, signed "Tiffany." **Price: $1,100**

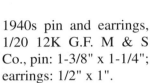

(A) (Photo courtesy Wm. Doyle Galleries, New York 9-19-90)

Retro-style wristwatch and earrings set, 14K yellow gold and platinum framed by a border of diamonds, fifty-six assorted baguettes, total approx. 4.00 cts., with 17 jewels per watch movement, approx. 32 dwt., the ear clips are enhanced with ten assorted baguettes, total approx. 1.50 cts. **Price: $3,500**

(D) (Jewelry Box Antiques)

Retro Modern necklace and earrings, 10K yellow gold, set with synthetic blue spinels, worn in the movie "Mr. and Mrs. Bridge." **Price: $295**

(D) (Jewelry Box Antiques)

1940s necklace and earrings, mkd. "1/20 12K G.F. on silver Carl-Art Inc., Providence, R.I," in original box, original price $21.50. **Price: $195**

Miscellaneous

(D) (Jewelry Box Antiques)
1930-1940 earrings, gold filled, 3/4" dia.
Price: $40

(D) (Jewelry Box Antiques)
1940s Retro Modern earrings, silver.
Price: $60

(D) (Jewelry Box Antiques)
1940s earrings, 14K rose gold with cultured pearls,
approx. 3/4" dia. **Price: $295**

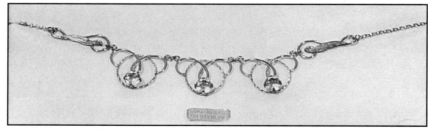

(D) (Jewelry Box Antiques)
1940s necklace, box marked "1/20 10K G.F. on sterling," aquamarine-
colored stones, lovely chain necklace. **Price: $195**

Section 2:

100 Years of Cameos

The story of the tiny works of art referred to as "cameos" is one that reaches far back into history. The Egyptians used intaglio cut stones (a stone cut with a deep design) as seals. Gradually, intaglio cutting evolved into a more complex relief carving (cameos). The earliest cameos were carved in stone and represented characters from Greek and Roman mythology. The stone cutter's best efforts were used to depict the favorite stories of the gods and goddesses.

Archaeological excavation during Napoleon's reign had awakened an interest in the ancient art. Napoleon enjoyed wearing cameos and giving them as gifts to his favorite people. In 1805, he initiated "A Prix de Rome" to encourage stone engraving. About that same time a public school founded by Pope Leo XII was opened in Rome for the study of cameo engraving. It was highly sucessful.

The new cutters were inspired by the ancient motifs and produced many neoclassical designs. Even Napoleon was depicted in stone cameos dressed as a Roman emperor.

Cameos made lovely, portable souvenirs for tourists visiting the ruins of Pompeii and Herculium. When travelers returned home, their friends were enchanted with these small works of art. Within a short time, Italian cameo artists had shops in England, France, and America. These craftsmen carved cameos in the ancient styles or any other designs the purchaser might select. The January 1850 issue of *Godey's Magazine* included the following note, "Peabody the celebrated cameo portrait cutter, 140 Chestnut Street, is kept busily engaged with the portraits of some of our most eminent citizens." Many famous people amassed huge cameo collections. Napoleon, the Duke of Marlborough and Catherine the Great all had "cameo cabinets."

As cameos became more plentiful, the cutting of cameos changed from being an art form into being merely decorative. The subject matter gradually changed from that of classical inspiration, to portraits and characters in Literature and Biblical scenes. Eventually the most popular motifs were those of romanticized women. The 19th century began with a man as a favorite subject and ended with the bust of a woman being the most popular.

It didn't take long for the workmen to realize that cameos carved from shells would be plentiful enough to meet the increased demand for more cameos at less expensive prices. Women wore cameos set in rings, brooches, earrings, and bracelets. Men had them set into watch fobs, rings, and pins. The carvers used the shells of the black helmet, horned helmet and the pink and white queen's conches, which were so plentiful in the seacoast towns of Italy.

Cameos are made by cutting away background material to make a design in relief. In stone cameos, a banded agate is often used. The lighter band is used for the figure of the cameo. The remainder is carved away to expose the darker ground. In shell and stone cameos, the true artist takes advantage of different layers and faults in the material to enhance the design.

Quite often I am asked, "Which is more valuable, a shell cameo or a stone cameo?" I ask them in return, "Which is more valuable, a watercolor or an oil painting?" They sometimes reply, "Well, it depends on who painted it and how well it is done." To this I reply, "The same is true of a cameo." After all, a well-executed cameo is a tiny work of art.

If all other factors are equal, a stone cameo is more valuable than a shell one. Cameos depicting full figures and scenes are more valuable than those that show a head or bust only. But remember, all other factors must be equal and the workmanship comparable. Stone cameos were cut from onyx, agate, sardonyx, cornelian, coral, lava, jasper, malachite, ivory, tortoise shell, rock crystal, jet, moonstone, emerald and other precious stones. They are generally more valuable than those made of shell. But the medium is not nearly as important as the artistry. The best way to judge a cameo is to examine it with a good magnifying glass. Graceful, smooth-flowing lines with much detail are signs of a good one. The inferior ones seem to have sharper lines, fewer details, and a harsh look. Be sure to hold the cameo to the light and examine it for possible cracks.

Many antique cameos were reset in the late 18th and early 19th century. Some craftsmen were expert at copying antique pieces. This makes accurate dating almost impossible. However, there are usually some clues to help determine age.

If a cameo is made of lava, it is almost certainly Victorian. Other clues are: the style of design (Greek, Roman, etc.), types of clothing and hair styles on the figures, and the motif and construction of the mounting. If the cameo is mounted as a brooch, carefully examine the pin and hook. Safety catches are a twentieth century adaptation. If the cameo has one, then it is either not older than the early nineteen hundreds or a new catch has been added. If it is an addition, this can usually be ascertained by more careful examination. Look for signs of soldering. Often the new catch is attached to a small plate jointed to the back of the brooch. Next look closely at the pin. Notice what kind of hinge it has. If the sharp point of the pin extends past the body of the brooch, it is an "oldie."

Gold, silver, pinchbeck, gold-filled, cut-steel and jet were some of the materials used for mounting cameos. The type metal used can often give an indication of when it was made. If the mounting is pinchbeck, it was probably made between the early seventeen and the mid-eighteen hundreds. Gold electroplating was patented in 1841, so, if the piece is plated, it was made after that date. Nine karat gold was legalized in 1854. A piece stamped 9K would have to be made after that date.

A popular metal used for mountings in the 1880s was silver, but this does not mean that all cameos mounted in silver were made at the time. All the clues have to be examined before a judgment on age can be made. A circa date must never be determined by any one clue.

Scenic cameos are generally more valuable than bust cameos. A very popular motif around 1860 was what is known as "Rebecca at the Well." There are many variations on this theme, but they usually include a cottage, a bridge and a girl.

Technically, a cameo is made by cutting away the back ground of a material to make a design in relief, but there are some items called cameos that do not fit this description. Josiah Wedgewood's factories produced jasper-ware plaques in blue and white and black and white. These had the look of a cameo, but they were molded. These massed produced "cameos" were originally very inexpensive, but today they are quite collectible.

Another type of counterfeit cameo is created by gluing a molded glass cameo (usually a bust) onto a glass or agate background material. Sometime this can be mistaken by the untrained or unaided eye to be an "undercut" cameo which was a style popular during the 1860-1870s. Be assured that with practice and good magnification they become easily detected.

Unfortunately, the art of cameo cutting has continued to decline. But as the supply of well-executed cameos has declined, the demand has continued to rise. Consequently nicely carved cameos have risen steadily in value.

One time I was in Italy, I found only one cameo artist whose work I admired. I purchased one of his shell cameos (unmounted) for $400. Remember, it was not mounted, but it is beautiful, and I consider it a bargain.

Bracelets

(D) (Jewelry Box Antiques)

1860-1870s bracelet, yellow gold filled mesh with hand-carved black/white cameo, 1-1/4" approx. width.

Price: $495

(D) (Camille Grace)

1900-1915 jointed bracelet, gold filled with cameo, 1" x 1-1/4".   **Price: $340**

(C) (Cindy Stokes)

1940s bracelet, gold over brass, set with 3 hand-carved shell cameos, faux pearls and imitation lapis and garnets, 9 plaques, 7-1/2" x 1".   **Price: $200**

(D) (June O'Donnell)

1930-1940s bracelet, gold over brass bangle with hand-carved shell cameo, 1" w.   **Price: $125**

(D) (Lucille and Sam Mundorff)

1860-1870 bracelet, 22K gold lava cameo, 7/8" x 1", band 1" x 1/2".

Price: $1,800

(C) (Susan Bergmeier)

1940s bracelet, gilt silver with hand-carved shell cameo's depicting the 7 days of the week. Brought back from WWII.

Price: $650

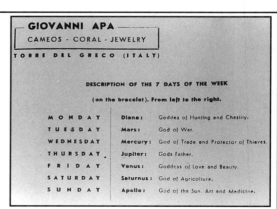

GIOVANNI APA

CAMEOS - CORAL - JEWELRY

TORRE DEL GRECO (ITALY)

DESCRIPTION OF THE 7 DAYS OF THE WEEK

(on the bracelet). From left to right.

MONDAY	Diana:	Goddess of Hunting and Chastity.
TUESDAY	Mars:	God of War.
WEDNESDAY	Mercury:	God of Trade and Protector of Thieves.
THURSDAY	Jupiter:	Gods Father.
FRIDAY	Venus:	Goddess of Love and Beauty.
SATURDAY	Saturnus:	God of Agriculture.
SUNDAY	Apollo:	God of the Sun, Art and Medicine.

Description of the days of the week that came with the bracelet.

Brooches & Pins

Cameo and half pearl brooch and earrings, 14K yellow gold (earrings not pictured). **Price: $2,100**

(A) (Photo courtesy William Doyle Galleries, New York 12-7-89)

Early 1900s brooch, gold filled, shell cameo, 1-1/2" x 2". **Price: $295**

(D) (Jewelry Box Antiques)

(C) (W. Baldwin)

1920 brooch/pendant, 10K yellow gold mtg., shell cameo, 1-3/8" x 1-3/4". **Price: $525**

Early 1900s brooch, celluloid cameo, hook for pin is also celluloid, 1-1/2" x 2". **Price: $50**

(D) (Jewelry Box Antiques)

Mid 19th century brooch, gold oval with shell cameo of Bacchante, signed with mark of Castellani on the cone-shaped pin cap, £900. **Price: $1,600**

(A) (Photo courtesy of Phillips, London)

1920-1930 brooch, sterling bezel with nicely done shell cameo, 1-1/4" x 1-5/8". **Price: $325**

(D) (Jewelry Box Antiques)

1920s brooch, mkd. "sterling made in England," glass cover over plastic figure with shining blue background, 1-1/2" dia. **Price: $95**

(D) (Jewelry Box Antiques)

1850-1860 brooch, Pinchbeck mtg., shell cameo. 1-1/4" x 1-1/2".
Price: $295

(D) (Jewelry Box Antiques)

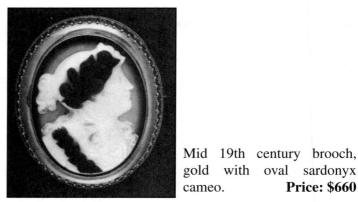

Mid 19th century brooch, gold with oval sardonyx cameo. **Price: $660**

(A) (Photo courtesy of Sotheby's, New York 10-6-83)

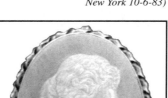

1860s brooch, yellow gold filled with hand-carved shell cameo, "Rebecca at the Well," approx. 2" x 1-5/8".
Price: $395

(D) (Jewelry Box Antiques)

1860-1880s brooch, 14K yellow gold with coral cameo, 3-1/2" x 2" approx.
Price: $795

(C) (Gale Wright)

(C) (Jeanenne Bell)

1850-1870 brooch, 14K gold, stone cameo with enameling, 1-1/4" x 1-1/2".
Price: $975

1860-1880s brooch, yellow gold filled mounting with hand carved shell cameo, 1-1/8" x 7/8".
Price: $190

(D) (Jewelry Box Antiques)

1840-1850 brooch, gilt mtg. with enameled leaves and molded cameo. **Price: $95**

(D) (Jewelry Box Antiques)

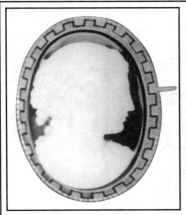

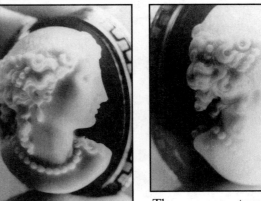

(C) (Lynn King)

1840-1860s brooch, 14K yellow gold set with hand carved stone cameo, 2-1/4" x 1-3/4". **Price: $3,000**

The cameo turned to show the numerous layers (or bands) in the stone with which the artist worked.

The cameo turned to allow the light to "glance off" its surface so that the details are more visible. A closer look at the details of the hair.

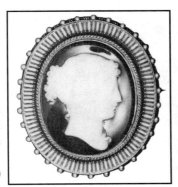

1880 brooch, gold with sardonyx cameo and pale blue and white enameling, £770. **Price: $1,370**

(A) (Photo courtesy of Sotheby's New York 4-14-83)

(C) (Camille Grace)

1860-1880 brooch, silver mtg., shell cameo, 1-3/4" x 2-1/4". **Price: $325**

(C) (W. Baldwin)

1860-1880 brooch, gold filled mtg., shell cameo, 2-1/4" x 2-5/8". **Price: $295**

(Private Collection)

1840-1860s brooch, 14K yellow gold with carved coral cherub, actual size approx. 2" x 1-1/2". **Price: $850**

(D) (Jewelry Box Antiques)

1860s brooch, yellow gold filled twisted wire bezel set with hand carved "Rebecca at the Well" motif in shell. **Price: $395**

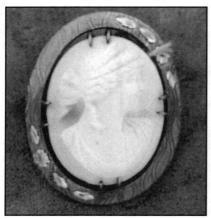

1910-1912 pin, gold over brass mounting with hand-carved pink shell cameo, 1-1/4" x 1" approx. **Price: $170**

1912-1920s cameo, white gold filigree mounting set with hand-carved shell cameo wearing diamond necklace, 1-1/2" x 2" dia. **Price: $800**

1912 pin, 14K yellow gold set with hand-carved shell cameo, 1-1/2" x 1-3/16". **Price: $450**

1920s pin, silver metal with marcasites and set with hand-carved shell cameo, 1-1/2" x 1-1/4". **Price: $325**

1930s pin/pendant, yellow gold filled with hand-carved shell cameo, 1-1/4" x 1". **Price: $175**

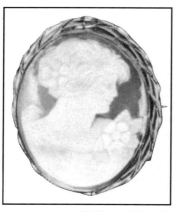

1920s pin/pendant, yellow gold filled mounting with hand-carved shell cameo, 1-1/2" x 1-1/4". **Price: $195**

1940s pin/pendant, gold over silver mounting with hand-carved shell cameo, 1-1/2" x 1-1/8". **Price: $225**

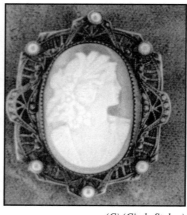

1920s-1930s pin/pendant, gold over brass mounting set with molded glass cameo and 6 half faux pearls, 1-1/2" x 1-1/8". **Price: $70**

(A) (Photo courtesy of Wm. Doyle Galleries, New York 9-21-83)

1860-1870 brooch, yellow gold with cameo and 6 assorted diamonds. **Price: $325**

(D) (Jewelry Box Antiques)

1840-1860 brooch, yellow rolled gold mounting set with "Three Graces" shell cameo, 2-1/4" x 2-1/8". **Price: $695**

(A) (Photo courtesy of Sotheby's, New York 10-6-83)

1850-1870 brooch, gold with oval sardonyx cameo, embellished with 4 seed pearls and 8 single cut diamonds. **Price: $990**

(C) (W. Baldwin)

Brooch/pendant, 1908-1917, 10K yellow gold, shell cameo, 1-7/8" x 2-1/2". **Price: $595**

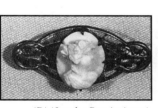

(D) (Jewelry Box Antiques)

1890-1915 brooch, gold over brass, coral cameo, 1-5/8" x 3/4". **Price: $150**

(C) (W. Baldwin)

Early 1900s brooch/pendant, 10K yellow gold mtg., shell cameo. **Price: $545**

(C) (W. Baldwin)

1900-1917 brooch/pendant, 10K yellow gold mtg., shell cameo, 1-1/4" x 1-1/2". **Price: $495**

(D) (Jewelry Box Antiques)

Early 1900s brooch, gold over brass with orchid enameled flowers with green emerald leaves, 2-3/4" x 1-5/8". **Price: $995**

(C) (Cindy Stokes)

1870-1880s brooch, 9K yellow gold mounting with hand-carved shell cameo, 1-5/8" x 1-3/8". **Price: $500**

Mid 1800s brooch, yellow rolled gold mounting set with beautifully done shell cameo. Center section is reversible so that the glazed compartment (reverse) can be worn in front, 2-3/4" x 2-1/4". **Price: $740**

(D) (Jewelry Box Antiques)

Code in Front of Name
(A) Auction House - Auction Price
(C) Collector - Collector Asking Price
(D) Dealer - Dealer's Asking Price

(D) (Jewelry Box Antiques)

1880-1900 brooch, gold over brass mtg. with celluloid cameo, 1-1/2" x 2". **Price: $95**

(D) (Jewelry Box Antiques)

1880-1890s brooch, 9K yellow gold with hand-carved shell cameo, 2-1/4" x 1-3/4". **Price: $600**

(D) (Jewelry Box Antiques)

1850s-1860s cameo brooch, yellow gold-filled, 2-5/8" x 1-3/4". **Price: $395**

(D) (Camille Grace)

1860-1870 brooch, gold filled mounting, shell cameo, 1-3/4" x 2". **Price: $325**

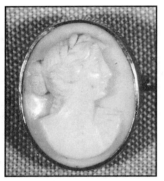

(C) (W. Baldwin)

Early 1900s brooch, 10K yellow gold mtg., coral cameo, 3/4" x 7/8". **Price: $325**

(C) (W. Baldwin)

1900-1917 brooch/pendant, 10K yellow gold mtg., coral cameo, 1" x 1-1/4". **Price: $525**

(C) (W. Baldwin)

Early 1900s brooch/pendant, 14K yellow gold mtg., stone cameo surrounded by pearls, done in Victorian style, 1-1/4" x 1-1/2". **Price: $2,400**

(D) (Camille Grace)

1880-1890s brooch/pendant, gold filled, shell cameo, 1-1/2" x 2". **Price: $395**

(C) (W. Baldwin)

1940s brooch, 14K gold with shell cameo, 1-3/8" x 1-3/4". **Price: $495**

(A) (Photo courtesy of Phillips, London, 6-21-83)

Early 19th century brooch, silver gilt frame with classical scene executed in blue and white shell cameo, original leather case. £650. **Price: $945**

(D) (Camille Grace)

1915-1925 brooch/pendant, 10K Wedgewood, 1-1/8" x 7/8". **Price: $425**

(C) (W. Baldwin)

1940s brooch/pendant, .925 silver, shell cameo, 1-3/8" x 1-3/4".
Price: $385

(D) (Jewelry Box Antiques)

1940s brooch/pendant, silver over copper mtg. with shell cameo, new 20" sterling chain, cameo 1-1/4" x 1-1/2".
Price: $195

(C) (W. Baldwin)

1915-1920s brooch, 10K yellow gold, pink coral cameo, 1-1/4" x 1-5/8".
Price: $600

(A) (Photo courtesy of Sotheby's, London 4-14-83)

Brooch/pendant, last quarter of 19th century, gold with sardonyx cameo, mounting embellished with rose-cut diamonds. £1,650.
Price: $2,940

(D) (Jewelry Box Antiques)

1915-1920s brooch/pendant, 10K yellow and green gold with pink coral cameo, 1-1/2" x 1-3/4".
Price: $600

(D) (Camille Grace)

1915-1920s brooch/pendant, 14K yellow gold, coral cameo, 1-1/2" x 1-5/8".
Price: $500

(D) (Jewelry Box Antiques)

1912-1920 brooch, 14K yellow gold set with hand-carved shell cameo, 1-1/2" x 1-1/8".
Price: $470

(C) (Jeanenne Bell)

1850-1860 brooch/pendant, 15K beautiful sardonyx cameo with graduation, 1-1/8" x 1-7/8".
Price: $1,400

(D) (Jewelry Box Antiques)

1912-1920 brooch, 14K yellow gold set with hand-carved shell cameo, 1-1/2" x 1-1/8".
Price: $470

(D) (Jewelry Box Antiques)

1850-1860 brooch, gold over brass with some gold ornamentation, stone cameo, 3" x 1-1/4".
Price: $325

(D) (Jewelry Box Antiques)

1915-1920s brooch/pendant, 10K yellow gold mtg., shell cameo, 1-1/4" x 1-5/8". **Price: $485**

(C) (W. Baldwin)

1915-1920s brooch/pendant, 14K coral cameo, 1-1/2" dia. **Price: $550**

(D) (Jewelry Box Antiques)

1920s brooch, sterling silver with hand-carved pink shell cameo, 2" x 1-1/2".

Price: $265

(D) (Camille Grace)

1915-1920s brooch/pendant, .800 silver, shell cameo, 1-1/4" x 1-3/4". **Price: $425**

(C) (Patricia Horton)

1855-1860s brooch/pendant, 15K yellow gold set with hand-carved shell cameo, Etruscan-style work on mounting. **Price: $1,875**

(C) (Glenda Read)

1920s brooch, yellow gold filled mounting with hand-carved shell cameo, 2" x 1-1/2". **Price: $270**

(D) (Jewelry Box Antiques)

1940s brooch, yellow gold filled mounting with hand-carved shell cameo surrounded by faux pearls, 1-3/4" x 1-1/4". **Price: $125**

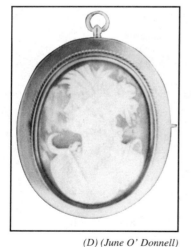

(D) (June O' Donnell)

1912 brooch/pendant, 14K yellow gold set with hand carved shell cameo, 1-3/4" x 1-1/2". **Price: $525**

(D) (June O'Donnell)

1912 brooch/pendant, 14K yellow gold set with hand-carved shell cameo, 1-3/4" x 1-1/2". **Price: $525**

(C) (Jeanenne Bell)

1860s brooch, 18K mtg., lava cameo, 1-3/4" x 2-1/8". **Price: $2,000**

Earrings

(D) (Jewelry Box Antiques)

1840-1860s earrings, made from collar buttons. **Price: $395**

1860-1870s earrings, 14K yellow gold set with hand-carved cornelian stone cameos. **Price: $895**

(D) (Jewelry Box Antiques)

(D) (Jewelry Box Antiques)

1940s earrings, gold over white metal with shell cameos on new 14K gold wires, 3/4" x 1-1/2" l. **Price: $225**

1870-1880s earrings, 18K yellow gold set with banded stone cameos, mounting embellished with taille d' epergne enameling and half pearls. **Price: $795**

(D) (Jewelry Box Antiques)

(C) (Gale Wright)

1920-1930 earrings, sterling silver mountings set with hand-carved shell cameos and marcasites, 2" l x 5/8" w. **Price: $295**

(D) (Jowsey & Roe, Whitby, England)

1860s earrings, jet with pink shell cameos, 2-1/4" x 1". **Price: $425**

(C) (Warren Boyce)

1930-1940s earrings, 14K yellow gold with hand-carved shell cameo. **Price: $395**

Necklaces

(D) (Jewelry Box Antiques)

1920s necklace, gold over brass with celluloid cameo, 1" x 1-1/4".   **Price: $200**

1915-1920s necklace, 10K white gold with some yellow gold, shell cameo and pearls, 1/2" x 5/8", original chain.
    Price: $445

(D) (Jewelry Box Antiques)

(D) (Jewelry Box Antiques)

1940s necklace, yellow gold filled with hand-carved shell cameo, 2-1/4" x 1-3/4".
    Price: $245

(D) (Jewelry Box Antiques)

1860-1870s necklace, yellow gold filled woven chain 8.53mm wide, 20" long, hand carved stone cameo drop.   **Price: $695**

(D) (Jewelry Box Antiques)

1932-1945 necklace, earrings, vermeil set with hand-carved shell cameos, necklace approx. 16" l with 1-3/4" x 1" and 2-1/2" x 3/8" cameos; earrings approx. 3/4" x 1/2".   **Price: $395**

1920s necklace, silver over brass, glass "stones" with white cameo heads, 15" l.
Price: $65

(D) (Jewelry Box Antiques)

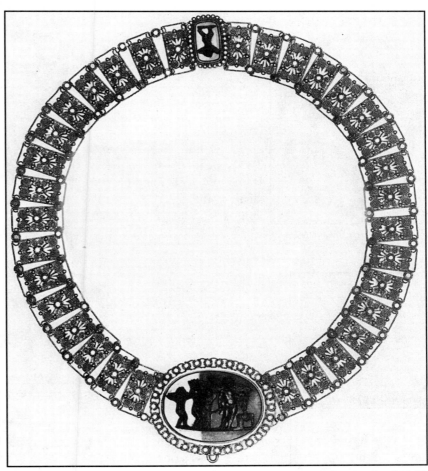

Early 19th century necklace, gold panel links with a central mount set with oval brown and black agate cameo "captor and captive," clasp has a cushion-shaped agate cameo. £1,050.   **Price: $1,870**

(A) (Photo courtesy of Phillips, London, 6-21-83)

Pendants

1840-1860 pendant, gilt brass mtg., Cornelian cameo, 3/4" x 1-1/3".
Price: $295

1850-1870 pendant, gold with oval sardonyx cameo of Roman maiden.
Price: $935

1850-1870s pendant/brooch, gold with sardonyx cameo of Hagar and Ishmael (some damage), Spaulding & Co.
Price: $990

1860-1870s pendant, 14K and yellow gold filled and gold over brass with hand-carved black/white stone cameo. Originally the bottom portion of an earring, it was made into a pendant.
Price: $350

1890s pendant, silver metal frame set with hand-carved shell cameo, 2" x 1-1/2" approx.
Price: $325

1908-1917 pendant necklace, 14K yellow gold mtg. coral cameo with 17" chain, 7/8" x 1".
Price: $545

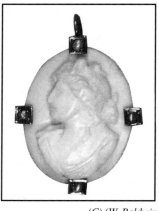

1890-1910 pendant, 14K yellow gold with 4 seed pearls and coral cameo, 7/8" x 1-1/8".
Price: $365

1920-1930 necklace, chain with drop of clear plastic with imitation jet cameo of plastic, chain 28" l, drop 2" w x 2-1/2" l.
Price: $95

(D) (Jewelry Box Antiques)

1890-1910 pendant, 14K yellow gold with hand-carved coral cameo, 1" x 3/4", chain yellow gold filled, 18" l. **Price: $325**

(D) (June O'Donnell)

1890-1910 pendant, 14K yellow gold with pink shell cameo and seed pearls and freshwater pearl as drop, 1" x 3/4" with 18" chain. **Price: $325**

(A) (Photo courtesy Phillips, London 9-20-83)

Mid 19th century pendant, gold with a black and white onyx cameo, frame enameled in pale blue and white, with earrings (not shown) and fitted case, £1,200. **Price: $2,135**

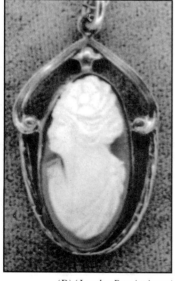

(D) (Jewelry Box Antiques)

1910-1920 pendant, yellow gold filled mounting set with hand-carved shell cameo, 1" x 5/8". **Price: $140**

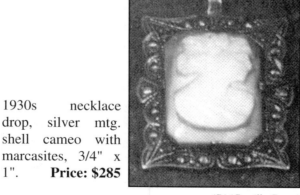

1930s necklace drop, silver mtg. shell cameo with marcasites, 3/4" x 1". **Price: $285**

(D) (Camille Grace)

(A) (Photo courtesy of Sotheby's New York 12-7-83)

Pendant/brooch, last quarter of 19th century, gold with hard stone cameo of Elizabethan lady. Embellished with 4 pearls and 8 old mine diamonds, reverse has glazed compartment and hinged pendant loop, "Tiffany & Co." **Price: $2,530**

1860-1870s, pendant/brooch, gold with sardonyx cameo, "The Triumph of Love." **Price: $1,540**

(A) (Photo courtesy of Sotheby's New York 12-7-83)

Rings

(D) (Jewelry Box Antiques)

1940s ring, 10K yellow gold cameo. **Price: $295**

(D) (Jewelry Box Antiques)

1920-1930s ring, 10K white gold mounting set with black/white stone cameo, 3/4" x 1/2". **Price: $450**

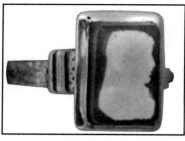

(D) (Jewelry Box Antiques)

1840-1860s ring, 11K yellow gold set with hand-carved stone cameo, 1/2" x 5/16" approx. **Price: $470**

(D) (Jewelry Box Antiques)

1930-1940s ring, 10K yellow gold set with hand-carved shell cameo, 1/2" x 3/8". **Price: $300**

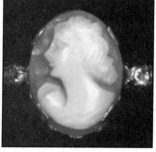

(D) (Jewelry Box Antiques)

1920-1930 ring, 14K R.G.P. shell cameo and 2 white stones, 1/2" x 5/8". **Price: $95**

(C) (Jennifer Hill)

1920s ring, 10K white gold filigree set with bloodstone intaglio. **Price: $395**

(D) (Jewelry Box Antiques)

1840-1860s cameo ring, 14K yellow gold set with hand-carved tiger eye. **Price: $545**

Opposite side of ring showing detail of cameo.

(D) (Jewelry Box Antiques)

1860-1880s ring, 14K yellow gold set with hand-carved shell cameo, "Rebecca at the Well." **Price: $390**

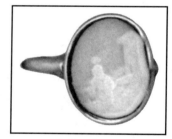

(D) (Jewelry Box Antiques)

1860-1880s ring, 14K yellow gold set with hand-carved shell cameo, "Rebecca at the Well." **Price: $390**

(D) (Jewelry Box Antiques)

1840-1860s ring, cameo, mounting 1940s, 10K yellow gold, Belcher black and white cameo. **Price: $450**

(C) (Silvia Goldman)

1920s ring, 14K white gold filigree with full figure cameo surrounded by seed pearls. **Price: $875**

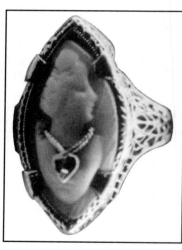

(D) (June O'Donnell)

1920-1930s ring, 14K white gold filigree set with cameo head, 1" x 1/2" navette. **Price: $595**

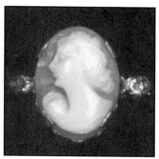

(D) (Jewelry Box Antiques)

1920-1930 ring, 14K R.G.P. shell cameo and 2 white stones, 1/2" x 5/8". **Price: $95**

(D) (Jewelry Box Antiques)

1870-1880s ring, 10K yellow gold set with hand carved stone cameo. **Price: $295**

(D) (Jewelry Box Antiques)

Early 1900s ring, 10K yellow gold filigree design mounting set with hand-carved coral cameo, 7/8" x 5/8". **Price: $395**

(D) (Jewelry Box Antiques)

1930-1940s ring, 10K yellow gold set with hand-carved shell cameo, 1/2" x 3/8". **Price: $300**

(D) (Jewelry Box Antiques)

1920-1930s ring, 18K white gold set with cornelian intaglio depicting a deer. **Price: $650**

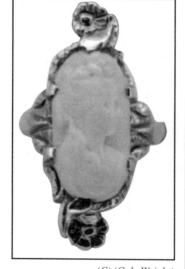

(C) (Gale Wright)

1890-1910 ring, 10K yellow gold set with hand-carved coral cameo, approx. 3/4" x 3/8". **Price: $395**

(D) (Jewelry Box Antiques)

1890-1910 ring, 14K yellow gold and green gold mounting set with hand-carved coral cameo. **Price: $425**

Close-up of coral cameo.

(D) (Jewelry Box Antiques)

Early 1900s ring, 14K yellow gold set with coral and seed pearls. **Price: $495**

Ring, side view.

(D) (Jewelry Box Antiques)

1940s ring, 10K yellow gold filled ring set with hand-carved stone cameo and black onyx. **Price: $795**

Flip ring, reverse side showing "note" tubes on each end to enable it to flip over.

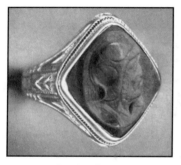

(D) (Jewelry Box Antiques)

1920s ring, 14K white gold set with tiger's eye cameo. **Price: $425**

(D) (Camille Grace)

1860-1870s ring, 18K shell cameo, massive mounting, cameo 1" x 1-1/4". **Price: $545**

(C) (Cindy Milliron)

1840s-1860s ring, 18K yellow gold set with hand-carved coral cameo. **Price: $795**

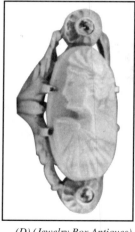

(D) (Jewelry Box Antiques)

1890-1910 ring, 18K yellow gold set with hand-carved coral cameo and 2 diamonds. **Price: $525**

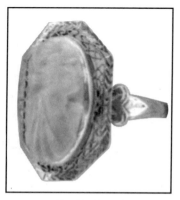

(D) (Jewelry Box Antiques)

1900-1920 ring, 10K yellow gold hand-carved coral cameo, 3/4" x 1/2" approx. **Price: $425**

(D) (Jewelry Box Antiques)

Portrait cameo carved from shell and mounted in a pinchbeck ring. Do you know his identity? If so, please let me know!

(D) (Jewelry Box Antiques)

1890-1917 ring, silver with gold ornamentation, imitation cornelian cameo is molded glass, drop 1/2" x 7/8". **Price: $115**

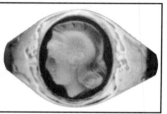

(D) (Jewelry Box Antiques)

1880s ring, 10K yellow gold set with hand-carved cornelian stone cameo. **Price: $425**

(C) (Kathy Haggerty)

1840-1860s cameo ring, 14K yellow gold "pancake" mounting with closed back and pierced shoulders set with a hand-carved stone cameo. The artist took the dark top layer and carved a helmeted soldier. In the next layer (white) is carved a female head and the background is grayish with a cornelian-colored layer behind it. This is one stone, not applied carvings, all hand done in the 1840-1860s time period. It measures approx. 21.56mm by 15.89mm. **Price: $1,325**

The proceeding banded agate double-headed cameo shown turned to the side to reveal the layers in the stone.

The opposite side of the same ring.

Sets

1850-1870 necklace and earrings, 15K sardonyx cameo, new wires on earrings, necklace drop 1" x 2", earrings 3/8" x 1". **Price of set: $1,600**

(C) (Barbara J. James)

(D) (Jewelry Box Antiques)

1932-1945 necklace, earrings, vermeil set with hand-carved shell cameos, necklace approx. 16" l with 1-3/4" x 1" and 2-1/2" x 3/8" cameos; earrings approx. 3/4" x 1/2". **Price: $395**

(C) (Jeanenne Bell)

Circa 1870s brooch and earrings, gold top with gold over brass backs and taille d' epergne enameling, centered with black/white stone cameos. **Price: $995**

397

Miscellaneous

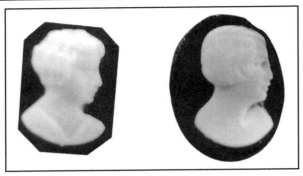

Black/white stone cameos, hair styles can sometimes be good indicators of circa. The ladies pictured with this "bobbed" hair cannot be any earlier than the 1920s. **Price: $175**

Two unmounted stone cameos, carved with a classical motif. **Price: $350**

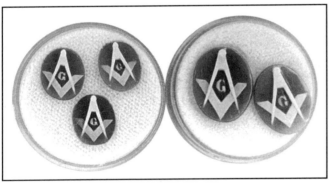

Five unmounted shell cameos, hand carved, probably carved for cuff links and shirt studs, mosaic motifs.
Price of set: $200

Code in Front of Name

(A) Auction House - Auction Price
(C) Collector - Collector Asking Price
(D) Dealer - Dealer's Asking Price

Banded agate portrait cameo.

Banded agate portrait cameo.

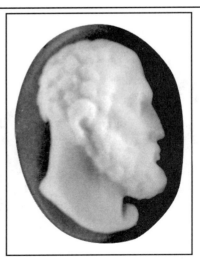

Banded agate portrait cameo.

Unmounted intaglio, depicting "Hermes" cut into bloodstone oval.

Price: $200

1860s slide and chain, gold top slide with enameling and stone cameo; chain is new gold filled, 52" l. **Price: $525**

Unmounted intaglio cut into bloodstone. **Price: $125**

Late 1800s tiger eye chevette cameo. **Price: $95-$150**

Full-figure stone cameo.

Price: $250

Section 3:

Manufacturing Techniques

The newest fashion is jewelry made by the electroforming process. It allows a big bold look without the heaviness of a solid piece. Just what is this electroforming process and why is it relevant to the construction of antique and collectible jewelry?

This new modern process was first patented in England in the 1840s. In the 1850s and throughout the end of the century, it was used to make copies of ancient and Celtic jewelry. Both the Victoria and Albert Museum and the British Museum have many fine examples of replicas made by using this process.

Although the process is widely used for industrial purposes, it has been dormant insofar as jewelry making is concerned for almost 100 years. Now once again it is coming into popularity as a jewelry manufacturing technique.

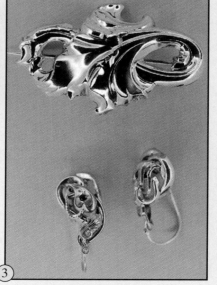

The CaSandra Collection by Carla Corporation.

There are two basic systems of electroforming: A hot bath method and a cold bath method. Both processes are used today to make unique one of a kind pieces and both systems start with a mandrel on which to electrically deposit the metal.

The mandrel can be made of wax, metal or any article (even a leaf) that the artist wants to be accurately replicated. It is coated with a layer of metallic solution so that when it is placed in a bath of electrolytic solution with a metallic anode the positively charged gold is deposited on the negatively charged mandrel.

In the hot bath system, a mandrel of white metal in the shape and finish needed for the final product is used. A gold electroplating of approximately 160 microns (about 4 to 6 thousandths of an inch) is electroplated to the mandrel.

Afterwards the mandrel is heated to its melting point and drained out through a hole left in the piece for that purpose. This process can result in beautiful hollow gold pieces of jewelry that are lightweight, but have the big bold look that is popular today.

For the cold bath system, a mandrel made of wax or plastic can be used. After a piece is finished, the mandrel can be eliminated or left inside the piece. Many antique pieces still contain their original wax mandrels.

This electroformed bracelet, circa 1840s-1850s is in extremely good condition. It still contains its wax mandrel and even though the gold deposit is thin, it is very durable and very comfortable to wear. **Price: $1,800**

Look at the fluid lines of this electroformed brooch and earring set from the 1840s-1860s. **Price: $995**

This is a simplified version of how electroforming is done. It is an expensive, labor-intensive process. Based on weight, electroformed pieces are at least double the price per penny weight of other manufactured pieces. Consequently, a piece should never be purchased with the consideration of weight. Instead, the customer should consider the uniqueness of the piece and its impressive look.

Have you ever wondered why so many fine examples of filigree rings and pins from the 1920s and 1930s have survived? They look lacy and delicate, but looks can sometimes be deceiving. These finely-detailed pieces were die-struck with such force that it has altered the atomic structure of the metal causing it to be denser and stronger. Consequently, it is heavier, tougher and more resilient and durable than a comparable cast piece. These are just a few of the reasons a die-struck piece can be more expensive and more valuable. Most pieces of antique jewelry were made by using one or more of these three methods: white metal spin-casting, electroforming, or die-striking/stamping.

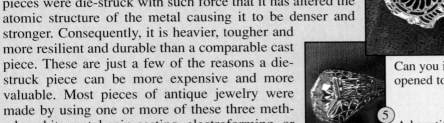

Can you imagine the number of windows that had to be opened to produce this beautiful lacy brooch?

A beautiful example of a die-struck ring.

This is a good example of how a filigree ring looks at the beginning of the process and as a finished product. The piece in my hand is called a "T" shank. It is a flat die-struck piece. The top of the "T" is one-half of the circumference of the top of the ring. After the piece is taken through the piercing process, the two halves are shaped and joined together at the top and bottom of the oval head. Then the bottom of the "T", which is the shank of the ring, is cut to the desired ring size and each half is curved and joined. The ring at the top of the picture was made in this manner.

This cameo mounting was made using a hand fabricated bezel, a ribbon twist flat wire and a twisted gallery wire with stamped flowers and leaves. It is 14kt gold; circa 1850s-1860s. **Price: $585**

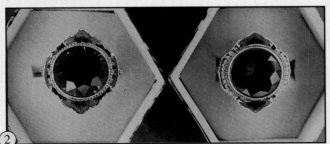

Because the die-making process was expensive, many manufacturers made up new "numbers" by varying the embellishments and ornamentations on a basic style already in their line. These two 14KT white gold rings were made using the same die. The different look of the head of the ring on the left was achieved by using seed pearls, which were strung on gold wire around the bezel of the amethyst. The synthetic sapphire ring on the right has more area for enamel work because of the absence of the seed pearls.

This photo shows the disassembled pieces. At the bottom left is the bezel that holds the cameo. Next the ribbon twist is set in place. Then the twisted wire with the stamped flowers and leaves are attached.

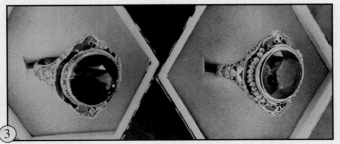

Side view of brooch showing the solder line on the bezel.

Circa 1860 brooch, rolled gold mounting with painting on porcelain. This piece has the same type bezel and ribbon twist as the above cameo. **Price: $295**

The shoulders of the ring have die-struck, pink gold ornamental pieces and the ring on the left has a green gold ornament in a different design. Both are beautiful variations of the same ring, circa 1920s-1930s. **Price: $995 and $895**

According to David Fiderman, the executive editor of *Modern Jeweler Magazine,* the theme song of die-striking should be the Johnny Mercer song "Something's Got to Give." For those of you who don't remember the popular tune from the 1950s, it goes something like this: "When an irresistible force such as you, meets and old immovable object like me, chances are as sure as you live somehow, somewhere, something's got to give!"

When the manufacturing process is striking, the moveable force is a steel "forcer" (male) and the immovable object is a steel die (female). If a sheet or strip of metal is put between them the "something that has to give" is always the metal. The shape created by this irresistible force is called a blank or a stamping. Often designs and hollows are created by the shaping and engraving of the punches used in cold forging (embossing) and the dapple-die. Before the computer age, a die-struck piece of jewelry often began when an artist sculptured a three dimensional design in steel referred to as a "hub."

This is a hub designed for the back of a hand mirror.

Two hubs used for ornamental pieces. These hubs and the preceding hub were on display at a special exhibit sponsored by the Providence Jewelry Museum in Rhode Island.

Before the steel hub can be used to make a die it has to be hardened by heating it in an oven at 1700 degrees. The hardened hub is then pushed by hydraulic pressure into soft steel to form a die. This new die is then hardened in the oven so that it can be forced into soft steel to produce a "forcer". After the forcer is hardened by heat, the two finished piece result in a "working piece" referred to as a forcer (male) and a die (female). The original hub is then carefully stored away to be used again if the die and forcer need replacing.

The preceding pieces were stamped on a machine much like this hydraulic one used today by Salvadore Tools and Findings. In earlier days, American factories were powered by water wheels that drove overhead shafting which provided power. After 1840, the English used steam power and continued to do so until electricity became prevalent.

This machine at the Providence Jewelry Museum is used to demonstrate to visitors how a pair of sterling earrings was made. The die is struck using 30 tons of pressure. Peter DiCristofaro, president of the Providence Jewelry Museum was kind enough to give me a guided tour of the exhibition and allow me to photograph.

This beautiful chatelaine notepad was assembled using silver stampings.

The backside of the piece shows the flat blank back of the pad and the embossed underside of the top. This top piece was done in one stamping between the working piece.

This photo shows the design stamped by the die and the strip of silver from which it was punched. The pieces at the bottom have gone through another machine that has "opened" some of the "windows" in the drop. There are still unopened windows in the piece that could be opened with yet another piercing tool.

8

Now we are ready to cast. Centrifugal, vacuum, or gravity casting can be used. Shown here is a centrifugal casting machine. The gold casting grain is heated by a torch in a crucible. Then the metal container is wound around and let loose. Using centrifugal force, the hot molten gold is literally flung into the cavity left in the investment by the "burned out" wax.

9

Next the investment is "quenched" in cool water. This not only cools the hot metal, but it causes the hard chalky investment to crack. Thus, the task of removing the rough casting becomes easier.

10

These rough, unpolished rings are still on their sprue. They are cast duplicates of the original waxes. Next they will be cut off and polished.

11

The piece is finished! The original model for this ring was die-struck. We will discuss that process later, but let's look now at how you can detect whether or not a piece has been cast.

12

Look closely at the backside of this bracelet. Can you detect the flow lines and porosity that are the tale-tale signs of the casting process?

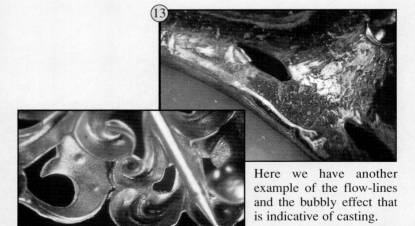

13

Here we have another example of the flow-lines and the bubbly effect that is indicative of casting.

14

Here is another example of porosity. Note the edges of the cut-out areas.

This method usually starts with an existing piece of jewelry or a carved wax from which a mold model is cast. A rubber mold is made by packing the model in a special rubber material and vulcanizing it in a mold maker. When finished, the model is cut out leaving an exact duplicate of the original.

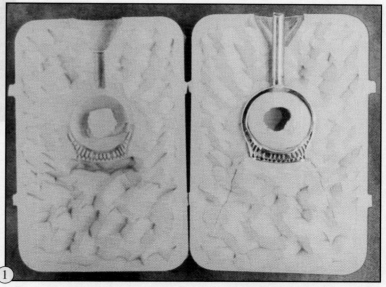

This picture shows the mold model (left) before it is removed from the mold. Notice the model has a metal rod attached to the base of its shank. This is called a "sprue" and it allows a channel to be formed in the mold so that wax can be injected.

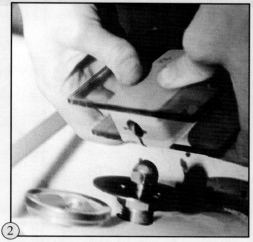

The mold is then injected with hot liquid wax to form a wax replica of the original model.

After the hot wax cools, it is removed from the rubber mold.

Then the wax is attached to a base.

Now the wax is ready to be invested. A white chalky "investment" powder is mixed with water to the desired consistency. Then the mixture is poured into a metal canister and completely covers the wax.

In to the oven it goes! To do a complete burn-out of the wax usually takes from 6 to 12 hours.

While the wax is in the oven, the jeweler can weigh the appropriate amount of gold needed to cast the piece.

JEWELRY MANUFACTURING AND CONSTRUCTION TECHNIQUES

There have been very few changes in jewelry construction basics in the last 4,000 years. A rudimentary knowledge of jewelry construction and manufacturing techniques is imperative if one truly wants to accurately identify and authenticate antique and period jewelry. This section is included to provide a basic overview of the methods most widely used including hand fabrication, casting, die-striking/stamping, electroforming, and white metal spin casting.

Here is a group of antique tools from the Providence Jewelry Museum in Rhode Island. All are still in production and most are used daily by many jewelers.

This is an etching of a jewelry workshop from the late 18th century (from Diderots' Encyclopedia). The jeweler's bench is situated beneath the window. The two glass globes on stands were filled with water and used to concentrate light on the work. The workmen are seated at semi-circular stations. Each work area has a bench peg, on which to steady the work piece, and a leather drape, to catch any scrap gold. The floor has a wooden grid to assure that gold dust or scrap would not be lost by clinging to the workmen's shoes. (A few years ago I was in the Jura Valley in Switzerland visiting some of the world's finest watchmakers. They had the same type flooring with the addition of a vibrating vacuum in the floor grid at the doorway.)

Hand Fabrication

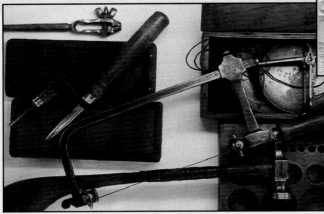

Let's look first at hand fabrication. A piece is said to have been handmade when a bench person makes the piece from start to finish.

He or she may purchase tubing or sheets of gold or may elect to alloy the metal and roll out the gold themselves.*

The designer/jeweler can start with a sketch of the piece and then select the stones and materials or begin with the stones and let them dictate the size and flow of the finished piece.*

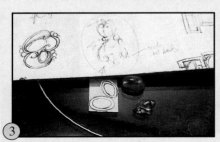

Here is the gold framework based on the preceding sketch.*

This is the finished amber pendant.*

A beautifully handmade and engraved ring shank, circa 1840s-1860s.

* Photos by Leslie Kinder-Anderson

White metal spin-casting is the construction method used to make much of the costume or fashion jewelry on the market today. Because old costume jewelry is so collectible, it is important to have a basic understanding of how it is made.

The white metal used in this process pertains to a mixture of a tin, lead, bismuth, antimony and cadmium. The tin content may vary from 17 to 92 percent, depending on the quality of the piece. Many quality white metal pieces have an 88 percent tin content. White metal melts at a temperature range of 520 degrees to 420 degrees.

As in most types of casting the process begins with a model of the piece to be produced. From this piece a model mold is made. Since 1937, rubber has been the choice material for molds. Prior to that year, bronze model molds were used.

Michael Salvadore, Jr., of American Jewelry Products, Warwick, RI demonstrates the cutting of a rubber mold.

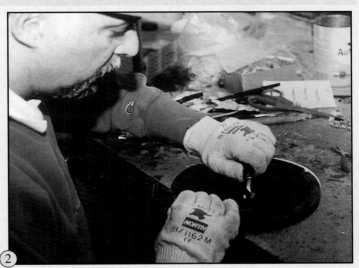

Here is an example of a bronze mold and a wax of the piece to be produced. These were on display at a special exhibit in Rhode Island sponsored by the Providence Jewelry Museum.

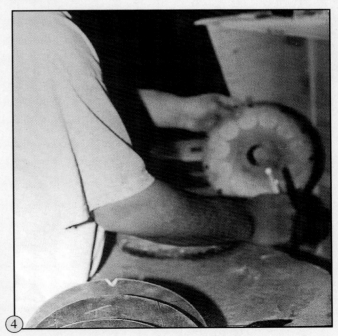

(Photo by Michael Salvadore, Jr.)

This picture shows the template used for the mold and two molds used to make parts of the same piece. Most molds are two parts (top and bottom) and look like a big, round, black pancake. In the center is shown the finished hinged, bangle bracelet.

This circular production mold could have as many as twenty cavities. This one has twelve. Before it is used to cast, it is dusted with powder to reduce surface friction and allow the metal to flow into the cavity.

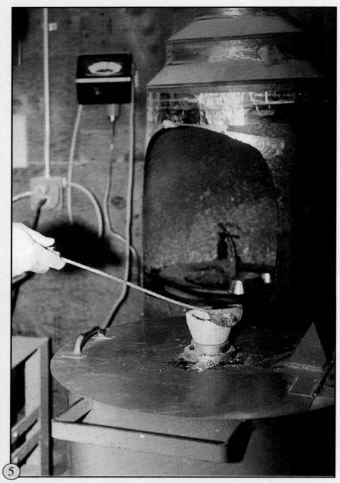

Next, the mold is placed in the spin caster and the molten, white metal is poured into the mold as it spins. The white metal cools in the mold in approximately 20 seconds. Then the pieces are broken off of the gates. After the piece is surface finished, it then goes to the plater for an electroplated metal finish.

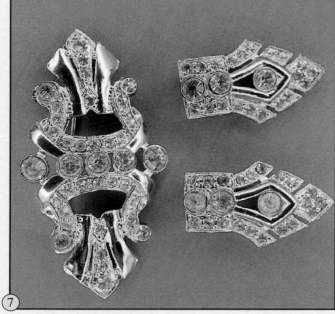

Description: When taken apart, it converts to a brooch and a set of dress clips.

Front of the brooch.

Here is the reverse side of the brooch.

Appendix 1:
Circa Dating Clues

Fittings and Findings

Catches

The following drawings represent the types of catches found on antique and period jewelry.

"C" Type

The "C" type is the earliest type of catch, but it can still be found on some new pieces.

open

ca. 1895

This type of catch was used for only a short period of time.

ca. 1890

I have found this type of catch on European pieces as early as 1896, but my research indicates they were not generally used in the United States before 1912. They continued to be popular throughout the 1920s.

This catch dates from the 1920s.

Tube or Trombone

**Tube or Trombone
ca. 1890**

The tube or trombone type was popular in the 1890s, but it can be found on many European pieces from the 1940s.

Hinges

There are two types of hinges found on antique and period jewelry.

Tube Hinge

The tube hinge is the earliest type.

Ball Hinge

The ball hinge has been used from the 1890s to the present.

Earring Findings

Here are the five principal types of earring findings.

Fish Hook

The fish hook is the earliest type of ear wire.

Kidney Wires

Kidney wires have been traced as far back as the 1870s. They are still popular today.

Threaded Stud

The threaded studs are circa 1890s. They are used today, but are smaller in diameter and the nut is usually a lighter weight.

Screw Backs

Screw backs date from 1909. They are still used, but are not common on new pieces.

1930-70 Ear Clips

Clips date from 1930-70 and are still used on some new earrings.

Findings not only help in circa dating, they can also give clues about any additions or alterations to the piece. If a piece has a safety catch, we know it is either a twentieth century piece or that the safety was added later. Whether or not it was a later addition can usually be ascertained by a careful examination. Look for signs of soldering. Often the new catch is attached to a small plate joined to the back of the brooch. This plate is a sure sign that the safety catch is not original.

Periods

Victorian

Queen Victoria reigned from 1837 until her death in 1901. Consequently, many pieces of jewelry can be referred to as Victorian. I have chosen to use Margaret Flower's divisions of Early Victorian 1837-1860, Mid-Victorian 1860-1885, and Late Victorian 1885-1901. I have added Edwardian 1901-1910 to the Late Victorian period. Keep in mind that there is never a clear-cut line dividing these periods, because some styles and motifs continued to be popular for a longer period of time in some areas. Styles also tend to overlap. A style that was waning in England could be at its peak of popularity in the United States.

Early Victorian: 1837-1860

Popular Motifs:
Classical Greek and Roman designs
Gothic and medieval designs
Garter jewelry
Grapes (usually formed of seed pearls)
Vines and leaves
Eyes (eye miniatures)
Hands
Knots of all types
Serpents
Hearts

Materials:
Gold (all colors except white)
Pinchbeck
Rolled gold
Gold electroplate (after 1841)
Jet
Gutta-percha
Bogwood or Bog Oak
Hair
Tortoise
Ivory
Aluminum (after 1855)

Embellishments:
Stones often cut in cabochon
Amethyst
Citrine
Coral
Garnets
Paste
Ruby
Topaz
Pique
Mosaics
Cameos (stone, shell, lava, coral)
Bloodstone
Cairngorm
Dark blue enameling

Mid-Victorian: 1860-1885

Popular Motifs:
Acorns
Amphorae
Anchor, heart, and cross
   (hope, love, and faith)
Beetles
Bells
Crosses
Etruscan motifs
Buckles
Fringes
Tassels
Monograms
Insects
Garter jewelry
Hearts
Serpents
Ram's head
Archaeological motif

Materials:
(see Early Victorian)
Bloomed Gold
Tiger Claws
Real Beetles
Amber

Embellishments:
(see Early Victorian)
All forms of enameling

411

Amethysts (sometimes incised with a flower motif)
Diamonds
Emeralds
Coral
Pearls
Sapphire
Turquoise
Cameos (done in amethyst, emerald, garnet, jasper, hematite, coral, agate, lava, and shell)
Intaglios
Lapis
Cornelian
Tourmaline
Spinel
Rock crystal
Aquamarine
Zircon (natural brown)
Demantoid garnets (after 1869)

Late Victorian and Edwardian: 1885-1910

I'm taking the liberty of combining these two periods. Officially Edward VII reigned from 1901-1910, but his influence was felt much earlier. Many Victorian motifs were reflections of his activities; e.g. racing motifs and good luck motifs. During this period, clothing was lighter and softer than it had been in almost a hundred years. The jewelry also became lighter in scale. Dainty pieces such as the lavalier became popular.

Popular Motifs:

Clovers
Crescent and stars
"Cross-over" designs
Hearts (single and double)
Birds
Flowers
Horseshoes and other good luck signs
Moon and owl
Man in the moon
Shamrocks
Sporting
Bats
Insects

Materials:

Gold (multicolored)
Platinum
Silver
Oxidized silver
Copper
Rolled gold
Celluloid
Watch cock covers
Gun metal

Embellishments:

Opals
Moonstone
Diamonds
Pearls
Peridot
Sapphires
Topaz
Amber
Glass
Jet
Turquoise
Garnets
Mother of pearl
Aquamarine
Crepe stone
Onyx
Amethyst
All forms of enameling

Art Nouveau: 1885-1917

Popular Motifs:

Female head
Serpents
Dragonflies
Interwoven, asymmetrical flowing lines
Flowers
Swans
Peacock
Bats

Materials:

Gold
Silver
Silver-plates
Gold-filled

Horn
Ivory
Tortoise

Embellishments:

Stones cut in cabochon
Opals
Moonstones
Pearls
Diamonds (usually small)
Pate de Verre
Glass
All forms of enameling
Rock crystal

Art Deco: 1920-1930s

Popular Motif:

Geometric lines
Abstract designs
Motifs denoting speed
Dramatic interplay of colors
Shimmery colors
Stylized floral motifs

Materials:

Platinum
White gold
Silver
White metal
Bakelite

Embellishments:

Emeralds
Ruby
Sapphire
Onyx
Diamonds
Rock crystal

Marcasites
Cornelian
Chrysoprase
Jade
Ivory

Retro Modern: 1932-1940s

Popular Motifs:

Stylized flowers
Cones
Spacecraft motif (my term)
Bows
Ovals with bows
Stylized feathers
Cornucopia
Birds
Bold Polish curves

Materials:

Yellow Gold
Green Gold   } → all often
Pink Gold   used in the
Sterling Silver} → same piece
Gold-filled   (after WW II)
Gold-plated

Embellishments:

Rubies
Diamonds
Blue sapphires
Pearls
Faceted and cabochon cut stones often in the
    same piece
Aquamarines
Synthetic stones

Appendix 2:
"What Is This Metal?"

This is one of the most important questions asked about old jewelry. The metal not only plays a major role in determining value, but it can also provide clues as to when and where a piece was made.

Almost everyone knows that a gold-plated ring is less valuable than one made of karat gold, but how can the average person tell the difference? What do the numbers and letters stamped on a piece mean? How can silver, white gold, and white metal be identified? This section will answer these questions and more.

To properly examine jewelry, a magnifying glass of some sort is needed. A jeweler's loupe is a good investment whether you are a collector or a curious owner. A 2-1/2 power loupe is adequate for examining most markings and is available at jewelry supply stores for less than $10. For examining stones, a 10 power loupe is recommended, and a good one can be purchased for less than $50. With these aids in hand, you are ready to examine the metal.

Gold

In the United States, the purity of gold is designated by karat. Pure gold is 24K, but, because of its softness, it is not suitable for making jewelry. Other metals such as copper, silver, nickel, and zinc are added to gold to strengthen it. What is added and how much is added, determine the color and karat of gold.

To make this easier to understand, let's take an imaginary ring and examine it. The color of the metal is immediately apparent. Gold comes in several colors, but let's pretend that this ring is pink gold. Inside the ring is stamped 10K. What do these things tell us? First, that the gold was mixed with copper, silver, and zinc to make yellow gold. The pink look was achieved by using a larger quantity of copper. The 10K mark assures that 41.67% of the metal is pure gold, and the other 58.33% is copper, silver, and zinc. It also indicates that the piece was made in the United States (other countries do not use 10K). A 14K stamping would mean that the ring contained 58.33% gold and 41.67% other metals. If the ring was marked 18K, it would contain 75% pure gold and 25% other metals.

In Europe, gold is stamped according to its fineness. Pure gold is 1000 fine; 18K gold is 75% or 750 fine. Consequently, an 18K ring made in Europe would be stamped 750.

Below is a chart of the most common karat markings:

US karats	Percent of gold	Fineness
24	100%	1000
22	95.83%	958
18	75%	750
15	62.50%	625
14	58.33%	583
10	41.67%	417
9	37.50%	375

The 375 at the bottom of the list is the English number for 9K. It will often be found enclosed in a rectangular box with other markings. These are known as hallmarks and are discussed under the silver heading.

414

Rolled Gold Plate

Always be sure to look for other letters that might be stamped next to the karat sign. A piece marked 14K R.G.P. is not 14 karat gold. The R.G.P. stands for rolled gold plate, which is made by applying a layer of gold alloy to a layer of base metal. This "sandwich" is then drawn to the thickness needed for the piece of jewelry. Rolled gold plating was very popular in the 1800s and early 1900s.

Gold Filled

Other letters that sometimes appear next to the karat number are G.F. This signifies the piece is gold filled. The name is misleading, because the piece is not filled with gold as the name implies, but is made by joining a layer of gold to a base metal as in rolled gold plating. The layer of gold used in R.G.P. is sometimes thicker than the one used in gold filled, making it more durable and more valuable. Again, the numbers tell how much gold and what karat of gold was used. A piece marked 1/20 12K assures that the alloy is 12 karat or 50% pure gold and the 1/20 of the total weight of the piece is 12K gold.

Electroplating

If the piece in question is marked 14K H.G.E., it has been gold plated. The initials stand for hard gold electroplated. It means that the piece is made of base metal that has been plated with a thin coating of gold by an electrical process.

Other Markings

In the late 1800s, many pieces were stamped "solid gold" or advertised as such. Some of these pieces were only 6K to 10K gold, and most were gold filled or rolled gold plate. A law passed in 1906 required the gold content be stamped on jewelry. Before that year, many pieces of gold jewelry were unmarked. For ways to determine whether an unmarked piece is gold, rolled gold plated, or gold filled refer to Appendix 3: "Is It Real?"

Pinchbeck

Pinchbeck is a very old metal rarely encountered today. The name is often misapplied to gold filled or rolled gold-plated items. It is not a plate or coating, but a solid metal made by mixing copper and zinc.

The formula, discovered by Christopher Pinchbeck (1670-1732), contained no gold; yet it looked like gold and wore well. The pinchbeck formula was a guarded secret passed down in the family, but other companies developed their own versions.

There were so many imitations that Christopher's grandson, Edward Pinchbeck, found it necessary to place this advertisement in the July 11, 1733 edition of the *Daily Post*:

> To prevent for the future the gross imposition that is daily put upon the public by a great number of Shop-Keepers, Hawkers, and Peddlers, in and about this town. Notice is hereby given, that the ingenious Mr. Edward Pinchbeck, at the 'Musical Clock' in Fleet Street, does not dispose of one grain of his curious metal, which so nearly resembles Gold in Color, Smell, and Ductility, to any person whatsoever, nor are the Toys (jewelry and trinkets) made of the said metal, sold by any one person in England except himself; therefore gentlemen are desired to beware of imposters, who frequent Coffee Houses, and expose for Sale, Toys pretended to be made of this metal, which is a most notorious imposition, upon the public. And Gentlemen and Ladies, may be accommodated by the said Mr. Pinchbeck with the following curious Toys: viz: Swords, Hilts, Hangers, Can Heads, Whip Handles, for Hunting, Spurs, Equipages, Watch Chains, Tweezers for Men and Women, Snuff-Boxes, Coat Buttons, Shirt Buttons, Knives and Forks, Spoons, Salvers, Buckles for Ladies Breasts, Stock Buckles, Shoe Buckles, Knee Buckles, Bridle Buckles, Stock Clasps, Knee Clasps, Necklaces, Corals, and in particular Watches, plain and chased in so curious a manner as not to be distinguished by the nicest eye, from the real gold, and which are highly necessary for Gentlemen and Ladies when they travel, with several other fine pieces of workmanship of all sorts made by the best hands. He also makes Repeating and all other sorts of Clocks and Watches particularly Watches of a new invention, the mechanism of which is so simple, and proportion so just, that they come nearer to the truth than others yet made.

The advertisement referred to necessary items for travel. Quite often copies of favorite pieces were made to wear on "travels." The gold ones were left safely at home. McKeever Persivial in his *Chats on Old Jewelry* states, "In those days when a journey of even a few miles out of London led through roads infested by thieves and highway robbers, careful folk preferred not to tempt these 'gentlemen of the road' by wearing expensive ornaments unless traveling with a good escort; so not only would a traveler with a base metal watch and buckles lose less if robbed, but owing to the freemasonry which existed between innkeepers and pestilence and the highwaymen, they were actually less likely to be stopped, as it was not worthwhile to run risks for such a poor spoil."

With the invention of the electro-gilding process in 1840, and the legalization of 9K gold in 1854, the use of pinchbeck declined and eventually became passe.

415

Pinchbeck is very collectible, but there are very few pieces available. Part of the fun of jewelry collecting are the "lucky finds." After viewing a few pieces, pinchbeck becomes visually identifiable. Until then, take care to buy from a knowledgeable dealer.

Silver

Silver is a precious metal that has always intrigued man. Because of this fascination, regulations have been applied to its use for centuries. After silver is mined, it is refined to .999 pure. Like gold, it is too soft to be used in this pure state. Instead it is mixed with other metals for strength.

Sterling

Sterling silver is .925 fine. This mixture of pure silver and copper has long been regarded for its fine beauty. The word donates quality of the highest standard. According to Seymore B. Wyler the word "sterling" was coined when King James brought in a group of Germans to refine silver for making coins. Since they were from the east, they became known as Easterlings. When a statute concerning silver was written in 1343, the first two letters were accidentally omitted. Hence the word sterling was first applied to silver.

A lion or leopard stamped into silver signifies sterling. In the United States, the word sterling is usually stamped into the piece. All new sterling is marked or punched to signify its credibility.

Hallmarks

Since the amount of silver involved greatly determines the cost of a piece and the average person could be easily fooled, laws were passed to insure a standard purity. As early as 1335, English law required silversmiths to punch or stamp their mark into any pieces made in their shop. By 1477, a leopard head stamp was required as proof that a piece met the accepted silver standards. In 1479, a letter designating the year of manufacture was initiated, making silver even more identifiable. These signs or hallmarks are still used today and provide clues as to when and where a piece was made.

In this hallmark, the first character, a lion passant, signifies the piece is sterling silver. The anchor is the mint mark for Birmingham, England,

and the letter date signifies that it was made in 1889-1890. Sometimes, but not always, the maker's mark is included in the hallmark. The style of the letter and the shape of the box in which they are placed are all important factors when reading a hallmark. Fortunately, there are several good books on hallmarks that include lists of date letters, mint marks, and makers. These provide invaluable aid in dating and identifying silver.

Items made of sterling get more beautiful as they are used or worn. With use, tiny scratches known as patina develop, giving the silver a warm, soft look. Only gold and platinum are more durable than silver, so do not be afraid to wear it.

Coin Silver

Quite often a piece of jewelry or a watch case will be marked coin silver or .900. This means the piece is 90% silver and 10% other metal. At one time, this was the standard content of silver coins. Thus, the name "coin silver" is synonymous with this percentage of silver items. In fact, this was so prevalent in England that a law was passed in 1696 making the standard for silver items higher (958) in silver content than coins. This did not eliminate the problem. Shrewd silversmiths continued to melt coins and add silver to bring the content up to standard. Since the act did not solve the coin problem, and the new "Britannia" was softer and less durable, in 1720, the higher standard became optional.

Silverplate

A method of silver plating was discovered in 1742 by Thomas Boulsover. While repairing a knife blade, he accidentally fused silver to copper. This accident was the beginning of the Sheffield Plate Industry in England.

In 1840, G.R. Elkington was granted a patent on a process for electroplating silver or gold to a base metal. This process uses electricity to apply a coating of silver to an article made of base metal. Although this coating is usually very thin, pieces more than a hundred years old are sometimes found in amazingly good condition. The most popular base metals were copper and German silver.

German Silver

The term German silver is a misnomer. German silver is not silver at all, but rather a combination of nickel, copper, and zinc. A German introduced it to England in the late 1700s. Because its color resembles silver, it made a perfect base for silver-plated items, hence the name German Silver. To confuse matters even more it is also known as gunmetal or nickel silver.

When a piece is marked E.P.N.S., it is electroplated nickel silver.

Vermeil

The French definition of vermeil (Vair-MAY) is "silver gilt." Items made of sterling silver and coated with gold were favored by French nobility during the reign of Louis XIV and throughout the 18th century. In the early 1800s, scientists discovered that the mercury used in the vermeil process was causing the jewelry workers to go blind and the process was banned. Consequently, very little vermeil was made in the nineteenth century.

In 1956, Tiffany's reintroduced vermeil. According to Joseph Puntell, the Tiffany factory developed a process using a plating of 18-1/2 karat gold covered with second plating of 22-1/2 karat gold. This new process provided the glowing look of the mercury process without its poisonous side effects.

Platinum

Platinum, one of the heaviest, most valuable metals known to man, was first discovered in 1557 by Julius Scaligerk, an Italian scientist. In the 1700s, Spanish explorers discovered deposits in Peru and called it "plata," their name for silver.

Platinum was used very little until the late 1880s. At that time, new developments in jeweler's equipment made it easier to work, and it became popular for mounting diamonds. By the 1920s, it was the most popular metal used in jewelry. Platinum's popularity caused white gold to become fashionable. Eighteen karat white gold was advertised as "a look-alike" for the more expensive metal. Platinum's durability made it an excellent choice for the filigree styles of the 20s and 30s.

During World War II, the use of platinum for jewelry was restricted by the War Production Board. The metal was needed for a catalyst in munitions' plants. Reluctantly jewelers turned to palladium, a related metal, as a substitute.

The same ore that yields platinum contains five other metals—iridium, palladium, rhodium, ruthenium, and osmiridium. They are known as the platinum group, of these, platinum, palladium and rhodium are widely used in jewelry.

Palladium

Palladium is one of the six metals in the platinum group. Even though it is harder, lighter, and less expensive than platinum, it has never been as popular.

During World War II, jewelry manufacturers turned to palladium when platinum was restricted. The public could not tell the difference, and palladium was 30% cheaper. Its weight is comparable to 14K gold. After the war full page advertisements were used to promote palladium, but it never gained full acceptance by the general public.

Rhodium

Rhodium is another of the six metals in the platinum group. Because of its hardness, it is often used as a plating. Quite often a piece will be marked "sterling silver rhodium finished" or "stainless steel rhodium finish." The abbreviated mark for rhodium is "Rh."

Appendix 3:
Is It Real?

This question is most often asked about stones. Because the answer can mean a big difference in value, it is most important that it be correct. The person most qualified to answer this question is a graduate gemologist, a person trained to identify and evaluate stones (a Gemological Institute of America graduate).

If you are a collector or a dealer, a good working relationship with a gemologist can be invaluable. Whether you own an extensive collection or just a few pieces that have been handed down in the family, an appraisal by a gemologist with a knowledge of antique and period jewelry is needed to assure proper insurance coverage. Most gemologists charge by the job or on an hourly basis. Appraisers who base their fee on a percentage of value, are not recommended.

To assure a good appraisal, look for a graduate gemologist who is a member of the "National Association of Jewelry Appraisers" and lists antique and period jewelry as one of his/her fields of expertise. This assures that the appraiser not only has superior knowledge in his/her area of certification, but has also completed courses on appraisal theory and ethics.

Imitation and Synthetic Stones

Genuine stones have been imitated for thousands of years. The Egyptians made glass imitations and endowed them with the same supernatural power as the genuine. Paste, a glass imitation gemstone, was widely used from the thirteenth through the seventeenth century. In the eighteenth century, Joseph Strass discovered that by adding a high percentage of lead to glass he could increase its brilliance, thus creating more beautiful imitations. By the early nineteenth century, a process for making synthetic rubies had been discovered. But it was almost another hundred years before they were commercially feasible for use in jewelry.

Synthetic stones are not imitations. Physically, chemically and optically, they are the same as the natural. By the use of heat and pressure, man has been able to speed up the process that takes nature thousands of years to produce.

When rubies were first synthesized in the 1800s, they were more expensive than the natural ones. In 1910, August Verneuil came up with the idea of using a smeltering torch that could provide heat equal to half of that produced by the sun. This new process produced stones at a much lower cost. Still they were so highly regarded that jewelers of the 1920s often set them in 18K gold mountings.

Synthetic spinels came on the market in 1926, followed by synthetic emeralds in the early 1940s, and synthetic star sapphires and rubies in 1947. The process for making synthetic diamonds was perfected in 1955. Today, most of the diamonds used for industrial purposes are synthetic.

Gem quality synthetic diamonds have been possible since the 1970s, but they are more expensive than the natural ones. Stones such as cubic zirconium (C.Z.s) and YAG are synthetic stones but they are not synthetic diamonds.

Doublets and Triplets

Before relatively inexpensive synthetic stones were available, a combination stone called a "doublet" was popular. The jeweler fused a layer of one stone to another, then faceted the stone as if it were one large stone. The most popular doublet was one using garnet and glass. It was used to imitate sapphires, topaz, emeralds, amethyst, rubies and of course, garnets.

A piece of green or blue glass with a red garnet top is intriguing. It takes a trained eye and close inspection to detect. Consequently, pieces of jewelry set with old doublets are quite collectible. Most people are fascinated by them.

The term "triplet" is used to describe a stone that is made up of three parts. This can mean three stones (genuine top and bottom with something else in between), or it can refer to two stones put together with a colored cement that provides the "stone's" color. Because synthetic emeralds are expensive, triplets made of quartz or synthetic spinel joined by emerald green cement are often encountered.

Tests for Stones

The first test for any stone is visual. Get out your 10 power loupe and look at the stone. There are many things to notice. When examining colored stones, look for color zoning. In layman's terms this is a variance of color. Usually there is more color or more intense color in some areas of the stone. This "zoning" (especially noticeable in amethyst) is an indication of a natural stone. Synthetic stones usually have more "life" and are evenly colored.

When examining the cut of a stone, notice whether or not there are sharp, precise lines. Natural stones have to be cut to their best advantage and are not always as precise as synthetic ones. Look for signs of layers that could mean a doublet or triplet. Chips and abrasions on the surface of a clear stone are usually in indication that the stone is not a diamond.

Next, look into the stone. Natural stones often have needle-like angular inclusions. Synthetics have curved lines or curved color bandings. Any stone made by a flame fusion process such as glass or synthetics will usually have round gas or air bubbles. (See figures)

Figures #1-5 are pictures taken under magnification of "glass used as gemstones." Reprinted from the G.I.A. study course on colored stones, they are courtesy of the Gemological Institute of America. Figures 1, 2, and 3 show differently shaped gas bubbles. Figure 4 shows swirl marks and flow lines. Figure 5 shows groups of "bubbles arranged in a feather-like pattern."

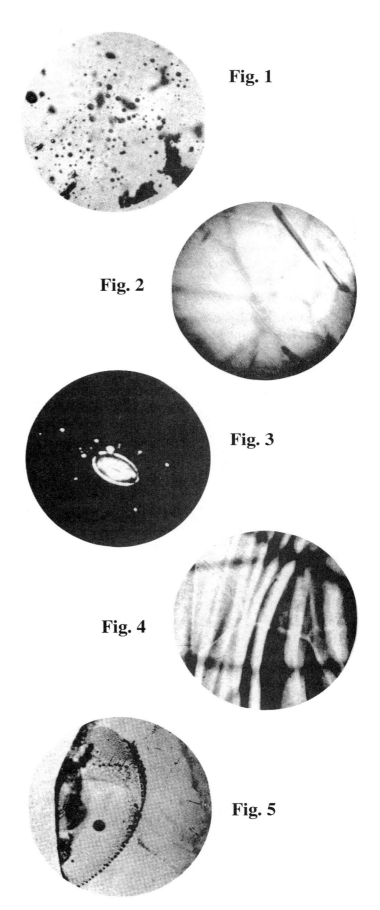

Fig. 1

Fig. 2

Fig. 3

Fig. 4

Fig. 5

Another more difficult test is one for "refraction." This is done by looking through the stone and focusing on a facet line (where two facets intersect). Slowly tilt the stone back and forth. If one looks like two or splits apart and comes back together, it is a doubly refractive stone. Peridot, topaz, tourmaline, emerald, quartz, amethyst, citrine, synthetic rutile and zircon are all doubly refracting stones. The last two are highly refractive and can often be identified by this test alone. Diamonds, garnets, spinels and glass do not double refract. Although this test does not give all the answers, its results are well worth the effort to become proficient.

There are many other tests used by the gemologist to determine stones. Synthetics have become so sophisticated that even an expert cannot be sure without the aid of expensive equipment. Today, a trained gemologist with a well-equipped laboratory is imperative for proper stone identification.

This is not to say, that the average person cannot learn to identify and enjoy stones. The best way to gain this knowledge is by becoming visually acquainted with the various stones. Take every opportunity to view and examine them. Antique shows and gem and mineral shows provide ideal opportunities to handle stones. Most dealers and participants are more than willing to share their knowledge.

Test for Diamonds

If you have a loose clear stone and want to know whether or not it is a diamond there are some simple tests that may help in this determination.

For the first test, draw a line on a sheet of white paper. Place the stone (table down) on the line. If the stone is a diamond, the line will not be visible. Any other clear stone will allow the line to show through.

The next test is done by placing the stone on a sheet of white paper and holding a penlight under it. Be sure that the light shines up under the stone. If the stone is a C.Z., YAG, or any other clear stone, the light will outline the stone and also show through the middle. If the stone is a diamond, the outline will show through but the middle will remain dark.

Another test is the "breath test." If breathing on the stone causes it to "fog" this is an indication that the stone in question is not a diamond. All these tests should be performed for the first time using stones that are known. This provides a chance to see the accurate reactions before testing an unknown stone.

An amazingly accurate determination of whether or not a stone is a diamond can be done with a small heat probe instrument. Diamonds are the most heat conductive of stones. Using this fact, the instrument has a small pen-like probe that heats up. When this point is placed on a diamond, the heat is transmitted away from the point, and triggers a beeping sound to signify that it is a diamond. When the probe is placed on any other clear stone the heat is not conducted and no sound is heard. It's a simple fun thing to see. Go to your local jeweler and ask him to demonstrate it.

Test for Amber

There are many tests to help determine the authenticity of amber. The Greeks were aware of its static electricity, so this was probably the first test. This version of the test was included in the February 1864 *Peterson's Magazine*:

> Our article on amber and amber combs last year brought out the inquiry by whether all combs, or other articles, represented to be amber, are so, or not. We replay that very many things sold as amber are imitations. A lady who has an amber necklace, which belonged to her ancestors, sends us the following as a sure method of testing amber. "Prepare a fine bit of split straw-piece of split straw an inch long-rub the article briskly with woolen or cotton cloth a few minutes; place it immediately in contact with one end of the straw, (the straw must not lie in the hand, but on a table, or any dry substance). If the beads or combs are really amber, they will lift the end of the straw, and sometimes the point of a very fine needle."

This test can be done today using bits of tissue paper. The problem is that some of today's plastics also have the same ability.

Another test is done by sticking a hot needle into an inconspicuous spot on the amber. If the piece is genuine, it will emit a pine-like odor. According to Marilyn Roos, an amber dealer, this test is not always conclusive because artificial amber made in Russia includes small bits of genuine amber. If the needle should hit any of these pieces, it would test authentic.

The only true test, according to Marilyn, is done with ether. She suggests putting a small amount on a cotton swab and applying it to the piece in question (in an inconspicuous place of course). If the piece is genuine, the ether will not affect it. If it is plastic, it will become sticky and the ether will eat into it.

Gutta-percha

Gutta-percha is one of the easiest plastics to identify. It is black or brownish black in color and very lightweight. When rubbed briskly on a piece of cloth, it emits the very distinctive odor of burnt rubber.

Ivory

Unless you are an expert, identifying ivory can be very difficult. A loupe for magnified viewing is a necessity. Elephant ivory has an "engine turned" effect when viewed under magnification. Figure 1a (on the next page) shows a piece magnified 15 times. Grain lines, shown in figure 2a (magnified 25x) are found in any true ivory. When ivory is touch with nitric acid, it effervesces—bone, vegetable ivory and plastics do not. (See photos on next page.)

Bone is often used to imitate ivory. Figure 4a shows a transverse section of bone magnified 25 times. A longitudinal section, magnified 50 times is shown in figure 5a. As you can see, it has an entirely different look than that of ivory.

The so-called vegetable ivories are fairly easy to identify. When a few drops of sulfuric acid are applied to this type of ivory, it turns a rosy color. True ivory will not be affected by the acid. Figure 6a shows a cross section of corozo nut magnified 25x. a longitudinal view of the vegetable ivory is seen in figure 7a. Figures 8a and 9a show the same views of the doum-palm nut. These pictures are courtesy of the Gemological Institute of America.

Jet

Bog oak, gutta-percha, onyx and black glass are all often misidentified as jet. Mr. Brian Fall, a volunteer at the museum in Whitby, was kind enough to share his method of identifying jet. He warned me that the test should be done with care so as not to destroy the piece.

Simply rub the piece across a piece of concrete (a sidewalk?). If it leaves a brownish black mark, the piece is jet. If it does not leave a mark it is some other material.

Jet can sometimes be identified by its weight. It has an extremely lightweight feeling, much like the feel of amber. Maybe this accounts for the misnomer "Black Amber" that is often applied to jet. Jet has sharp, precisely cut lines. Mold lines are an indication of glass.

Pearls

An imitation pearl can usually be detected by examining the hole through which it is strung. If it is a glass imitation covered with essence d' orient, a thin film can usually be detected.

Another test for determining whether or not pearls are imitation is done by rubbing them against your teeth. Imitation pearls will feel smooth while cultured or natural pearls will feel "gritty." With a little practice, one can become quite profi-

cient at this. This is an easy accurate way to tell the imitation from the cultured.

Cultured pearls are not imitation, and there is no visible difference between them and oriental pearls. Only an expert with the proper equipment (usually x-rays) is qualified to make this judgement. Since the price of cultured pearls is much lower than that of natural ones, always get an expert opinion, in writing, before making a purchase.

Other Tests

Quite a few materials can be tested by using a few items that you probably already have at home.

First get a pencil with an eraser on the end. Place the eye-end of a needle into the end of the eraser. Now all that is needed to complete this scientific testing unit is a lighted candle.

After heating the needle over the candle, place the hot point to an inconspicuous place on the piece of jewelry. The odor different materials produce can help you determine what it is.

Below is a list of several materials and their identifying odors. Always remember to stick the hot needle into an inconspicuous place:

Amber: Pine scent

Bakelite: Carbolic acid

Celluloid: Camphor

Jet: Burning coal

Tortoise Shell: Burning hair

If you are really interested in learning more about jewelry, learn to use your built in tools. The first tool is your eyes. Notice details. Learn to recognize styles. Visually compare pieces. Expose your eyes to good examples of jewelry by visiting art galleries (notice the jewelry worn in portraits), going to antiques shows and looking through old books.

The hands are another important tool in exploring jewelry. Learn the feel of a piece. Touch the finish. Feel the weight. The more you handle jewelry, the more adept you will become at judging it. Surprisingly enough, you may even get to the point where you can determine whether or not a piece is gold just by its feel.

The most surprising jewelry tool is your teeth. By touching a beaded necklace lightly against my teeth, I can distinguish between glass and plastic. Try it. Get used to the difference in the sound and feel of different substances against your teeth. I will admit this looks a bit strange. I have had people ask, "What in the world are you doing?"; but it does work. Again, it is something that has to be worked at, but it is well worth the effort.

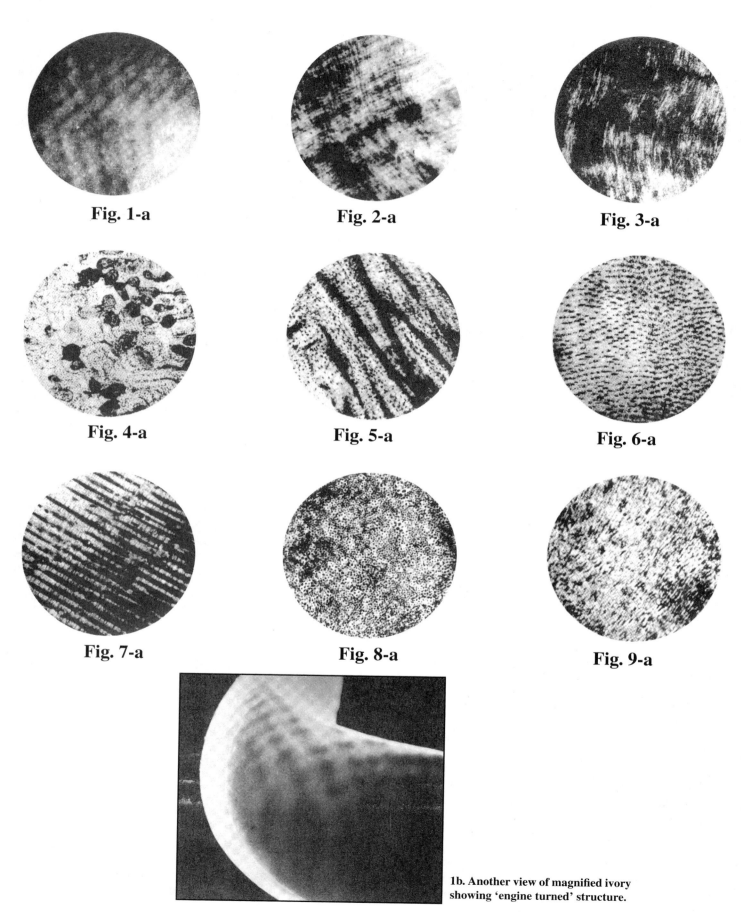

Fig. 1-a

Fig. 2-a

Fig. 3-a

Fig. 4-a

Fig. 5-a

Fig. 6-a

Fig. 7-a

Fig. 8-a

Fig. 9-a

1b. Another view of magnified ivory showing 'engine turned' structure.

422

Testing Gold

If a piece has no markings, there may be other clues to help determine the metal. First, examine it closely with a loupe. Look closely at the edges or any place that was likely to rub against things. Many times small patches of base metal are visible at these points. If the base metal is white and the piece is yellow gold, this is fairly easy, but to see brass or copper base metal under yellow is sometimes more difficult. The more accustomed your eyes become to noting subtle differences, the easier it will become. If there are no visible signs of wear, it is possible that the piece is gold. It is also possible that it is not.

There is only one true test for gold, and that is done with acid. Your jeweler can perform this test, and the charge is usually less than twenty dollars. But if jewelry is a hobby or if you are a dealer, it would be worthwhile to invest in a gold testing kit. A good one can be purchased at a jewelry supply store for less than one hundred dollars. This kit will have everything you need to test gold except the most important ingredient, acid. It can be ordered through your pharmacist or purchased pre-mixed at the jewelry supply store.

The first step in testing gold is to find an inconspicuous place on the piece of jewelry in which to file a groove or notch. Please take care where the notch is made. Many lovely antique pieces have been ruined by butchers who indiscriminately filed chunks. The groove is to get past any layer of gold in a gold filled piece. Apply a small amount of nitric acid to the groove. If the piece is gold over brass, it will bubble green; if a bluish color appears, the base metal is copper. When the piece is 14K gold or better, the acid keeps its clear water color. If, after a few minutes the spot darkens, this is an indication of 10K gold.

The exact karat can be determined by using the needles that come with the kit. With these needles a mixture, called Aqua Regis, (one part distilled water, one part nitric acid, and three parts hydrochloric acid) is used. Instructions are included in the test kit.

For those who do not care to invest in a gold test kit, there is a less expensive alternative. Simply purchase glass acid bottles and pre-mixed testing solution for 10, 14, 18 and 22 karat gold (less than $10 a bottle).

Nitric acid is still used to determine if the piece is gold. After the piece has tested gold, make a mark by rubbing the piece on a test stone. If the piece is 14K or better and a 14K solution is used, there will be no reaction. The mark will remain as visible as ever. Proceed by making another mark and using a higher karat solution until the mark dissolves. If an 18K solution dissolves the mark and the 14K solution does not, the piece is at least 14K. After testing, always rinse the piece with a mixture of baking soda and water to neutralize the acid.

Testing Silver

Although silver has been hallmarked and stamped for centuries, unmarked pieces are still encountered. If there is reason to believe a piece might be silver, examine it with a loupe. Look carefully at wear points to see if a base metal can be detected. If there are not indications of plating, a more extensive test is necessary.

For the serious collector or dealer, a pre-mixed silver test solution (available from jewelry supply stores for less than $10) is highly recommended. It can be an invaluable aid in deciphering silver content.

To test silver properly, a notch must be filed (in an inconspicuous place) in the piece being tested. Make sure the notch is deep enough to go through any plate or coating of silver. Apply the pre-mixed solution to the notch and wait a few seconds for the color reaction. If the piece is sterling, the solution will turn a dark red color. On 800 silver it turns brown. If the piece is palladium, there is no reaction. This simple inexpensive test can help make you an expert at evaluating silver content.

Misnomers

Inaccurate names are often applied to stones. They are usually used to give added importance and more sales appeal. These misnomers sometimes become so commercially accepted that the general public is unaware of what they are actually buying.

The following is a list of commonly accepted names and what they really are:

Alaskan diamond:	Rock crystal
Arizona diamond:	Rock crystal
Arkansas diamond:	Rock crystal
Arizona ruby:	Garnet
Belas ruby:	Spinel
Cape ruby:	Garnet
Cornish diamond:	Rock crystal
Goldstone:	An imitation adventurine
Herkimer diamond:	Rock crystal
Siberian ruby:	Tourmaline
Smokey topaz:	Smokey quartz
Synthetic aquamarine:	Aquamarine colored

A trade name people often wonder about is "Aurora Borealis." This name is applied to glass that has been coated with a compound to give it an iridescent look.

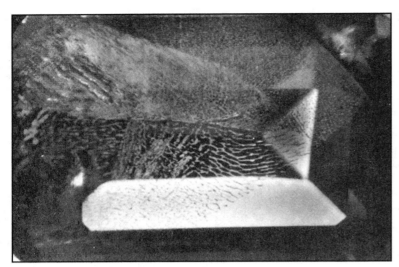

2b. Synthetic ruby magnified to show flux inclusions.

3b. Glass 'stone' magnified to show orange-pel effect and concave facets.

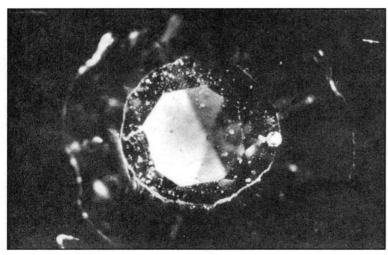

4b. Garnet and glass doublet. magnified view shows garnet top and trapped gas bubbles under garnet cap.

Appendix 4:

Makers' Marks, Trademarks & Designers' Marks

While some of the marks found on jewelry have been written about in the metals portion of this book, there are a number of other marks that are very important to the collector.

These are trademarks, makers' marks and designers' marks. All three can help date a piece and identify its origin, manufacturer, wholesaler or retailer. In the United States, trademarks became popular in the mid 1800s, but there were no laws making any marks compulsory before 1906. Consequently, there are many American pieces with no markings whatsoever.

English pieces with full hallmarks inform us of the date the piece was made, its metal content, the town in which it was assayed and its maker. Unfortunately, many pieces, especially designer ones, were never assayed. Glenais Wild of the Birmingham Museum in Birmingham, England told me this was because many times the maker's work was destroyed if for any reason the piece was slightly under specifications. This is also the reason that designers such as Lalique and Fouquet often pierced or engraved their marks.

Other markings can also be confused with trademarks. The French used an eagle's head as a gold quality mark, an owl's head in an oval for imported goods and the head of Mercury with a number on goods to be exported. Until the late 1800s, Russia used town marks with the numbers 56, 72, and 92 indicating 14K, 18K and 23K gold content.

Marks used to signify towns were as varied as a hand for Antwerp and a pineapple for Augsburg. Some town marks can be confused with American trade marks if one is not experienced in identifying marks. This section was added so the reader might become curious about the various marks on a piece of jewelry. Hopefully, it will kindle an interest that will cause the reader to be aware of any markings. Markings can help answer the question: "Who made this piece and where was it manufactured?"

This section of short biographical sketches is by no means complete. Some designers and makers are included because of the important part they played in the history of jewelry. Some firms are included because their inexpensive mass-produced pieces have become quite collectable.

The makers and firms are listed in alphabetical order within the Victorian time period. The Art Nouveau and Arts and Crafts are also alphabetized and separated. The American companies are grouped together at the end of this section.

Victorian

Boucheron

This French firm was founded in 1858 by Frederic Boucheron (1830-1902). Over the years some of the best designers of the day were at work in the Boucheron workshops. A London branch of the company was opened on New Bond Street in 1907. Boucheron is noted today as a designer of luxury and medium priced jewelry. Mark: BOUCHERON

John Brodgen

John Brogden was in English goldsmith and jeweler working in London from 1842 to 1885. His "archaeological" style pieces were prized for their beautiful filigree and granulation gold work. In 1867, his work earned him a medal at the Paris Exhibition. Two fine examples of his work are in the Victoria & Albert Museum in London. Mark:

Castellani

Castellani is one of the most famous names in jewelry of the nineteenth century. The Castellani story began in 1814, when Fortunato Pio Castellani (1793-1865) started to work in his father's jewelry workshop in Rome. He quickly acquired the status of master goldsmith and opened his own shop on the Via del Corso.

Fortunato Pio's friend, patron and associate, Michelangelo Caetani, Duke of Sermonita (1804-1883), was instrumental in igniting Castellani's interest in archaeological jewelry. He arranged for Castellani to be present (in an advisory capacity) during the excavations of the Reguline Galassi tomb.

Castellani became fascinated with the beautiful Etruscan granulation and he was determined to find the technique used in this gold work. In Umbria, he found artists using methods similar to the Etruscan work and persuaded them to come and work with him in Rome.

Because of the political situation in Italy, Castellani's shop was closed from 1840 to 1858. During this time, Fortunato Pio retired, leaving Casa Castellani in the hands of two of his eight sons, Alessandro (1924-1883) and Augusto (1829-1914).

These sons were extremely interested in archaeological jewelry and enthusiastically continued and expanded upon what their father had begun.

Augusto managed the business and strove to carry on his father's tradition. Later, he became the Director of the Capitolini Museum in Rome.

Because of his political involvements, Alessandro was in prison from 1850 to 1858. During his exile from Rome, he continued to research and study. Setting up a workshop in Naples, he continued his experiments with granulation. In 1862, he published a pamphlet "Antique Jewelry and its Revival"

to accompany the Castellani display at the London Exhibition. This pamphlet was reprinted again in Philadelphia in 1876. Alessandro published a catalogue "Italian Jewelry as worn by the Peasants of Italy, collected by Signor Castellani," in 1868.

Both Augusto and Alessandro were collectors. Augusto's Collegione Castellani was sold to the Louvre in 1860. Alessandro's Estruscan style jewelry was acquired by the British Museum in London and by the Villa Guilea Museum in Rome. Marks:

Child and Child

This firm of silversmiths and jewelers was established in London in 1880. They were located at 35 Alfred Place, Kensington from 1891 until they discontinued business in 1916. Known for high quality enamel work they were patronized by Royalty. Mark: a stylized sunflower, the stalk flanked by the initials c & c on each side of the stem.

Peter Carl Fabrege (1846-1920)

Volumes have been written about this Russian goldsmith and jeweler. Hopefully, the reader will take the time to learn about this artist by reading some of the books that include photographs of his lavish work. Two of these are: *Carl Fabrege: Goldsmith to the Imperial Court of Russia* by Kenneth Snowman, and *Fabrege and His Contemporaries* by Henry Hawley published by the Cleveland Museum of Art. A little booklet *Fabrege* available through the Victoria and Albert Museum in London contains a list of Fabrege's work masters and their marks. I highly recommend it. Mark:

ФАБЕРЖЕ

Froment-Meurice

Francois Desere Froment-Meurice was the son of France Froment a French goldsmith who had been in business since 1774. After the death of his father, his mother married Pierre-Meurice, who was also a goldsmith. Francois Desere went to work in his stepfather's workshop and added Meurice to the Froment name. Francois Desere Froment-Meurice is said to have studied drawing and sculpture. His work shows evidence of this.

In 1839, he exhibited pieces done in the Gothic Revival style for which he is noted. He was often referred to as the "Cellini" of the nineteenth century. He was much admired by his contemporaries. His enameled Renaissance style pieces are truly treasures.

Emile Froment-Meurice (1837-1913) took over the family business a number of years after his father's death. He displayed jewelry at the Exposition Universelle in Paris in 1867. The pieces were executed in the styles made famous by his father. In about 1900, he began to experiment with the new Art Nouveau designs. Marks: Both father and sons: FROMENT MEURICE

Giuliano

Carlo Giuliano is another outstanding name in nineteenth century jewelry. Born in Naples, it is believed that he met Alessandro Castellani and worked in his shop there. It was probably Alessandro who instigated Giuliano's move to London. It is evident that Giuliano worked for Casa Castellani in London.

From 1867-1874, his work was sold by prestigious firms such as Robert Phillips, Hunt and Roskell, Harry Emanuel and Hancocks. Pieces bearing his mark were sold in fitted cases imprinted with the retail firm's name. Harry Emanuel exhibited some Giuliano pieces at the L' Exposition of 1867 in Paris.

In 1874-1875, Carlo set up his own retail shop at 115 Piccadilly. Here in luxurious surroundings he sold his tiny works of art to some of Britians most prominent families.

His sons, Carolo Joseph and Arthur Alphonse, joined him in the business and continued it after his death in 1895. The firm was relocated in 1912 at #48 Knightsbridge and was closed in 1914. Marks:

A. W. N. Pugin

Augustus Wilby Northmore Pugin (1812-52) was a multi-talented Englishman who designed silverware, scenery, ironwork, jewelry, dresses and part of the Houses of Parliament. His writings included *Designs for Gold and Silversmiths*, 1836; *The True Principles of Pointed or Christian Architecture*, 1841; *The Glossary of Ecclesiastical Ornament and Costume*, 1844; and *Floriated Ornament* in 1849.

He was responsible for reviving the art of enameling and for making the Gothic style popular in England. His famous set of marriage jewelry was exhibited at the Mediaeval Court at the Crystal Palace in 1851. John Hardman & Co. in Birmingham, England executed most of his designs. Mark: (AWP monogram)

Art Nouveau
Designers, Manufacturers, and Retail Firms

Edward Colonna

Edward Colonna was a German born (1862) decorative designer whose work spanned both the Art Nouveau and Art Deco period. After finishing his architectural training in Brussels, he came to America (1882) and worked for a company founded by L.C. Tiffany. While living in Ohio, he wrote a booklet entitled *Essay on Broom Corn*. The booklet of Art Nouveau designs was inspired by the interlaced lines formed by the stalks of corn which were used to make brooms.

In 1898, he traveled to France and designed jewelry for Maison de l' art Nouveau. The book *Modern Designs in Jewellery and Fans, 1903*, by Gabriel Mourey pictures several of his pieces. Mourey states, "His works have this great charm in my eyes, that they are neither showcase jewels or mere bejoux de parade, things intended solely for display. As a rule, they are quiet and practical." After Bing's shop closed in 1905, Colonna returned to America. Mark: COLONNA (stamped) SANB (in a diamond, the mark for Maison de l' art Nouveau)

Wilhelm Lucas van Cranch

Wilhelm Lucas van Cranch (1861-1918) was a German painter and jeweler. His Art Nouveau jewelry designs are said to have an "air of decadence." He won a gold medal in Paris in 1900. Mark: WLC (in monogram)

Theodor Fahrner

Theodor Fahrner (1868-1928) was a jewelry manufacturer in Pforzheim, Germany. His mass-produced jewelry was usually done in low-carat gold or silver. He used designers from the artist's colony in Darmstadt. The book *Modern Designes in Jewellery and Fans, 1903*, pictures two pieces of jewelry executed by this firm. One of these pieces was designed by J. M. Olbrich. Mark:

Lucien Gaillard

Lucien Gaillard (born 1861) was a French silversmith, jeweler and enameler who inherited a jewelry business in 1892 that had been founded by his grandfather in 1840. His talents as a silversmith were praised at the 1889 Paris Exposition.

A friend, Rene Lalique is credited with persuading him to try designing jewelry. In about 1900, he opened a workshop where he experimented with materials such as horn and ivory. In 1904, he won first prize for jewelry at the Paris Salon. Mark: L. GAILLARD (engraved)

Rene Jules Lalique

The foremost designer of the Art Nouveau period was Rene Jules Lalique (1860-1945). At an early age, he exhibited a talent for art. At age 16, he was apprenticed to Louis Aucoc.

In 1885, he acquired a fully equipped workshop. Here he designed and made jewelry for such firms as Cartier, Boucheron and Aucoc. Much attention was drawn to his work in the 1890s when the illustrious Sarah Bernhardt became his patron. A series of 145 pieces of jewelry, which took him 17 years to complete, is now housed at the Foundacion Gulbenkian in Lisbon. Any study of Art Nouveau jewelry is incomplete without a survey of his work. Mark:

R. LALIQUE
LALIQUE
R.L.

Liberty & Co.

Liberty and Company in London, England, had a most important influence on the Art Nouveau style. Before anyone had ever used the term Art Nouveau, the style was being offered by this company. In fact, the Art Nouveau style was known as "stile Liberty" in Italy for quite some time.

A. L. Liberty had always been intrigued by the designs of the Orient. He had been employed by Farmer and Rogers when they purchased part of the Japanese exhibit from the International Exhibition of 1862. When he opened his own shop in 1876, it was devoted exclusively to goods from India, Japan, and other parts of the Orient. The aesthetics patronized his shop, and it became a dominant force on the fashion scene.

In 1899, Liberty introduced a new line of jewelry under the name "Cymric." This jewelry was designed by a group of designers connected with the Arts and Crafts movement including Arthur Gaskin, Bernard Cuzner and Archibald Knox. Most of these pieces were manufactured by W. H. Haseler and Son in Birmingham.

Cymric jewelry is described in a Liberty & Co. advertisement as "an original and important departure in gold and silver work. In this development there is a complete breaking away from convention in the matter of design and treatment which is calculated to commend itself to all who appreciate the note distinguishing artistic productions in which individuality of idea and execution is the essence of the work." Liberty & Co. jewelry may bear the Haseler mark or one of the Liberty marks. Marks:

LY & CO (in a triple diamond)
CYMRIC (trademark registered with the Board of Trade in 1901)
W. H. H. (for W. H. Haseler)

Murrle, Bennett & Co.

According to Viviene Becker, this firm was strictly a wholesaler of jewelry and not a manufacturer. The firm was founded in London in 1884 by a German (Murrle) and an Englishman (Bennett).

They sold all styles of jewelry including the New Modern designs associated with the Arts and Crafts movement. Most of the pieces were made in Pforzheim, Germany. Pieces bearing the Murrle,

Bennett & Co. mark are sought after by collectors.
Mark:

Otto Prutscher

Otto Prutscher (1880-1961) was a pupil of Josef Hoffman in the Wiener Werkslatte. He was an architect and a jewelry designer. His designs were executed by Rozet & Fischmeister, a Viennese jewelry firm.

In the book, *Modern Designs in Jewellery and Fans, 1903*, W. Fred makes this comment on Prutscher's work: "Otto Prutscher's necklaces and rings are remarkable alike for this beauty and harmonious variety of their coloring. He uses enamel to a great extent and also quite small precious stones. Very uncommon, too, is the way in which he employs metal, though only enough of it to hold the enamel in place. It would appear as if the artist had in his mind a vision of the women who are to wear his work, who are too tender and frail to carry any weight, so that the use of much metal in ornaments for them would be quite unsuitable." Mark: OP (in a square monogram)

Louis Comfort Tiffany

Louis Comfort Tiffany (1848-1933), the eldest son of C. L. Tiffany, was a painter, interior decorator, designer, glass maker and jeweler. In 1879, he founded Associated Artists, an interior design firm. His decorative work reflected his interest in and his love of Japanese art. In 1889, he associated himself with another exponent of the Oriental Samuel Bing, owner of Maison de l' art Nouveau.

Tiffany studios started making jewelry in 1900. L. C. Tiffany became the manager of the company's jewelry workshop when his father died in 1902. Marks: Louis C. Tiffany (in italics); LCT, Tiffany & Co.

Philippe Wolfers

Philippe Wolfers (1858-1929) was a Belgian jeweler who was also trained in art and sculpturing. He designed for his family firm and enjoyed working with ivory. He designed a series of Art Nouveau jewelry and marked it with his special mark to distinguish it from the pieces done for the family firm. In the book, *Modern Designs in Jewellery and Fans, 1903*, F. Khnopff gives his opinion of Wolfer's work:

M. WOLFERS seeks his inspiration in the study of the nature and the forms of his marvelous domain, and his vision of things is specially defined in his jewels. The detail therein contributes largely to the spirit of the entire work, which borrows its character from the decoration itself or from the subject of that decoration. He never allows himself to stray into the regions of fancy; at most, he permits his imagination to approach the confines of ornamental abstraction. Nevertheless, he interprets Nature, but is never dominated by it. He has too true, to exact a sense of the decorative principle to conform to the absolute reality of the things he admires and reproduces. His art, by virtue of this rule, is thus a modified translation of real forms. He has too much taste to introduce into the composition of one and the same jewel flowers or animals which have no parallel symbol or, at least, some family likeness or significance. He will associate swans with water-lilies—the flowers which frame, as it were, the life of those grand poetic birds; or he will put the owl or the bat with the poppy—the triple evocation of Night and Mystery; or the heron with an eel—symbols of distant, melancholy streams. He rightly judges that in art one must endeavor to reconcile everything, both the idea and the materials whereby one tries to make that idea live and speak.

Mark: PW (in a shield with the words 'exemplaire unique')

Arts And Crafts
Designers and Manufacturers

The Arts and Crafts movement was a reaction against the dehumanization of man by the machine. It was not a period style, but a movement that began in the late 1850s and continued until the 1920s.

Influenced by the writing of John Ruskin (1819-1900) and the philosophy of William Morris (1834-1896), its exponents believed that there should be no distinction between the designer and the craftsman, and that the best art was achieved when artists worked in partnership.

These artists formed guilds and lived and worked together. Their dreams of bringing art to the common man by executing ordinary items in honest and hand-crafted designs were never fulfilled, because the expense involved in hand crafting the items made them unaffordable to the very class for which they were intended. Hollbrook Jackson in this book *The Eighteen-Nineties*, published in 1913, has this comment about the movement:

The outward effect of this search for excellence of quality and utility in art was, however, not so profound as it might have been. This is explained by the fact that the conditions under which Morris and his group worked were so far removed from the conditions of the average economic and industrial life of the time as to appear impractical for general adoption. They demonstrated, it is true, that it was possible to produce useful articles of fine quality and good taste even in an age of debased industry and scamped counterfeit workmanship; but their demonstration proved also that unless something like a revolution happened among wage-earners none but those of ample worldly means could hope to become possessed of the results of such craftsmanship.

Today many of these pieces are not only collectable—they are also affordable. If you find the style of Arts and Crafts jewelry appealing, I urge you to buy it. I feel sure that good examples are destined to appreciate in value.

C. R. Ashbee

Charles Robert Ashbee (1863-1942) was the cornerstone of the Arts and Crafts movement. He founded the School and Guild of Handicraft in 1887-88 which served as a "training ground" for young exponents of the movement. Ashbee was an admirer of Cellini and translated and published Cellini's treatises in 1898. A copy of this fascinating work was published by Dover Publication in 1967. It gives an excellent account of how jewelry was made in the sixteenth century. Ashbee designed most of the jewelry executed by the Guildsmen. He exhibited at the Vienna Seccession Exhibitions number VIII, XV, XVII and XXIV, and with the Arts and Crafts Society from 1888.

Aymer Vallance, writing about British Jewelry in *Modern Designs in Jewellery and Fans, 1903*, had this to day about Ashbee's work:

AMONG pioneers of the artistic jewelry movement, Mr. C. R. Ashbee holds an honorable place. He stood almost alone at the beginning, when he first made known the jewellery designed by him, and produced under his personal direction by the Guild and School of Handicraft in the East End. It was immediately apparent that here was no tentative nor half-hearted caprice, but that a genuine and earnest phase of an ancient craft had been reestablished. Every design was carefully thought out, and the work executed with not less careful and consistent technique. In fact, its high merits were far in advance of anything else in the contemporary jewellery or goldsmith's work. The patterns were based on conventionalized forms of nature, favorite among them being the carnation, the rose and the heartsease, or on abstract forms invited by the requirements and conditions of the material—the ductility and luster of the metal itself. Most of the ornaments were of silver, the surface of which was not worked up to a brilliantly shining burnish, in the prevalent fashion of the day, but dull polished in such wise as to give the charming richness and tone of old silver work. Mr. Ashbee also adopted the use of jewels, not lavishly or ostentatiously, but just wherever a note of color would convey the most telling effect, the stones in themselves, e.g. amethysts, amber, and rough pearl, being of no particular value, save purely from the point of view of

decoration. Novel and revolutionary as it were, at its first appearance, the principles underlying Mr. Ashbee's jewellery work— viz, that the value of a personal ornament consists not in the commercial value of the materials so much as in the artistic quality of its design and treatment—they became the standard which no artist thenceforward could wisely afford to ignore, and such furthermore that have even in certain quarters become appropriated by the trade in recent times.

Mark: CRA (pricked or scratched); GOH ltd (registered 1898)

Birmingham Guild of Handicraft

This firm of craft jewelers was founded in 1890. The guild became part of Gittins Craftsman Ltd. in 1910. They had a reputation for making good quality handmade jewelry. Mark: BGOH (in a square)

Bernard Cuzner

Bernard Cuznar (1877-1956) was an English silversmith and jeweler. While serving an apprenticeship as a watchmaker, he went to night school at the Redditch School of Art. Soon he gave up watchmaking in favor of silversmithing. Cuznar was strongly influenced by Robert Catterson Smith and Arthur Gaskin. Various Liberty & Co. designs have been attributed to him. In 1935, he published an illustrated book of designs entitled, *A Silversmith's Manual*. Cuzner was head of the metalwork department of the Birmingham School of Art from 1910 until he retired in 1942. Mark: BC

Arthur and Georgie Gaskin

Arthur Gaskin was born in Birmingham, England in 1862. In 1883, he was a student at the Birmingham School of Art. Here he met Georgie Evelyn Cave France (1868-1934). Their mutual interest in design, art and illustrating brought them together, and on March 21, 1894, they were married. Arthur was a "born teacher" and was assistant master at the Central School from 1885 until 1903. From 1903-1924 he was headmaster and teacher at the School of Jewelers and Silversmiths.

Both Georgie and Arthur entered their work in national competitions. In 1899, they decided to learn to make jewelry. Commenting on the production of this jewelry Georgie wrote in 1929, "In the jewelry I did all the designing and he did all the enamel, and we both executed the work with our assistants."

In the March 1903 issue of *The Magazine of Art,* an article written by Aymer Vallance states:

...public demand for the jewellery is such that strenuous effort is needed by Mrs. Gaskin, who has a gift for divining the individual wants of her clients, to maintain in every case that touch of personality which contributes no little to the attractiveness of her work. I have always thought that jewellery, requiring as it does dainty taste in the designing and delicate manipulation in execution, is an industry specially suited to lady artists, and it is surprising how few comparatively appear to give it a thought. Mrs. Gaskin's achievements ought to show what can be done by anyone possessed of the above qualifications.

This same author had this to say about the Gaskins in *Modern Designs in Jewellery and Fans, 1903*:

> Mr. Gaskin came to the conclusion that it was of little benefit for a draughtsman to make drawings on paper to be carried out by someone else; studio and workshop must be one, designer identical with a craftsman. It is not very many years since Mr. Gaskin, ably seconded by his wife, started with humble, nay, almost rudimentary apparatus, to make jewellery with his own hands; but the result has proved how much taste and steadfast endurance can accomplish. Their designs are so numerous and so varied—rarely is any single one repeated, except to order—that it is hardly possible to find any description that apply at all. But it may be noted that, whereas a large number have been characterized by a light and graceful treatment of twisted wire, almost life filigree, the two pendants here illustrated seem to indicate rather a new departure on the part of Mr. Gaskin, with their plates of chased metal, and pendants attached by rings, a method not in any sense copied from, yet in some sort recalling the beautiful fashion with which connoisseurs are familiar in Norwegian and Swedish peasant jewelry.

Mark:

C. H. Horner

C. H. Horner is a collectable name in English jewelry. He designed his own pieces and his factory produced them from start to finish. This vast array of items included pendants, brooches, chains and hat pins. Most pieces were done in silver and embellished with enamel. The winged scarab and insect motif were frequently used. Horner pieces are available at London Street Markets and are reasonably priced. Mark: C. H. (Chester assay)

Fred I Partridge

Fred I. Partridge was an English metal worker and jeweler who worked from about 1900 until 1908. In 1902, he went to work with C. R. Ashbee and the Guild of Handicraft. Partridge was influenced by the work of Lalique and his work reflects this interest. Partridge married May Hart, a Birmingham trained enameler, in 1906. They set up a business on Dean Street in Soho. From this location they supplied pieces for firms such as Liberty & Co. Mark: PARTRIDGE

Edgar Simpson

Edgar Simpson was an English designer who worked from about 1896 until 1910. He was one of the original designers at the Artificers Guild when it was founded in 1901. Eventually, he became their chief designer. A good example of what his contemporaries thought about his work can be gleaned from this excerpt from an article by Aymer Vallance published in *Modern Designs in Jewellery and Fans, 1903*:

> MR. EDGAR SIMPSON, of Nottingham, is an artist of great gifts, as his drawings and, still more, the specimens of his actual handiwork here illustrated fully testify. Many excellent designs lose vigor and character in the process of execution from the original sketch; but Mr. Simpson, on the contrary, manages to give his designs additional charm by the exquisite finish with which he works them out in metal. Particularly happy is this artist's rendering of dolphins and other marine creatures; as in the circular pendant where the swirling motion of water is conveyed by elegant curving lines of silver, with a pearl, to represent an air bubble, issuing from the fish's mouth.

Mark: an Artificers Guild with EDWARD SPENCER DEL in a circle

Henry Wilson

Henry Wilson (1864-1934) was an English sculptor, architect, metalworker and jeweler. He established a workshop in 1890 and joined the Art Workers Guild in 1892. He taught metalworking at the Central High School of Arts and Crafts from 1896 to about 1901. Wilson exhibited with the Arts and Crafts Society from 1889, and became its President in 1915. His book on design and techniques entitled *Silver Work and Jewellery* was published in 1903.

A hair ornament attributed to Henry Wilson was sold by Phillips Blenstock House, London on July 7, 1983 for $1,958. This description was furnished by Phillips: "A good Art and Crafts gold, silver, plique-a-jour and opal hair ornament attributed to Henry Wilson on stylistic grounds, the crescent-shaped top inset with three circular plique-a-jour plaques decorated in pink, green and turquoise with tulips, flanked by gold florets and silver leaves, with an oval opal cabochon below and tortoise shell tines to the comb, 17 cm long." Mark: H.W. (in a monogram)

The American Arts And Crafts Revival

In Chicago, the Arts and Crafts movement was well received by those who shared its philosophy of social and cultural reforms. After a visit in the 1880s to C. R. Ashbee's Guild in London, Jane Addams became an advocate of the Arts and Crafts Movement. She was instrumental in fostering the movement in America. When Ashbee came to the United States in 1900, he lectured at the Chicago Art Institute and stayed at the Hull House, a settlement run by Jane Addams. The Chicago Arts and Crafts Society was founded there in 1897.

For more information about the Arts and Crafts revival in America I urge you to read *Chicago Metal-Smiths* by Sharon Darling, published by the Chicago Historical Society in 1977. It offers valuable insight to the movement and its exponents. Many of the designers and manufacturers listed in this book are sure to become even more collectable. The book offers excellent photographs of the makers' marks.

The Kalo Shop

Clara Black named the shop she founded in 1900 "Kalo," a Greek word meaning beautiful. At first, the shop produced leather items and woven goods but when Clara married George S. Welles, a metalworker in 1905, her interest turned to metalwork and jewelry.

All the items produced by the Kalo shop were handmade. The couple set up a school and workshop known as "The Kalo Art-Craft Community" in their Chicago residence.

Jewelry bearing the Kalo stamp is much sought after by collectors. Since jewelry constituted about half of the company's total sales, pieces are still available at reasonable prices. Mark: KALO

Florence Koehler

Florence Koehler (1861-1944) was a jewelry designer and craftswoman who lived and worked in Chicago. She was one of the leaders of the Arts and Crafts revival in America and one of the founders of the Chicago Arts and Crafts Society.

Sharon S. Darling's "Chicago Metal-Smiths" lists her as Mrs. F. H. Koehler and states that she was, "...mentioned as a successful local metalworker and jewelry maker in an article by Harriet Monroe 'An Experiment in Jewelry'" (*House Beautiful*, July 1900).

Art Deco Retail Firms

The Art Deco period style was reflected in the jewelry made by leading jewelry firms such as Bocheron, Cartier, Chaumet, La Cloche, Mauboissin and Van Cleef & Arpels. Some important designers of the period were George Fouquet, Gerard Sandoz, Jean Despres and Raymond Templier.

Cartier

This firm was founded in 1847, when Louis Francois Cartier opened a small shop in Paris. In 1898, the company relocated to 13 Rue de la Paix. A London branch was opened in 1902 followed by the New York branch in 1903. Cartier is credited with making the first wristwatch in 1904. The firm executed some of the finest examples of Art Deco jewelry.

Marks: LFC (in a diamond shaped shield);
AC (with a hatchet)

Chaumment & Cie

This French firm was founded in 1780 by Erienne Nitot. The company was commissioned to make the Emperor's coronation crown and sword after Nitot assisted an accident victim who turned out to be the First Consul Napoleon Bonaparte. They also executed the wedding jewelry for Marie Louise in 1810. In 1875, they opened a showroom in London. Their Art Deco pieces were most sophisticated.

Georg Jensen

Georg Jensen (1866-1935) was a Danish goldsmith and silversmith who opened a shop bearing his name in 1904. He designed, made and sold jewelry and silverware. His distinctive style is still evident in the work produced by the firm today. Mark: Jensen; GJ

La Cloche

La Cloche was both a manufacturer and retailer of Art Deco jewelry. Founded in Madrid in 1875, the Paris branch was opened in 1898. The firm was known for its high fashion style executed in the finest materials and embellished with colored gems and diamonds.

Van Cleef & Arpels

This French firm was founded in 1906. It is credited with creating the first "minaudiere." In 1930, this name was trademarked by them. Their main office is still in Paris, but they have branches in London and New York.

Collectible American Marks

Black, Starr & Frost Co., New York

This firm of goldsmiths and jewelers was established in New York in 1810 and known as "Marquand & Co." In 1839, the company's name was changed to "Ball, Thomkins and Black," and in 1851, it was changed to "Ball, Black & Co."

The name "Black, Starr & Frost" was with the company from 1876, until it merged with the Gorham Corporation in 1929. Their customers were prestigious and pieces from their stock were often illustrated in fashion magazines of the day. Mark:

Gorham Corporation Inc., Providence, R.I.

This company, founded by Jabez Gorham in 1815, is included in this section because of some jewelry it produced in the late nineteenth and early twentieth century. This jewelry was designed by a group of artists under the direction of William C. Codman and executed by a group of silversmiths selected by Edward Holbrook. The pieces were marketed under the name MARTELE and are quite collectable. They were usually made of silver, silver gilt or copper. The few pieces with stones were set with the colorless ones most popular during the Art Nouveau period.

Marks:

Wm. B. Kerr & Co.

This firm of goldsmiths, silversmiths and jewelers was founded in Newark, New Jersey in 1855 by William B. Kerr. The company mass-produced pieces in the neo-Renaissance style and the Art Nouveau style. The Gorham Corporation purchased the company in 1906. Today, pieces baring the Kerr trademark are prized by collectors. Marks:

(Discontinued)

Jewelry Box Antiques, Inc., Kansas City, Missouri

This is definitely the newest of collectable trademarks. It is the trademark of my revival jewelry lines which premiered in November 1993. I have 3 different lines, they are:

Classics: A revival of styles from the 1840s thru the 1940s. All are executed in 18K gold and platinum.

Classics Collectables: These pieces made of 14K and 18K gold feature an original antique or vintage item as a central motif or component.

Vintage 'N Vogue: A fashion line of jewelry inspired by the styles from the 1840s thru 1940s.

These lines all proudly display our trademark on authentically inspired revivals. Mark:

C. L. Tiffany

In 1853, C. L. Tiffany founded Tiffany & Co. Prior to that year he had been in partnership with J. B. Young (1837) and J. L. Ellis (1850). Pieces bearing the Tiffany name can best be dated by following the progression of moves by the company:

1853-54:	217 Broadway
1854-1870:	550 Broadway
1870:	Union St. and 15th St.
1868:	London branch opened

Tiffany & Co. exhibited at the Exposition Universelle in Paris 1867, and at the Philadelphia Centennial Exposition of 1876. In 1878 and 1889, they won gold medals in Paris.

Special marks were added to Tiffany & Co.'s usual markings for pieces made for the 1893 World's Columbian Exposition in Chicago, the 1900 Exposition Universelle in Paris, and the 1901 Pan American Exposition in Buffalo. These are shown below. Marks:

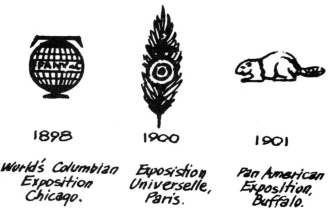

1898
World's Columbian Exposition Chicago.

1900
Exposistion Universelle, Paris.

1901
Pan American Exposition, Buffalo.

Unger Brother

This firm of silversmiths and jewelers has a very collectable trademark. Unger Brothers began making jewelry in 1878. Eugene and Frederick Unger opened a shop at #18 Crawford St. in Newark, New Jersey in 1881. P.O. Dickinson, the company's chief designer, was issued a series of patents for Art Nouveau jewelry design in 1903. The company mass produced these designs in silver and silver gilt from 1904 to 1910. In 1914, they discontinued the manufacturer of jewelry. Marks:

(Old Mark.)   (Old Mark.)   (1904)

Wayne Silver Co.

This firm was founded in Honesdale, Pennsylvania in 1895. They are described as making, "fancy and useful articles of silver, not plated." Records indicate that they discontinued business after the turn-of-the-century. Mark:

Whiting & Davis Co., Inc.

This company was founded in 1876 in Plainville, Massachusetts. In 1907, C. A. Whiting became owner, shortly after this, the first chainmail mesh machine was developed and Whiting & Davis became the world's largest manufacturer of mesh products.

Many fine examples of their early bags have survived. These are eagerly sought after by collectors, because of their beauty and durability. New bags manufactured by this company are sold in many major department stores.The company also produces a line of antique and museum reproduction jewelry. Mark:

Glossary

A

Algrette: Jewels mounted in a shape resembling feathers or a feather motif.

A-jour Setting: An open work setting in which the bottom portion of the stone can be seen. Also a setting in which the metal has open work.

Albert Chain: A watch chain for a man or a woman with a bar at one end and a swivel to hold a watch at the other.

Alma Chain: A chain with broad ribbed links.

B

Baguette: A stone cut in the shape of a narrow rectangle.

Banded Agate: Agate which has bands of lighter and darker colors. It can be onyx (black/white), cornelian (orangish red/white), or sardonyx (brown/white).

Bangle: A rigid bracelet often tubular and hinged.

Basse-taille: An enameling technique in which a translucent enameling is applied to an engraved metal surface.

Baton: A stone cut in the shape of a long narrow rectangle.

Beauty Pins: Pins popular from the mid 1800s until after the turn of the century. Usually under 2" long with rounded ends.

Belcher Mounting: A claw type ring mounting on which there were many variations. Popular from the 1870s thru 1920s.

Benoition Chain: A chain worn suspended from the top of the head that encircled the head and dropped down onto the bosom.

Bezel: A metal rim which holds the stone in a ring, a cameo in its mounting or a crystal on a watch.

Black Amber: A misnomer for jet.

Bloomed Gold: A textured finish on gold that is created by immersing in acid to give it a matte pitted effect.

Bog Oak: Wood preserved in the bogs of Ireland and used to make jewelry during the Victorian era.

Bohemian Garnet: A dark red pyrope garnet.

Brilliant Cut: A cut that returns the greatest amount of white light to the eye. It usually has 57 or 58 facets. Usually used for diamonds or other transparent stones.

Briolettes: A teardrop-shaped cut covered with facets.

Brooch: An ornamental piece of jewelry which has a pin back for affixing it to clothing or hats. Usually larger in scale than the ones referred to as "pins."

Brooch-watch: A watch with a brooch affixed so it is worn as one would wear a brooch.

Bulla: A round ornamental motif found in ancient jewelry.

C

Cabochon: A stone cut in round or oval shape in which the top is convex shaped (not faceted).

Cairngorm: Yellow brown to smoky yellow quartz named after the mountain range in which it is found in Scotland.

Calibre Cut: Small stones cut in the shape of squares, rectangles or oblongs used to embellish jewelry.

Cameo: A layered stone in which a design is engraved on the top layer and the remainder is carved away to reveal the next layer, leaving the design in relief. Also done in shell, coral and lava.

Cameo Habille: A type of cameo in which the carved head is adorned with a necklace, earrings or head ornament set with small stones.

Cannetille: A type of metal decoration named after the type of embroidery made with fine twisted gold or silver thread. It is done using thin wires to make a filigree pattern. Used frequently in England in 1840.

Carat: A unit of weight for gemstones. Since 1913 one metric carat is one fifth of a gram or 200 milligrams.

Carbuncle: Today used to refer to a garnet cut in cabochon. In the middle ages it referred to any cabochon cut red stone.

Cartouche: An ornamental tablet used in decoration or to be engraved, usually symmetrical.

Celluloid: One of the first plastics. A compound of camphor and gun cotton. Highly flammable.

Champlive: An enameling technique in which enamel is put into areas engraved or carved into the metal

Channel Setting: A type of setting in which stones of the same size are held in place by a continuous strip of metal at the top and bottom literally creating a channel for the stones.

Chasing: The technique of embellishing metal by hand using hammers and punches to make indentations: thus raising the design.

Chatelaine: A metal clasp or hook worn at the waist from which hang a variety of useful items suspended by chains.

Chaton: The central or main ornament of a ring.

Cipher: A monogram of letters intertwined.

Claw Setting: A style of ring setting in which the stone is held by a series of vertically projecting prongs.

Clip: A piece of jewelry resembling a brooch but instead of having a pin stem to fasten into clothing it has a hinged clip that hooks over and into the fabric. Very popular from the 1920s: 40s. Some-times made a brooch that incorporated a double clip. It could be worn as a brooch or disassembled and used as a pair of clips.

Cloisonne: An enameling technique in which the enamel is placed into little preformed compartments or cells built on to the metal.

Collet Setting: A ring setting in which the stone is held by a circular band of metal.

Coronet Setting: A round claw setting in crown like design.

Cravat Pin: The same as a tie pin.

Creole Earrings: A hoop style in which the metal is thicker and wider at the bottom than at the top.

Croix a la Jeanette: A piece in the form of a heart from which a cross is suspended. A form of French peasant jewelry. Circa 1835.

Cross-over: A style of ring, bracelet or brooch in which the stone set decorative portions overlap and lie alongside each other.

Crown Setting: An open setting resembling a crown.

Cultured Pearl: A type of pearl induced and stimulated by man to grow inside a mollusk.

Curb Chain: A chain in which the oval flattened links are twisted so that they lie flat.

Cushion Cut: A square or rectangular shape with rounded corners. Also called "antique cut."

Cut Steel Jewelry: Jewelry made of steel studs which are faceted. Popular from the 1760s until the late 19th century.

Cymric: A trade name used by Liberty & Co. for articles sold by them which were designed and manufactured by English firms. The name was adopted in 1899.

D

Designer: A person who designs jewelry. Occasionally they were also makers of jewelry.

Damascene: The art of incrusting metals with other metals.

Demi-parure: A matching set of jewelry consisting of only a few pieces such as a necklace with matching earrings or a bracelet with matching brooch.

Demi-hunter: A watch with a lid over the face in which there is a circular hole in the middle to expose the hands of the watch.

Dog Collar: A type of necklace consisting of rows of beads or a wide band worn snugly around the neck.

Doublet: An assembled stone consisting of two materials, usually garnet and glass.

E

Edwardian Jewelry: Jewelry made during the reign of Edward VII, 1901-1910, that does not fall into the "Art Nouveau" or "Arts and Crafts Movement" category.

Electro-plating: The process of covering metal with a coating of another metal by using electrical current.

Electrum: A pale yellow alloy made by mixing 20% gold and 80% silver.

Enamel: A glass-like material used in powder or flux form and fired on to metal.

Engine-turning: Decoration with engraved lines produced on a special lathe.

Engraving: A technique by which a design is put into a metal surface using incised lines.

Eternity Ring: A ring with stones set all the way around. Symbolizing the "never ending" circle of eternity.

F

Fede Ring: An engagement ring which features two hands "clasped in troth."

Ferronniere: A chain that encircles the forehead as portrayed in Leonardo da Vince's "**La Bel Torronnier.**" A 16th century adornment, it was revived during the Victorian era.

Filigree: Ornamental designs made by using plain twisted or plaited wire.

Fob: A decorative ornament suspended by a chain usually worn with a watch.

Foil: A thick layer or coating used on the back of stones to improve their color and brilliance.

French Jet: It is neither French nor Jet, instead this term usually refers to black glass.

G

Gate: A channel in a mold through which the molten metal flows during the white metal spin-casting process. Also refers to that part of the cast piece that is wasted.

Gilloche: Engraved decoration of geometric design achieved by engine turning. Usually used as a base for translucent enamel.

Girandole: Brooch or earring style in which 3 pendant stones hand from a large central stone.

Gunmetal: An alloy of 90% copper and 10% tin that was very popular in the 1890s.

Gutta-percha: A hard rubber material made from the sap of a Malayan tree. Discovered in the 1840s, it was used for making jewelry, statuary and even furniture.

Gypsy Setting: A type of setting in which the stone is set down flush in the mounting.

H

Hairwork Jewelry: Jewelry made using hair worked on a table or jewelry that incorporates hair and was worked on a palette.

Hallmark: A group of markings used on silver or gold in England since 1300 to designate the fineness of the metal, the town in which it was assayed, and the name of the maker.

Holbeinesque: A style of jewelry popular in England in the 1870s. Its inspiration was from the design of Hans Holbein the Younger.

Hunting Case: A watch that has a lid covering the face. A case spring is activated by pushing on the crown causing the lid to pop open.

I

Incise: A line cut or engraved in a material.

Intaglio: A design cut below the surface of stone. The opposite of a cameo.

Intarsia: The use of stones to make a picture by cutting them out and inlaying them flushed into a background stone.

J

Jabot Pin: A type of stick pin worn on the front of ladies blouses.

Jet: A very light weight black or brownish black material which is a variety of the coal family.

K

Karat: Pure gold is 24 karats. The karat of gold alloy is determined by the percentage of pure gold. For instance 18K gold is 750 parts pure gold and 250 parts other metal or 18 parts pure gold and 6 parts other metal.

L

Lava Jewelry: Jewelry made of the lava from Mr. Vesuvius. Usually carved into cameos or intaglios and sold as souvenirs of the "grand tour."

Laveliere: A light scaled necklace usually consisting of a pendant or pendants suspended from a chain. In the 1890-1910 era it usually had a baroque pearl appendage. The word is probably derived from the Duchess de la Valliere, a mistress of Louis XIV.

Line Bracelet: A flexible bracelet composed of stones of one size or graduating in size, set in a single line.

Luckenbooth Brooches: So called because they were sold in street stalls (Luckenbooths) near St. Giles Kirk in Edinburg. The motif usually consisted of one or two hearts occasionally surrounded by a crown. When the motif included the initial "M" the brooch was referred to as a Queen Mary Brooch.

M

Macle: A flat bottomed diamond crystal.

Mandrel: A replica made of wax or white metal used as a core onto which metal is deposited during the electroplating process.

Marcasite: A misnomer that is now commonly accepted trade name for pyrite. Popular from the 18th century onwards.

Marquise

Marquise: A boat shaped cut used for diamonds and other gem stones. Also called a "navette" shape.

Memento Mori: "Remember you must die." Grim motifs such as coffins, skeletons, etc. Worn as a reminder of ones mortality.

Millegrain: A setting in which the metal holding the stone is composed of tiny grains or beads.

Mizpah Ring: A popular ring of the 19th century consisting of a band with the word **Mizpah** engraved across the top. "May the Lord watch between me and thee while we are absent from the other."

Mosaic: A piece of jewelry in which the pattern is formed by the inlaying of various colored stones or glass. Two types of mosaic work are Roman and Florentine.

Mourning Jewelry: Jewelry worn "in memory of" by friends and relatives of the deceased. Often sums of money were set aside in one's will to have pieces made to be distributed to mourners attending the funeral.

Muff Chain: A long chain worn around the neck and passed through the muff to keep it secure.

N

Necklace Lengths: Choker-15 inches, Princess-18 inches, Matinee-22 inches, Opera-30 inches, Rope-60 inches long.

Nickel Silver: A combination of copper, nickel, zinc and sometimes small amounts of tin, lead or other metals.

Niello: A decorative technique in which the metal is scooped out (in the same manner as champlive) and the recessed area is filled with a mixture of metallic blue black finish. The technique dates back to the Bronze Age. Good examples of this work can be found in the Siamese Jewelry of the 1950s in this book.

O

Old Mine Cut: An old style of cutting a diamond in which the girdle outline is squarish, the crown is high and the table is small. It has 32 crown facets plus a table, and 24 pavilion facets plus a culet.

P

Paste Jewelry: Jewelry which is set with glass imitation gems. Very popular in the 18th century, it provides us with many good examples of the jewelry from that time period.

Parure: A complete matching set of jewelry usually consisting of a necklace, earrings, brooch and bracelet.

Pate de Verre: An ancient process in which glass is ground to powder, colored, placed in a mold, and fired. It was revived in the 19th century and used to make many pieces of Art Nouveau jewelry.

Pave Setting: A style of setting in which the stones are set as close together as possible, presenting a cobblestone effect.

Pebble Jewelry: Scottish jewelry (usually silver) set with stones native to Scotland. Very popular during the Victorian era.

Pendeloque: A faceted drop shaped stone (similar to a briolette) that has a table.

Pietra-dura: (Hard Stone). Flat slices of chalcedony, agate, jasper and lapis lazuli used in Florentine mosaic jewelry.

Pinchbeck: An alloy of copper and zinc invented by Christopher Pinchbeck in the 1720s that looked like gold. It was used for making jewelry, watches and accessories. This term is very misused today. Some dealers refer to any piece that is not gold as "pinchbeck."

Pique: A technique of decorating tortoise shell by inlaying it with pieces of gold and silver. Popular from the mid 17th century until Edwardian time.

Platinum: A rare heavy, silvery white metallic element which is alloyed with other metals and used to make fine pieces of jewelry.

Plique-a-jour: An enameling technique that produces a "stained glass effect" because the enamel is held in a metal frame without any backing. An ancient technique, it was revived and used extensively by Art Nouveau designers.

Poincon: A French term for the mark on French silver similar to the English Hallmark.

Posy Ring: A finger ring with an engraved motto (often rhymed) on the inner side.

R

Regard Ring: A finger ring set with 6 stones of which the first letter is each spell REGARD. The stones most commonly used were: Ruby, Emerald, Garnet, Amethyst, Ruby and Diamond.

Repousse Work: A decorative technique of raising a pattern on metal by beating, punching or hammering from the reverse side. Often called embossing.

Rhinestone: Originally rock crystal found along the banks of the Rhine river. Today, a misnomer for colorless glass used in costume jewelry.

Rhodium: A white metallic element that is part of the platinum group. Because of its hard reflective finish it is often used as a plating for jewelry.

Riviere: A style of necklace containing individually set stones of the same size or graduating in size that are set in a row without any other ornamentation.

Rose Cut: A cutting style in which there are 24 triangular facets meeting at the top with a point. The base is always flat. Diamonds cut this way are usually cut from macles.

Ruolz: A gilded or silvered metal named after the inventor of the process who was a French chemist.

S

Sautoir: A long neck chain that extended beyond a woman's waist. Usually terminating in a pendant or tassel.

Signet Bangle: A hinged tubular bracelet with a central plaque for engraving. Very popular in the 1890-1910 time period.

Signet Ring: A ring with a central plaque on which ones initials were engraved. Sometimes a seal or crest was used.

Scarf Pin: A straight pin approximately 2-1/2 inches long with a decorative head. It was used between 1880-1915 to hole the ties in place. It is the same as a tie pin.

Seed Pearl: A small pearl weighing less than 1/4 grain.

Shank: The circle of metal that attaches to the head of a ring and encircles the finger.

Sprue: A rod attached to the base of a mold model to provide a channel in the mold through which the wax can flow. This sprue also becomes a part of the wax and consequently a part of the casting.

Star Setting: A popular setting in the 1890s in which the stone is placed in an engraved star and secured by a small grain of metal at the base of each point.

Stomacher: A large triangular piece of jewelry worn on the bodice and extending below the waistline. An 18th century style that was revived during the Edwardian period.

Swivel: A fitting used to attach a watch to a chain. It has an elongated spring opening for attaching the watch. The swivel allows the watch to hang properly.

Synthetic: A man-made material with the same physical, chemical and optical properties as the natural. Not to be confused with imitation.

T

Taillé d Epergne: An enameling technique in which engraved depressions are filled with opaque enamel.

Tiffany Setting: A round six prong mounting with a flare from the base to the top.

Trademark: The mark registered with the U.S. Patent Office that identifies a wholesaler or retailer.

V

Vermeil: Gilded silver. Sterling silver with a gold plating.

W

White Gold: An alloy of gold, nickel and zinc developed in 1912 to imitate the popular platinum.

White Metal: A base metal of tin, lead, bismuth, antimony and cadmium used in the manufacturing of costume jewelry. The tin content can vary from 17 to 92 percent. It can be electroplated to any color desired.

Selected Bibliography

I. Art and Style

Barelli, Renoto, *Art Nouveau,* Fulthan, Middlesex, Hamlyn House, 1969.

Batterbery, Michael, *Twentieth Century Art,* New York, McGraw-Hill Book Co.

Battersly, Martin, *Art Nouveau,* Middlesex, Hamly House, 1969.

Buel, J. W., *The Magic City,* St. Louis-Philadelphia: Historical Pub. Co., 1894.

Grief, Martin, *Depression Modern,* New York, Universe Books, 1975.

Treasures of Tutankhamun, New York, The Metropolitan Museum of Art, 1976.

Warren, Geoffrey, *All Color Book of Art Nouveau,* London, Octopus Books Limited, 1972.

II. Catalogues

Benjamin Allen & Co., Wholesale Jewelers Cataloque, Chicago, 1947.

The Brecker Book 1947, Wholesale Catalogue, Chicago, Austin N. Clark, 1946.

Criterion Illustrated Wholesale Catalogue, Chicago, Rahde-Spencer Co., 1929.

The Crystal Palace Exhibition Illustrated Catalogue, London 1851.

"The Art Journal" Special Issue New York, Dover Publications Inc., 1970.

Hen & Haynes, Jewelry & Opticians, Gift Suggestions 1916, Chillicothe, Ohio, New York, The United Jewelers Inc., 1916.

Marshal Field & Co. 1896 Illustrated Catalogue, Edited by Joseph J. Schroeder, Jr., Chicago, Follett Publishing Co., 1970.

R. Chester Frost & Co. 1896 Illustrated Catalogue, Chicago, Illinois, Manufacturing Jewelers, 1896.

Montgomery, Ward & Co., Fall & Winter 1928-29 Cataloque #109, Kansas City: Montgomery Ward & Co., 1928.

Montgomery, Ward & Co., Fall & Winter 1931-32 Catalogue #115, Kansas City: Montgomery Ward & Co., 1931.

Montgomery, Ward & Co., Spring & Summer 1946, Kansas City: Montgomery Ward & Co., 1946.

Montgomery, Ward & Co., Fall & Winter 1958-1959, Kansas City: Montgomery Ward & Co., 1958.

C.B. Norton Illustrated Jewelry Catalogue, Kansas City: 1923.

C.B. Norton 1924-Illustrated Jewelry Catalogue Kansas City, Mo.: 1924.

The Ring Mounting Salesman, issued by Graffe & Stanik. Chicago, Ill.: 1920.

Sears, Roebuck & Co., Fall & Winter 1933-34, Kansas City: Sears, Roebuck & Co., 1933.

Sears, Roebuck & Co., Fall & Winter 1935-36

Sears, Roebuck & Co., Fall & Winter 1936-37, copyright by Sears, Roebuck & Co., 1936.

J.R. Wood & Sons Jewelry & Diamonds Catalogues, New York: 1927.

Otto Young & Co., 1888, Chicago, Illinois Chicago: J.L. Regan Printing Co., 1888.

III. Fashions

Carter, Earnestine. *The Changing World of Fashion,* New York: G.P. Putman's Sons, 1977.

Gold, Annalee. *75 Years of Fashion,* New York: Fairchild Publications Inc., 1975.

Fifty Years of Fashion, New York: Fairchild Publications Inc., based on material that appeared originally in *Women's Wear Daily.*

IV. General Antiques

Three Centuries of American Antiques, by the editors of American Heritage. New York: Bonanza Books, 1979.

The Connoisseurs Complete Period Guide, edited by Ralph Edwards and L.B. Ramsey New York: Bonanza Books, 1968.

Bishop, Robert and Patricia Coblentz. *The World of Antiques, Art and Architecture in Victorian America,* New York: E.P. Dutton, 1979.

Depperd, Carl W. *Victorian, The Cinderella of Antiques,* New York: Doubleday & Co., 1950.

Lavine, Sigmund A. *Handmade in America,* New York: Dodd, Mead & Co., 1966.

McClinton, Katharine Morrison. *Antiques Past and Present,* New York: Branhall House, 1971.

Mebane, John. *Treasures at Home,* New Jersey: A.S. Barnes & Co. Inc., 1964.

Norbury, James. *The World of Victoriana,* New York: Hamlyn House, 1972. A beautiful book filled with interesting information.

Peter, Mary. *Collecting Victorian,* New York: Frederich A. Praeger Pub., 1968.

Pevsnev, Nicholaus. *High Victorian Design,* London: Architectural Press, 1951.

Shull, Thelma. *Victorian Antiques,* Vermont: Charles E. Tuttle Co., 1963.

V. Jewelry

Armstrong, Mary. *Victorian Jewelry,* New York: McMillian Publishing Co., 1976. A beautiful book about jewelry.

Becker, Vivienne. *Antique & Twentieth Century Jewellery,* Second Edition, N.A. G. Press Ltd., 1922.

Beuer, J. and A. *A Book of Jewels,* Prague: Artia, 1966.

Brenda, Klement. *Ornament and Jewellery,* Prague: Svoboda, 1967. Archeological finds from Eastern Europe.

Bradford, Ernle. *English Victorian Jewellery,* New York: Robert M. McBride & Co. Inc., 1957.

Bradford, Ernle. *Four Centuries of European Jewellery,* Great Britain: Spring Books, 1967.

Burgess, Frederich W. *Antique Jewelry and Trinkets,* New York: Tudor Publishing Co., 1919.

Bury, Shirley. *Jewellery 1789-1910, Vol I & Vol. II,* 1991.

Curran, Mona. *A Treasury of Jewels and Gems,* New York: Emerson Books Inc., 1962.

Curran, Mona. *Collecting Antique Jewellery,* New York: Emerson Books Inc., 1964.

Evans, Joan. *A History of Jewellery 1100-1870,* Boston, Mass.: Boston Book and Art Publications, 1970.

Gene, Charlotte. *Victorian Jewelry Design,* Chicago: Henery Regnery Co., 1973.

Goldemberg, Rose Leeman. *Antique Jewelry, A Practical and Passionate Guide,* New York: Crown Publishers, 1976.

Flower, Margaret. *Victorian Jewellery,* New York: Duell, Sloan and Pearce, 1951.

Fregnac, Claude. *Jewellery From The Renaissance to Art Nouveau,* London: Octopus Books, 1973.

Giltay-Nijseen L. Jewelry New York: Universe Books, 1964.

Hornung, Clarence P. *Antique and Jewelry Designs,* New York: George Braziller, 1968.

Jessup, Ronald. *Anglo-Saxon Jewellery,* United Kingdom: Shire Publishers Ltd., 1974.

Kuzel, Vladislav. *A Book of Jewelry,* Prague: Artia, 1962.

Miller, Anna M. *Cameo's Old & New,* Von Nostrand Rhinhold, 1991.

Percival, MacIver. *Chats on Old Jewellery and Trinkets,* New York: Frederich A. Stokes Co., 1902.

Peter, Mary. *Collecting Victorian Jewellery,* New York: Emerson Books, Inc., 1971.

Sataloff, Joseph and Alison Richards. *The Pleasures of Jewelry & Gemstones,* London: Octopus Books, 1975. A beautifully informative book.

Schumann, Walter. *Gemstones of the World,* New York: Sterling Publishing Co., 1979. A great new book on gems.

Smith, H. Clifford. *Jewellery,* New York: G.P. Putnam & Co., 1908.

Jewelry Ancient to Modern, New York: Viking Press in cooperation with the Walters Art Gallery, Baltimore, 1979.

VI. Magazines

Adrian, "Setting Styles Through the Stars," *Ladies Home Journal,* Feb. 1933, pgs. 10-11.

Bliven, Bruce. "Flapper Jane," *The New Republic,* Dec. 9, 1925, pgs 65-67.

Case, Tina Bailie. "Fashion Primer for Winter," *Independent Women,* Nov., 1937, pgs. 348-50.

Hampton, Edgar Lloyd. "A 1200 Mile Style Parade," *Nation's Business,* April, 1937, pg. 78.

Hageland, Ruth. *Country Gentleman,* Sept., 1934.

Koues, Helen. "The Reflector of the Times," *Good Housekeeping,* May, 1935, pgs. 62-63.

Lewis, Mary. "Culottes for Action," *Collier's Magazine,* May 9, 1942, pg. 50.

Mollay, Anne Shirley. "Jewels for the Yuletide," *Country Life,* Dec., 1926, pgs 88-90.

Ray, Marci Beynon. "The Jewel for Every Occasion," *The Delinator,* April, 1928, pg 35.

Read, Helen Appleton. "The Exposition in Paris," *International Studies,* Nov., 1925, pg. 93.

Robinson, Selma. "Glowing Compliments," *Saturday Evening Post,* Sept. 29, 1934, pg 26.

Samberg, Ronben. "Costume Jewelry," *Fortune Magazine,* Dec., 1946, pg. 140.

"The Neo-Modern School," *The Delinator,* Oct., 1936, pg. 32.

"Crazy over Jewelry," *Collier's Magazine,* Dec. 15, 1943, pg. 93.

American Magazine March, 1948, pg. 118.

Business Week, Sept. 19, 1938; Sept. 5, 1942; Feb. 2, 1943; April 17, 1943; Sept. 2, 1944.

Collier's Magazine, July 26, 1947, pg. 34.

The Delinator, Oct., 1936.

Fortune Magazine, Jan., 1937; May, 1946; Dec., 1946.

Frank Leslie's Illustrated Newspaper, Jan. 5, 1878 through Nov. 23, 1878.

Godey's Lady's Book, Philadelphia, January-December, 1850; January- June, 1859; New York, July-December, 1896.

Gleason's Pictorial Drawing Room Companion, Oct. 8, 1853.

Good Housekeeping, May, 1939.

Harper's Magazine, New York: Harper & Brothers, January-December, 1876, July, 1877.

Life Magazine, June 27, 1949, pg. 93; April 21, 1952; April 26, 1954, pg. 129; Sept. 10, 1956, pg. 49.

The Literary Digest, Nov. 21, 1925; Jan. 16, 1926.

Look Magazine, May 31, 1955.

Newsweek, Aug. 1, 1955; May 5, 1958.

Time Magazine, Sept. 8, 1942, pg. 64; April 13, 1942, pg. 18.

The Young Ladies Journal, January-December, 1887.

VII. Metals

Bradbury, Frederich. *Bradbury's Book of Hallmarks* Sheffield, England: J.W. Northend Ltd., 1928.

Wyler, Seymour B. *The Book of Old Silver,* New York: Crown Publishing Inc., 1937.

VIII. Personalities

Bently, Nicholas. *Edwardian Album,* New York: Viking Press, 1974.

Pearsall, Ronald. *Edwardian Life and Leasure,* New York: St. Martin's Press, 1973.

Purtell, Joseph. *The Tiffany Touch,* New York: Random House Inc., 1971. (A good book on the famous Tiffany's.)

Starchey, Lytton. *Queen Victoria,* New York: Harcourt, Brace & Co., 1921.

IX. The Times

The Fabulous Century by the editors of Time-Life Books. Vols. 1-VI. New York: Times Inc., 1969.

The Centennial Portfollio; A Souvenir of the International Exhibition in Phil. Philadelphia: T. Hunter, 1876.

Life History of the United States Vols. 1-12. New York: Time Inc., 1964.

Brunhammer, Yvonne. *The Nineteen Twenties Style,* New York: Paul Hamlyn, 1969.

Dickens, Charles. *David Copperfield,* New York: Simon & Schuster, 1959.

Jenkins, Alan. *The Twenties,* New York: Universe Books, 1974.

Jenkins, Alan. *The Thirties,* New York: Stein & Day Publishers, 1976.

Partridge, Bellamy, and Otto Bettmann. *As We Were: 1850-1900,* New York: McGraw-Hill Book Co., Inc., 1946.

Randel, William Pierce. *Centennial American Life in 1876,* New York: Chilton Book Co., 1969. (A most informative book.)

Notes

1 *The Crystal Palace Exhibition Illustrated Catalogue,* London 1851. *The Art Journal Special Issue*; New York; Dover Pub. 1970, pg. 127.

2 *Godey's Lady's Book.* June 1855, pg. 501

3 *The Centennial Portfollio; A Souvenir of the International Exposition in Philadelphia* Pennsylvania: T. Hunter, 1876, no page number.

4 Ibid.

5 Ibid.

6 Patridge, Bellamy and Otto Bettman. *As We Were: 1850-1900,* New York: McGraw-Hill Book Co., 1969, pg. 140.

7 *McCalls Magazine,* May, 1909.

8 Buel, J.W. *The Magic City, St. Louis*, Philadelphia: Historical Publishing Co., 1894, pg. 2.

9 Ibid., no page number.

10 *The Columbian Exposition Album.* Chicago: Rand, McNally & Co., 893.

11 Burl, J.W. op. cit., no page number.

12 Jenkins, Alan. *The Twenties,* New York: Universal Books, 1974, pg. 66.

13 Adrian. "Styles Through the Star," *Ladies Home Journal,* February 1933, pg. 10.

14 Read, Helen Appleton. "The Exposition in Paris," International Studio Nov., 1925, pg. 95.

15 *Business Week,* Sept. 5, 1942, pg. 64.

16 Ibid.

17 *Business Week Magazine,* Feb. 27, 1943, pg. 51.

18 *Newsweek,* May 5, 1958, pg. 98.

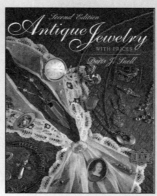

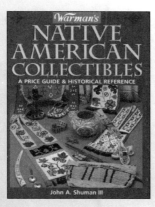

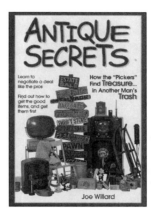
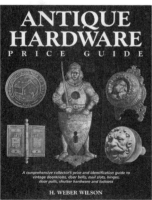